MYTHS OF THE CHICAGO SCHOOL OF SOCIOLOGY

In memory of my dad
Aveley Walter Harvey
whose encouragement
made this possible.

Myths of the Chicago School of Sociology

LEE HARVEY
Department of Sociology and A.S.S.
City of Birmingham Polytechnic

Avebury

Aldershot · Brookfield USA · Hong Kong · Singapore · Sydney

Published by

Avebury

Gower Publishing Company Limited,
Gower House
Croft Road
Aldershot
Hants GU11 3HR,
England

Gower Publishing Company,
Old Post Road
Brookfield
Vermont 05036
United States of America.

British Library Cataloguing in Publication Data
Harvey, Lee, 1949-
   Myths of the Chicago School of Sociology
   1. Chicago school of sociology
   I. Title
   301'.01   HM22.U5

Library of Congress Cataloging in Publication Data
Harvey, Lee, 1949-
   Myths of the Chicago school of sociology
   Bibliography: p.
   Includes index
   1. Sociology--United States--History. 2. Chicago
school of sociology--History. I. Title
HM22.U5H37 1987   301'.0973   86-33497

ISBN 0-566-05398-5

Printed and bound in Great Britain by
Athanaeum Press Ltd, Newcastle-upon-Tyne

Contents

Acknowledgements   vi

1. The 'Chicago School'   1

2. Chicagoans as ameliorists   23

3. Chicagoans as ethnographers   47

4. The quantitative tradition at Chicago   74

5. Chicagoans as atheoretical empirical researchers   109

6. G. H. Mead and the Chicagoans   154

7. Chicago dominance   176

8. Schools and metascience   213

Appendices   221

References   300

Index   331

Acknowledgements

My thanks to all those who helped in the research for this
book. In particular, thanks to the very helpful staff of the
Special Collections Department, University of Chicago Regenstein Memorial Library, who greatly facilitated my archive
research. Thanks to James Coleman for his very informative
recollections, to Morris Janowitz and Martin Bulmer for their
assistance and suggestions. Thanks also to Library staff at the
City of Birmingham Polytechnic notably Jane Richards and
Michael Shoolbred for their extensive assistance in searching
out references, and to Jean Wood (who has now escaped to sun-
nier climes) for similar help in the early stages. Especially,
I would like to thank Martyn Hammersley for his invaluable
contribution over the last eight years. The City of Birmingham
Polytechnic provided financial assistance, for which I am
grateful. Thanks also to my family and friends who encouraged
the endeavour, especially my mother, Kathleen Harvey, friends
and colleagues Ardha Best, Mike Little and Nick Stanley for
being so positive about my work. Most importantly to Morag
MacDonald who had not only to live with this book but also
contributed enormously to the empirical data collection.
Without her support, assistance and patience the work would not
have been completed.

1 The 'Chicago School'

Introduction

The 'Chicago School of Sociology' means a number of different things to different people. References to the 'Chicago School' in the literature are quite varied and the constructions of the 'school' are very much a function of the commentator's academic endeavour, predeliction and preconceptions as well as a view of what a 'school' of sociology is and what purpose and role it plays in the history of sociology.

This book directs itself to examining the preponderant constructions of the 'Chicago School' which have grown up over the last quarter century. Before beginning this examination, some introductory remarks about the nature of 'school', the academic concerns of those who refer to a 'Chicago School' and the type of construction of a 'Chicago School' are necessary.

The concept of 'school'

The concept of school is widely used in attempts to understand the history and contemporary structure of sociology. For the most part it is used informally, without definition, to refer to groups of sociologists assumed to be sharing a certain perspective and perhaps a particular institutional location. This casual approach to the term has lead to a plethora of different concepts trading under the same label. This has tended to handicap, rather than help, those sociologists and historians of the social sciences who have attempted a more rigorous analysis using the concept of 'school' as a metascientific category. [1]

The casual approach to the term school involves nothing much more than a process of grouping together practitioners into convenient pigeon-holes in order to boundary, and thus facilitate, a sociological or historiographical analysis. The nature of a 'school', when the term is used in this casual way is determined by the structure of the pigeon holes, rather than by any explicit thesis about, either, the internal structuring of a research unit, or of any thesis about the nature of scientific knowledge and its development.

The term 'school', when appropriated in this rather informal way, has been used to group people together to show similarities in style, approach, epistemology, theoretical concerns, or substantive interests. Such groupings may be restricted to people working in the same place at the same time (e.g. The Centre for Contemporary Cultural Studies). Alternatively, 'school' might refer to a number of 'generations' of practitioners bounded by a particular institutional affiliation (such as the Frankfurt School) or 'allegience' to a recognised central figure (such as the Durkheimian School and the Parsonian School). Or, a 'school' may be used to refer to contemporaries scattered across a number of institutions but who are seen as having some sort of identifiable common core (e.g. the structural functionalists). A wider meaning still occurs where the core is seen to span a period of time and space such that members could not possibly have worked either together, or in the same environment, but have been identified as having adopted some tenets which stand independently of the research situation. This last is usually referred to as a 'school of thought' (e.g. Marxism, or Pragmatism). 'School' has also been used in conjunction with groupings of people circumscribed by national boundaries (e.g. Polish School of Sociology; Soviet Sociology; The French School of Sociology) [2].

However, there have been attempts to develop the idea of 'school' and make it into a more rigorous metascientific concept. Approaches that use the 'school' as some form of metascientific unit prescribe the nature of the school in explicit terms which are informed by both the internal structure and dynamic of the social unit and by a thesis about the nature of the growth of social scientific knowledge (Mullins, 1973; Radnitzky, 1973; Tiryakian, 1979a; Besnard, 1983; Bulmer, 1984a). The development of this more rigorous metascientific concept of school owes a lot to the debate in the philosophy of science, in particular to Kuhn's (1962, 1970) 'paradigm' thesis and to Lakatos' (1970, 1975) 'methodology of scientific research programmes' (see Harvey, 1985, 1986).

The result has been a number of related, but distinct ideas as to what constitutes a viable metascientific unit. These range from 'invisible colleges' (Price, 1963, 1965; Crane, 1972) through 'networks' (Mullins, 1973) to 'schools' (Tiryakian, 1979a, 1979b; Bulmer, 1984, 1984a). While substantial differences exist between these various metascientific units they have certain elements in common. Although differing in scope, they are all closely defined concepts and they each prescribe the criteria for demarcation of any co-operating group as a metascientific unit. All see research units as integrally related to the development of science and all delimit their respective metascientific unit to a group of communicating researchers.

The metascientific construct of 'school' is the narrowest of these units and tends to refer only to people who work in a closely defined institutional context and/or in close association with a dominant leader figure. Metascientific schools have thus been likened to 'schools of art' with a charismatic leader by those who adopt the concept [3], while those less sympathetic see schools as insular, rather like religious sects (Krantz, 1971a; Crane, 1972; Lakatos, 1975).

While not everyone agrees as to the exact nature of 'schools', Tiryakian's (1979a) model has proved popular among sociologists and historians of sociology. His is a rather rigid model, however, and Bulmer (1984a) has developed it into a more flexible construct (Harvey, 1986). Bulmer suggests that a number of features are likely to be present in some form if the social grouping can be said to be a 'school'. A 'school' has a central figure around whom the group is located, who is an inspiring and effective leader, whose school it essentially is, and without whom the school begins to break up. The school needs an infrastructure which includes a propitious academic and geographic location, institutionalised links with existing bodies, external financial support and a means of disseminating its work. A school must attract students and develop an intellectual attitude and be open to ideas and provide a climate for 'intellectual exchanges between the leader and other members of the group'. A school is thus a more closely-knit group 'than is usual in academic departments or disciplines' (Bulmer, 1985, p. 67) [4].

Constructions of the 'Chicago School'

The different constructions of the 'Chicago School' cover a wide span of time and focus on different aspects of the institutional context and work undertaken by the Chicagoans. This section examines these constructions and suggests a typology which reflects the concerns of the commentators.

Arguably, constructions of the 'Chicago School', like any other 'school', are guided by some kind of view (even if not very clearly defined) of the nature and role of 'schools' in the generation of social scientific knowledge. These constructions are, however, also effected by the general academic enterprise in which the construer is engaged. The extent to which 'school' is defined, rather than is used in a casual fashion, is dependent upon the academic enterprise being undertaken. There are, perhaps, four academic activities of sociologists which lead to constructions of a 'Chicago School'.

First, a construction of the 'Chicago School' is offered in a general way in the presentation of sociology as an academic enterprise, notably in introductory texts. Most construals of this kind are fleeting and cursory references which seem to pass on accepted 'wisdom' without really investigating the nature of the sociological work undertaken by the Chicagoans. Perhaps one should simply discount these throw-away references, but given that they persist, and are part of students' initial orientation to the subject matter, they serve to perpetuate myths about the 'Chicago School'. This type of introductory level or passing comment almost always uses a casual notion of 'school' Such references tend to re-present a rather one dimensional view of the work of the Chicagoans, often selecting out members in a fairly random way as indicative of some early attempt to explain social behaviour. Depending on the orientation of the author, Chicago is invoked as an exemplar of participant observation, of empiricism, of deviancy study, of urban sociology, and so on. Usually, the connotation is that the work was descriptive, or reformist, or unsystematic and lacking in rigour. The studies produced by the Chicagoans are not infrequently portrayed as rather quaint, unscientific curios. In this kind of construal the 'Chicago School' is represented as either a group of people, or as a set of tenets guiding practice.

A second set of construals are those developed by historians of sociology. These are usually much better researched, although a surprising number are reliant upon a few secondary sources. Of course, history is an interpretive process and there can be no definitive statement about the nature of the 'Chicago School'. Thus, researched historical accounts do not stand in isolation but are related to other concerns. Such concerns are, for example, an overview of the historical development of sociology in the United States (Martindale, 1976; Coser, 1971); or a thesis on the development of sociological methodology (Easthope, 1974); or a biographical account to which the 'Chicago School' was germane (Matthews, 1977; Raushenbush, 1979) or a specific history of the 'Chicago School' (Faris, 1967; Bulmer, 1984). The use of the term 'school' here is again usually a casual reference, a developed metascientific concept of 'school' is rare (e.g. Bulmer, 1984). The casual use of 'school' in this context tends to reflect preconceived ideas about the nature of the development of either the theory or practice of American sociology. It tends to rely heavily on the 'presentist' idea that sociology has developed relatively smoothly over time through a succession of 'great men' passing on 'great ideas' up to the present.

A third set of construals come from those proclaiming some sort of Chicago heritage. These have, in the main, been of three sorts. First, those who have constructed a 'Chicago School' of Urban Sociology (Hunter, 1980); second, those who have created a 'Chicago style' ethnography (Madge, 1963; Dreitzel, 1970; Bogdan and Taylor, 1975); third, those who have created a 'Chicago School' of symbolic interactionism (Meltzer et al, 1975). We shall look at these in more detail, below, when considering specific constuctions of the 'Chicago School'.

Fourth, construals of the 'Chicago School' occur as a result of metascientific analyses about the nature of the development of sociological knowledge in the United States (Mullins, 1973; Tiryakian, 1979a). This approach adopts an explicit notion of 'school' or research unit as central to a thesis about the growth and development of scientific knowledge. The metascientific analysis engages the research environment in an attempt to construct a history that does not take-for-granted a cumulative 'great man' approach to the history of science. The 'Chicago School' is often used as a case study in such metascientific analyses. This kind of work is particularly concerned with the institutional context, the roles, and the activities of the research group at Chicago. It has been effective in casting doubts on the validity of the taken-for-granted views of the 'Chicago School'. However, far too often, these metascientific analyses, too, seem to have been undertaken with a limited amount of first hand research.

A 'Chicago School'?

There is a widespread view amongst sociologists that there was a 'Chicago School' of sociology in a sense that implied more than a a number of scholars in a university department. However, doubt has been cast on this presumption, not least by people closely linked to the so-called 'Chicago School'.

In the introductory note to his book which sets out to evaluate Chicago sociology, Kurtz (1984, p. 99) writes

> I use the term "Chicago School" throughout this volume with some hesitation. Although it is a convenient, frequently employed term, the reader should not assume that it indicates a monolithic, homogeneous tradition. Like all

"schools" of thought, the Chicago school evaporates under close inspection

Throughout the history of the Department of Sociology at the University of Chicago there have been disclaimers of the idea that the Chicagoans represented a homogenous body of sociologists. As early as 1911, Small (1911, p. 634) noted that

> There is quite as much difference of opinion in matters of detail between members of our sociological staff as will be found between representatives of different institutions.

The notion of a 'Chicago School of Sociology' was not an issue in 1911, and, indeed, even in the 1920s during the 'Golden Era' of the 'School' Cavan (1983) noted that she could not ever recall hearing the term 'Chicago School'. Wirth and Hughes, both students in the twenties and later tenured members of the Chicago faculty were also apparently sceptical of the idea of a 'Chicago School'.

> When I was a graduate student at Chicago, one of the people who was really considered to be a leader in a 'Chicago School of Sociology' was Louis Wirth. And Louis Wirth used to say that he was constantly amazed at being told that he was part of the Chicago School of Sociology, because he couldn't imagine what he had in common with all those other people. (Becker, 1979, p. 3)

> I don't remember where or when I first heard of the Chicago School. That phrase was invented by others, not the Chicago people. I suppose there was some sense in the term, but it implies more consensus than existed. (Hughes quoted by Cavan, 1983, p. 408).

Hughes confirmed this view in 1969 when he indicated that he still disliked talking of a 'Chicago School' or 'any other kind of school' (Hughes, 1980, p. 276).

Janowitz (1966) also raised doubts about the extent to which the Chicagoans could be seen as a school.

> it is a disputable question whether there was a distinct or unified Chicago approach to sociology ... the Chicago school contained theoretical viewpoints and substantive interests which were extremely variegated.

And the official brochure of the Department of Sociology at Chicago for 1981-82 also noted that 'the department has never been dominated by a single individual or by a single school of thought.'

Perhaps more important than the recollections and reassessments of the people at Chicago is the documentary record. In the light of his reported view, it is not surprising that Wirth (1947), in his review of the history of sociology (1915-1947), makes no reference to a 'Chicago School' or a particularly unique practice located at the University of Chicago. Nor indeed, did ex-graduates who produced sociology texts refer to a 'Chicago School' or a 'Chicago Approach'. For example, Hiller's (1933) Principles of Sociology and Young's (1949) Sociology discuss the work of the Chicagoans in some detail, but never in terms of them being a 'school'. In Hiller's book Park, Burgess, Thomas, and Cooley get far more references than any one else (except Sumner) and Young has an extensive discussion of urban sociology which includes the works of the Chicagoans among others. Neither, however, separate the 'Chicago School' from other American sociologists. Similarly, McKenzie's contribution to the President's Research Committee on Social Trends (1933) about developments in metropolitan communities makes no reference to a 'Chicago School' although it discusses in some detail the various analyses of the city of Chicago undertaken through the University of Chicago.

Even more surprising than the lack of reference to a 'Chicago School' in the published literature is the almost total lack of any such reference in the Chicago archives. The Special Collections Department of the Regenstein Library at the University of Chicago [5] contains an extensive collection of the papers of the Chicago faculty since the University's inception. In my examination of a large number of documents in the Collection I found no references at all to a 'Chicago School' (or any similar construct) prior to 1939, and on material up to 1955 references to anything like a 'Chicago School' were very rare indeed. It is interesting that the isolated reference I found to a 'Chicago School' on a document written by Park (1939) refers in fact to the Society for Social Research at the University and was written by Park, at Wirth's request, as an overview of the history of that Society. It seems that Park (five years after leaving Chicago) saw the Society as embodying 'The Chicago School', a term which he had probably heard elsewhere. The document only refers to the notion of a school once, in passing, and makes no attempt to elaborate a thesis about such a 'School'. As Park (1939, p. 1) recalled, the Society for Social Research was organised in the Fall of 1921, and its aim was to bring together interested and competent researchers (students and staff).

Research in the social sciences at Chicago began before the organization of the Society for Social Research. However, the particular type of research that has been identified with the "Chicago School" has found in this Society, in its

7

Institute, and its publications an effective organ of ex-
pression. The Society was originally organized to stimulate
a wider interest and a more intelligent co-operation among
faculty and students in a program of studies that focused
investigation on the local community. [6]

The Society saw itself as an open discussion forum and as a
'clearing house of ideas' (Bulletin of the Society for Social
Research, June, 1929) and this is most indicative of the nature
of the 'Chicago School' (see Appendix 3). Indeed, The Bulletin
of the Society for Social Research [7], makes no reference at
all in any issue to a 'Chicago School', or a 'Chicago Approach', or to a specifically 'Chicago Sociology'. The openness
of the Society, reflecting the Chicagoans approach to sociological enquiry, explains why there are virtually no references
to a 'school' in the archive material of the Chicagoans. The
Chicagoans did not detatch themselves from prevailing approaches to sociology, but, as we shall see in chapter seven, openly
engaged in the development of mainstream sociology. The Chicagoans did not see themselves as sect-like. It seems that if
there was any 'school' of sociology associated with Chicago, it
was not a deliberate construction of the Chicagoans nor did it
reside in an insular group. Rather than a sect like insularity,
the Chicagoans favoured an open and critical approach to sociology.
Arguably, the diverse activities and interests of the Chicagoans belies the idea of a 'school', and it is clear that the
term was one rarely used by the Chicagoans themselves. Such
usage, by them, tends to have been retrospective and casual and
perhaps no more than an indicator of institutional affiliation.
Some outsiders, on the other hand, it seems, did regard
sociology at Chicago as representing some sort of caucus or
distinct school. The first published reference to a 'Chicago
School' appears to have been in 1930. According to Cavan (1983)
it occurrred in Bernard's (1930) article on 'Schools of Sociology'. This appears to have been a fairly isolated reference
in the literature.
Nonetheless, there does appear to have been a notion in the
1930s of a Chicago group of sociologists of some sort and, even
if the Chicagoans did not see themselves as a school, they were
seen in that light by outsiders. The extent to which this
recognition represented academic or political concerns, however, is less clear [8].
There was, at least until the 1950s, no real consensus by
outsiders as to the nature of the 'Chicago School', nor was it
a generally used term. For example, even by 1940, Wilson of
Harvard in writing to Burgess to recommend William F. Whyte to
Chicago made no mention of a 'Chicago School' nor an exclusive
style of sociology at Chicago. Indeed, Wilson (1940) saw Colum-

8

bia and Chicago as offering the same opportunities for Whyte, and not as antithetical institutions. It seems, then, unlikely that there was any recognition of a 'Chicago School' much before 1935 and that any references to it up to the 1960s were unsystematic, vague and devoid of the implications that have become associated with it over the last quarter of a century.

Designations of the 'Chicago School'

While the extent to which the Chicagoans saw themselves as a 'school' is unclear, others have claimed to have identified the 'school' and its characteristics. Different people, different histrorical periods, different substantive and theoretical concerns and different ways of working have been specified under the banner of the 'Chicago School'. These reflect the ways in which the school has been designated and I have grouped these varied designatory processes together into two broad types, the historical group and the bonded group.

The historical group

The simplest kind of construction of a 'Chicago School' merely logs the (significant) figures of the tenured faculty for any given period of time. Thus for Anderson (1983), a student at Chicago in the 1920s, the 'School' consisted of the members of the teaching faculty who appeared to have the most impact on the way sociology was taught and researched while he was there. Anderson designated Small, Park, Burgess and Faris as the 'school'. There is no particular 'Chicago core' evident in the work of the four faculty he designates either theoretically, empirically or epistemologically.

A more extensive historical group construction is provided by those sociologists who refer to a number of generations of Chicago sociologists (Tiryakian, 1979a; Becker, 1979; Kurtz, 1984). Three and sometimes four generations are identified. The first generation consists of the tenured staff and their students up to 1914, principally Small, Henderson, Thomas and Vincent. These are seen as the founders of a 'Chicago Approach' in the sense of promoting empirical enquiry and concentrating attention on the city of Chicago (Dibble, 1972; Diner, 1980). The second generation usually includes Park, Burgess, Ellsworth Faris and, in some accounts, William Ogburn. These four staff members and their students are seen as developing the embryonic concerns of the first generation (Faris, 1967; Carey 1975). Out of these came the third generation, principally graduates who, often after a short absence, returned to Chicago and became tenured. Notable here are Blumer, Wirth, Hughes and Stouffer. The fourth generation again tended to be students of the third generation, but often developed much of their sociology away from Chicago. Becker, Strauss, Goffman and Janowitz are among the most clearly identified members of the fourth generation Chicagoans.

This approach divides the personnel into a relatively simple temporal sequence, identifying the dominant characters at each phase of the Department's history. Very different groups of people and ways of doing sociology have, then, been credited with the same label. Nonetheless, this 'historical group' designation tends towards a view that the period from 1915 to 1933, the period of Park's tenure, was the era of the classic 'Chicago School'. This period, known as the 'golden era' (Cavan 1983), is identified as being the time when the 'School' was most active in its empirical enquiry, and, during which time, its more famous studies were produced. Indeed, many discussions of the 'Chicago School' really only see the school as operative in terms of the work carried out in the 1920s and early 1930s, particularly that guided by Park and Burgess (Madge, 1963; Hunter, 1983).

The bonded group

Commentators who concentrate on the 'golden era' tend towards a view of the 'Chicago School' as a bonded group rather than simply an historical grouping. The group at Chicago is seen as bonded together in one of three ways.

First, and most popularly, through the specification of a network owing allegience to a leader figure.

> Most of the important people around Chicago had studied, or been closely associated with [Park], and that made an enormous difference. Because with all their differences with respect to methods of research, and one thing and another, they all essentially looked at things the way the old man had looked at it, and he had a very comprehensive view. (Becker, 1979, p. 5)

In their biographical accounts, both Matthews (1977) and Raushenbush (1979) see the 'Chicago School' as a group around Park. Tiryakian and Bulmer, in constructing an explicit meta-scientific school, identify Park as the leader figure of a bonded group. Faris's (1967) historical account of the period 1920 to 1932 also identifies a core bonded group around Park.

Second, through specification of set of concepts and values.

> The Chicago School may be considered a "school" rather than a solidarity group committed to a particular point of view, in that it represented a vertically bonded network of practitioners located in and identified with a specific

institution, all of whom shared near identical beliefs and ideas. (Thomas, 1983a, p. 390)

An example of a rather narrow designation of a 'Chicago School' as a bonded network of this sort is provided by Blumer (1972) [9] who suggested that Park, Burgess and Faris made up the 'Chicago School'. Blumer excluded Ogburn who was a tenured colleague of the others because although the others had different approaches, Ogburn, as a statistician, was more concerned with 'so-called objectivity' than 'dealing with the whole process whereby action came into being' (Blumer, 1972, p. 13). [10]

Third, through an approach to a set of substantive issues

In a sense there was a School of Sociology at Chicago, given form by the Park and Burgess Textbook and by the Polish Peasant. Add to this the demand for empirical work focussed on the 'untouched' city of Chicago. (Cavan, 1983, p. 411).

This third type of approach to a bonded group is popular amongst those who reconstruct Chicago heritages such as the development of Chicago symbolic interactionism; the reconstruction of an urban studies heritage; and the reconstruction of a 'Chicago style' ethnography.

The 'Chicago School of Symbolic Interactionism'. The development of symbolic interactionism is closely linked to the 'Chicago School' (Manis and Meltzer, 1978; Snodgrass, 1983). A number of different varieties of symbolic interactionism have been identified of which the Blumerian or 'Chicago School' approach is seen as of major importance and often portrayed as at variance with the 'Iowa School' (Meltzer et al, 1975; Littlejohn, 1977; Carabana and Espinosa, 1978)

Such designations of a 'Chicago School' are constructions linked to a specific form of symbolic interactionism which has roots in practice at Chicago. However, such constructions do more than refer to a given style of interactionism. They do three other things. First, they imply a heritage which links Blumerian and post-Blumerian symbolic interactionism to the development of sociology at Chicago. Second, in so doing, these constructions provide Blumerian symbolic interactionism with legitimacy. A view of Chicago sociology is reconstructed which locates the concerns of the symbolic interactionists as the principal concerns of the Chicagoans (e.g. Rock, 1979). The third effect of this reconstructed heritage is to award a role to Mead in the history of the development of sociology at Chicago in the 1920s that it seems likely he did not have (Lewis and Smith, 1981; Harvey, 1985). It seems that 'present-

ist' designations of the Chicagoans, for the purposes of legitimating a particular style of symbolic interactionism, have
tended to determine the nature of the history of the school
(Bulmer, 1984a). The construction of a symbolic interactionist
heritage is considered in more detail in chapter six which
looks at the role of George Herbert Mead in the Chicago School.

'The Chicago School of Urban Studies'. While much of the work
of the Chicagoans of the 1920s has been forgotten, their contribution to urban sociology has been kept alive in the sociological imagination.

> By the end of the 1950's, it would have appeared to the
> intellectual historian that the Chicago school of urban
> sociology had exhausted itself. Even at the University of
> Chicago, the intensive and humanistically oriented study of
> the social worlds of the metropolis had come to an end. The
> older figures had disappeared one by one, and a new gener-
> ation of sociologists were interested in quantitative meth-
> odology and systematic theory. A few disciples of the
> traditional approach carried on in the shadows of the
> university or were scattered through the country.
> But intellectual traditions are transmitted and transformed
> as much by the intrinsic vitality of their content as by
> the institutions of academic life. A mere decade later the
> themes of a reconstructed urban sociology are once again at
> the center of social science thinking. (Janowitz, 1968, p.
> vii)

The view of the Chicagoans as preoccupied with the concerns
of urban sociology (the metropolis, the community, urban policy
and institutions) is indicative of a view that sees the 'Chicago School' as at the heart of a tradition of sociological
enquiry which focuses on the urban environment. In a sense,
there is some validity in this view of the attentions of the
Chicagoans as Park (1939) pointed out when summing up the
development of sociology at Chicago in the 1920s. However, it
is not all the story, as we shall see in later chapters, and
does tend to give a misleading picture of the work and concerns
of the Chicagoans. To identify the 'Chicago School' in terms of
'urban studies' and isolate Park, Burgess and Wirth (Philpott,
1978; Slattery, 1985) is to generate a misleading heritage
which may give legitimacy to an urban studies tradition but
also serves to generate myths about the 'Chicago School'.

'The Chicago School of Ethnography'. For a number of years,
there has been a general view, of American sociology as encom-
passing a methodological divide. The division into qualitative
and quantitative camps is often construed in terms of institu-

tional affilliation with Chicago as the champion of ethnography
and Columbia as the flag-bearer of quantitative approaches. We
shall investigate this more fully, from the point of view of
Chicago, in chapters three and four. This has, however, led to
reconstructions of am ethnographic heritage, and the 'Chicago
School' is frequently seen as a central pillar in such a heritage. More specifically, there have been claims recently that a
'New Chicago School' emerged in the 1950s and flourished in the
1960s and 1970s. In the main, this new school was not based at
Chicago although it derived from there. Laperriere (1982), for
example, argued that the 'New Chicago School' of sociology
arose in the United States in the 1950s. It attempted to break
the hold of 'quantitative' sociologists on the discipline,
which had coincided with the theoretical sterility of sociology. She argued that the 'New Chicago School' aimed to develop a
systematic, open and empirical approach to theory construction.
This allowed them to take into account the richness of social
reality while adopting rigorous sociological method. The 'New
Chicago School', she argued, was characterised by a more systematic and wider approach than that exhibited by other qualitative sociologists.

In effect, this designation of a 'New Chicago School' is
reflected in the accounts of those commentators who talk of the
'late Chicago School' or of the labelling theory of the 'Chicago School'. This is primarily in terms of the work of Becker,
Geer, Strauss, the later work of Hughes and his students, and
the emergence of the 'dramaturgical approach' found in Goffman,
Duncan and Burke (Littlejohn, 1977; Dotter, 1980). This idea of
a new school tends to disengage the 'fourth generation' Chicagoans from their earlier heritage while at the same time looking to Chicago to provide a heritage for ethnographic work. The
disengagement is on two fronts. First, it argues for a dis-
tinctly qualitative approach at variance to prevailing sociological enquiry. Second, it raises issues of objectivity and
the engagement with the perspective of the subject. In short,
the construction of an ethnographic heritage, tends to raise
participant observation to the ideal method, and seeks to find,
in the earlier 'Chicago School', the genesis and patronage of
this method. This, as we shall see, is at variance with what
the Chicagoans were actually doing. Becker's (1967) explicit
demand to make it clear 'Who's Side Are We On ?' contravenes
the earlier non-aligned search for 'objectivity' at Chicago
(Carey, 1975) and participant observation was not the only, or
even major, approach of the Chicagoans up to 1940. This notion
of a 'New School', then, construes a Chicago tradition of
qualitative sociology, which the fourth generation have developed, not as the dominant approach, but as a radical alternative in a discipline becoming increasingly sterile as a result
of an overcommittment to 'reliability' and 'validity'. [11]

13

The assumption among historians and sociologists of sociology is that there was a 'Chicago School' of sociology and that it had a considerable bearing on the development of American sociology during the first half of the twentieth century. However, the exact nature of the 'school' and the impact it had are not clearly defined. As we have seen, a number of different sorts of reconstructions of the school have been developed.

In the light of the various partial constructions outlined above, it is perhaps opportune to outline who the Chicagoans were before going on to investigate their work.

A brief chronology of the Department of Sociology at the University of Chicago

When Albion Small was appointed head professor of the Department of Sociology and Anthropology at the University of Chicago in 1892 it was the first sociology department to be established in a university anywhere in the world. Along with Small in the Department in its first year were six other people. Charles Henderson was associate professor of social science, later to become head of the Department of Ecclesiastical Sociology (1906) subsequently renamed Practical Sociology (1913). Marion Talbot was assistant professor in sanitary science; in 1903 she moved to the newly created Department of Household Administration. E.W. Bemis who was an associate lecturer in political economy was a member of the extension staff in sociology. W.I. Thomas was a fellow in the Department. He received his doctorate in 1896, was slowly promoted to a professorship (1910) and stayed on in the Department until forced to resign in 1918. In addition there were two anthropolgists, Frederick Starr, assistant professor and curator of the museum who remained in the Department until he retired in 1923 and G.H. West, docent for three years. (Appendix 1 contains full details of the information provided in this summary).

Small remained head of the Department and professor until 1925 during which time approximately thirty people were listed in the annual Official Publications of the University of Chicago as sociology teaching staff along with another three anthropologists. At no time, however, did the sociology group consist of more than half a dozen people. W. I Thomas was to emerge as the major theoretician in the early period of the 'Chicago School' and his impact on conceptual development at Chicago was to be profound. We shall examine this in some detail in chapter five. Apart from Thomas, the main appointments made during Small's headship were probably Vincent, Burgess, Park, Bedford and Faris. George Vincent, who co-authoured a sociology text book with Small (Small and Vincent, 1894), was a graduate student in 1893 who became a tenured member of staff at Chicago

14

until 1908. He became professor and Dean of the Faculty of Arts, Literature and Science in 1907 before leaving to become President of the University of Minnessota. In 1917 he was appointed as President of the Rockefeller Foundation (Diner, 1980).

E.W. Burgess was also a Chicago graduate student and received his doctorate in 1913. He was appointed in 1917 as an assistant professor and remained in the Department until 1951. Following his retirement in 1952 he remained active as an emeritus professor into the 1960s. His long term involvement with the Department, covering some fifty years, made him an important figure in its development.

An equally important appointment, initiated by Thomas (Matthews, 1977; Raushenbush, 1979), was that, in 1914, of Robert Park. Initially appointed as a professorial lecturer, Park became a full professor in 1923. He is regarded by a number of commentators (Faris, 1967; Matthews, 1977; Coser, 1971) as the prime force behind the rapid development of empirical study in the Department during the 1920s. Park retired in 1933 and became attached to the Tuskegee Institute although he remained professor emeritus until his death in 1944.

S.W. Bedford was another long term appointment made under Small. He was associated with the Department over a twenty year period until his resignation in 1925. His principal interest had been urban sociology and his teaching actually gave an impetus to the area which is most usually associated with the 'Chicago School' (Diner, 1980). However, he published very little and did no empirical research and perhaps for this reason is not often regarded as a significant figure in the development of sociology within the Department. Faris (1967, p. 32) mentions Bedford once, referring to him as an instructor. Bedford was, in fact, an associate professor when he resigned [12].

Apart from Ira Howerth and Anne Marion MacLean who taught in the extension division, other members of the Department, excluding fellows, recorded in the Official Publications up to 1925 were C. Zeublin, A.F. Bentley, J.H. Raymond, H. Woodhead, G.Taylor, M.S. Handman, C. Rainwater, F. Znaniecki, F.N. House and E.N. Simpson. In addition Edith Abbott taught part time in the Department as a lecturer in methods of social investigation until 1920 while also assistant director of The Chicago School of Civics and Philanthropy (from 1908). With the formation of the School of Social Science Administration in 1920 she left the Department of Sociology and Anthropology.

One other major appointment was made during Small's leadership. Following Thomas' departure, Ellsworth Faris was appointed professor in 1920 and became Head of Department in 1926, a position he retained until his own retirement in 1939. During this period the Department of Sociology and Anthropology split into two separate departments (1929) and the Sociology Department finally appointed its own quantitative expert, W.F. Ogburn in 1927.

Chicago graduates from the 1920s who were to become professors and exercise some considerable influence on the Department were Louis Wirth, Herbert Blumer, Samuel Stouffer and Everett Hughes. Wirth was granted the doctorate in 1926 and, after two years at Tulane returned to Chicago in 1931 and became a full professor in 1940 following Ogburn's own promotion to Head of Department. Blumer gained his doctorate in 1928 and remained at Chicago. Blumer took over the teaching of Mead's social psychology course following Mead's death in 1931. Blumer's own promotion to full professor was not until 1947, at which time Ernest Burgess had taken over the headship of the Department. Stouffer, who had been an instructor for two years following the award of the doctorate in 1930, was reappointed at Chicago in 1935 as a full professor. Hughes received his doctorate in 1928 and left Chicago to teach at McGill University in Canada before returning to take up the appointment of assistant professor in 1938. He was eventually appointed to full professor in 1949 and became head of the Department for three years from 1954 to 1957. He retired in 1961.

Hughes was succeeded as head of Department by Philip Hauser, who was awarded a doctorate in 1938. He had been an instructor in the Department for five years prior to that and was reappointed in 1947, in the first year of Burgess' headship, as a full professor.

Burgess' headship also saw the inauguration of more varied developments in the Department and the growth of a number of associated staff involved in a variety of projects. One of these was the National Opinion Research Centre, whose directors were C.W. Hart (1954) and P. Rossi (1962) and whose senior study directors included S.A. Star (1954), E.S. Marks (1954), J. Elinson (1955), E. Shanas (1958), L. Kriesberg (1960), J. Feldman (1961) and J.W. Johnstone (1962). Another development was the Industrial Relations Centre, in 1955, for whom C. Nelson was Director of programme evaluation. Other projects included the Chicago Community Inventory; the Population Research and Training Centre (E. Kattagawa, 1956 and O.D. Duncan, 1959); the Farm Study Centre (E. Litwak, 1954); and Community Studies Inc. of Kansas City, Miss., (with whom Howard S. Becker was associated).

Another thirty people were also employed in a lecturing capacity in the Department of Sociology from 1926 to 1954. Of these, the following spent five years or more lecturing in the Department: E.H. Sutherland (1930-34), M.M. Davis (1932-37), E.S. Johnson (1933-41), C. Shaw (1935-1957), J.D. Lohman (1940-1956), E.A. Shils (1940-7 and 1957 onwards) [13], W.F. Whyte (1944-48), L. Goodman (from 1950), D. Horton (1948-57), D.G.

Moore (1950-55), N. Foot (1952-56) and W. Bradbury (1952-58).

The Department also employed teaching assistants (who are listed in the Official Publications between 1922 and 1932) and research fellows. Of the one hundred and eighty five fellows listed in the Official Publications up to 1952, eighteen went on to develop an academic career at Chicago.

In addition to the resident staff, the Department invited eminent sociologists from other institutions to teach, especially during the summer quarter (a system relatively unique to the University of Chicago). Among the twenty five different sociologists listed in the Official Publications who provided such courses were E.A Ross of Leyland Stanford University (1895), Lester Ward of the Smithsonian Institute (1896) Talcott Parsons of Harvard (1937) and Paul Lazarsfeld of Columbia (1949).

The work of the Chicagoans will be examined in detail in the next chapters and some of the myths about the Chicago School that have grown up over the last half century will be investigated.

The myths of the 'Chicago School'

The varied designations of the 'Chicago School' constructed as a result of different academic endeavours have lead to the emergence of a number of taken-for-granted conceptions of the school. These conceptions have taken on the character of myths [14], and are seen as emblems of a distinctive sociological approach. The prevalent taken-for-granted views of a 'Chicago School' raise metascientific questions. The designation of a 'Chicago School' is not independent of a view of the activities, approach and impact of the school. In effect, certain preconceptions are amplified by the designation of the work of the Chicagoans as reflecting a school. So, the designation of the 'Chicago School' and the myths of the 'School' are interdependent. What is taken to constitute the 'School' is influenced by what commentators take as characteristic of its work, while the myths about the school are amplified by specific widespread designations (Harvey, 1981, 1983; Lofland, 1983).

In assessing the sociological practice at Chicago, I have taken recourse to primary sources in order to assess secondary accounts. I have grouped various conceptions about Chicago together, to suggest five principle myths that underpin many of the constructions of the 'Chicago School'. These myths overlap and are, to some extent, contradictory. This is because they are not all directed to the same ends, nor arise as a result of the same endeavours.

These five myths are:

(1) that Chicago sociologists were primarily social ameliorists, sympathising with Progressive or liberal ideas and
concerned to resolve social problems.

(2) that Chicago sociology was dogmatically qualitative and
had no interest in quantitative techniques of social research and, indeed, were openly hostile toward them.

(3) that Chicago sociology had no strong theoretical orientation and its work, in the main, constituted a descriptive
exercise. Such theories as it did produce were little more
than ideal type models (notably the 'concentric zone' thesis) with little explanatory power.

(4) that Chicago sociology is closely associated with symbolic interactionism and dominated by the epistemological
perspective of G. H. Mead.

(5) that the 'Chicago School' dominated American sociology
until the mid-1930s and then went into decline and became
isolated mainly because it retained an old fashioned, unscientific, approach to sociology.

The following chapters examine each of these myths in detail
and the last chapter assesses the role that 'school' has played
in helping generate such myths and casts doubt on the concept
of school as currently utilised in the sociology of knowledge.

Notes

[1] The usage of the term metascience reflects that outlined by
    Radnitzky (1973). It is research into science as a develop-
    er of knowledge. Etymologically, it is something coming
    'after' science, or 'about' science. Science is here taken
    to refer to any empirically grounded area of enquiry,
    through which theoretical statements about the nature of
    the world (physical, natural or social) are made. This
    position is synonymous with such terms as 'Wissenschaft',
    'scienza' and 'nauka'.

[2] Szacki (1975) suggests that schools are also construed in
    terms of substantive content of a research area.

[3] Tiryakian (1979a) referred to the surrealists around Breton
    and Bulmer (1984a) referred to the Bauhaus School and the
    Impressionists. Besnard (1983) also likens sociological

schools to schools of art.

[4] Both Tiryakian's and Bulmer's criteria for schools are the result of an inductivist generalisation from a few cases.

[5] The University of Chicago, Joseph Regenstein Memorial Library, Special Collections Department houses an enormous amount of archive material covering the span of this study. I am grateful for the assistance afforded by the staff of this department in accessing source material.

[6] The Department of Sociology and Anthropology inaugurated a Society for Social Research in 1921. Membership was open to all social researchers (graduates and staff), election to the society was fairly straightforward and new members were constantly being added. Graduates and staff remained members after they moved away from Chicago. By 1926 there were around one hundred and fifty members. Subscription, payable annually, was a nominal $1. Each year, from 1923, Summer Institutes were held which lasted about three days and included a substantial proportion of invited visiting speakers, some of whom were members. The format of the regular weekly meetings changed over the years, but generally they were addressed by graduates, staff, or outside speakers on matters of research practice, findings or philosophy. The society served to keep members informed of current research ideas and work in progress and also functioned as an informal network with contacts around the country. Hughes (1980) noted that while he was away in Canada he kept in constant touch with the University through the Society for Social Research. The society also performed one other major function, that of arranging discounts on text books and research monographs. Appendix 3 contains details of the Society for Social Research including the Constitution and a membership list.

[7] The Society for Social Research produced a Bulletin in 1926 and continued to do so two or three times a year throughout the period of this study. The circulation list included current and past Chicago graduates.

[8] The political nature of outsider designations of the 'Chicago School' is considered in more detail in chapter seven, which looks at the so-called 'coup' in the American Sociological Society. It is notable that Bernard does not refer to a 'Chicago School' of sociology during his engagement with the Chicagoans at the time of the 'coup' in 1935 (Lengermann, 1979) although he does refer to our 'Chicago friends'.

[9] In 1972 James Carey interviewed a number of ex-graduates who had been at Chicago in the 1920s. The transcripts of these tape recorded interviews are lodged in the Special Collections Department of the Regenstein Library, University of Chicago.

[10] Certainly, Park and Ogburn never worked together during the six years they were both at Chicago, as Ogburn recalled.

When I went to the University of Chicago in 1927, September, Professor and Mrs. Park gave a large party in the first part of November to which neither I nor my wife was invited. I was sensitive on this point. Next I was told that repeatedly by various persons that Park spent a good deal of time in his classes belittling statistics and pointing out their limitations. I was invited to the University in part to teach statistics since none had ever been taught in sociology and none was then taught in any other social science. Perhaps I displayed too much missionary zeal for Park, who questioned whether there was any need of teaching statistics, so I was told. Next, one day he came in my office with a hand full of books and asked me to review them for the American Journal of Sociology, and then proceeded to tell me how to do it and what was expected of me. I took the books but never reviewed them. Though Park was twenty years older than I, I had been a full professor at Columbia for ten years, and was quite intellectually mature.... I never forgave Park, which is a trait very marked in me, not to forgive or forget a slight. I wish I were different and had not been so sensitive in regard to Park.... So I never saw Park except at meetings or greeted him as he passed. Oh yes, he did invite me once with all the department to his house and I went. I think Park was a great teacher for the few. (Ogburn journal, 4th and 5th April, 1955)

[11] Arguably, the journal Urban Life represents the coming together of the reconstruction of an ethnographic tradition with an urban studies one. The journal supposedly provides an outlet for sociologists who are continuing the 'Chicago Approach' to the investigation of the urban environment. The journal was inaugurated following the short lived endeavours of a group of 'Chicago Irregulars' in 1969, who aimed at 'reviving an ethnographic tradition' and encouraging works of 'Chicago informed urban ethnography' (Thomas, 1983a, p. 391). According to Lofland (1980, pp. 251-2), The 'Chicago Irregulars' were a group 'born in the living room of Sherri Cavan's San Francisco home on April 11, 1969,

when Sherri Cavan, John Irwin, John Lofland, Sheldon Messinger, Chet Winton, Jacqueline Wiseman, and I met and agreed that a "mutually supportive association of sociologists and others interested in the study of natural settings, everyday life, everyday worlds, social worlds, urban lifestyles, scenes, and the like" was in order. It died in late 1969 or early 1970 when the energies required to keep it going simply ran out. In between it turned out three newsletters (mailed to a continually growing list), held several seminars, started an archives (long defunct), and, most memorably, organized the Blumer-Hughes talk [of 1st September 1969].'

Sheldon Messinger, introducing the Blumer-Hughes talk added that the 'Chicago School Irregulars' had 'had the strong feeling that there is a substantial group of people in sociology for whom the Chicago School is still a very viable institution, notwithstanding the spread of its members away from Chicago to Berkeley and Brandeis, to name two places.... The group is devoted to keeping the Chicago School tradition alive. Many of the people in it do what is nowadays called ethnography - in the old days it was called nosing around. Others, who aren't themselves doing ethnography, are reading about it, talking about it, and trying to keep up the standards established many years ago by people at Chicago' (Messinger, 1980, p. 254).

During the talk, Hughes was disparaging about attempts to preserve a tradition but told the group 'go ahead and be a Chicago School if you like.' (Hughes, 1980, p. 277)

By 'recreating' a 'Chicago urban ethnography' these irregulars are constructing a heritage and providing a legitimation for their work. Thus, possibly, Urban Life presents nothing more substantial, by way of an elucidation of the 'Chicago Approach', than a picture of Chicago which fits in with its own requirements as a vehicle for ethnographic urban researchers.

[12] Blumer (1980b) and Hughes (1980) recalled their time at Chicago in a talk in 1969. They made jocular references to 'someone who taught urban sociology', but were unable to recall Bedford by name. Bulmer (1984) pointed out that Bedford was forced to resign as he did not fulfil the criteria for a member of staff Small required of him.

[13] Bulmer points out that Sutherland was a research professor in the Division of Social Science from 1930-35 and that Shils' original appointment was on the Committee on Social Thought. (Correspondence 1.4.1985). The information in the text derives from the Official Publications of the University of Chicago.

[14] Myth does not refer here to the original anthropological sense of 'fabulous narration' a sense in which it is still commonly widely used. Nor does it refer to a 'distorted' thesis about the origins of humanity. In short, myth does not mean either fable or legend. Nor is myth used simply to mean a deliberately false account or belief. It is used in the sociological sense of a pervasisve taken-for-granted account. This reflects, for example, the work done in analysing the mythical element of media messages. Thus myth is used in the sense of generalised connotation (Barthes 1967, 1974; Centre for Contemporary Cultural Studies, 1978; Larrain, 1979). This raises questions about the relationship between myth and ideology, the nature of ideology and the relationship between ideology and knowledge. These important questions, however, go beyond the scope of this analysis of the role of 'school' in the production of scientific knowledge and the particular account of the 'Chicago School'.

I have identified five myths, although I do not claim that they are exhaustive. Similarly, I take the point that one must be careful not to construct 'straw-man' images. However, I cannot agree at all with Denzin (1984, p. 1431) who, in a review of Lewis and Smith (1981), argues against any myths surrounding the 'Chicago School'. Whether Denzin is simply referring to the myth Lewis and Smith project around the role of Mead or whether he is suggesting that the 'Chicago School' is not characterised by myth at all, is not clear. However, the substantive point is that in analysing myths the historian must avoid the construction of the myth.

2 Chicagoans as ameliorists

The myth

The 'Chicago School' of sociology has often been associated with both amelioration and social reform. Friedrichs (1970, p. 73), for example, characterises the leaders of the 'Chicago School' as 'prophetic seers dedicated to the progressive amelioration of social ills', and Madge, (1963, p. 125) talks of the 'Chicago School's' 'faith in human betterment'. Tiryakian (1979a) linked the 'School' with civic reform and a number of other commentators refer to the Chicagoans involvement in, or concern with, amelioration and reform (Berger and Berger, 1976; Molotch, 1976; Castells, 1977; Greeley, 1977; Philpott, 1978; Brake, 1980; Kuklick, 1980).

Often, amelioration and reform are conflated in the literature on the history of sociology, and especially in relation to Chicago. For example, Hunter (1983, p. 473) observed

> The concluding chapters of Zorbaugh's [1929] study, as did most analyses of the early Chicago social scientists (Hunter, 1980), turned to the issue of applying his knowledge and insights to ameliorative social reform.

A clearer understanding of the role of reform in the development of sociology in the United States and the role of the Chicagoans in the development of sociological theory is facilitated if a distinction is made between reform and amelioration. Amelioration is taken here to be action guided by personal ethical values and a sense of Christian mission. Usually, ameliorative practices are linked to charitable works. Social reform, on the other hand, is linked to civic action and aimed at longer term structural change [1]. However, the distinction between the two did not become clear until at least the 1920s. Lapiere (1964), indeed, suggested that sociology did not escape reformism until much later.

> As you no doubt learned in your first course on the history of sociology, American sociologists of the first two decades of this century were - with some few exceptions, of which Cooley is the only one who comes to mind - just moralistic reformers in scientists' clothing. What you may not know, or at least not fully appreciate, is that well into the 1930s the status of sociology, and hence of sociologists, was abominable, both within and outside the academic community.
> The public image of the sociologist was that of a blue-nosed reformer, ever ready to pronounce moral judgements, and against all pleasurable forms of social conduct. In the universities, sociology was generally thought of as an uneasy mixture of social philosophy and social work.

Lapiere further suggested that it was only through the work of individuals using quantitative methods and located in isolated, mainly 'one man' departments, that sociology threw off this image. Yet this contradicts what the Chicagoans believed themselves to be doing. They, like other pioneers in the field, were concerned to establish a scientific approach to society devoid of ameliorative or reformist interests.

The view of Chicago sociology which suggests they were reformist or ameliorist is primarily aimed at the early years of the 'Chicago School', from the inception of the department in 1892 to the end of the 'golden era' (Faris, 1967; Cavan, 1983) around 1933. It tends to encompass the work of Small and Henderson, through to Burgess. The later work of the Chicagoans, especially as embodied in the deviancy studies of Becker in the 1950s, is seen to be explicitly antimeliorist (Gouldner, 1973).

Arguably, however, Chicago sociology was never committed to amelioration although some of the very early work encouraged by Henderson was possibly mediated by an interest in intervention. Chicago's involvement in reform was tempered by a concern with objective science and, from at least the first world war, it consistently adopted an attitude of 'detached' sociological enquiry, reflecting changes throughout the discipline. An analysis of the research conducted at Chicago will indicate the extent to which reformist tendencies were evident and illustrate that the 'School' changed its position in relation to

24

reform in a way which paralleled American sociology as a whole.

Small and Henderson and Christian reform

The 'golden era' of the 'School' (1918-33) was the period in which the shift from reform to 'objective research' was completed (Cavan, 1983, p. 407). The earlier founding period, during which time Small and Henderson were most influential, was, arguably, inclined more towards reformist ends and was close, at times to ameliorative concerns (Matthews, 1977, p. 93). Henderson, in particular, saw sociology as interwoven with Christian reform and, under the auspices of his role as University chaplain, published an article in which he wrote that 'God had providentially placed the social sciences at the disposal of reformers' (Henderson, 1899). Henderson had had a long experience of practical philanthropy before moving to the University. The city of Chicago itself was noted for its involvement in ameliorative issues and reform movements in the first decades of the century. There was a rapidly growing number of voluntary and civic organisations in the immediate pre-first world war period and, gradually, a more systematic programme of civic reform developed (Diner, 1975). Henderson had close ties with two such prominent organisations: Jane Addams' 'Hull House' and Graham Taylor's 'Chicago Commons'. He was impressed by the social surveys undertaken by them and promoted similar empirical work at the University. He argued that first hand observation and intimate experience of daily life as experienced by the 'poor, the socially deviant and the distraught' was essential as a basis for Christian reform.

However, the work undertaken in these early studies encouraged by Henderson (and Talbot), whilst motivated by 'reformist' concerns, were not all, however, simplistic ameliorative undertakings. For example, MacLean (1910) researched women in the labour force with a view to examining the role of trade unions. For her, trade unions represented a rational strategy of industrial betterment in which the employee rather than the employer was the motivating force. So, even at this early stage, the encouragement of first hand investigation was directed towards an understanding as well as the alleviation of problems.

Small, too, argued forcibly for empirical research and encouraged first hand investigation. He advocated an 'objective' approach to social enquiry and, while he believed that sociology must be essentially Christian, 'distrusted the preachers of the Social Gospel' (Matthews, 1977, p. 95). Barnhardt (1972) recalled that Small was not at all keen on his attending Matthews' course on 'The New Testament and Social Problems' in the Divinity School, nor a course on social work with Breckinridge. Small thus distanced the sociological work of the department from social work and the religious concerns of the University.

Between 1895 and 1915 Small and Henderson attempted to reconcile the debate between the naturalist sociologists and the Christian reformers (Inskeep, 1977). They refused, on the one hand, to confine sociology to the New Testament scriptures, nor, on the other, would they sacrifice spiritual answers entirely. Post Darwinian naturalism and New Testament spirituality both held self evident natural truths for Small and Henderson, and they were not prepared to limit their insights to a unidimensional approach. Thus, Small and Henderson promoted Christian concerns, but in the context of an understanding of social processes.

Many of Carey's (1975) interviewees indicated, however, that by the 1920s the religious connotation was less evident. Indeed, they claimed that the Department tended to ignore religion, in the sense that there was no attempt to develop an attitude to sociology or social problems which ostensibly reflected religious concerns. The bitter struggle between evolutionism and fundamentalism had been resolved in the former's favour and Chicago adopted an evolutionary approach, and with it a kind of 'religious indifference'.

The Department had been established at a time when sociology and Christian reform were seen as compatible and its faculty composition was influenced by this perceived relationship. As the new century unfurled, sociology and reform were less closely allied. Indeed, at Chicago, a separate department of Ecclesiastical Sociology was established in 1904, later to become the Department of Practical Sociology (1913). Henderson was professor of the department and it is notable that, after his death in 1915, the course structure in the Department of Sociology, with which he had still been closely linked, was revised. Courses which linked sociology with religion and reform were dropped or began to fade out. Thus, Small's own course on the 'Ethics of Sociology' was never actually taught, and Burgess's 'The Causes and Prevention of Poverty' ran only rarely in the next decade. 'Problems and Methods of Church Expansion', 'Contemporary Charities' and 'Family Rehabilitation' rapidly disappeared and, like 'Church and Society', were not taught by mainstream sociology staff. The later reorganisation of courses in 1924 saw a pronounced distancing of sociology from social reformism (see Appendix 4), and the establishment of a more 'scientific' approach to sociological enquiry.

> The conflicting interests of human betterment and objective studies were apparent from the beginning. The purpose of sociology was not humanitarianism or social reform, but an understanding of human behaviour.... Small... set the stage for an objective research approach. (Cavan, 1983, p. 409)

Small, arguably, had always seen sociology as an objective science in its own right, and not just as an extension of moral philosophy, although ethical considerations pervaded his sociology (Dibble, 1972). In arguing for the founding of the American Journal of Sociology, Small noted that

> every silly and mischievous doctrine which agitators advertize, claims sociology as its sponsor. A scientific journal of Sociology could be of practical social service in discrediting pseudo-sociology and in forcing social doctrinaires back to accredited facts and principles. (Small, 1895)

For Small, sociology was a scientific and ethical discipline oriented towards reform based on sound knowledge. Ethical considerations, for Small, provided the basis for decisions about what areas of enquiry were suitable for sociology, while enquiry should proceed scientifically. The canons of science advocated by Small were value neutrality, objectivity, and theoretical analysis. Value neutrality meant non-partisanship, objectivity meant rooting assertions in empirical evidence rather than conjecture, and he saw science as necessitating inductive theorising not just the collection of 'raw facts' (Small and Vincent, 1894). He saw science proceeding through the correlation of facts, through a procedure that would allow for the grasping of meaning embedded in facts.

Small maintained that the worth of scholarly research lay in its objective, non-partisan perspective. The more a work took into account diverse views the more objective Small saw it to be. He expected sociological research to take into account the wider social milieu, yet be empirically grounded, as he noted in a letter to Harper in 1891

> I would never grant the doctorate to men of the microscope alone, but would insist that they shall have acquired a sharp sense of relation of what their microscope discovers, to the laws of society as a whole. (Small, 1891)

Thomas and the demand for pure research

With the death of Henderson and the waning of Small's influence, Thomas became prominent at Chicago during the first decade of the twentieth century. His was an important role in the transformation of sociology into an 'objective empirical' discipline.

> He was dedicated to the belief that sociology had to have a subject matter and a body of empirical findings.... But his

position was not that of a narrow empiricism such as later characterized much of American sociology. He was a man genuinely interested in broad explanations, but prepared to confront social reality at each point in the research process. (Janowitz, 1966, pp. ix and xxix)

He reasserted Small's contention that understanding of the social world must precede social action and that objective research was the goal of sociologists. He extended this to the point of shelving Small's ethical concerns and, in this, reflected the prevailing attitude towards social science. Objectivity, in the sense of impartiality, had become a major concern and directive for social research (Bernard and Bernard, 1943; Schwendinger and Schwendinger, 1974; Furner, 1975). Thomas replaced particular ethical considerations with a more general concern with social control. For the Chicagoans who followed him, sociology was inexorably linked to social control rather than amelioration or reform.

'When sociology emerged as an intellectual discipline, the idea of social control was a central concept for analyzing social organization and the development of industrial society' (Janowitz, 1978, p. 27). Social control, in its classical sense referred to the self regulation of a society, in accord with 'desired principles and values' (Vincent, 1896; Ross, 1901) [2]. Although by no means a radical sociological perspective, social control does not imply a reactionary position. Rather social control involves the constituent groups of a society acting in a manner commensurate with acknowledged collective goals. Social control can be conceived as resting on a value commitment to reduce coercion, while accepting a legitimate system of authority, and to eliminate human misery, while recognising the persistence of some degree of inequality (Janowitz, 1978, p. 30).

Ross (1901) moved the concept of social control into the centre of sociological analysis, but it was Cooley and Thomas who developed the concept. For Cooley, social control and the notion of self were interrelated. The self grew through interaction and social control was essential in this process. Conversely, self-control was fundamental for social control (Cooley, 1920). Thomas argued that sociologists as well as public servants of various sorts should aim to develop effective rational control in social life (Janowitz, 1975, p. 37). For Thomas, social control depended on the effective linkage of ecological, economic and technological factors. Social disorganisation resulted when these factors did not mesh together.

In his review of the origins of the Society for Social Research at the University of Chicago, Park (1939) suggested that Thomas provided the basis for work done at Chicago. This involved not only the role of sociology in the process of social control but also the distancing of sociology from reformist concerns.

> It is in the work of W.I. Thomas, I believe, that the present tradition in research at Chicago was established. .... His **Source Book for Social Origins** (1909) ... introduced a point of view from which society, with its codes, conventions, and social programs, was regarded as a natural phenomenon, the result of purely natural processes. From this point of view society ceased to be a body of legal conventions or moral ideas which sociologists were seeking to criticize...
> He wanted to see, to know, and to report, disinterestedly and without respect to anyone's politics or program, the world of men and things as he experienced it. (Park, 1939, pp. 1-2)

Thomas was, then, instrumental in the advocacy of direct, detached, first-hand experience of the social world (Park, 1939; Hayner, 1972). Thomas advocated empirically informed theorising and saw himself as a scientist of society. He hoped his work would provide a sound basis for social policy (Janowitz, 1966) and he saw sociology as providing the laws by which change could take place. These laws were not seen by Thomas as completely deterministic but merely as providing the frame within which action would be constrained. These laws would provide the basis for social control, the principal objective of sociological enquiry. Empirical analysis of concrete historical situations in the manner of the objective sciences would permit the discovery of these laws.

> By following the example of the physical sciences and accumulating the largest possible amount of secure and varied information and establishing general and particular laws which we can draw on to meet any crisis as it arises, shall we be able to secure a control in the social world comparable to that obtained in the natural world, and to determine eventually the kind of world we want to live in. (Thomas, 1917, p. 188)

To achieve this, Thomas argued that sociology should concern itself with 'pure' research and should not worry about direct social utility. Drawing parallels with the physical sciences he argued that research in the social sciences should proceed irrespective of practical applicability. Sociologists should not be dependent on practice, particularistic reform should not inform sociological endeavours. He argued that if we recognise that social reform is to be reached through the study of behavior, and that its technique is to consist in the creation of attitudes appropriate to desired values, then I suggest that the most essential attitude at the present moment is a public attitude of hospitality toward all forms of research in the social world. (Thomas, 1917, p. 188)

Thomas's own major empirical work (Thomas and Znaniecki, 1918; Thomas, 1924) reflects his concern with producing theoretically informed analyses of social phenomena (Bulmer, 1984; Kurtz, 1984).

This concern with social research rather than with instrumental studies, while not the only consideration underpinning research in the department, became established among the Chicago sociologists and, indeed, within the social sciences at Chicago in general. Bedford's resignation, for example, after twenty years in the department, following Small's retirement, was possibly as much to do with his lack of interest in 'pure sociology' and too great a social work orientation (Barnhardt, 1972), as it was a result of moral improprieties (Bulmer, 1984).

In the 1920s there was considerable competition amongst leading graduate departments, vying for theoretical leadership in their field. The University of Chicago as a whole was keen to stake a reputation. The faculty committee report of the Commission on the Graduate Schools of the University of Chicago, (26th October 1925) stressed knowledge for its own sake rather than applied knowledge with practical applications, and recommended that graduate courses be organised to foster such research. Indeed, in the Ogg Report (1928) on the extent and nature of research in the humanities undertaken at American Universities, Chicago and Columbia were identified as in the forefront of the development of 'pure learning'.

Park's anti-reformism

Park endorsed Thomas' perspective (Blumer, 1980b) and reflected the development of American sociology in general. Park's approach to social analysis had evolved from his news-reporting concern to expose social ills, to doing something about them in his work at Tuskegee, to beginning to understand the processes which bring about social problems. He had reached the threshold of the last stage when he moved to Chicago, to a department that he saw as clearly espousing a theoretical rather than an ameliorative perspective.

Looking back, Park (1939, p. 2) noted that he had always been of the opinion that sociology as a mere 'science of social

welfare' would be ineffective as a contributor to social welfare because it would be limited to practical affairs and
lacking a fundamental theoretical base.

> The conception of sociology which made it a science of
> welfare would have limited research to practical problems,
> as they were conceived by various social agencies. In so
> doing it tended to discourage that intellectual interest
> and natural curiosity which had been so largely responsible
> for the growth of science in other fields (social anthropo-
> logy for instance) which have not been dominated by practi-
> cal and ethnocentric interests to the same extent that is
> true of sociology in the United States.
> It was in his Social Origins that Thomas seems definitely
> to have broken with the American tradition that identified
> sociology with social politics and limited social research
> to so-called 'social problems. (Park, 1939, p. 2)

Park indicated that Social Origins (Thomas, 1909) served to
shift the focus of attention of sociology and to revive a
scientific interest in social processes and turn sociology away
from social reform and 'social welfare'. Park's analysis denies
the assumption sometimes made that empiricism at Chicago was a
function of reform initiatives. For him, empirically grounded
study served to reveal the 'real world' of social relations,
and illustrate the essentially limited and misconceived world
view of 'do-gooder' reformers.
Park identified with Thomas' view of sociology; he was a
vociferous supporter of the dictum of non-alignment, and is
reported (Faris, 1967; Coser, 1971) to have been displeased by
students who espoused reformist sentiments.

> Park was just vicious in his attack on social workers and
> reformers and do-gooders. They were lower than dirt. The
> thing to do was get out and know what life was like. His
> students got this attitude quite readily from Park and
> Thomas also. (Cottrell, 1972)

Apparently, Park commented that Chicago had suffered more at
the hands of 'lady reformers' than from gangsterism, and Blumer
(1972) recalled that there was hostility between Park and
Breckinridge (Head of the School of Social Science Administration). Sociology students, while able to take courses in other
departments, were discouraged from taking social work courses.
This antagonism towards social work was about 'science'.

> Park was decisive in his view that in order for reforms to
> have reasonable chances of being successful... they should
> be grounded upon a scientific knowledge of human society

and settings in which the reform efforts were to be undertaken. (Blumer, 1972, p. 8)

In the wake of the race riots of 1919 [3] Park advised Johnson, the associate executive secretary and black co-director of
the commission of investigation, to study race relations with
the same detachment that a biologist might adopt in dissecting
a potato bug (Turner, 1967, p. xvi). Johnson apparently adopted
a dispassionate 'cold-blooded' approach (Faris, 1967, p. 131)
and was attacked for being a 'calm student' rather than an
'active reformer' (Bracey et al., 1973, p. 15). Park, while
interested in Johnson's work, actually maintained a distance
from the commission investigating the Chicago race riots, although asked for advice on the nomination of the executive
secretary. As he was the foremost authority in Chicago on race
relations, this distancing seems peculiar. However, the commission was 'clearly the idea of reform minded civic leaders'
(Bulmer, 1981), and Park was more interested in illuminating
public opinion than direct social improvement.

Park fought vehemently against reformist crusades and endorsed Thomas' pioneering approach to the science of society. Park
was, at times, somewhat aggressive in making this view quite
clear to his students, especially those who espoused reformist
sentiments. Park's research tended to be informed by policy
problems, underpinned by a concern with social control, but
conducted with varying degrees of detachment from policy implications. At root, all problems of society were, for Park,
problems of social control (Park, 1967). He did not equate
social control with conformity; rather, social control was
about collective problem solving (Janowitz, 1975). For Park,
the usefulness of social science lay not in its immediate
ameliorative or reformist application, but in its ability to
cast light on public opinion. For example, in his survey of
'Chinese, Japanese and British Indian' residents on the Pacific
Coast, (Park, 1926) sponsored by the Institute for Social and
Religious Research, Park insisted on a disinterested survey
while the sponsors wanted to use it as a means of educating the
public. Park argued for a study which took popular views about
ethnic minorities at face value and then attempted to understand why and how such opinions emerged (Matthews, 1977, p.
114).

Thus, Park's own work, as well as that of his students, was
directed at the sociological analysis of social problems. He
insisted that any commentary on 'social ills' be pitched at a
holistic level and related to the idea of social control.

Though the outsider would never have suspected it, he
embarked upon his career with a passion for social reform
and ended it with the same goal to improve the human lot.

But he was never a 'for God-saker', as he used to refer to
the crusaders who ignored reality. His interest in the
solution of problems of human interrelationships was chast-
ened by the recognition of the facts of life and the nature
of social change. He was a disciplined humanitarian.
(Wirth, 1944, p. 3) [4]

While Small had increasingly argued for the development of
sociology independent of ameliorative concerns, he had been
constrained by ethical considerations. Thomas had pushed
Small's scientific concern away from its ethical constraints by
arguing for 'pure' research as fundamental for the understanding of social problems and as a basis for sound policy decisions. This suited Park who increasingly advocated the practice
of a disinterested sociology.

I think, like all young newspapermen, he thought that the
power of the press was something and he could really get
things done in the world by exposing it, and so on. I think
that he just sort of found out that that wasn't the case
and retired into a scientific attitude. The thing to do is
to understand these processes and when we understand them
then we will be able to control intelligently and rational-
ly. That was the general mind set I got from him. So reformism was in ill-repute. (Cottrell, 1972)

Park, then, was opposed to piecemeal and theoretically unin-
formed social action. Park advocated a 'big picture' perspective. For him, social action needed to be rooted in a sound
understanding of social processes. Park, like Thomas, saw the
pure dimension as preceding the policy dimension of research.
'Even Park would say that once we know what is going on you can
use this knowledge to support some kind of rational social
order' (Cottrell, 1972).
Park wanted a clear distinction between social science and
reformism, not out of any notion that sociologists had no role
to play in reform, but because reform would be served better if
social science developed independently of reformist constraints
and perspectives. By the late 1920s, the issue of the reform
element of sociological enquiry was of secondary importance at
Chicago.

We were committed sociologists, we didn't think of it being
opposed to social reform or even really consider social
reform as such. (Faris, 1972)

By the time I got to Chicago I pretty well made the kind of
transition that I think a lot of people made from a kind of
religious motivated interest to do something about the ills

of society to a scientific orientation. What is it that makes the thing tick? (Cottrell, 1972)

The idea as I saw it was that sociology was not an applied science, its function was not to bring about changes in society but describe society accurately and presumably, then, if you wanted to become a society changer you could do so by stepping out of the description role and going into the action role. (Dollard, 1972)

Burgess and action research

Of the sociologists at Chicago through the 1920s, Burgess was perhaps more concerned with the policy implications of research than other faculty members. He tended more towards evaluative or 'action research' (Hayner, 1972).

Burgess was much more explicit. In fact Burgess was always somewhat suspect among his more 'objective scientific colleagues' as being a little bit too much motivated by wanting to save the family, or cure delinquency, or help social workers do their jobs better because he always had a very practical flair, everything he did he was really very atheoretical and eclectic. (Cottrell, 1972)

Burgess had close ties with a number of city-based social and ameliorative organisations; had contacts with local and national social work agencies; and, up to the 1930s, had reasonably friendly relations with the social workers in the university. He encouraged Hayner and Johnson, for example, to take courses in case work in the School of Social Science Administration in the early 1920s despite a certain distancing of the sociologists and social workers (Hayner 1972; Johnson, 1972).

There wasn't much friendly contact between the social work school and the department of sociology. Park was always very nasty in his comments about the social work profession. Burgess, they got along better with Burgess because Burgess did work with social agencies and was sympathetic to their problems and did think that investigation should throw light on what you could do about immediate practical problems in the family and delinquency and that sort of thing... Only Burgess had a real interest in the Chicago Area Project. (Cottrell, 1972)

Nonetheless, despite Burgess's apparent leanings towards 'reformism' this was not reflected in the work of the students at Chicago in general. There is little evidence to suggest that either ameliorative or reformist concerns were an important factor in graduate research at Chicago after 1915. Of the the forty two Ph.D. theses examined in detail, only three (7%) directed some attention towards reform, while twelve explicitly disassociated themselves from reformist concerns and the re-maining twenty seven had nothing to say on the subject.

Burgess may have been more concerned with the application of sociology than most of his associates. Nonetheless he had varied research interests of both a theoretical and a practical nature, which included work on crime and delinquency, the family and the community. His work tended to have fairly direct policy implications but was also concerned with social control (in the mould of Thomas and Park), and was underpinned by theoretical concerns. For example, he addressed the possibility of developing a more effective and rational basis for communal life in the increasingly fragmented urban metropolis, arguing for a coincidence of administrative areas and 'natural' commun-ities (Burgess, 1926a), while at the same time developing an 'ideal type' model of city growth (Park and Burgess, 1925). This zonal model he was to continue to develop for more than a quarter of a century (Hunter and Goldman, 1973).

In the 1930s, Burgess shifted more towards study of specific social problems, notably delinquency research. His approach was both policy influenced and theoretically grounded. On the one hand he was involved in an experimental programme of delinquen-cy control (The Chicago Area Project) and instrumental in developing predictors of success in parole for prisoners (Bur-gess and Tibbits, 1928) which the Illinois Board of Pardons and Parole adopted in 1933 and 'has used ever since' (Burgess, 1941). On the other, his theoretical interests in the 'deviant person' and the ecological analysis of deviancy were developed by the Illinois Institute for Juvenile Research (Shaw, 1930, 1931, 1938; Shaw et al., 1929; Shaw and McKay, 1942) with which he had close links, and by his students, notably Landesco (1929).

In his research on the family, Burgess again adopted this dual approach. He prepared the ground for studies of the family which persisted well into the 1960s. Burgess saw the family as an interacting unit, and was principally concerned with the dynamics of the modern family as it confronted changing socio-economic and cultural conditions (Cottrell, 1972). Burgess hypothesised that each type of natural area had a distinctive pattern of family life, and Mowrer (1927), one of his students, tested this out in Chicago. Burgess was concerned with the nature and functioning of the family and thus emphasised the need for analysis of the internal dynamics of the family unit (Burgess, 1926b; Dollard, 1931). In view of the widespread prediction by social scientists in the mid 1920s that the end of the family was imminent, Burgess (1926c) analysed the breakdown of marriage, looking for indicators of success (Burgess and Cottrell, 1936, 1939), in a similar fashion to his earlier prediction studies of parole success (Burgess and Tibbets, 1928).

> The practical value of the parole probation procedure induced a similar practical slant in the approach to the marriage study. The emphasis, therefore, was not on testing theoretically derived hypotheses so much as on identifying efficient predictors. (Cottrell et al., 1973, p. 75)

Many of the social problems that prompted study by graduate students in Chicago from 1915 to 1930 under the guidance of Burgess (see Short, 1971; Cottrell et al., 1973) were indeed a response to reformist concerns, for example, Cressey's study of 'Taxi Dance Halls' (Cressey, 1929), and the work of Shaw (1930). Much of the funding of such research, especially in the period up to 1924, came from private or ameliorative sources. Anderson (1983) recalled that the money for his study of Hobohemia (1923) came privately from Dr. W. A. Evans, and Shaw's studies were initially prompted by the interest of the Chicago Women's Club (Burgess, 1925). This was later incorporated under the auspices of the Chicago Juvenile Protective Agency with which Burgess had close ties and which also supported the work of Cressey.
Nonetheless, despite undertaking research linked to such agencies to a greater degree than did his colleagues, Burgess remained a social scientist first, and social reformer second, and insisted that his students adopt a similar distancing from reform. This is evident, for example, in the research on taxi-dance halls undertaken by Cressey (1932). The conclusion to Cressey's study sums up the approach to applied social research in the 'Chicago School'. Cressey noted that the taxi-dance hall developed naturally in the urban environment and should be considered as a problem of the modern city just like

> the problem of crime, of vice, and of family disorganization, we find in the taxi-dance hall the same forces which operate in all city life.... Toward misconduct such as is associated with the taxi-dance hall it would be easy to advocate some form of repression. But a policy involving repression alone would never be wholly successful. It does not get at the heart of the problem, for the problem is as big as the city itself. (Cressey, 1932, p. 287)

However, despite this liberal scientism, Cressey finished by suggesting that the needs of the taxi-dance hall patron should be met more 'wholesomely', following a thorough investigation, but that in the interim they should be condoned conditionally

as they 'serve the legitimate interests of men whose needs are
not met elsewhere' (Cressey, 1932, p. 291).

The taxi dance hall study reflects the concerns of many of
the sociologists at Chicago in the 1920s. A spirit of scientific enquiry was dominant, but a sense of social responsibility
still informed the interests of the graduates.

> A lot of my friends all seemed to have been challenged by
> having rejected a former kind of religio-moral orientation
> ... and we all still, underneath, we wanted to do some
> good, we wanted to make the city better, solve the problems
> of the family, do something about crime and so on... If you
> could get at these problems by a scientific objective
> rational approach analysing and working out.. you could
> avoid seeing the possibility that you might be a communist
> ... We were rebelling [through] this detached objective
> rational scientific way.... (Cottrell, 1972)

While Burgess had social work contacts and was interested in
the 'amelioration of social ills' (Short, 1973) it is question-
able whether even he adopted a wholly applied perspective.
Throughout his career he was also concerned with the development of sociology as a science and this appeared to take on
more importance over time. During the thirties Burgess shifted
to more 'rigorous scientific' methods and gradually loosened
his connections with the social workers

> Social workers weren't on good terms with sociology, they
> disliked Burgess very strongly.... I don't know what Bur-
> gess had done to offend them. Maybe Shaw did, Shaw was
> Burgess's protege... I think it was Breckinridge showing a
> fairly good statistical relationship between broken homes
> and delinquency. Shaw made a study where he just showed how
> defective that was. I think that infuriated her.... There
> was no real conflict between social work and sociology, I
> think we just ignored each other. (Faris, 1972)

Certainly, by the 1940s, the emphasis in the department as a
whole had shifted irrevocably away from reformism and any such
concerns were expunged from Burgess's proposal to the Rockefeller Foundation in 1941. In it he argued for the necessity of
basic research rather than policy research on 'transitory mat-
ters'. By this time, if not earlier, Burgess' primary concern
as a sociologist was to extend the frontiers of scientific
knowledge (Burgess, 1941). [5]

Burgess' early links to ameliorative and social work agencies
were related to his involvement in the Local Community Research
Committee the work of which was, to a large extent, tied up
with the concerns of city based social agencies.

The Local Community Research Committee and reformism at Chicago

The Local Community Research Committee was very important during the 1920s in attracting research funds to the social sciences at Chicago. Research monies were of two sorts, grants from the Laura Spellman Foundation and matched funds from local agencies. Both types were channeled through the Committee. Funding from the Laura Spellman Rockefeller Memorial Foundation was initially directed towards substantive problems related to children, the aged, immigrants, leisure and recreation, poverty, and neighbourhood relationships (Bulmer, 1980, p. 72). Thus, the sphere of research funded from this source was limited.

Similarly, the organisations contributing matched funds to the research of the Local Community Research Committee were primarily social agencies (Smith and White, 1929). The matched funding procedure accounted for about half the total funding of the projects under the Local Community Research Committee (Bulmer, 1980, p. 78). Matched funding tended to place the initiative for research in the hands of the community, who in effect made requests for services, sometimes to the detriment of less immediately applied research (Smith and White, 1929). (See Appendix 2 for full details of funding and publications related to the Local Community Research Committee).

An examination of the work published by social researchers funded by the Local Community Research Committee shows a heavy practical, reformist orientation. Of the forty-eight books or contributions to books published under the auspices of the Local Community Research Committee from 1923 to 1929, thirteen were on social welfare, nine on sociology, eight on politics, eight on business studies, three on geography, two on economics, one each on the census and on history. Of the forty one journal articles published under its auspices, ten were sociology articles, eight of these published by Burgess and two by Frazier. Thurstone, the psychologist, published thirteen articles and the publishing locations of the total article output clearly indicates that sociology was a peripheral rather than a central concern of the Committee. Even the three articles published in the American Journal of Sociology were by non-sociologists. Of research in progress in 1929, only seventeen (22%) of the seventy eight projects were sociological compared to economics (29%) and welfare projects (23%) [6]. Of this sociological work in progress, about half were M.A. theses and most of the rest was quantitatively oriented work undertaken or inspired by Ogburn. Much of the non-quantitative sociological work carried out in conjunction with the Local Community Research Committee seem to be 'social reformist' at least in conception if not their final presentation (e.g. Reckless, 1925; Conway, 1926; Leiffer, 1928; Cressey, 1929; Scott, 1929).

The Local Community Research Committee had both positive and negative consequences for 'pure research'. It did serve to establish the principle of co-operative social science research. It served as an embryonic organisation for the administration of such research. It encouraged a greater concern with methodology, and particularly provided opportunities to develop quantitative techniques (Bulmer, 1981a; 1984). It encouraged, if further encouragement was needed, empirical research in the social sciences. More importantly it enabled this research by attracting funds.

On the other hand, the Local Community Research Committee did not provide an academic forum. It had occasional discussion meetings to review progress, at which time the only satisfaction voiced was with its administrative role. It seemed not able to fulfil a consultancy, stimulatory, monitoring or, in any sense, an academic role. Even its organisation seemed to be ad hoc, Cottrell (1972) recalled that the organisation was loose and informal, with decisions often being made by telephone. Further, the nature of the funding attracted by the committee meant that reformist motivated research was prominent in the work supported by the Committee.

The role of the Local Community Research Committee seems to have been primarily, if not exclusively, administrative and directed towards fund raising, especially attracting research commissions and funds from outside, usually civic and 'caring' agencies. The result was a concentration on policy oriented research, rather than the more 'objective scientific' research which was encouraged and fostered through the Social Science Research Committee at Chicago, in the post 1930 period, in line with the policy of the Social Science Research Council.

However, the Local Community Research Committee did not generate research funds which, by any means, occupied all the research time of the sociologists at Chicago. Nor, where they were involved, did they get absorbed into reformist concerns at the expense of the development of sociological theory. For most of the sociologists the Local Community Research Committee was kept at a distance even where it did supply the money to enable their research.

Up to 1927, Burgess was the only sociology faculty member involved with Committee, and this was mainly due to his contacts with outside agencies. Park, notably, seems to have remained detached from the Committee. Ogburn became involved after 1927, encouraged by the Committee's sponsorship of the quantitatively oriented Thurstone and Schultz as research professors. It was only after 1929, when the Local Community Research Committee was terminated and reborn into the the Social Science Research Committee at Chicago in accord with the growing role of the Social Science Research Council nationally, that sociologists became more involved, and Faris, Wirth and

Ogburn in addition to Burgess served on it between 1929 and 1940.

Despite its importance in generating funds and promoting 'social' as opposed to 'sociological' research, the Local Community Research Committee did not create an institutional environment which fostered a reformist rather than a theoretical climate within which the sociologists had to work. It did not serve to inhibit sociological research through an encouragement of extensive involvement in ameliorative concerns. Amongst the sociologists, it was really only the work of Burgess and some of his students that may have been affected, but on balance, Burgess and most of his students still undertook scientific rather than ameliorative research.

The Society for Social Research and reformism

The Local Community Research Committee was a base for getting funds, but not a forum for ideas or analysis of work. In the Chicago context this was done through the Society for Social Research. If any organisation can be said to be representative of the 'Chicago School's' approach to amelioration then it is the Society for Social Research, rather than the Local Community Research Committee. Curiously ignored, the society was clearly the major academic clearing house for sociological and other social scientific research at Chicago for thirty years (Bulmer, 1983). Indeed, it provided the institutional focus for the development of the sociological work done at Chicago. The annual Institutes of the Society allowed Chicago to keep in touch with research elsewhere and also provided a window onto research developments at Chicago. Its orientation was firmly 'scientific'; social reform was kept at arms length. Sociology was distanced from central and municipal administration and was seen as distinct from the 'generalizations of the practical man' (Bulletin of the Society for Social Research, June, 1932). This concern with 'pure research' continued the Thomasian heritage and was put most forcefully to the Society by Ogburn when he commented that he 'deplored the obsession with practical ends as diverting attention from more fundamental studies' (Bulletin of the Society for Social Research, June 1930, p. 3).

The meetings of the Society between 1924 and 1935 do not indicate any real concern with reform. Of the one hundred and thirty six meetings over this period on which information was available, only 16 (12%) were directed to reformist or welfare concerns. Of these, twelve were given in the period 1924-26 and none of the addresses after 1933 could be construed as concerned with welfare or reform issues. Fifty per cent of all addresses that were presented to the Society which dealt with reform were presented by external, non-academic speakers, including all those addresses on reform issues presented after 1930. Only two sociology students addressed the Society about reform concerns and none of the sociology faculty did. The real concerns of the Society were the development of an 'objective' methodology and the consideration of the nature of scientific sociology (see Appendix 3).

Conclusion

As the nature of the concept of 'objectivity' changed, and as a more 'scientistic' approach to sociology emerged, so American sociology became more remote from social reformism. This is reflected in changes of attitude towards amelioration and reform. These two concepts took on divergent connotations during the first fifty years of the twentieth century as applied to social science. While the earlier concerns of sociology were highly influenced by Christian ethics and the desire to improve the lot of humanity, this ethical utopianism lost its momentum when confronted by the radical disavowal of religious concerns in Spencer's so-called 'Social Darwinism'.

While meliorists still probably formed the majority of American sociologists by 1910 (Matthews 1977), there was a gradual shift towards a more 'disinterested' approach which reflected the concerns of laissez-faire capitalism. The movement towards an 'objective' social science increasingly displaced ethical considerations in the wake of the first world war, and the distinction between amelioration and social reform became clearer (Rucker, 1969; Dibble, 1972; Carey, 1975; Furner, 1975). Charitable works, the essence of amelioration in the nineteenth century, were seen as incidental to the sociological endeavour, and while amelioration, as practiced by various organisations and analysed by academic departments, attempted to move beyond the administration of charity, there was still a strong sense in which amelioration was seen as 'doing good', as alleviating hardship. It was still integrally linked with voluntary organisations and unable to overcome the taint of amateurism, of partisanship, of interference. The 'revelatory' nature of the presentation of ameliorative enquiry, usually through the assemblage of 'facts' derived from statistical surveys designed to illustrate the extent of deprivation, and the ad hoc approach to social problems, detached ameliorative work from either theoretical concerns or an integrated social policy.

Sociology began its detachment from this charitable orientation by becoming more involved in social surveys (Burgess, 1916). Sociology provided a wider theoretical focus for amelioratively motivated enquiry towards social policy; the 'revelatory facts' were put into a wider context. This reform oriented work differed from the amelioration studies in that it attempted to seek causes in terms of generalisable social phenomena rather than in terms of particular situations. Reform was thus linked to sociological theory. Ethical judgements, partisanship and personal advocacy drifted more into the background. Analysis was aimed at a societal level, with a view to suggesting action.

Sociology in the United States moved towards an 'objective pure science approach' in the 1920s. This was made easier by the adoption of the 'disinterested' laissez-faire attitude in the stead of religiously based morals (Farberman, 1979). Over time, then, the Chicago sociologists revised their research practice, their methodological presuppositions and theoretical orientations to accommodate these changes [7]. The concern with social control was the focus through which the transition from social reform to social science was made at Chicago.

So, then, whatever reform orientation, motivation or consideration the Chicago sociologists espoused was mediated by an overriding concern to develop an 'objective science' of sociology. This dated back to Small, was carried through by Thomas and developed by Park and Burgess and their students. Whatever reform intent these students may have had was, for the most part, subverted to broader sociological concerns. This is especially noticeable in the potentially partisan studies which Park encouraged his students to undertake. He considered that developing a detached attitude to an area in which the researcher had some familiarity would provide insights that went beyond the mask of surface appearance. The work of Horak (1920), Hayner (1923), Young (1924), Thrasher (1926), Wirth (1926) and Frazier (1931) [8] are testimonies to the effectiveness of the approach and the adherence to objectivist demands. The Chicagoans were not primarily proponents of social reform. Rather, they were first and foremost detached enquirers into the social world, reflecting the growing 'scientific' concerns of the profession. They were not simply reformers dressed in scientists' clothing.

Notes

[1] Janowitz (1975) argues that social reform is guided by a concern with social control. He went on to argue (Janowitz, 1978) that social control served as a central concept in the development of sociological theory in the United States. He suggested that social control has been a 'sensitizing concept' or 'theoretical orientation' of sociology from the inception of sociology until the 1960s. Social control, he suggeted, emerged as a central theoretical

thrust by which sociologists sought to integrate substantive and theoretical interests. Sociological theory up to 1930 was heavily dominated by the concept of social control and this was also used as a 'vehicle for joining sociological analysis to "social problems" and social policy' (Janowitz, 1975, p. 40).

However, as we shall see, it is the theoretical analysis of social change and disorganisation which lead the Chicagoans, especially Thomas, to advocate an approach to sociology that did not concern itself with the direct, practical reformist potential of its enquiry. Thus Thomas' concern with social control and disorganisation is similar to Durkheim's concern with collective order and anomie.

[2] The opposite of social control is social coercion (Janowitz, 1978, p. 28). It is not social chaos. Indeed, social disorganisation is an inevitable aspect of control, societies will not always be in equilibrium.

[3] The Race Riot in Chicago in 1919 lasted from 27th July to 8th August. It resulted in thirty eight deaths, (twenty three blacks, fifteen whites) injury to 537 people (342 black) and made around one thousand people homeless. This was the first serious large scale race violence in Chicago. Although the loss of life and destruction had been extensive, martial law was not introduced. The riots were investigated by the Chicago Commission on Race Relations which produced a report of nearly seven hundred pages entitled 'The Negro in Chicago' (1922). The Commission was set up three weeks after the riots by the governor of Illinois following pressure from the Union League Club. A white lawyer chaired the Commision which consisted of six black and six white commissioners. Graham R. Taylor was appointed as executive secretary. He was a journalist and his responsibility was to write the report. Charles S. Johnson was associate executive secretary. Johnson was a graduate in sociology from the University of Chicago and he was the architect of the research programme, assisted by advice from Robert Park. (For more detail on the race riots see Waskow (1967), Tuttle (1970) and Bulmer (1981)).

[4] As a journalist Park had been a 'muckraker', particularly towards the Congo, with the avowed aim of exposing the appalling situation in that country. He wrote a serious of articles advertising the atrocities in the Belgian Congo which were designed to 'prepare the way for political reform action' (Faris, 1967, p. 28). Even at this stage, however, Park located the atrocities in a bigger picture, noting that the Belgian Congo was not unique but that it

43

was the inevitable result of 'more sophisticated peoples' invading the territories of 'more primitive peoples' in order to exploit their lands and, incidentally, to 'uplift and civilize them' (quoted in Faris, 1967, p. 29). His work at the Tuskegee Institute, although 'detached', was also geared to getting a better deal for blacks (notably through promoting self-help). Throughout his race relations work, however, Park attempted to retain a 'big picture' perspective and was opposed to piecemeal reform. Park saw racial equality as synonymous with democracy, and despite casual observations and perspectives which may now seem to be somewhat racist, his endeavour was directed towards the ending of prejudice. This is reflected in the obituary article written by Horace Cayton, in which he noted that while Park was economically conservative, or even reactionary, he had an altogether different view of race relations. Cayton quoted from a letter written by Park.

Democracy is not something that some people in the country have and others not have, not something to be shared and divided like a pie - some getting a small piece and some getting a large piece. Democracy is an integral thing.... The Negro, therefore, in fighting for democracy for himself, is simply fighting the battle for our democracy... If conflicts arise as a result of efforts to get their place it will be because the white people started them. These conflicts will probably occur and are more or less inevitable but conditions will be better after they are over. In any case, this is my conviction. (Park, 1944)

[5] Burgess was an experienced proposal writer by 1940 and one must read the proposal as that of someone who has a good idea of what kind of application is likely to attract funds.

[6] The classification of publications is based on (a) the series published by the University of Chicago Press in which they appeared, (b) the content of the article as indicated by title and sub-title (c) by inspection of the publication where (a) and (b) did not provide a clear indication.

[7] There are those who argue that Chicago was reformist despite itself. Kuklick (1980) maintained that the 'Chicago School' developed a form of 'reform Darwinism'. Irrespective of any ostensive reform concerns, the approach had direct policy effects. For example, following their research into 'natural areas' of Chicago, property valuation became addressed in terms of the race and character of the

mortgagee thus encouraging the institutionalisation of racial discrimination. Similarly, the movement of population through housing areas has become a self-fulfilling prophecy with further discriminatory results, including the subsidising of the middle classes. Greeley (1977), points to the 'Chicago School's' disorganisation thesis as responsible for augmenting nativists' reactions to immigrants. While the racial inferiority of non-Anglo Saxons was being promoted by, for example, the Dillingham Commission, the disorganisation thesis indicated that such immigrants were also culturally inferior. This provided a rationalisation for the Americanization movements of the early decades of the century, to which the race relations cycle theory addressed itself. Philpott (1978) reflected these sentiments too in addressing the way in which vested interests conspired to keep Chicago's slum dwellers in their run down neighbourhoods. Chicago sociologists, he intimated, naively contributed to this conspiracy through the provision of legitimating criteria. Prominent amongst these was the idea that ethnic groups all passed through a ghetto stage before the ethnic groups naturally disintegrated. Ghettos, Philpott argued, only ever really existed for the black population. For the rest the ghetto was a 'state of mind' rather than a geographic concentration. Ethnic identity could be maintained without the burden of becoming ghetto inmates with its associated economic oppression. The Chicagoans, through their 'middle class oriented studies' of the colourful areas of the city, inadvertently provided grist to the segregation mill. Carabana and Espinosa (1978) had also developed a similar line of critique in respect of symbolic interactionism arguing that it does not provide for a critical consciousness that can perceive of contradictory expectations. It represents, they claim, classic individualist contractualism, reducing personality to instincts. It is essentially 'reformist American individualism' providing a rationale for commercialisation. These criticisms, which have the benefit of hindsight, do suggest that the Chicagoans' apoliticism (Carey, 1975) probably unwittingly served conservative reformist ends. The Chicagoans, along with the majority of sociologists at the time, imagined that empirically based, disinterested research was fundamental to scientific sociological enquiry and the Chicagoans did not develop a critical methodology (Thomas, 1983b).

[8] Madge (1963, p. 110) noted of Thrasher that he 'was committed to a certain point of view in relation to gangs, which he found morally odious and difficult to view objectively.' Yet Thrasher restricted himself to footnote comments about

the 'intolerable' impact of racketeering and crime on the United States. Such comments were also 'objectified' by referring to the cost of crime, which, for example, in 1931 was estimated by the National Commission on Law Enforcement and Observance in excess of one thousand two hundred million dollars.

3 Chicagoans as ethnographers

The myth

One of the most common views of Chicago sociology is to see it as embodying a qualitative approach to sociology and thus at variance with a 'quantitative tradition' embodied in the approach adopted at Columbia. (Glaser and Strauss, 1967, p.vii; Berger and Berger, 1976, p.48). In this chapter the nature of the ethnographic work undertaken at Chicago will be examined. Chapter four will take up the 'forgotten tradition' of quantitative social research at Chicago.

Chicago is portrayed as rooted in 'qualitative sociology' (Deutscher, 1973, p. 325; Mullins, 1973; Tiryakian, 1979a, p. 227; Wiley, 1979, p. 56; Kuklick, 1980, p. 207). Some commentators suggest that map drawing, life history collection and even walking (Bell, 1977, p.52) were the major preoccupations of the Chicago sociologists (at least until 1930); while others imply that the Chicagoans were principally, if not exclusively, participant observers (Madge, 1963; Pusic, 1973; Bogdan and Taylor, 1975; Meltzer, et al., 1975; Rock, 1979). This methodological aspect of the myth of the 'Chicago School' is the most enduring and specific.

The idea of Chicago as the bulwark of ethnography is usually supported through reference to the work of three people at Chicago, namely Thomas, Blumer and Park. The latter is popularly seen as having instituted a programme of research which led to the adoption of participant observation. The views on ethnography of these three key figures, along with that of other

47

significant figures in the history of Chicago, will be examined below. The extent to which the Chicagoans relied on participant observation will be explored and the approaches adopted at Chicago will be put into the context of American sociology as a whole in order to assess the extent to which Chicago sociologists offered something methodologically unique.

The nature of ethnography

Part of the problem in assessing the methodological tendencies of the Chicago sociologists lies in the confusion over the use of terms. Ethnography has emerged, in the 1980s, as a term preferred to 'qualitative approach' but is no clearer in its delimitation of methodic practice or methodological tendency. Hammersley and Atkinson (1983, p.1) pointed to the diversity of usage of the term 'ethnography'.

> There is disagreement as to whether ethnography's distinctive feature is the elicitation of cultural knowledge (Spradley, 1980), the detailed investigation of patterns of social interaction (Gumperz, 1981), or holistic analysis of societies (Lutz, 1981). Sometimes ethnography is portrayed as essentially descriptive, or perhaps as a form of storytelling (Walker, 1981); occasionally, by contrast, great emphasis is laid on the development and testing of theory (Glaser and Strauss, 1967, Denzin, 1978).

The tendency in most approaches to ethnography is to view it as somehow opposed to the 'positivist' approach to sociology embodied in the 'quantitative tradition'. Ethnography is seen as aligned with 'naturalism' and concerned with 'meanings' rather than 'causes'. It is viewed as aiming essentially at an understanding of the processes of interaction and the way people construe their world in interactive settings. In this sense, ethnography is usually contrasted with the attempt at causal abstraction associated with quantitative research practice.

There are probably as many definitions of participant observation as a method as there are participant observers, and any general definition is bound to be disputable. The terms 'ethnography' and 'participant observation' are often used interchangeably. Both imply certain methodic practices and a methodological attitude. The distinction between ethnography and participant observation has become blurred. Ethnographers participate 'overtly or covertly, in people's daily lives for an extended period of time, watching what happens, listening to what is said, asking questions; in fact collecting whatever data are available to throw light on the issues' (Hammersley and Atkinson, 1983, p. 2)

Involvement, observation and an insatiable eclecticism, all elements of participant observation, seem to be covered by this definition. The re-emergence of the term ethnography draws methodic practice, such as non-participant observation, in-depth interviewing, into a common sphere with participant observation. Although there is no agreement on what ethnography or participant observation attempts to do, I would argue that the core of the modern concept of ethnography is 'getting out among the subjects of enquiry' in such a way that their perspective is engaged. Participant observation is thus the exemplary method.

However, the term participant observation has changed over time, and has not always been associated with the current wide notion of research practice associated with ethnography. Thus retrospective reconstructions sometimes attach current meanings to past research practice and in so doing are misled by them.

Lindeman (1924) first published an account of participant observation as part of his critique of current methods of investigation, notably the absurdity of surveyors in regarding their scheduled questions as free from bias. He argued for more emphasis on observation. But for Lindeman, observation was a form of asking questions and involved two things. First, the 'objective observation' of all external phenomena connected with behaviour and, second, 'participant observation from the inside'. For him, no one could do both and so joint investigations were imperative. Lindeman's approach was essentially behaviourist and concerned with the 'objective' observation of behaviour from two perspectives. The participant nature of the participant observation Lindeman recommended required no engagement with the subject's perspective.

Subsequently, in the 1940s, participant observation tended to mean the adoption of a role that would enable one to participate, to varying degrees, in the life of the subjects, in order to get first hand information (Daniel, 1940) usually as an adjunct to other research methods, notably the use of documentary material from other sources, such as case records. Only during the 1950s did participant observation emerge as a potentially exhaustive method in its own right (Becker and Geer, 1957), and with it the varied and extensive nature of the enterprise. Along with this came the ostensive engagement with the issue of the subject's perspective, expounded forcefully in Becker's (1967) question 'Whose Side Are We On?'.

The emergence of participant observation in its own right was related to the critique of 'positivism' and the emergence of 'naturalism'.

Participant observation research still produces much ethnographic description but its keynote has shifted to a more

'phenomenological' register, in which the texture of symbolic exchanges is highlighted in order to display the
practical committment of individuals to making their own
sense out of their social encounters. (Butters, 1973, p. 2)

Thus participant observation involved a 'style' of sociological
research

characteristically used for seeking analytic descriptions
of complex social organisations. This style emphasises
direct observation, informant interviewing, document analysis, respondent interviewing, and direct participation, and
is made possible in large part by repeated, largely social
interaction with members of the organisation under study.
The use of these techniques is organised by unusual research design in which hypothesis generation, data gathering and hypothesis testing are carried on simultaneously at
every step of the research process. (Butters, 1973, p. 1)

In this sense, participant observation research was not a
conspicuous feature of American sociological research at Chicago or elsewhere until the second half of this century. The
excursions into this form of research were fairly rare and
virtually non-existent prior to 1940. An examination of some
early examples of studies generally assumed to be based on
participant observation research will illustrate the gulf between the approach adopted and the 'naturalistic' concerns now
apparently central to participant observation. If these studies
(Anderson, 1923; Cressey, 1929; Zorbaugh, 1929) are participant
observation studies they are so only in the limited sense of
'first hand descriptive studies' and not in the sense of engaging the perspectives of the subjects in the field situation.
First, however, the notion of case study, a far more familiar
term and technique for Chicagoans, will be considered.

Case study

Rather than participant observation, early 'ethnographic' work
was oriented towards 'case studies' in which the collection of
'life histories' were regarded as important (Platt, 1981). The
core of case study research was the extraction of contextualis-
ed 'attitudes' [1]. The formation of attitudes both in terms of
the impact of personal experience and social mileu, were seen
as crucial for an interactionist sociology [2].
 Certainly for Thomas, at least initially, the optimum approach was to concentrate on life histories. These would reveal
the processes by which individual attitudes were mediated by
social values, and vice versa.

We are safe in saying that personal life-records, as complete as possible, constitute the perfect type of sociological material, and that if social science has to use other
materials at all it is only because of the practical diffi-
culty of obtaining at the moment a sufficient number of
such records to cover the totality of sociological problems, and of the enormous amount of work demanded for an
adequate analysis of all the personal materials necessary
to characterize the life of a social group. If we are
forced to use mass-phenomena as material, or any kind of
happenings taken without regard to the life histories of
the individuals who participate in them, it is a defect not
an advantage of our present sociological method. (Thomas
and Znaniecki, 1918, Vol 3, p. 1)

This statement has to be put into context. First, it is the
only time that such a forceful advocacy of life history is set
out in the Polish Peasant, and Thomas did not repeat it in his
work throughout the twenties, indeed his position, in practice,
was far less dogmatic (Thomas, 1928). Second, it prefaces the
one complete life history included in the first edition of the
Polish Peasant and is clearly designed to legitimate the inclusion. In the second edition the life history was shifted from
its central position and located at the end of the last volume
as a kind of appendix. In practice, Thomas and the other Chicagoans rarely used complete life histories.

There was an appreciation at Chicago of the problematic
nature of life history records, which was to lead to the development of attitude scales. (Thomas and Znaniecki, 1918;
Stouffer, 1930; Burgess, 1944a). Life history collection was
cumbersome, requiring vast resources and patient and very co-
operative subjects. Second, it was retrospective and therefore
suspect because of unconscious distortions of reconstruction.
(Although, for the same reason possibly revealing of social
phenomena, as the psychoanalytic case study is revealing of
'suppressed causes' of 'disturbance'). Third, it was difficult
to use for generalisation.

Consequently, there was a tendency to approximate the life
history approach, and this is evident from the Polish Peasant
onwards. The collection of surrogate life histories in various
forms became a hallmark of sociology in the United States for
more than a decade, despite a retention of the idea that life
experiences as expressed by the subject provide the essential
base for eliciting subjective meaning (Burgess, 1944a). The
approximations took the form of case studies of one sort or
another as there was no definitive view of the course methodic
practice should take in order to gather life experiences.

In their research on the problems of adjustment facing Polish
immigrants to the United States, Thomas and Znaniecki had

relied heavily on correspondence between Poles in the United States and in Poland. This data constituted a 'slice' of life history pertinent to the research area. The surrogate life histories provided by the letters revealed the personal attitudes and social values to which they responded.

Later, in his work on female delinquents, Thomas (1924) used court and social work records. These case records provided a ready source of material for the elaboration of the theory of social disorganisation and accompanying thesis of 'wishes' in the particular area of delinquency. Such case records were abbreviated life histories which bore upon the issue at hand. (They were, of course, uncritical sources but the aim of qualitative research has not been with structural critique).

The nomothetic orientation of 'Chicago Ethnography'

The interactionist sociology undertaken by the Chicagoans, although 'qualitative', reflected nomothetic concerns. The principles of an interactionist sociology which underpinned Chicago sociology, as Park (1939) has suggested, derived from Thomas and are set out in the 'Methodological Note' (Thomas and Znaniecki, 1918). Thomas' perspective involved three central features. First, that sociology take account of subjective aspects of human interaction as well as objective ones, incorporating attitudes as well as values. Thomas thus explicitly 'codified' the prevailing sentiment among sociological researchers by objectifying and locking the 'moralistic' concerns of reformers into humanistic empirical enquiry. Second, that social control, the principal aim of sociological enquiry, could only be approached through the discovery of social laws and that subjective perceptions must be incorporated into these laws. Third, social laws must relate to the social rather than personal mileu.

> The chief problems of modern science are problems of causal explanation. The determination and systematisation of data is only the first step in a scientific investigation. If a science wishes to lay the foundation of a technique, it must attempt to understand and to control the process of becoming. Social theory cannot avoid this task, and there is only one way of fulfilling it. Social becoming, like natural becoming must be analysed into a plurality of facts, each of which represents a succession of cause and effect. The idea of social theory is the analysis of the totality of social becoming into such causal processes and systematisation permitting us to understand the connections between these processes. (Thomas and Znaniecki, 1918, p. 36)

This central concern, however, was mediated by the need to account for the subjective nature of social interaction. So, while the physical sciences provided the model for scientific enquiry into the social world, their example, Thomas argued, should not be adopted uncritically. In what amounted to an attack on those who would adopt an objectivist 'Scientific Method' which aims to find 'the one determined phenomenon which is the necessary and sufficient condition of another phenomenon', Thomas pointed to the fundamental difference between physical and social science which is that

> while the effect of a physical phenomenon depends exclusively on the objective nature of this phenomenon and can be calculated on the ground of the latter's empirical content, the effect of a social phenomenon depends in addition on the subjective standpoint taken by the individual or the group toward this phenomenon and can be calculated only if we know, not only the objective content of the assumed cause, but also the meaning which it has for the given conscious beings ... A social cause is a compound and must include both an objective and a subjective element, a value and an attitude. (Thomas and Znaniecki, 1918, p. 38)

Attitudes involve a process of individual consciousness which 'determines real or possible activity of the individual in the social world'. Values are data 'having an empirical content accessible to members of some social group and a meaning with regard to which it is or may be an object of activity'. Social values are different from objects in as much as the latter have no meaning for human activity. The incorporation of meaning into the causal process was fundamental for Thomas and those who followed him at Chicago. The analysis of social activity in terms of values and attitudes implied, for Thomas, an holistic approach. Prefacing a position which C. Wright Mills (1959) was to restate and expand, Thomas argued that, in studying society, 'we go from the whole social context to the problem, and in studying the problem we go from the problem to the whole social context' (Thomas and Znaniecki 1918, p. 19). And, in such a procedure, Thomas claimed, one should proceed as if one knew nothing of the area, for the most usual illusion of science is that the scientist simply takes the facts as they are, without any methodological presuppositions and 'gets his explanation entirely a posteriori from pure experience' (Thomas and Znaniecki, 1918, p. 37). On the contrary, Thomas asserted that a fact is already an abstraction and what one must attempt is to develop this abstraction methodically rather than presume that the uncritical abstractions of common-sense are adequate. This systematic process of abstraction must be done because 'the whole theoretical concreteness cannot be introduced into science'.

Central to this endeavour, then, is the need to ensure that 'our facts must be determined in such a way as to permit of their subordination to general laws' for a fact that cannot be treated as a manifestation of a law (or several laws) cannot be explained by causal processes. Following upon this proposition, Thomas, predating Popper, further asserted a 'falsificationist' principle. In noting the problem of generalising laws that are initially manifest in particular spheres, Thomas suggested that the social scientist assess the core concepts of the proposition embodied by the particular law and, should such concepts relate to other circumstances, present the law in general terms. The social scientist is therefore essentially in a position to make bold conjectures, but such conjectures must be refutable: and further, because of the ethical and moral consequences of the application of generalisable social laws by social practitioners it is necessary that

> besides using only such generalisations as can be contradicted by new experience [the scientist] must not wait until new experiences impose themselves on him by accident, but must search for them, must instigate a systematic method of observation. And, while it is only natural that a scientist in order to form an hypothesis and to give it some amount of probability has to search first of all for such experiences as may corroborate it, his hypothesis cannot be considered fully tested until he has made subsequently a systematic search for such experiences as may contradict it, and proved these contradictions to be only seeming, explicable by the interference of definite factors. (Thomas and Znaniecki, 1918, p. 65)

Early interactionism, via the work of Thomas, involved a nomothetic view of sociology based on empiricism, but one mediated by a concern that mental capacities be incorporated. Individuals through reflection can transcend social values and indeed transform attitudes. Causal relations need to take account of this.

In order to understand social phenomena, Thomas argued that one needs to be able to explore the structural determination of action and its social psychological aspects. This may best be done by concentrating on the individual case and relating the biography to its social constraints as manifest in social values. This reflects the much later view by Mills (1959), (although without developing any critique of social structure or seriously questioning the adequacy of nomological perspectives in science).

Thomas's methodological presuppositions were not, then, a refutation of nomological principles per se, but rather an attempt to develop them. Nonetheless, Thomas and the later Chicagoans are often portrayed as being overly concerned with the subjective at the expense of the objective aspects of the social world.

Other interactionists reflected Thomas' concerns, notably Park and his students. Like Thomas, they, too, adopted a nomothetic approach. Park was not a 'verstehen' or phenomenological sociologist, although his period of study under Simmel had informed his sociological perspective. Park never developed an epistemology which detached explanation from understanding, and while sceptical of the possiblity of quantifying social phenomena and their interrelationships and thus of elaborating causal relationships, he never forsook the nomological premise of social science.

Park's approach was the elaboration of observable phenomena within a 'big picture', relying heavily on an underlying social disorganisation thesis. Contextualisation, with an emphasis on history, was central to this endeavour. Life history, recorded interview and case study, in one form or another, were important to this contextualising process.

The distinction between the case study approach and participant observation is examined in more detail below with reference to particular work at Chicago.

Participant observation at Chicago

There is a widespread assumption that 'Chicago sociology' was not only predominantly ethnographic and hostile to quantification, but that its predominant methodic practice was participant observation. For example, Cavan (1983) suggested that besides case study and statistics there was another method which was the result of Park's interest and influence and that was 'observation, participant and otherwise'. This method, Cavan claimed, was neither formalised nor named at the time but was the basis for a number of studies including Anderson (1923), Thrasher (1927), Zorbaugh (1929), Cressey (1932), Young, P., (1932), and Reckless (1933). However, it was left to Becker, she suggested, to give participant observation more formal shape (in the 1950s). Zorbaugh's work, in particular, has been taken as an exemplar of the participant observation approach of the 'Chicago School' (Madge, 1963; Hunter, 1983).

However, an examination of textbooks, methodological writings and substantive works suggests that the view of the 'Chicago School' as participant observers is misleading (Harvey, 1981; Platt, 1982). The early use of participant observation was not always conscious, was more related to case study and does not fit current conceptualisations of the method.

Nonetheless, there are some grounds for arguing that participant observation in the loosest sense is evident in the work of the Chicagoans from the beginnings of their empirical endeavours. MacLean (1910), for example, engaged in a series of short-term participant observer experiences as an employee in various industries in her survey of women in the labour force and this approach was representative of research carried out in Chicago in its very early days (Fish, 1981).

In his review of the early period of the 'school', Park (1939, p. 3) suggested that around 1910 there was a boom in graduate students going into the social sciences but that apart from 'applied social science' courses with their atheoretical orientations, there was

> no special provision for students who wanted to study a living society and no opportunity ... to study social problems in the field, or so to speak, "on the hoof".
> Chicago University provided that possibility, following Thomas' innovative development of the tradition he 'inherited' from Small, Henderson and Abbott. (Park, 1939, p. 3)

However this did not mean that the second decade of the century saw a blossoming of a relatively well established participant observation study tradition. The study of 'social problems on the hoof' is indicative of the growing concern to establish an empirically based social science. At its most radical this implied getting out and seeing what is going on. But such observation rarely involved any degree of active participation.

Of the forty two theses surveyed in detail, only two (5%) utilised complete participant observation (both after 1940), six (14%) used some kind of partial participant observation [3] while another seven (17%) employed casual observation, relied on past personal involvement or used the report backs of other observers. Nearly two thirds (64%) made no use of observation as a technique at all (see Appendix 6).

Even the 'golden era' of the 1920s was not a period in which participant observation blossomed. Cavan's (1983) suggestion, for example, that Thrasher's (1926) Gang was a participant observation study is dubious. On the face of it, a thesis entitled The Gang would seem perfect for such a method, but the subtitle A Study of 1,313 Gangs In Chicago belies this assumption. Nobody could observe so many gangs as a participant. The study was not so much an insider account of ganglife as a sociology of 'the gang as a type of human group' (Thrasher, 1927). As Park (1927) put it in the editor's preface

> The title of this book does not quite describe it. It is a study of the gang, to be sure, but it is at the same time a study of "gangland"; that is to say, a study of the gang

and its habitat, and in this case the habitat is a city slum.

The book deals with the natural history of the gang, including an attempt at typification; life in the gang; organisation and control in the gang; and the gang problem. Despite being hailed as 'an advancement in the general-survey and case study method' and as 'superior to earlier studies of the gang in that its conclusions grow out of concrete material' (Rice, 1931), Thrasher obtained most of his information through interviews. He interviewed about one hundred and thirty people consisting of sixty one gang members, a large number of social workers who made available case material, a dozen policemen, half a dozen politicians and a number of others such as lawyers and club owners. The material gathered in this way was used qualitatively rather than quantitatively and was augmented by the written life histories of twenty one of the gang boys, newspaper reports, and a mere ten of Thrasher's own observations (Madge, 1963). However, Thrasher was very concerned about the accuracy of his work and its objective scientific status.

> Such formulations as are presented, however, must be regarded as tentative hypotheses rather than as scientific generalizations. Certain of the suggestions made here may prove fruitful in dealing with the practical problems which the gang forments, but the investigation has probably raised more questions than it has answered. Too great precision, furthermore, must not be claimed for the materials collected, although every effort has been made to render them accurate. The study is primarily an exploratory survey designed to reveal behavior-trends and to present a general picture of life in an area little understood by the average citizen. (Thrasher, 1927, author's preface.)

Reckless' study of vice, also cited by Cavan as a participant observation study, also lacked participation to any degree. His dissertation, presented in 1925, had to rely primarily on official statistical sources. In the preparation of his book, published in 1933, he was able to augment this original study with case material made available from social workers. The study was directed to providing a picture of the location and degree of concentration of prostitution in Chicago and to assessing whether there was any correlation between vice and demographic features of Chicago as revealed by census material.
The difference between the observational approach adopted by the Chicagoans in the 1920s and that of more recent ethnographers is further illustrated by examining, in depth, three works supposedly indicative of Chicago participant observation studies and with much stronger claims to the method than Thrash-

er's or Reckless' research.

The core features of participant observation, as discussed above, are direct observation through a participating role which enables the organisational and symbolic processes of a group under study to be scrutinised in order to assess the meanings in use that define the subjects perspective of their social mileu.

The Hobo as a participant observation study

The Hobo, by Nels Anderson (1923) is often cited as an early example of Chicago ethnographic work. Usually it is seen as representing the beginning of the published participant observation studies, and being the forerunner of the kind of work undertaken by Becker and others in the 1950s and 1960s. However, there are considerable differences between the later participant observation studies and Anderson's work, to the extent that in terms of the current meaning of the term, The Hobo was not a participant observation study at all.

Anderson did not live as a hobo but rather stayed in a hobo hotel in hobohemia, which is counter to the taken-for-granted view even of people who were at Chicago at the same time as Anderson. In recalling the hobo research, Johnson, for example, implied that Anderson collected information as a 'complete participant observer'.

> I shared a room when I first got to Chicago with Nels Anderson. He was the hobo. He had hoboed all over the country. And he hoboed from Utah to Chicago. And he spent the previous night, before I first met him, sleeping under a concrete ledge around the smoke stack of the university power plant... He said he was used to that kind of thing because he was always sleeping outdoors or under a railway bridge with a bunch of hobos, warming up food in a tin can, and all that. Anderson did his dissertation on the hobo, he wanted to supplement his information with some surveys of hobos down in what you could call hobohemia, down at South Halstead Street. So several times on weekends he would go down there and I would go with him. We got a room in one of those cheap rooming places, almost like a flop house. We'd spend a couple of days just going around talking to people. And he established rapport very quickly with them because he was a very folksy kind of man. Maybe, Friday or Saturday night we would visit, so-called, 'Hobo College'. On one occasion he was asked to say something and he got up and gave a very nice little talk. (Johnson, 1972)

Anderson had, apparently, 'jumped a freight train' from Utah in order to get to Chicago and had encountered hobos. He may also have adopted this form of travel on other occasions but in no way, as he pointed out himself, could he be said to have taken on the role of a hobo for research purposes (Anderson, 1983). Before starting his study he had worked in a 'Home for Incurables' in Chicago which had put him in contact with hobos and it was through this contact that he developed his research. His approach was not participant observation of hobo life, rather, it was observation of hobos in an institutional setting with a heavy reliance on informal, in-depth conversations with residents. Like many of Park's later students, Anderson researched an area to which he already had access.

Neither Anderson, nor any commentators at the time referred to his work as involving participant observation. Mention of his work in the Bulletin of the Society for Social Research made no mention of participant observation. Nor did his style of work reflect the concerns of participant observation practitioners of more recent decades except that, somewhat against the tenor of the times, he was sympathetic to his subject. This made the 'insider' report he wrote, based primarily on his discussions with hobos encountered at work and in the hotel, appear to be a dispassionate, 'scientific' document. This appearance was amplified by the study being clearly at variance with what the University, at the time, saw as appropriate fields of study for its graduate students. Anderson (1983) suggested that his lack of moral stance appealed to Park and Burgess who made the decision to publish the work. They saw his study as scientific despite Anderson's lack of any substantial sociological background or use of sociological concepts. Indeed, Anderson suggested that the book was scientific without him having to work on it, simply because his background and approach was unlike that of the predominant 'clergy' at Chicago [4]. Its candid abandonment of conventional ameliorative wisdom seems to have been its main appeal for Park and Burgess.

The book simply stated what hobos did, what types of hobos there were, how they lived in both cities and rural areas, how they were seen by other non-hobo sectors of the community, and concluded with an assessment of why hobos were disappearing which concentrated on the lack of demand for migrant labour. In short The Hobo was a detailed descriptive account which analysed the usefulness of the hobo and their increasingly rapid disappearance. It lacked sociological 'pretentiousness' and was primarily a report of the state of affairs which challenged some of the taken-for-granted notions about hobos.

Working in the home had been an important factor in Anderson attracting the research funds but Anderson's decision to research the hobo was not one developed through any direct affiliation to the University of Chicago. It arose as the consequence of discussions with a Dr. Reitman who was interested in the subject of the hobo and raised the money for a study from his friend Dr. W.A. Evans and placed the money with the United Charities of Chicago. The director of the United Charities was Joel Hunter who became the treasurer of the hobo study committee to whom Anderson was responsible. The other two members of the committee were Reitman, the 'authority on the area and its inhabitants' and E.W. Burgess who, as 'scientific advisor' and chairman provided the link with the Sociology department at the University. Notably (and rarely, see also Blumethal, 1932a) Anderson's study was published as a book by the University of Chicago Press before he was awarded the M.A. for the work (1925).

As the study was based on his work in the home and the contacts this generated rather than as the result of any direct participation as a travelling and working hobo, there is very little grounds for according The Hobo the status of an early representative of a 'Chicago School' participant observation studies tradition.

The Taxi-Dance Hall as a participant observation study

The Taxi-Dance Hall (Cressey, 1929) is sometimes seen as a clear early attempt to develop participant observation at Chicago. It is seen, in particular, as an early example of participant observation of a deviant situation. The study has a strong claim in this respect because it involved a decision to engage in unobtrusive participation. Nonetheless, it is a relatively isolated study of this kind. Furthermore, the term participant observation is never used by Cressey nor did the Bulletin of the Society for Social Research refer to it as a participant observation study. Moreover, the extent to which the research represented even an embryonic participant observation study, in the sense explored above, is at least debatable.

The sensitive nature of Cressey's enquiry required subterfuge, but Cressey's comments show that the data came from many more sources than secret participant observation.

> Most of the data upon which this study is based was secured from the case records of social agencies, notably the Juvenile Protective Association, and from the reports of observers and investigators. Published material upon such a new phenomenon as the taxi-dance hall was found to be scanty and of little value; and formal interviews were abandoned as unsatisfactory. (Cressey, 1932, preface)

Cressey points out that co-operation was not forthcoming and so the decision was made to carry out the study without the co-operation of proprietors and in spite of the deliberate opposition of some of them. This lack of co-operation made it logistically impossible to secure what otherwise would have been desirable statistical data. The research was forced to adopt other approaches. Nonetheless, Cressey assures the reader that the 'considerable amount of case material which has been amassed' over five years (of which only a small amount is included in the text) 'afford a reasonable basis for the validity of the generalizations made'.

The observational method finally adopted was outlined by Cressey as follows

> Observers were sent into the taxi-dance halls. They were instructed to mingle with the others and to become as much a part of this social world as ethically possible. They were asked to observe and keep as accurate a record as possible of the behavior and conversations of those met in the establishments. Each observer was selected because of his past experience, his training and his special abilities. These investigators made it possible to gather significant case material from a much more varied group of patrons and taxi-dancers than could have been secured by any one person. The investigators functioned as anonymous strangers and casual aquaintances. They were thus able to obtain this material without encountering the inhibitions and resistance usually met in formal interviews. Further, the independent reports from different observers upon their contacts with the same individual made possible a check upon the consistency of the documents obtained. Moreover, this information concerning patrons and taxi-dancers made it feasible to secure much ancillary data from the records of social agencies. (Cressey, 1932, preface)

This research clearly does involve the collection of ethnographic material through secret participant observation type approaches and, in the same mould as Anderson's study of The Hobo, the point of view of the participants appears to be taken into account. Indeed, Cressey discussed the observational element of his research, in an unpublished paper (Cressey, 1983), in terms of the role of the stranger in interactive situations (Bulmer, 1983a).

However, this methodic orientation does not transform the research into a participant observation study in the current sense because Cressey's observers were more in accord with Lindeman's 'objective observers' than participant observers (Madge, 1963, p. 119). Despite appearances, the study differs from later participant observation studies on four important counts. First, the participant observation material was support data for case records. Second, it was regarded as somewhat suspect as research material and needed a great deal of cross-verification. Third, ironically, a preconceived moral position which regarded the halls as 'unwholesome' (if temporarily un-

avoidable) underpinned the research. Fourth, while the requirements of patrons were considered, no attempt was made to engage
the perspective of the female taxi-dancers. They were talked
to, but only in order to provide classificatory schemes, to
assess why they adopted the profession and so on, but never in
terms of adopting the dancers' points of view.

The Gold Coast and the Slum as a participant observation study.

A similar conclusion emerges from the study of Zorbaugh (1929)
The Gold Coast and the Slum, the third 'exemplar' of early
'Chicago School' participant observation studies, (Madge, 1963;
Hunter, 1983). This study was of the extremely diverse area of
Chicago known as the Near North Side, which lies just north of
the central business district (the Loop). The area, one and a
half miles long by one mile wide, is on the shore of Lake
Michigan and in the 1920s its economic prosperity and consequent social standing declined rapidly as one moved inland from
the shore. Lake Shore Drive, known as the Gold Coast, was a
highly desirable residential area. Backing on to this was an
area around Clark Street that had become a rooming house district and beyond that was 'Little Italy', a slum area that had
gone through various transitions but was, at the time of Zorbaugh's study, primarily a Sicilian enclave. Incongruously, the
'bohemian' area, known as Towertown, lay in the middle of the
slum area. This was, according to Zorbaugh, a rather second
rate community of artists. The Near North Side was thus an area
of extremes.
    The study was primarily concerned to provide a detailed
description of the complexities of the Near North Side, and to
that end was broken down into an examination of each of the
four sections separately. A considerable amount of the empirical evidence consisted of demographic data and ecological analysis. The types of shops on North Clark Street, for example,
were used as indicative of the area. The high concentration of
cheap lunch rooms and restaurants was related to the rooming
house district where residents had little or no opportunity to
prepare meals for themselves.
    The latter part of the study included an historical case
study of the Lower North Community Council, which ultimately
failed, and which Zorbaugh used to illustrate his conclusions
about the inadequacies in local community institutions throughout the area.
    Although Zorbaugh made himself familiar with the area under
investigation, he did not undertake the kind of participant
observation of a community that was to be attempted later by
Blumenthal, Warner and the Lynds. The source data for his study
came principally from documents provided by residents, from
life histories collected, presumably, by the author, and from

case histories, particularly those in the files of the United Charities. For example, when discussing the Gold Coast, Zorbaugh relied heavily on fourteen anonymous written contributions. The life histories included one provided by a pawnbroker and another by a 'charity girl'. However, it is not clear whether they were written by the contributors or compiled by the researcher on the basis of extensive interviewing.

Further evidence came from a large number of essays written by school children; from a school census probably conducted on behalf of the board of education; from comments to census workers; from key informants; from personal documents such as letters; from existing records, such as the 'Illinois Lodging House Register'; and from the records of the Juvenile Protective Association. A survey of the rooming houses was also undertaken, but the information gathered from this appears to be little used, and there is no clear indication of the kinds of questions asked, the sampling procedure or the number of respondents involved. Very little of the evidence presented in the study seems to have been direct observation by the author.

While a descriptive ethnographic account, it was preoccupied with an ecological analysis rather than the perspective of the subjects. Throughout, there is a taken-for-granted view that the area was 'disorganized' and that it represented the antithesis of what a community ought to be. However, Zorbaugh was at pains to point out that he was not comparing the area with an idealised community; rather, taking on Park's approach, he argued that it was necessary to accept the cultural traditions of the community as they are and attempt to understand them. To that end it was necessary to discover the nature of the community, how it operated and the impact of industrialisation upon it. Nonetheless, Zorbaugh was far more concerned with a generalised descriptive account than any insider attempt to unravel the perceptions of the subject groups. There is nothing in the methodology of the study to suggest that Zorbaugh was a part of the area. Thus, in current terms, it does not constitute a participant observation study.

Participant observation and community studies

Apart from within the field of community studies, participant observation was not a term widely used, nor a method greatly indulged in, either at Chicago or within American sociology in general, prior to the 1950s. In confronting the labelling of early 'Chicago School' studies as participant observation, I am not simply questioning the appropriateness of an elusive label. What is fundamentally at issue is whether the Chicagoans adopted the style of 'qualitative' methodology that is conventionally attributed to them, and out of which a retrospective

heritage of participant observation studies has been constructed.

The nearest the 'Chicago School' got to establishing an
ethnographic tradition of participant observation studies was
through its endorsement of community studies, with Blumenthal
pioneering in his Small Town Stuff (1932a). The first reference
to a participant observer study in the Bulletin of the Society
for Social Research was to Blumenthal's work. In the June
edition of the Bulletin for 1931 Blumenthal was listed as a new
member with, as research topic, 'A Participant-Observer Study
of a Small Town'. In the next edition, in the list of books
available through the Society, was the following entry

> Albert Blumenthal: Small Town Stuff
> The result of two and a half years of systematic investiga-
> tion, this is the first work to apply the participant-
> observer method of the anthropologist to the study of the
> small community in our civilization. (Bulletin of the So-
> ciety for Social Research, Jan. 1932, p. 3)

Besides being only the second reference to participant observation in the Bulletin this announcement also pointed to the
fact that Blumenthal's research was as much influenced by anthropology as the ethnographic work of Park's students.

There were fairly close links between anthropology and sociology at Chicago [5]. There was a single Department of Sociology and Anthropology until 1929. After the split into two separate departments, Radcliffe-Brown taught in the Department of
Anthropology for six years and was followed by Lloyd Warner (in
1935) who was Professor of Anthropology and Sociology. Both
Radcliffe-Brown and Warner taught 'a lot of sociologists to be
interested in doing field work' (Becker, 1979) and Polsky
(Lofland, 1980, p. 278) recalled that rubbing shoulders with
the anthropologists was an important element in the development
of field research. In the 1930s there was a growth of community
study type field work, notably the anthropological work of
Redfield in Mexico and the studies of the South carried out by
W. L. Warner and his associates, which was paid for 'by the
W.P.A. and other of those kinds of Government funds for relief'
(Becker, 1979). This research led on to the work of Dollard and
the Lynds outside Chicago. This was not, however, in any sense
a dominant tradition at Chicago.

> Middletown didn't immensely impress Chicago people, Burgess
> spoke favourably of it, but it was so much description and
> so little generalisation, there wasn't much sociology you
> could hang on to. It was too specifically descriptive of a
> little town in Indiana. (Faris, 1972)

These community studies unlike the early Chicago studies (of the 1920s) involved researchers leaving Chicago and living in the community chosen for analysis. While reflecting some of the earlier concerns of the Chicago studies of particular communities, such as Wirth's Ghetto and Horak's The Assimilation of the Czechs in Chicago, the work done by Blumenthal was different in many ways, not least because he, unlike Horak and Wirth, actually went to live in, and become part of, the community. The approach adopted by Blumenthal had been suggested in embryonic form by Zorbaugh in his study of the Gold Coast and the Slum, but Blumenthal went much further in his analysis of the structure and organisation of Missoula, Montana.

In a letter to Burgess mailed from Philipsburg, Montana and dated 20th April 1929 Blumenthal discussed methodology. He referred to spot maps of the community, which he took for granted as a methodological device, but asked if photographs may not be used, in particular, the use of an aerial photograph as the basis for such a spot map. Blumenthal reckoned that such a photograph would give a far better idea of the community than the conventional spot map. He thought that the photograph would be particularly illuminating in the kind of intimate study that he was undertaking. Blumenthal was particularly concerned about the secrecy of his work. He noted (Blumenthal, 1929) that he had intended the first chapter, of what became Small Town Stuff, to be on methodology but

> further thought has convinced me that the principal part of such a chapter would have to do with the role of the investigator in making the study and should thus be kept relatively secret. For, the DeGraff incident is suggestive of what could happen to me and my family if the true nature of my activities become public. [6]

He even suggested writing two theses, a formal one and a secret one kept at the Department of Sociology which would be 'replete with life history materials'.

Blumenthal unabashedly asserted that his work was methodologically innovative in terms of the manner by which he had gathered data, and emphasised the reflexivity of his work, but did not, at that time, refer to it as participant observation.

> It seems to me that the most promising results of my study is that of breaking the ground for the development of a technique of making intimate studies of small communities. And as I have suggested, the role of the investigator plays a very important part in his final product and should be thoroughly exposed in an adequate study which avoids the common fallacy of sociologists -- that of assuming a too nearly absolute objectivity on the part of the social

researcher. To that end, the document which I have entitled 'A Diary of Topics of Conversation and my Reactions upon Them' reveals a method of bringing out the role of the investigator if he faithfully records his attitudes, how he is treated, et cetera. (Blumenthal, 1929)

Blumenthal wanted to include six detailed life histories, a male and female from each of the following age categories; grade school child, young adult and mature adult who had lived in the community a long time. He referred to one document which

illustrates the use of the continued interview and its function of bringing a degree of intimacy which cannot be attained in a single interview. It is the most concrete revelation I have ever encountered and only my peculiar role as confidant could have enabled me to secure it.

Although Blumenthal was unsure what to call his methodology, it does seem to have been an early example of participant observation. Besides actually living in the community and participating in its day to day activities, Blumenthal also argued for a clear contextualisation of the data collection process. Rather than the 'objective observation' of earlier studies, Blumenthal was concerned to engage the perspectives of the subjects, and considered his own involvement to be a crucial procedure for acheiving this. For him, the novelty of his approach lay in his acceptance of the subjective role of the researcher. This role, he suggested, needed to be adequately documented so that the empirical data could be approached critically by others. In this respect he prefaced the perspective that became popular a quarter of a century later and directed towards all forms of sociological enquiry by Myrdal (1968, 1970).

Participant observation and the 'Chicago School' approach

Participant observation was not, then, a recognisably Chicago research practice until at least into the 1940s. Thus, at the 1939 conference on the Polish Peasant study, which concentrated on the human document as a research tool, a forum at which methodological issues were extensively discussed, there was but a single mention of participant observation, and this in reference to documents collected in an extensive survey in Sweden

The Swedish material has an all-round superiority in the fact that it includes the medical examination, the life history, the controlled interview, the letters to relatives, friends, sweethearts, lawyers, etc., and the testimony of 'participant observers'. (Social Science Research Council, 1939, p. 133)

Furthermore, there is in the transcript of the conference virtually no reference to a specifically Chicago approach with the exception of two references, by Thomas, both to the collection of human documents in the early part of the century

This movement toward the collection of human document material was going on inevitably, anyway, that is, in Chicago. So this work was merely another influence on the concrete trend in sociology....[besides the Swedish study and a collection of material from the Jewish Daily Forward] it is not necessary to mention the important collection of human documents by sociologists of the University of Chicago where the practice has been extensive and refined. (Social Science Research Council, 1939, p. 130-2)

Participant observation was still unusual at Chicago in the 1940s. For example, in his doctoral thesis submitted to the Chicago sociology department in 1940, Daniel adopted a mixture of methods including participant observation. Far from taking the method for granted, Daniel tentatively referred to the 'participant observation type method', as though it were not common-place.

Indeed, it was Whyte (1943) who probably provided the first example of a 'pure' participant observation study. Even so, this was not at the instigation of the University of Chicago, as correspondence between Burgess and Wilson (Wilson 1940) indicates. Indeed, Wilson talked of Whyte's study not as emulating the Chicago approach but rather 'you see his technique is the interview technique like Bakke's of Yale'. The only 'concession' Wilson made to a Chicago orientation is to say that Whyte is 'from the sociological or socio-economic aspects of current phenomena, on what I might call the clinical side, which has been favored by W. I. Thomas and Park and you.'

Whyte, himself, noted that 'I owe a great personal debt to Conrad M. Arensberg, now at Columbia University, from whom I learned my field-work techniques' (Whyte, 1955, p. vii). And it was Whyte, in his methodological appendix to the second edition of **Street Corner Society** (Whyte, 1955), who was one of the first researchers to discuss the problems of participant observation directly and in some depth. This belies the view that 'in the period from 1920 to 1940 people who called themselves students of society were familiar with personal documents and participant observation' (Bogdan and Taylor, 1975, p. 4).

Although he completed his research as a Chicago graduate student, Whyte had begun his study of an area of Boston as a Harvard graduate. The only contribution that Chicago seemed to have made to Whyte's discussion of participant observation methodology was indirectly through Arensberg having worked on Warner's 'Yankee City' research. This further supports my suggestion that participant observation at Chicago resided in its community studies.

It would seem, then, that the first classic 'pure' participant observation study was neither conceived at Chicago, nor, in terms of field work orientation, did it owe much, if anything, directly to a Chicago tradition. [7]

While Blumer suggested the efficacy of observational studies in the 1940s, and a 'tradition' of symbolic interactionist observation research ostensibly deriving from Chicago emerged in the 1950s, there is little to suggest that the 'Chicago School', prior to 1940 was single-mindedly pursuing participant observation research [8]. When Becker undertook ethnographic research in the late 1940s and early 1950s he studied the 'classics' of social research

> such books as **Street Corner Society**, the **Polish Peasant in Europe and America**, and back I should say to Charles Booth and Henry Mayhew was something that a lot of us read. You know, taking that to be a kind of model of how ethnography might proceed, of the kind of detail that one would want to know about people living in a city, for instance, or about occupation. (Becker, 1979, p. 7)

The 'Chicago tradition' prior to 1940, then, was broadly ethnographic rather than specifically concerned with participant observation. It aimed at finding out things 'you hadn't thought of' rather than adopting the insider perspective of the subjects. That was to occur later when 'ethnographic research began to be informed by multiple theoretical viewpoints' (Becker, 1979, p. 9).

Indeed, as late as the 1960s there was considerable advocacy of participant observation as an appropriate and novel method of research. Notable is Polsky's (1971) advocacy of participant observation for the study of deviance. He claimed that the naturalistic perspective was little used and the main target of his critique was the well known and highly regarded criminological work of Sutherland. Similarly, as late as 1969, Coleman pointed to the lack of 'in situ' observation which is commonly regarded as the hallmark of Chicago sociology. Coleman (1969) noted that sociologists have inadequately used observation, rather they have tended to depend on individual's reports of their own behaviour, (through questionnaires, life histories, interviews). Not enough, he suggested has been done on observation in situ. He pointed to the doctoral work of both Stinchcombe and Barker on high school students and children respectively which used direct observation and to

the work of Garfinkel and his students, in which the investigation presents verbal stimuli, not as an interviewer,
but as a member of the same social system.... More useful,
however, than at least the existing disappointing results
of Garfinkel's work is the work in participant observation
carried out by such sociologists as Howard Becker, and work
described by Webb, Campbell, Schwartz and Sechrest in **Unobtrusive Measures.** (Coleman, 1969, p. 112)

Coleman may have underplayed the extent to which, by the late
1960s, participant research had been used, but even so his
comments on the relative novelty of direct, in situ, observation belies the view that such an approach is intrinsic to the
Chicago heritage. The problem in the past, he argued, was that
observation was difficult because there were few aids. This, he
argued, had changed thanks to electronic aids, awareness of
time sampling, space sampling and sampling of roles and so on,
all of which increase reliability and validity.

Without doubt some of the work done at Chicago involved
methods more usually located within ethnographic orientations.
However there is very little to suggest that Chicago adopted
other than a nomothetic perspective on the analysis of the
social world until the 1930s, when, in embryonic form, a proto-
phenomenological scepticism began to emerge in the work of
Blumer and Wirth. (This is examined further in chapter five).
Prior to this, the interactionist perspective, reliant as it
was upon Thomas' general sociological orientation, clearly
adopted nomothetic principles, and with it a degree of methodological eclecticism, as will be illustrated below, with few
pieces of work that could be described as adopting a single
method.

However, that does not mean that there were not clear preferences expressed by members of the Department for particular
methodic devices. On the one hand, Park used to adopt an attitude of extreme scepticism towards statistics, which became
more acute as he grew older (Matthews, 1977); while Ogburn, on
the other, was keen to develop the measurement of social phenomena. Burgess, tended to mediate between the two and make use
of qualitative and quantitative techniques.

Ogburn knew very little of the Park sociology and Park knew
nothing of statistical methods. I think Park would sometimes make some grudging remark about it, disapproving of
the fad for statistics. Ogburn was a Southern gentleman and
he generally didn't make personal remarks about anybody,
but his wife did. And the bitter personal feelings between
the wives suggested that underneath both men had some
feeling about the matter but on the surface they both co-
operated well and I once overheard a good part of a depart-

ment meeting and everything went well. (Faris, 1972)

Although the 'Chicago School' myth would have it otherwise, the Chicagoans were as involved in developing quantitative techniques as they were in qualitative procedures. There were debates at Chicago, and there was, it seems, 'a tension in the Department about the Ogburnian's and Parkian's' (Cottrell, 1972). However, there is little evidence that any long standing alliances or factional divisions characterised the department. 'I'm not sure that they grouped into factions very much, at least I wasn't aware of it' (Faris, 1972). Importantly, there was no division into competing nomothetic and ideographic camps at Chicago. 'The two sides, the statistical and the social interactionists both wanted to build a scientific sociology' (Dollard, 1972).

In effect there were three debates at Chicago, those relating to quantification and the associated discussions about the efficacy of case studies and statistics, those relating to instinct theory, and those, somewhat more bitter and less resolvable, revolving around Freud's theories. Of these, the instinct theory debate was the least active. Instincts, for many, were a dead issue as Faris had laid to rest the residual instinct notion embodied in Thomas's wishes. The other two debates were active.

> Park would preside and he would rumble on about stupid Freudians and statisticians, but Burgess would nod as if he was approving of what Park said and he would look across to where some of us were sneaking out and getting courses on statistics and courses on Freud and he'd twinkle because he was doing the same thing.... He got very interested in the Freudian contribution to sociology, to social theory. (Cottrell, 1972)

The Chicagoans role in developing quantitative techniques is explored in chapter four. Chapter five takes up the theoretical debates which involved Freudianism.

Notes

[1] Case study refers to individual cases, particularly infor-
    mation achieved through personal documents either existent
    or derived through interview or written by the respondent.
    This usage does not not necessarily coincide with current
    usage. Chapin (1920) referred to case study as a 'technique
    for an intensive and many-sided study of the individual
    compared to the sampling of a group and the enumeration of
    a community. In the 1920s, too, 'field work' referred to

all empirical data collecting techniques, unlike its more usual usage today which implies ethnographic study, rather than scheduled interviewing.

[2] Interactionist sociology is the term used for sociological perspectives which were concerned primarily with social interaction. This was grounded in German social philosophy and American pragmatism (Rock, 1979). Interactionist sociology has taken various forms, but in the early period at Chicago its principles are clearly stated in Thomas and Znaniecki (1918). The work of the Chicagoans can be identified as broadly interactionist. Out of this (as Fisher and Strauss (1979) suggest) emerged a specific approach labelled symbolic interactionism, which was developed as much away from Chicago as at it.

[3] Complete participant observation refers to those instances where the researcher takes on the role of the group under observation and joins in on a more or less full time basis. Partial participant observation are those situations where the researcher merely engages as a participant observer on a part time or convenience basis.

[4] Anderson was not an atheist or agnostic and he suggested that he had a two year struggle relating his social scientific and notably Darwinian evolutionary views to his Mormon fundamentalist background. This reflects similar views of graduates of the 1920s, as seen in chapter two.

[5] Robert Redfield was Park's son-in-law. Park had apparently encouraged Redfield to take up anthropology and 'Park's sociology became clearly reflected in the series of Mexican community studies by Redfield, whose book Folk Culture of Yucatan is dedicated to Park'. (Faris, 1967, p. 101). Redfield, like many of the sociologists, had attempted a classification system of communities, based on his research in Mexico.

Faris, argues that sociology at Chicago was deeply rooted in cultural anthropology. Thomas' (1909) Social Origins and Ellsworth Faris' work reflect this anthropological root. Faris opened up the way for the establishment of a strong Anthropology section by bringing Fay Cooper Cole to Chicago. The Department separated into a Sociology Department and an Anthropology Department in 1929, but many students took courses in both areas and there were close links between the two Departments. A number of members of the Society for Social research were anthropologists.

[6] DeGraff was a graduate student at Chicago who was awarded

71

his Ph.D. in 1926 (DeGraff, 1926). What exactly the 'De-Graff Incident' amounted to is not clear as no other reference to it could be traced.

[7] When Whyte was awarded a three year junior fellowship at Harvard, following his graduation from Swathmore in 1936, he decided he wanted to research a slum district with a view to investigating racketeering. Whyte was an economist not a social researcher and when he located 'Cornerville', which he thought looked just like he imagined a slum area should, he had no real idea how to go about his research. In 1936, there was little existing literature to help him. Apparently only two published studies were available, **Middletown** by the Lynds (1929) and **Greenwich Village** by Carolyn Ware (1935). Neither of these were what Whyte wanted as they focused on social problems and not social systems. He wanted to see how a local community worked rather than investigate its particular social difficulties (Madge, 1963, p. 213). As Whyte acknowledged, it was Conrad Arensberg, another junior fellow at Harvard, who was to be a big influence on his approach. Arensberg, along with Solon Kimball had adopted an anthropological approach to the study of a community in Ireland (Arensberg and Kimball 1940). So Whyte did not derive his method from the Chicagoans, he did not seem to consider their work to be of the kind of direct involvement research that he intended. This is a little surprising. Perhaps his lack of sociological background left him without the knowledge of the Chicago studies. Perhaps, in 1936, the Chicago studies were not seen as participant observer studies. Or perhaps Whyte dismissed them, too, as social problem research. It is, nonethless, surprising that he was apparently unaware of Blumenthal's **Small Town Stuff** (1932a) which was concerned with the social sytem, rather than the problems, of a small community. In the event, due to force of circumstance, Whyte adopted a different approach to participant observation than the Lynds, Ware or Arensberg. His approach was to move into the close community of a particular group of people and rely heavily on a key informant and sponsor. He had not planned to operate in this manner but took full advantage of the opportunity when it arose. The result is the classic study (Whyte 1943a) to which a lengthy methodological appendix was added when it was published in its second edition in 1955. For the first time, we have an account of what it is like to research a group of people from ones own society with which the researcher has intimate contact. Many such studies have been done subsequently, but there were no such close and complete participant observation studies done at Chicago, or elsewhere,

prior to Whyte's research in the late 1930s.

[8] As late as 1947, Wirth (1947) in reviewing the development
of sociology over the previous thirty years suggested that
not only had there been a move towards specialising in
specific areas but also that sociologists needed specialised skills for empirical work. Wirth listed such skills
which did not include participant observation as such and
was dominated by quantitative techniques; social statistics, sampling, population analysis, personal documents,
prediction methods, attitude testing, public opinion polling, questionnaire construction, field interviewing, and
the mapping of social relations.

4 The quantitative tradition at Chicago

Introduction

The 'Chicago School' is rarely associated with the development or even use of quantitative techniques. As we saw in chapter three, the myth is that Chicago was the home of ethnographic research. Thomas's assertion of the 'perfect' nature of life history as a source of data, Park's apparent opposition to statistics and Blumer's attacks on variable analysis have all been taken as indicative of an antipathy towards quantification by the 'Chicago School'. This ignores the extensive development and use of statistics at Chicago (Bulmer, 1981a, 1984).

It must be remembered, too, that up to 1930 there was relatively little use of statistics by American sociologists at all. The Committee on Social Statistics of the American Statistical Association noted, in 1929, that more sociologists ought to be interested in statistics, as well as vice versa. To that end it felt the need for 'an appraisal of the extent to which statistical methods have already been developed, utilized or foreshadowed in a variety of social and sociological studies' (Rice, 1930). In December of 1929, for the first time, the American Sociological Society and the American Statistical Association had joint sessions, to discuss statistical method, at their annual meetings.

Duncan and Duncan (1934, p. 212), in their longitudinal survey of the interests of members of the American Sociological Society, between 1928 and 1931, concluded more sociologists have an interest in social psychology than any other subject, but their major interest is in social work. This being the case, those who look with disdain upon social work and social problems, and pin their hope for a "scientific" sociology on statistical sociology will find little comfort or satisfaction in these findings.

Although it is clear from inspecting their work that the Chicagoans made widespread use of official statistics in various ways, the assumption made by commentators is that the Chicagoans tended to make use of statistics as descriptive rather than analytic tools. This view further suggests that the development of quantification by the Chicagoans was quite different from the post war expansion centering at Columbia and initiated by the developments in public opinion polling. The use of statistics by the Chicagoans is usually not seen to fall into this mould. Chicago sociologists, it is assumed, did not specify hypotheses for rigorous statistical testing, develop the large scale scheduled interview of a representative sample, rigorously assess the relationship between correlation and causality (and thus criteria for causality attribution), define concepts operationally nor, therefore, develop accurate measurement techniques and advanced statistical analysis.

Thomas and the case study versus statistics debate.

As has already been demonstrated, Chicago sociologists were not opposed to a 'falsificationist' nomothetic basis for sociological research. Scepticism about statistical approaches thus reflected, not an opposition to the fundamental attempt to construct causal or pseudo-causal relationships in sociology, but rather a scepticism that statistical methods could adequately grasp the subjective aspect of interaction (communication), hence the initial concern with life history. However, as indicated above, Thomas was more concerned with the attitude-value relationship rather than with a particular method. Later, as attitude testing became more sophisticated he raised no objection to it provided it could generate the information required.

It is my experience that formal methodological studies are relatively unprofitable. They have tended to represent the standpoint developed in philosophy and the history of philosophy. It is my impression that progress in method is made from point to point by setting up objectives, employing certain techniques, then resetting the problems with the introduction of still other objectives and the modification of technique. For example, Galvani or someone else gets a reaction from a frog's leg ... this may suggest to Pfeffer or Verworn the application of electricity ....

In all of this, there is no formal attention to method but the use of some imagination or mind from point to point. The operator raises the question, at appropriate points , 'What if,' and prepares a set-up to test this query.

Similarly, in our own line, some of us, in connection with some experience, raised a question, 'What would happen if we were able to secure life records of a large number of persons which would show their behavior reactions in connection with their various experiences and social situations ?' After some experimentation, yourself [Park], Shaw and others have been interested in the preparation of very systematic and elaborate life-histories. In this connection it is noted that the behavior of young persons is dependent upon their social status and the regions in which they live. Studies are then made from the ecological standpoint. It is discovered that children brought into the juvenile court are predominantly from certain localities in the city. The rate of delinquency is related to gang life and gang life is related to localities. Thrasher then makes a study of the gang from this standpoint. As comparative observations multiply, Shaw undertakes to determine how the cases of boys brought into the juvenile court for stealing are connected with their gang life and determines that 90 per cent of these boys did their stealing in groups of two or more. In the search for causes of delinquency, it then appears that the delinquent and nondelinquent are often very much alike in their behavior reactions. It is then recognized that it is impossible to study the delinquent population without at the same time studying the nondelinquent, and at present we have introduced the plan of using nondelinquent groups as a control in connection with studies of the causation of delinquency.

In all this, also, we move from point to point without necessarily any formidable attempt to rationalize and generalize the process. It is only in fact, so far as sociology is concerned, since we abandoned the search for standardized methods based largely on the work of dead men, that we have made the beginnings which I have indicated. (Thomas, 1928.)

Indeed, Thomas came more and more to accept the possibility of quantitative techniques providing the kind of material life histories provided and this was very much a concern of the Chicago sociologists for two decades; a concern which was shared by the wider sociological community. Throughout the twenties a general debate on the relative merits of case study and statistics centered on the reliability of case study data

(Cooley, 1928; Shaw, 1931; Rice 1931) [1].

In 1930 two Ph.D theses at Chicago independently undertook empirical investigations of the extent to which attitude testing schedules were able to provide equivalent data to the self composed life history. Stouffer, in his influential thesis, demonstrated that, for some kinds of attitudes, the administratively easier test instrument was as good as the life history record, although perhaps less subtle in the case of extreme attitudes. Brown (1930) also included an assessment of life history and attitude surveys which suggested that for delicate areas the life history was more accurate, although he deferred to Stouffer (1930), in a footnote, as being a more rigorous study in respect of 'straight forward attitudinal statements'. However, this analysis did not ring the death knell of life history (Cavan, 1983). Stouffer still saw a role for it and Burgess, in particular, was concerned to integrate case study and statistics in a synthesis. Indeed, the personal document was still a central feature of methodological discussion a decade later (Social Science Research Council, 1939).

There was no attempt at Chicago to establish a position which gave primacy to case study rather than statistical work, nor was the debate about the two methods indicative of competing camps.

> Sutherland ... was a most knowledgeable person in criminology... he was brought up to Chicago and he sort of laughed at these debates about case studies versus statistics. He just plodded right along and got case studies when he damned pleased and wanted them and used statistics and was always trying to get a little more statistical methods too. (Cottrell, 1972)

> We had a few sessions on statistics versus case studies and most of us students regarded that as light entertainment because we found both of them useful and didn't think of it as versus. Blumer, however, stayed fairly big with this versus statistics and I think still is today. Blumer did not pick up the tight methods and has sort of gone out on a limb. (Faris, 1972)

The consolidation of case study and statistics, indeed, seems to have begun early at Chicago. Howard Jensen, a doctoral student in the latter half of the second decade of the century apparently

> felt that statistics were important although he was not willing to give them first place in his interest. He was a humanist... and he used statistics only to further that interest. But he was not narrow minded on the subject. He

felt that both things were important, the other thing being case study, of course. (Mrs. H. Jensen, 1972).

Bingham Dai obtained his doctorate in 1937 for his research into opiate addiction in Chicago (Dai, 1937). This research in progress he reported to the summer Institute of 1935 and an article on it in the Bulletin noted that the study consisted of two parts '(i) the analysis of statistical data regarding drug addiction, and (ii) case studies based upon the long interview' (Bulletin of the Society for Social Research, June 1935). [2]

Chicagoans were, thus, more likely to adopt methods according to circumstance rather than opt for either side of the case study versus statistics debate.

Subsequently, the case study-statistics debate shifted emphasis from a concern with the efficacy of statistics in the collection of attitudinal data to a concern with the definitive nature of concepts. Statistical analysis of schedules required that concepts be definitive and that they be predetermined by the interviewer. The debate on 'operationalisation' was indicative of this reorientation of the case study-statistics debate. It was not one concerned with establishing the primacy of quantitative approaches over qualitative ones per se, but rather of the possibility of a falsificationist science requiring conceptual explication and accurate measurement, (Lundberg, 1936; Waller, 1936).

Blumer responded vigorously to the movement towards operationalisation of concepts by arguing that concepts in sociology were primarily 'sensitizing' and not definitive (Blumer, 1931) [3]. This line of debate was not concerned with the efficacy of statistics in assessing attitudes, but cast doubt on the possibility of formulating concepts to a degree that measurement would be at all meaningful. Case study and other ethnographic techniques, it was argued, offered a sounder way of generating 'sensitizing' concepts.

These two phases of the debate as to the efficacy of statistics and the possibility of definitive concepts were engaged in as fully at Chicago as elsewhere and there was no 'Chicago' view which, as the myth suggests, saw the 'Chicago School' as defenders of case study and opposed to statistics. In terms of their work, the Chicagoans were more likely to adopt methods to suit circumstances rather opt for either side of the case study versus statistics debate.

Park's approach to quantification

Park is cited as a clear opponent of statistics and as providing a heritage that disdained the use of quantitative techniques.

For Park, statisticians were worse than dirt, that they really never knew the phenomena they were studying. He made great point of the difference between knowledge about something and aquaintance with the phenomena. (Cottrell, 1972)

He communicated this forcibly to some of his students and redirected their research methods, as Hayner recalls

You had to start with a map so I got one of these big maps of Chicago and spotted all the hotels in the Chicago area ... I was going to cook up a questionnaire to these places. Park put his thumb on that. He wasn't into statistics, you know. You don't want to do it that way. You have to get out and visit these people and talk with them. There are all kinds of people in the hotel. Put yourself in their place. Be a good reporter. (Hayner, 1972)

Indeed, his disdain of statistics also affected his personal relationships, according to Faris.

Park asked me how my thesis was coming along and I told him I hadn't done anything because I was getting too interested in statistics and that destroyed my relation with Park for three years.... He was anti-statistical, I didn't realise I was hurting his feelings but he didn't approach me any more and he didn't notice me in the corridors, not until my final examination on my thesis. He liked my work, he got immediately warm again and gave me a friendly compliment and was personally warm to me ever since. (Faris, 1972)

However, Park's position was not so straightforward as these accounts suggest. He noted (Park, 1939, p. 3) that as early as the 1890s he had an 'understanding of the significance and the possibilities of the social survey as an instrument for social investigations'. Like Thomas, he was sceptical of the uncritical adoption of the practice of the physical sciences and wanted the subjective element taken into account (Wirth, 1944). The social survey, he felt, could provide some useful information but that it only showed the surface of appearances and that it masked the meanings that underlay the aggregates. Nonetheless, he approached surveys and statistics critically rather than rejecting them outright. He even taught a course entitled 'The Survey' from 1915 to 1922 (with the exception of 1921) which looked at the 'uses and practical limitations of the Social Survey' and described and compared 'technical devices for the analysis, description and presentation of sociological data with reference to the different fields in which they have been practically employed'. Thus estimating 'the value for science and for social reform of the results obtained' (Univeristy of Chicago, Official Publications, 1915). The ending of this course in 1922 was the result of the development of Park's collaboration with Burgess on the teaching of a course entitled 'Field Studies'. Begun in 1917, Burgess joined Park in teaching it in 1920, and this became the only methods course in the department until 1927, and was the basis of Palmer's handbook (1928).

It would be possible to assume from this that Park saw little potential in the social survey and that, with Burgess, encouraged 'field work' which moved away from statistical concerns. The well-known studies of the 'golden era' could, then, be seen a result of this 'qualitative' orientation. While having some credibility, this interpretation accounts for only part of the story. Hughes recalled that during the period 1923 to 1927 he had a course on the social survey with Park (which was, presumably, part of the field studies course).

> It was a field operation and he introduced us to the volumes of Booth's Life and Labour of the People in London and Rowntree's study of poverty and other British studies of this kind and the Pittsburgh survey and the Springfield survey... he used these surveys emphasizing, incidentally, the demographic, statistical side of them as well as this dynamic human side. It's a mistake to think that Park was neglecting that side. (Hughes, 1980, p. 270)

Although the Department of Sociology had no statistician of its own until 1927, despite Small's repeated requests for one dating from 1915, Chicago sociology students were directed towards the statistics courses in other departments, notably Thurstone's course in the psychology department (Blumer, 1972) and Field's courses in the economics department (Bulmer, 1981a; Cavan, 1983). Field, in fact, developed his course to make it more suitable for social science students rather than specifically for economics graduates. While statistical techniques were taught elsewhere an understanding of them was expected of sociology students. Their active involvement in the development of small area statistics and in the Chicago Fact Books reflect the encouragement of statistical expertise and appreciation of it within the Department.

Park encouraged Charles Johnson, the joint executive secretary of the commission to investigate the Chicago race riots to investigate the riots using statistical techniques and Park, himself, employed a mixture of case study and statistical analyses in the 1925 West Coast survey of Japanese immigrants (Matthews, 1977) which was published in 'Survey Graphic' (Park, 1926). As part of this study, Park encouraged Bogardus to produce a quantitative indicator of social distance which later became the 'Bogardus Social Distance Scale'. On his return from the Institute of Pacific Relations held in Honolulu in July 1925, Park spoke of the 'unusual opportunities in Honolulu at the present time to study sociological problems as controlled experiments.' (Minutes of the Society for Social Research, 29.10.1925).

Park also tried to get Hughes to do a mathematical study of land values in a large city because he thought it would be the best statistical index to city growth. 'As you have no doubt heard, he didn't believe in statistics, but he wanted me to do that thesis just the same' (Hughes, 1980, p. 256).

Other students of Park and Burgess (e.g. Mowrer, 1927; Thrasher, 1927; Cavan, 1928) made use of statistical techniques in the early 1920s (before Ogburn joined the staff). Mowrer, for example, began his research on family disorganisation in 1920 which set out on a search for a 'fundamental and scientific analysis of marriage disorganization ... by an examination of statistics and statistical methods as these could be applied to the phenomena of divorce and desertion' (Mowrer, 1927).

Ogburn and the nurturing of quantitative techniques

Even if Park was opposed to, or at least sceptical of, statistical approaches other Chicago sociologists, notably Ogburn, were not ignoring statistical developments during the 1920s and 1930s.

> Ogburn was doing empirical work, which is not what we would call experimental work today, he was just manipulating countings that had already been made for other purposes by the government. But he was squeezing theoretical material out of the census and other government methods of counting. (Dollard, 1972)

> Ogburn represented a counterweight to the anti-statistical orientation Park represented and set the tone in the department for quite a while of being anti-statistician. Yet Faris insisted that it wasn't a good idea to have a sociologist falling behind because he didn't have good statistical training, so they brought Ogburn on and Ogburn made quite a splash and attracted some very good students. (Cottrell, 1972)

The development of quantification in sociology at Chicago received a boost from the employment of Ogburn who moved from Columbia with a well established reputation. Indeed, Ogburn contributed a chapter on 'Statistical Studies on Marriage and the Family' to the text that resulted from the work of the American Statistical Association's Committee on Social Statistics (Rice, 1930) and had been editor of the **Journal of the American Statistical Association.** He turned down the chairman-ships of sociology departments at Michigan and Minnesota (Og-burn 1929b) in order to come to Chicago where he took responsi-bility for the development of quantitative techniques and of quantitatively based research in the department. Nonetheless, the development of a statistical perspective, he recalled, was not easy.

> On coming to the University of Chicago I found a much more hostile attitude toward statistics than I ever had at Col-umbia. Yet I fought the battle, taught all the statistics in the Sociology Department, and participated generally in the statistical work of University Committees. (Ogburn journal, 13th June 1952)

The arrival of Ogburn, while clearly a boost for quantifica-tion in Chicago sociology, was not simply the arrival of a statistician. Ogburn had rejected the idea of restricting his intellectual development by being nothing but a statistician as early as 1912 (Ogburn journal, 13th June 1952). With the de-pression Ogburn spent more time on substantive sociology and became particularly interested in technology and social change. Eventually he lost track of developments in statistical theory and gave up teaching the subject altogether.

Some commentators, have suggested that Ogburn's development of statistics represented a split in the department. As Ogburn's influence began to be felt towards the end of the 'golden era'

> statistics gained favour... and life histories began to fade as a primary means of study, to be replaced by the collection of comparable data from a number of cases that were subjected to statistical analysis.... Ogburn's arrival gave impetus to the quantitative analysis of social data and thereby contributed to the decline of case studies. (Cavan, 1983, p. 414).

Cottrell (1972) also suggests that the impact of Ogburn was to lead to a methodological split with him developing his own group of quantitatively oriented students. Such a view, which implicitly prevails as part of many designations of the 'Chica-go School', gives credence to the view of the school as retain-ing 'anachronistic ethnographic techniques' for 'unscientific reformist' purposes (see chapter seven).

However, such views are misleading. Small had wanted a stat-istician in the department for more than a decade.

> Ogburn was recruited because sociology did not have a course in statistics... the realisation came up that it was

an important subject and the realisation was there that Chicago ought to bring in some outsiders.... Columbia was the other strong department in the country... probably my father heard it from somewhere that Ogburn was dissatisfied at Columbia and it might be a good chance to raid... Ogburn really wanted to stay at Columbia but wasn't really decided. There was feeling against him there.... It was my father's initiative that got Ogburn here... he probably talked the others into it. (Faris, 1972)

Blumer (1972) thought that Burgess had pushed for Ogburn's appointment more than anyone else but that it had been a consensus of the Department that such an appointment was necessary as their was a gap to be filled. Ogburn moved rapidly to promote a more positive image of quantification in sociology, but was not acting either to reverse a trend, or in isolation. If Park and Blumer had reservations, in the main Ogburn's arrival was seen as advantageous for sociology at Chicago. The Society for Social Research, through its Bulletin, welcomed Ogburn and advertised and promoted his courses.

Ogburn's impact was substantial and went beyond the mere importation of statistical expertise. His involvement in the department and outside was notable and he tended to adopt wide horizons. 'His concepts were primarily national whereas the others were local' (Dollard, 1972). Ogburn was directly involved in ongoing research in the department as well as his own heavy committments which included the President's Committee on Social Trends. He wrote to Ruth Newcomb on October 17th 1929

I am working this Fall on the planning of a survey of recent social changes to be conducted under the auspices of President Hoover. I'm just finishing up the study on the comparative strength of the various forces operating in the Presidential election of 1928. I'm also hoping to finish up a study on the business cycles and politics. I have also worked during the past month of the quarter and during two and one half months of the Summer quarter on outlining the report for a plan for a nationwide cost of living study with particular reference to its scope and method. This was done for President Hoover at the request of Secretary Wilbur. (Ogburn, 1929)

One avenue of his involvement in research at Chicago was through the Local Community Research Committee, which he joined as soon as he settled in. Ironically, in view of its general tendency, the Local Community Research Committee actually provided a focus for the development of quantitative research techniques. In the period from his appointment in 1927, to the demise of the Committee in 1929, Ogburn had begun three studies

under the auspices of the Committee and two of the more quantitative students, Stephan and Tibbits, were involved in two
other projects. The Committee was also responsible for establishing research professorships in the social sciences, two of
whom, Thurstone and Schultz, were predominantly involved in
quantitative research.

The Local Community Research Committee was a major force in
the development of quantitative research methods at Chicago
(Bulmer, 1981a, 1984). The committee gave considerable financial support to quantitative research in the social sciences at
Chicago. The funding of large scale politics surveys, the
purchase of census tract data, the appointment of support staff
(crucial for the time consuming process of attempting factor
analytic and multi-variate techniques by hand), and the provision of physical facilities for research, notably computational
machines and the space to house them, were important contributions of the Local Community Research Committee

This involvement of the Local Community Research Committee in
the developement of quantitative techniques towards the end of
the 1920s is reflected in White's (1929a, p.25) summary. He
noted that the social sciences have not ordinarily been thought
of as using or needing laboratory equipment and that

> social scientists regularly treat the community as a clin-
> ic, diagnosing on the basis of existing knowledge and
> insight, and prescribing with what wisdom they may possess
> for social ills.
> In a more precise sense, however, the social sciences have
> now reached the point where it is open to use laboratory
> methods. Mr. Gosnell's experiment with a section of the
> Chicago electorate, applying a known stimulus under con-
> trolled conditions, reveals the social scientist at work in
> an out-of-door laboratory; the various analyses of person-
> ality, including the application of the technique of the
> psychologist and psychiatrist, involve laboratory technique
> and equipment provided in the new Social Science Building.
> It may be more accurate to refer to this building .... as a
> workshop. (White, 1929a, p. 31)

A further indicator of Ogburn's involvement in the interdisciplinary nature of the development of quantitative techniques
at Chicago can be seen in his collaboration with the economics
department in reconstructing their written quantitative methods
paper for the doctorate. What had once been a combined account-
ancy and statistics paper was restructured into two self contained papers with the statistics element greatly enhanced and
including time series analysis, index number construction,
multiple and partial correlation and probability distributions.
Ogburn was also quick in requesting additional full time

support in the quantitative area and circulated the department with a draft memorandum (c. 1928) entitled 'Preliminary Draft of the Statistics Proposal'

> It is highly important that a man in statistical mathematics be added to the mathematics department, this is the first wish of all of us. If, however, it is not possible to arrange for this a man should be added to the economics business staff who is very strong on the mathematics side. There should be centralised operations of all elementary and intermediate statistics work in economics, sociology, psychology, commerce and administration and social service administration. The really advanced work should be given in a new building in connection with research projects. (Ogburn, 1928).

In the event, the Social Science Research Building was erected for such advanced social scientific work in 1929 and contained an advanced statistics laboratory. Ogburn, who had responsibility for the 'image' of the Social Science Research Building, managed to persuade his colleagues that a suitable motto would be an annotated quote from Lord Kelvin, 'When you cannot measure * your knowledge is * meagre * and * unsatisfactory *', which is engraved on the outside of the building.

Ogburn's interdisciplinary perspective did not, however, have priority over his sociological concerns. Apart from taking on R. E. L. Faris as a statistics assistant in October 1929, he developed various new courses in the department. Ogburn's arrival, having been announced and welcomed in the Bulletin of the Society for Social Research in 1927, was followed up in January with an article which noted that

> The University has announced a new course in methods of research for the first term of the Summer Quarter, 1928, which it is hoped will be of interest to members of the Society for Social Research, and to others who expect to attend the sessions of the Institute next August. (Bulletin of the Society for Social Research, January, 1928)

The course, which was taught by Ogburn, was aimed at graduate students who had some experience in, and who were carrying on, independent research work and who wanted to meet others engaged in the same or related lines of enquiry. The course consisted of lectures, demonstrations and a twice weekly clinic, plus individual counselling from instructors. The course had been prompted by

> The steady accumulation in recent years of maps, statistics and local studies at the Social Research Laboratory of the

University; the interesting investigations now in progress
at the Institute for Juvenile Research... and the increasing number of social investigations carried on by other
local institutions.
The purpose of the new course in methods of research is to
extend and complete the program of the Institute of the
Society for Social Research; to make it a center where
students may meet; a clearing house where methods of research may be compared and criticized. (Bulletin of the
Society for Social Research, January, 1928)

The April 1928 issue of the Bulletin of the Society for
Social Research called attention once again to the new course
in 'Methods of research in the social sciences'. This was but
one of a number of new courses in quantitative methodology
which were to blossom at Chicago. In 1927 Ogburn offered an
introductory course in statistics which he taught until 1929.
Stouffer, one of Ogburn's graduate students, took over the
teaching in 1930. When, in 1932, Rice spent a year at Chicago,
the course title was changed to 'Statistical sociology'. Ogburn
continued teaching the new course until 1934. During his year
at Chicago, Rice also ran a course entitled 'Measurement in
social politics'. Running parallel to the introductory course
was a course entitled 'Statistical methods' ('Methods of quantitative sociology', after 1932) which either Ogburn or Stouffer taught from 1927 to 1945 (with the exception of 1931,
1943).
Ogburn was supposedly to provide a course on the 'Statistics
of social maladjustment' when he first arrived at Chicago but
this was never given, although he did teach a course on 'Sociology and the social sciences' in which he demanded a more
'exact' approach to social scientific data and enquiry. In
1929, he began an advanced course in 'Research in quantitative
sociology' which was available most years until 1940 and in
1936 Ogburn gave a course on 'Partial correlation analysis'
which he repeated each year he was available until 1945.
In 1931 Ogburn first offered a course on 'Statistical problems' which he taught between 1932 and 1935, before it became a
more specific course in the 'Measurement of relationships' in
1937 and was taught until 1942. Stouffer taught this course in
1938 and had earlier taken the 'Statistical sociology' course
in 1935. These were but a part of Stouffer's prolific involvement in teaching quantitative methodology courses in the mid to
late 1930s. In 1935 he started a courses on 'Sampling in social
research' (which was later taught by Williams in 1948 and
1949), 'Quantitative studies in the family', 'Quantitative
criminology', as well as a course on the 'Applications of
probability to sociology' which changed to 'Quantitative aspects of social problems' the following year. In 1938 he inaug-

urated 'Quantitative studies in social psychology' and in 1939 he took over and revamped Park's old course in 'Human migrations' before, a year later, focussing upon 'Quantitative studies in social organisation' and 'Statistical problems of governmental research'. Teaching developments in this field, however, were thwarted by the War and Stouffer's involvement in government research culminating in his leave of absence for government service in 1944 and 1945.

The courses Stouffer began in 1936 on 'Quantitative problems in population', 'Quantitative studies in population and human ecology' and 'Dynamics of population' initiated a series of courses on population in which Hauser and Duncan were heavily involved. In 1948 Hauser taught 'Comparative population structure and dynamics', 'Quantitative methods for population research' and 'Seminar in the analysis of census data' as well as the introductory course to the study of population human ecology. Hauser had already offered a course on statistical sources in 1947 and followed it up with one specifically on 'Sample surveys as a research method' in 1949. In 1950 he took over a course on the 'Design of research' which Goodman had started in 1947.

Other sociologists who took on the teaching of quantitative methodology courses [4] included Williams, Kittagawa and Hart. Williams taught 'Methods of quantitative sociology' in 1947, 'Introduction to statistical reasoning', and 'Mathematics essential to elementary statistics' in 1948. Kittagawa also taught these courses during the next three years. In 1948 the more advanced statistics courses were 'rationalised' into three successive courses 'Statistical methods of research' parts I to III, and taught initially by Williams and Kittagawa before becoming the province of Goodman. The latter also developed a course on statistical inference (in 1951) and on 'Recent advanced methods' in quantitative research a year later. In 1949, Lazarsfeld was a visiting lecturer from Columbia and offered a course on 'New developments in attitude measurement' and a year later Hart (director of the National Opinion Research Centre) gave a course on 'Research in public opinion'. (Appendix 4 provides full details of courses offered in the Sociology Department of the University of Chicago).

Burgess as the barometer of methodological tendencies

If Park, on balance, was hostile to statistics, Burgess certainly was not. Before coming to Chicago, Burgess had been involved with social surveys and statistics. He had worked with J.J. Sippy on the Belleville Survey (1913) and with F.W. Blackmar on the Lawrence Social Survey of 1916 (Burgess 1916). He encouraged students to make use of statistical data wherever appropriate. He was very much involved in developing census data for sociological use. 'Burgess, it may fairly be claimed, was the father of modern census tract statistics, both by example and as a co-ordinator of pressure on the Bureau of Census in drawing up their plans for 1930' (Bulmer, 1981a, p. 315).

Burgess, in conjunction with Newcomb, produced analyses of the 1920, and 1930 censuses (Burgess and Newcomb, 1931, 1933), and encouraged the analysis of the 1934 census (Newcomb and Lang, 1934). In conjunction with this Newcomb was awarded the 'University prize for originality in research ... for his contribution of a "Single Numerical Index of Age and Sex Distribution of Population"' (Bulletin of the Society for Social Research, Dec., 1930).

Burgess' request for funding from the Social Science Research Council (Burgess, 1935a) for research that would lead to the presentation of materials on city growth, movement of population and formation of local communities by sector, prepared the ground for the later Fact Books of Chicago (Wirth and Furez, 1938; Wirth and Bernert, 1949; Hauser and Kitagawa, 1953; Kitagawa and Taeuber, 1963) [5]. His involvement with census analysis at a multi-disciplinary level goes back at least to 1924. As chairman of the Chicago Census Committee, Burgess circulated a paper (3/6/1924) to the Social Research Committee of Political Economy, Sociology and Political Science Departments on the development of the Chicago census. This committee was the forerunner of the Local Community Research Committee and Marshall, Merriam and Burgess were the executive committee.

> Burgess was very instrumental in encouraging students who had been brought up to make case studies and to get qualitative data and that sort of thing to try and translate them into a more quantifiable form and to pay some attention to the statistics. He was much influenced by Ogburn, much encouraged I should say, he was already aware of the uses of quantified material, he was very much aware of the usefulness of the census data and that sort of thing and of course our delinquency area studies ... Yes, that preceded Ogburn ... Park was mainly grumbling about people who started on a problem with lets get some quantitative data, he wanted to start with 'lets find out about the way this person ticks' and get inside of him and inside of his community and find out what is going on. And if you have to use quantitative data [then] use it in the light of what you know, not start out with it and cover over your ignorance about it, as is what goes on with a lot of figures. So we were already using rather elementary quantitative material. And that was, I think, becoming more impressed on Faris, as Chairman, to get a statistician. (Cottrell, 1972)

Ogburn had a considerable impact on Burgess when he arrived, and Burgess supported Ogburn. He encouraged the development of multiple factor analysis by his students, and learned the technique from Lang and Cottrell, whom he had encouraged to attend Ogburn's class. 'Actually we were the first sociologists to use factor analysis on sociological data in the marriage prediction studies. It was not a central thing but a technique we tried out and got some help in the interpretation of the data (Cottrell, 1972).

Burgess had taken the opportunity, as a full professor, of attending Ogburn's quantitative courses and utilised the extensive quantitative expertise available at Chicago in his own research. This is clear from the development of his marriage adjustment research. In an enclosure to a letter to Wirth, Burgess (1935b) referred to the initial study of prediction of marriage adjustment he had undertaken in collaboration with Cottrell. The aim was to predict, at the time of marriage, the success or failure of the relationship. He referred to the fact that approximately one thousand schedules were secured and that a high degree of reliability was found 'as indicated by coefficients of correlation ranging from .86 to .96'. The construction of a 'marriage adjustment index out of eighteen items in the schedule' allowed for assignation of numerical values to adjustment in marriage. Thus they were able to identify the factors making for success in marriage. The further development of the research was in terms of weighting the most important factors and combining them 'for prediction by the method of partial and multiple correlation'.

The association between Ogburn and Burgess persisted until their retirement in 1952. In 1950, for example, Ogburn recorded that

> one of Burgess's students, Strauss, did some research once on the reasons for choosing a mate for marriage. He investigated three reasons.... I rang Burgess yesterday and suggested that he have another research done on these same couples to see which class of choice yielded more stability and which showed more separations and divorces. (Ogburn journal, 11th November, 1950)

Throughout, however, Burgess was concerned to ensure the mutual development of case study and statistics. In the development of a book on the 'Family in the Urban Community', for example, Burgess (1935c) proposed that the volume 'makes use of both statistics and case study material'. Over a thirty year period Burgess consistently argued for a methodological eclecticism and against monism. In many respects Burgess's methodological comments are a barometer of prevailing direction of methodological concerns in sociology in America from 1920 to

1950.

For Burgess development of prediction studies was of the highest 'theoretical and practical importance. Increase in the efficiency, precision, and scope of prediction is a chief aim of the social sciences as it is of all science' (Burgess, 1941 p. 55). This involvement in prediction studies and the development of quantitative research alongside case study was also reflected in his teaching. From 1919 to 1941 Burgess had taught on the 'Field studies' course which gradually became a student practical, in that it was 'designed to provide direction and suggestion for either special research or a community survey' (Burgess, 1952). In 1940 he began teaching 'Methods of sociological research' which was described as

> Methods of historical research, field observation, mapping, interviewing, evaluation of human documents, and case study as used in sociology -- especially in human ecology and social psychology -- and the relationships of these methods to statistical procedures. (Burgess, 1952)

This course continued until 1944 when Burgess taught 'Introduction to statistical sociology', until 1947, which involved

> Practical methods of analysing sociological data -- the questionnaire, graphical presentation, interpretation of statistics, the nature of statistical evidence, statistical fallacies. (Burgess, 1952)

Meanwhile he began a course on the 'Problems and methods of prediction' (1941) which was concerned with the theory of prediction and forecasting and included a comparison of 'statistical prediction and forecasts from case studies'. Burgess was proud of his role in pioneering prediction studies (Burgess, 1941) and either directly, or through his students, was involved in a number of such studies in various areas including school and college success, occupational adjustment, criminal recidivism, mental breakdown, adjustment in army camps, juvenile probation, adult probation, cadet camps, and selection of occupation. The first marriage prediction study ever undertaken in 1931 was published in a report by L.S. Cottrell and Burgess in 1939 entitled 'Predicting Success or Failure in Marriage'. A progress report on this study to the Social Science Research Committee at Chicago in the Winter Quarter of 1931 noted of the study that

> its objective is to work out a method for predicting the statistical probabilities both (a) of the continuance of the marriage status and (b) of happiness in marriage....
> The schedule of eight pages is placed in the hands of per-

sons who have been married from two to five years....
The revised schedule includes the shorter personality test
by Professor Thurstone which it is believed will be a valuable addition to the study.
In addition to securing these schedules, a small number of
case studies have been secured partly for the purpose of
checking the schedule. (Burgess, 1931).

Burgess' prediction studies had a wide impact, for example
the work of Lewis Terman ('Psychological Factors in Marital
Happiness') and E. Lowell Kelly ('Study of Engaged Couples')
used the Burgess-Cottrell scale of marital adjustment, while
Clifford Kilpatrick (University of Minnesota) and Harvey Locke
(Indiana University) undertook similar marriage study work
(Burgess, 1941).
These studies gradually became a test of the case study as a
means of objective data gathering, as Burgess turned more and
more towards a factor analytic, correlational study of prediction. He noted that the prediction work was related to other
work going on at the University of Chicago which

has been most helpful in the development of methods of
research. W.F. Ogburn, who has carried on considerable work
in the prediction of political behavior has given valuable
advice in the initial development of both the parole and
marriage studies. L.L. Thurstone and his students have been
of great assistance particularly in the application of
methods of factor analysis (in our first study) and of
matrix algebra (in the present study) to problems of prediction. S.A. Stouffer, who has developed a significant
mathematical formula for the prediction of intermigration
between cities has been increasingly helpful in giving
advice and suggestions upon problems of statistical and
case-study prediction. His interest in the possibilities of
interrelating statistical and case-study techniques goes
back to his doctoral dissertation [1930]. He has had a long
interest in the problems of prediction as indicated by
certain of his published papers. Dr. David Slight, who has
given valuable advice on psychiatric aspects of the project, has shown a strong interest in which I equally share
in the possibilities of working out a joint project on
psychiatric and sociological phases of behavior important
for prediction. (Burgess, 1941, p. 58-59) [6]

Clearly, then, the Chicagoans, not only made extensive use of
statistics in the inter-war period, but also developed the
rigorous hypothesis testing and cumulative theory development
principles which later came to be identified so closely with
the post 1945 'Columbia School'.

In his account of prediction studies, Burgess specified the following stages. Stage one is to locate the best criteria of adjustment. The second stage is to isolate the best predictive factors on three fronts: the past experience of subject; the present personality traits; and contingency conditions. The third stage is the combination and weighting of predictive items, using 'factor analysis and matrix algebra' (Burgess, 1941 p. 53). The fourth stage is the assessment of the

> feasibility of prediction from intensive case studies to discover dynamic factors difficult to arrive at by sched-ules and to reduce to statistical formulations either (i) by case study analysis alone or (ii) in conjunction with statistical techniques (Burgess, 1941 p. 54)

Chicago sociologists generally aimed at explanatory accounts in the Thomasian mould. Burgess (1944a) provided a clear desig-nation of the explanatory process in quantitatively oriented nomothetic sociology when he outlined the five steps in any factor analytic causal attributable study. These are

1. selecting criteria (of success) [Y]
2. selecting determining factors [Xs]
3. establishing temporal precedence
4. correlating each X with Y
5. combining (useful) Xs into a prediction score for use on others not in the study.

This outline closely parallels the Columbia model of operat-ionalised non-spurious time prioritised correlation. (Labowitz and Hagedorn, 1971; Hirschi and Selvin, 1972; Boudon, 1974).
The Chicagoans were also quite aware of the potential or possibilities of the large scale scheduled interview or quest-ionnaire survey. Indeed, the earliest development of this form of data gathering for social scientific rather than official purposes was the work done through the Local Community Research Committee in the politics department at Chicago (see Appendix 2). The close interdepartmental ties, meant that the large scale survey was an accepted and developed tool of social science at Chicago (Bulmer, 1981a). Burgess was very interested in developing the technique and had been since his early invol-vement in social surveys (Burgess, 1916). By the early 1920s he was considering the likely effectiveness of a large scale interview based sociological survey (Burns, 1924).
Burgess's views on technique tended to be very flexible, his main concern was that society be conceived of as an organism rather than as an aggregate of atomistic units. He was pre-pared, then, to countenance any method that may be of use in developing sociological theory within this overall perspective.

Thus he embraced all methodological developments, including advanced statistical techniques, provided that they did not swamp his underlying methodological concerns. Thus he noted that factor analysis assumes

> that factors operate in the individual case as in the average of all cases in the sample of the population upon which predictions are based. This assumption does violence to the clinically-minded person who perceives in each case a unique configuration of dynamic factors. (Burgess, 1944a, p. 30).

In a paper read to the Annual Meeting of the Iowa Association of Economists and Sociologists in 1927 Burgess had asserted the need for empirical work in sociology and his fundamental view of the organic nature of society. He addressed himself directly to the role of statistics and argued that they had tremendous potential and utility if used in conjunction with other techniques and were located within the theoretical perspective he advanced. To adopt an atomistic statistical monism was, for Burgess, to ignore the relationships that lay beneath the surface of ostensive appearances. In this, he reflected Park's Jamesian concern about the 'reality behind the mask' and Thomas's distinction between attitude and value. He argued that statistics alone were inadequate because it was important to

> recognise that quantitative methods deal in the main with the cruder, more external aspects of human behavior, and that some other more sympathetic and discerning method is necessary to probe beneath the surface and to depict and analyse the inner life of the person. (Burgess, 1927, p. 112).

His suggestion had been to proffer a mixture of case study and statistics and he argued that the two were not incompatible techniques. He reminded his audience that Le Play (commonly regarded, at the time, as the 'father' of statistical analysis in social science) introduced case study as the 'hand-maiden of statistics' and that Healy's well known statistical analyses into the causes of delinquency were elaborated by the use of case study material, which acted to provide Healy with the insights his statistical analyses alone were unable to provide. Burgess was not simply advocating uncritically or naively the use of case studies. He argued, for example, that they provided a way of testing hypotheses, and suggested that the first systematic use of case studies in this respect had been the **Polish Peasant** study (Thomas and Znaniecki, 1918). Burgess also pointed to the suggestions of Karl Pearson that scientific method involved classifying facts, noting mutual relations and describing their sequences, and argued that case study provided just such a facility.

Burgess did not assume that case study was an established technique, however.

> The assumption sometimes made that case studies and statistics were opposed to each other, or that statistics succeeded case studies in the 1920s, does not correspond to reality. Case studies and statistics developed side by side and supplemented each other. Students might use both approaches in their dissertations, as I did in my dissertation on Suicide. (Cavan, 1983, p. 414)

The debates about the relative merits of statistics and case study that peaked at the end of the 1920s and the mid 1930s were not debates about an old established method (case study) being superseded by a new growing method (statistics). As Burgess argued, the systematic use of case study as a method was in its infancy in 1927 and, like the rapidly expanding field of statistics, needed to be developed and nurtured. He advocated quite specifically that the two techniques be embraced jointly.

> It is probably sufficient to point out that the methods of statistics and of case study are not in conflict with each other: they are in fact mutually complementary. Statistical comparisons and correlations may often suggest leads for research by the case-study method, and documentary materials as they reveal social processes will inevitably point the way to more adequate statistical indicies. (Burgess, 1927, p. 120).

This is a position that Burgess addressed himself to consistently for the next 20 years. Throughout he attempted to develop research which adopted the complementary approach, his emphasis shifting, as he became more and more involved with prediction studies, to evaluating the efficacy of each method for predictive purposes. Thus, as part of his research outline in 1944, he pointed to how his results will provide an assessment of whether 'prediction by case-study analysis of dynamic factors is superior or inferior to prediction by statistical techniques' (Burgess 1944a, p. 54).

Even at this stage, having made enormous use of multivariate analysis, factor analysis and other statistical techniques, Burgess is reluctant to concede ground to quantification and treads the delicate line that divided the two sides of the **Polish Peasant** debate (Social Science Research Council, 1939).

The main research method relied upon by students of person-

ality, social organization and disorganization and collective behavior has been the personal document. Through letters, interviews and life histories data have been obtained
by which the processes of personal and social interaction
might be analyzed. Once a process is identified and defined
then it is possible but often difficult to develop statistical methods for more precise and accurate measurement as
in the case of ideal type concept already discussed. (Burgess, 1944a, p. 21).

Burgess persisted in his advocacy of the synthesis of case
study and statistics and pointed to how such interrelation may
be achieved. He maintained that case study is a useful adjunct
to statistics at an exploratory level and that it is useful for
interpreting statistical findings which would otherwise be
unintelligible. Of central importance for Burgess in the further use of case study was whether or not the problems of
explanatory generalisation from case study data may be resolved. Burgess admitted that the strongest supporters of case
study are those interested in idiographic rather than nomothetic study. Burgess himself, reflecting the long tradition at
Chicago, is interested in nomothetic study and conceded that

> so far the data available in comparison of statistical and
> case study predictions appear to indicate the superiority
> of quantitative methods. This seems in large part due to
> the difficulty of controlling the personal equation of the
> clinical investigator who tends to judge cases on the basis
> of his training or personal experience. (Burgess, 1944a, p.
> 31).

In this respect Burgess tended to underplay the shift in the
debate, fostered by Blumer, which centered on the conceptualisation process. However, he referred to the 'conceptualisation'
debate when addressing the penchant for scaling. He warned
against the vogue of scale construction lest it proceed without
'due care for careful development of prior conceptualisation'.
It was the critique of conceptualisation, especially of the
problems and aims of operationalisation, which lay at the heart
of the differences between quantifiers and methodological sceptics such as Blumer and Lerner (Social Science Research Council, 1939).
Burgess was both alert to, and interested in, developments in
quantification in the social sciences outside of Chicago, notably the mathematical orientation espoused by Lundberg (1929,
1936, 1942) and attempted by Dodd (1940) and the sociometry of
Moreno. Burgess saw sociometry as predated by Bogardus' 'Social
Distance Scale' but as being a more systematic development of
it. Burgess argued that sociometry contributed to the bridging

of the gaps between social analysis and statistics by concentrating on group interactive processes rather than the conventional approach of statistical analyses which was to deal with aggregates of atomistic items. Thus he saw great potential in sociometry as a methodological tool in his advocacy of an eclectic approach.

However, this did not deter him from his main concern and contention that statistics and case study are mutually complementary. He argued that case studies suggest problems for quantitative analysis which need case studies to interpret results fully, which leads to more problems, and so on. In other words, the interactive use of case study and statistics is compatible with a cumulative development of knowledge model. Such a model underpinned American sociological research for half a century and became embodied in middle range theorising (Merton, 1948). This is further discussed in chapter five.

The examination of the role of the Chicagoans in empirical social research and the development of methodology has indicated that Chicago sociology did not exhibit tendencies towards a single methodic approach. Rather, it tended to be eclectic, and certainly changed throughout the first half of the century. The Chicagoans tended to integrate both the subjective and the objective aspects of the social world and in doing so were not particularly unique (see Social Science Research Council, 1939). They were very much aware of methodological debates and this is reflected in the discussions in the Society for Social Research at Chicago. In its regular meetings and annual institutes, both with a large proportion of visiting speakers, current debates were vigorously enjoined.

Methodological debates in the Society for Social Research

The regular meetings of the Society for Social Research were very much concerned with methodology. They were forums which engaged different research ideas, techniques and procedures. As the Bulletin announced on a number of occasions, there was a diversity of opinion on methodological issues which ensured healthy, and lengthy debate.

> During the Autumn Quarter (1931) from 30 to 60 people attended each meeting an increase of from three to five fold over the meetings of five years ago. Never during this quarter did the discussion cease before the time of adjournment. (Bulletin of the Society for Social Research, January 1932).

The talks given during 1929 provide an example of the engagement with the developing statistical approach. These meetings were reported in the Bulletin (1930) as excellently attended and with 'enough conflict of ideas to insure lively and critical discussions'. The talks included F.N. Freeman from the School of Education on a statistical study of foster children; L.L. Thurstone from the Psychology Department on a statistical technique for comparing I.Q. of younger and older children; a debate between Blumer and T.C. McCormick on the logic and scope of statistical methods; and E. Faris critically examining the value of life history documents as data in social psychology. Nearly all the talks that year were concerned with methodological considerations. The year was rounded off by a farewell dinner for Park prior to his trip to Asia and Park summed up the tendency in the Department by urging 'sociologists not to lose their human interests while amidst their abstractions and their measurements' (Bulletin of the Society for Social Research, 1930, p. 3).

Rather than advocate impressionistic research, the Chicagoans, as the meetings of the Society for Social Research show, were very concerned with methodological aspects of research. Indeed, in the person of Ogburn, the Chicagoans were represented by a severe critic of impressionistic research. As is clear from the minutes of his address to the Society for Social Research (6th March 1933) about his involvement in the President's Social Trends research, Ogburn was far from happy with the contributions of many of the researchers to the Social Trends study. As chairman of the committee on research he was in the position of having to sharpen up the research, which he said he did by posing the question 'How do you know it ?'. He noted, scornfully, that only approximately twenty per cent of researchers could forecast on the basis of their study, and that much of the reporting provided a false impression.

The extent of the methodological debate is evident in the number of meetings in which methodological discussion was the prime focus. Forty five (33%) of the addresses were mainly concerned with methodology. In the period up to 1930 nearly half (48%) of all meetings had an address in which methodology was a major concern. After 1930 the proportion dropped to a third (32%). While the addresses directed to methodology were mainly from sociology staff and students (48%), other Chicago faculty contributed considerably (31%). While about one in three of all academic addresses (faculty and students) were directed to methodology, the ratio dropped to one in five for external, non-academic speakers. Members of the Society were more than twice as likely to address the meetings on methodological issues (65%) than non-members (35%). (See Appendix 3).

In all, thirty five (26%) of the talks given to the society were entirely devoted to methodological issues, these included two searching addresses by Blumer. The first (23rd November 1931) was in relation to his research into the effects of motion pictures on attitudes, in which he collaborated with Hauser. They used a combination of life histories and question-naires. Blumer criticised existing methods of examining mass data. The case method

> does produce a comprehensive record of individual exper-ience, but attempts to classify such data into types have been disappointing. The statistical method is too abstract, limited to one or two points, and provides a formula which is interpreted in the light of individual experience. Alternatively, Dr. Blumer suggested the collection of a large number of anonymous personal narratives related to the particular experience under investigation. If in these records an extreme form of experience appears in a few cases this may be indicative of a tendency toward the particular type of experience. (Bulletin of the Society for Social Research, Jan 1932)

The second (4th March 1935) was on

> "The Search for Method in Sociology". Preoccupation with method is not due to dissatisfaction with results obtained within the field of sociology. Rather it is born out of a desire to be accepted as "scientific" by other sciences. Such courting of favor has had disadvantageous consequen-ces. Sociologists tend to become constantly dependent upon other sciences for the framework inside which their work shall go on. They become exceedingly self-conscious regard-ing method and thus are led to restrict the area of their investigation to such problems as will easily lend them-selves to methods and techniques accepted without question by other sciences. They have come to place an exaggerated importance, for instance, upon quantitative procedure, As witness the present extensive volume of statistical work. Its extent cannot be explained by its success inside the field of sociology, but by reference to the prestige of the physical sciences .... The discussion which followed Pro-fessor Blumer's talk revealed ... interesting differences of opinion. (Bulletin of the Society for Social Research, March 1935, p. 4)

It is notable, in this, that Blumer made a comment on method-lead enquiry that C. Wright Mills (1959) found it necessary to restate a quarter of a century later. In addition, Blumer's (1931) celebrated paper 'Science Without Concepts' was first presented at the Ninth Annual Institute of the Society for Social Research (1930).

The concern with methodology in the Society reflects the discussion of methods and methodology in the doctoral disserta-

tions at Chicago. The sample of theses shows that thirty two
(76%) discussed methods and twenty one (50%) included methodological or epistemological discussions. Methodic discussion
increased from sixty five per cent up to 1940 to ninety per
cent of theses after 1940, there was a less dramatic and statistically insignificant rise in methodological discussion from
forty eight to fifty five per cent over the same period, (see
Appendix 6).

Chicago eclecticism

The dichotomisation of the history of sociological research in
the United States into qualitative and quantitative approaches
(Mullins, 1973) embodied in a view of a methodological struggle
between Chicago and Columbia, is not tenable (Wilson, 1940;
Coleman, 1980). Indeed, by the 1950s, when Columbia was at its
peak, Chicago had been developing quantitative studies for a
considerable time. The review of the methodological interests
of some of the key figures at Chicago clearly belies the idea
that Chicago was out on a limb compared with the rest of American sociology. Nonetheless, there are commentators who suggest
that such was the case especially after 1930 when its dominance
of the discipline is seen to draw to a close. This is investigated in chapter seven below.
   The Chicagoans did not represent one side of a dichotomised
view of methodic practice. The 'Chicago School' was not simply
anti-statistics. The rapid development of statistical analysis
in social science generated some reaction from interactionists
who were sceptical about, or hostile towards, what they saw as
a tendency to set aside the subjective element. Burgess is the
archetypal case, despite a positive attitude towards the potential of statistics, he also displayed a certain scepticism
towards quantitative techniques. In this he reflected not only
Park and Thomas but the prevailing attitude within the discipline. His changing stance, however, from initial scepticism of
statistics to enthusiastic usage in prediction studies is indicative of the changing nature of the view of sociology as
science in the United States.
   Shaw is a prime example of the eclecticism of Chicago sociologists. In his studies in the late 1920s and 1930s he utilised
spot maps, statistics and case studies. He was not prepared to
abandon case study for statistics maintaining that the

   case study method emphasises the total situation or combination of factors, the description of the processes or
   sequence of events in which the behavior occurs, the study
   of the individual behavior in its total setting, and the
   analyses and comparison of cases leading to the formulation

of hypotheses. (Shaw, 1931, p. 149).

Shaw was a student of Burgess who, as suggested above, can be seen as the barometer of methodological change at Chicago. A barometer affected not only by local pressure but also by changes in the wider sociological mileu. Burgess was far from alone in adopting this eclectic approach. Wirth, for example, in outlining a study of the black community in Chicago in 1939 indicated the use of three methodological approaches. These were the 'methods and concepts of the students of human ecology', 'the viewpoints and methods of those who have approached modern communities from the standpoint of the cultural anthropologist' and the 'life history method'. This necessitated three sources of data, statistics, interviews and life histories.

> The statistical material provides the background for the entire research. A statistical study of the growth of the Negro community has been made, as well as an ecological, a demographic and an occupational study. All available statistical sources are being used to check the interview materials and non-statistical data. The interview method has been relied upon to define and document the description of the social structure. The persons interviewed have been selected with reference to the various fields of major interest into which the study is divided. Approximately eight thousand interviews have been taken in the community. Life histories ranging from one hundred to seven hundred and fifty pages in length, were obtained from twenty five persons. These have been of value in showing the impact of the culture upon the individual by portraying the social structure as it appears to the individuals living in it, and by indicating the adjustment of the individual to the culture, its sub-societies, and the total society throughout his life career. (Wirth, 1939).

The sample survey of doctoral theses (Appendix 6) clearly reveals the eclectic nature of the methods adopted at Chicago. Only two theses were dependent on a single method and just five more relied on two methods. The data generation devices utilised by the Chicagoans surveyed range from literature review (adopted by 90%) through historical analysis (59%), document analysis (51%), informal interviews (43%) observation (36%), scheduled interviews (31%), life histories (30%), to questionnaires (14%).

Preference for methods shifted over time with literature review, historical analysis and document analysis dropping from a major technique adopted by between forty and sixty per cent of authors prior to 1940, to a mere five to twenty per cent.

after 1940, and life history dropped out altogether as a major technique, being replaced by informal interviewing of a less strenuous type (a rise of from 5% to 50%)

Conversely, scheduled interviewing, and participant observation which had not been used at all as a major technique before 1940, were adopted as a major technique after 1940 in sixty five per cent and twenty five per cent of theses respectively. Questionnaires increased in major usage from nine to twenty per cent in that period.

The interdisciplinary network of quantifiers at Chicago.

The Chicagoans, then, contributed considerably to the development of quantitative as well as qualitative techniques, although this element of their work is rarely emphasised, perhaps because of its interdepartmental character (Bulmer, 1981a). Thurstone's work on attitude scaling, factor analysis and multivariate analysis and the adaptation of the advanced correlation techniques of Pearson and associates for sociology by Ogburn, Stouffer and other, and the development of prediction studies in which Burgess was involved were important contributions to the development of quantitative analysis in sociology in the United States. The development of the 'Columbia style' had been predated by interdisciplinary work at Chicago. Central to this was not only Thurstone's work but also the large scale surveying in politics. As suggested above, the large scale social survey, while not used by the sociologists at Chicago, was developed in the politics department, with whom Ogburn had close ties (Merriam and Gosnell, 1924; Gosnell, 1927 and White, 1929). A further important development was the critical work of Stouffer on case history (i.e application of attitude testing to sociology) and the incorporation of the advances in British statistics following his year in London (1931-32) studying with Pearson, Yule, Fisher and Bowley.

Ogburn had a mediating role in all this, being a tutor and advisor to Stouffer, adapting and developing some of Thurstone's work (Ogburn, 1929c), assisting Burgess, and generally promoting statistical analysis. His own particular interest was in longitudinal analysis, notably time series analysis embodied in the social trends work. He co-ordinated the social trends contibutions to the American Journal of Sociology, one issue each year from 1927 to 1934 was on social changes, and was heavily involved in the work on the President's Committee on Social Trends.

There was no suggestion, at least until the 1950s, that Chicago sociology was 'non-quantitative'. Chicago had no repute for being hostile to statistics amongst contemporaries in the 1940s, rather the reverse was more likely the case given the reputation of Ogburn, Stouffer, Stephan and later O. D. Duncan and Fisher. The analysis of the 'coup' of 1935, in chapter seven, points to an alliance between the Chicagoans and other quantitative sociologists. In addition there were strong quantitative social science links provided through the interdepartmental research committees. Indeed, when Wilson wrote to Burgess in 1940 to recommend Whyte, one of the reasons was because 'I think he feels he needs more statistics than he has had.' The quantitative research at Chicago was not, then, undertaken by individuals working in isolation. Rather there was a strong network of quantitative practitioners within the University.

This can be seen in the close ties between quantifiers at Chicago, notably Ogburn, Thurstone, Gosnell, Douglas and Schultz and the connections they made with the departments of mathematics and biology served as a supplementary interdepartmental network which developed considerable research work. These ties were not merely transitory and there seemed to be a genuine concern that this area of work be harmoniously promoted at the highest level. As late as 1945 Stouffer, serving in the research unit of the War Department at Washington, wrote to Walter Bartky head of the Department of Mathematics at Chicago to recommend Guttman.

> Guttman's primary interest is in making basic contributions to social science. In that connection, he is, of course, very much interested in probability theory as well as in the theory of measurement. At the University of Chicago he would be a yeast which would have its influence throughout the social sciences. It seems to me that he would be a most useful addition to the committee on mathematical statistics, as well as to the social science division, and the critical Chicago atmosphere should stimulate him to continual new creative development. (Stouffer, 1945).

The development of quantitative techniques at Chicago has perhaps become a 'lost heritage' because of its interdisciplinary nature. However, given the long term of this development and the significant role played by Chicago personnel in the development of quantification in social science, this seems a rather too simple answer. Quantification at Chicago has, arguably, been deliberately ignored by historians who have been more concerned to explain the relationship of symbolic interactionism to the early 'pragmatic' base in the department, and thus have served to project an illusory view of Chicago as overly concerned with qualitative research.

Conclusion

It would seem that the idea that Chicago sociology was remote from the concerns of quantitative sociology has arisen through various factors. Artificial divisions have been created by historians in charting the history of social research in America and the 'Chicago School' has been located on one side of these divisions. So the 'School' is seen as supporting case study rather than statistics, as undertaking participant observation research rather than quantitatively based surveys, as ignoring quantitative techniques rather than developing them. The single most powerful component of this view is the assumed 'anti-statistical' perspective, derived from Thomas and Park and proposed as an alternative to 'positivistic' sociology in the work of Blumer. This avowed qualitative perspective is seen as clearly indicative of the school and opposed to the development of quantitative methods.

Such a perspective distorts the sociological enterprise at Chicago, not least by assuming a coherent 'School' opposed to prevailing methodological, epistemological and theoretical concerns of the discipline at large [7]. Such a position is presumed to be reflected in the advocacy of the theories of G. H. Mead by the Chicagoans. The following sections will explore the epistemological and theoretical orientations at Chicago, in relation to the perspectives in sociology in the United States in general. The role of Mead, in particular, will then be critically assessed. The discussion above has suggested that in terms of method and the development of quantification in sociology, Chicago was an integral part of American sociology.

Furthermore, the Chicagoans did not develop a phenomenological alternative to the prevailing nomological approach. Indeed, a cumulative theory model, grounded in a falsificationist approach to theorising can be seen to have underpinned the work of Chicago sociologists and was intrinsic to the general approach adopted in the United States. This will now be examined in more detail.

Notes

[1] There are various notions about the wars and battles fought between the quantitative and qualitative traditions and the exponents of particular positions reconstruct these encounters to project their side in the most favourable light. This leads to contradictions and confusions. Some wars are forgotten, other battles given exceptional prominence, and so on. Thus Blumer is seen as a major standard bearer of qualitative sociology by some historians of sociology, the early Chicago School, by others. Yet others do not seem to

distinguish between the two. Howard Becker is sometimes portrayed as the principle mover in a late rearguard action mounted by qualitative sociologists which became, eventually, necessary following the coup in the American Sociological Society in 1935. Others regard this as superficial posturing, the war having already been lost in the case study vs statistics and life history vs attitude scale debates of the 1929-1931 period. Ethnomethodologists, on the contrary, see the real battle beginning only in the late 1960s when, for the first time, the focus of qualitative sociological enquiry was radically questioned. In short, battle has been joined since sociology became an empirically orientated pursuit in the United States and will probably continue to be joined while a nomological presciption informs all spheres of science.

The reconstruction of the qualitative-quantitative debate has frequently been in combative terms but this tends to exaggerate the division. While certain elements in American sociology have conflicted, there is an enormous middle ground which has tended to avoid such conflict. Eclecticism of method, and a lack of epistemological dogmatism has prevailed rather than rigid adherence to singular orientations. This has been, possibly, at least in part, a function of the distance American sociology (and social psychology) has maintained from its European counterpart. American sociology has not developed a full fledged phenomenological, structural, hermeneutic or critical-dialectical sociology and has maintained a nomological orientation.

[2] Dai, had reported on his research to the Society for Social Research in April and the minutes record that it was a study based on 'a mass of statistical data' and 'repeated, or protracted interviews with addicts', fifty of whom have been interviewed once a fortnight for a year. In addition

statistical data is being collected for a five year period from 1928-34 on 1219 cases from the Narcotic Bureau and 326 pedlars from the same source, 834 cases from psychopathic hospital, 429 cases from the city police records, 118 cases from the Women's Reformatory at Dwight, 193 cases from the Probation Office, 70 cases from the Municipal Psychiatric Clinic and a few cases from a Behavioral Clinic for a ten year period from 1923 to 1934 and 359 cases from the Keeley Institute (Minutes of the Society for Social Research, April 8th 1935)

The types of conclusion drawn from the data are simple correlational, e.g. addicts live primarily in the zones of transition, very few crimes of violence are committed by drug addicts, most addicts start between the ages of 20 and 25, the majority of Chicago addicts were born in other states, addiction is negatively correlated to level of formal educational qualification. In the same year Lindesmith (1937) also received a doctorate for research on opiate addiction, a study which was more dependent on in depth interviewing.

[3] Blumer actually used these terms in a paper of 1954. However, he developed the thesis much earlier in Blumer (1931) and later specifically addressed social psychology (Blumer, 1940). In the paper of 1931 he concluded 'What I would declare, then, is that to use concepts in science as natural ultimates instead of tentative convenient conceptions, or to be uncritical or unreflective as to their import, is not likely to lead to genuine understanding and control'. (Blumer, 1931, p. 170).

It was to this sentiment, that Lundberg responded in 1936 with his comments on operationalisation which Blumer (1940, p. 182) discounted arguing that

The improvement in judgement, in observation, and in concept will be in the future, as I suspect it has been in the past, a slow maturing process. During the process the concept will continue to remain imprecise, but it should remain less so as observation becomes grounded in fuller experience and in new perspectives. Even though imprecise, the concept will serve, as it does at present, to help direct the line of observation and to help guide the forming of judgements involved in that observation.

[4] Ogburn gave up teaching statistics some time before his retirement to concentrate on his substantive interests in sociology. In his journal he reflected on whether he had made the correct decision.

Last evening, Rubyn, Harriet Welch and I had dinner at the Quadrangle Club. Nearby at a table for four sat R.A. Fisher, famed statistician with Allen Wallis and Thurstone, two U. of C. statisticians. Allen Wallis is editor of the American Statistical Journal and Executive Secretary of the U. of C. Committee on Statistics. Thurstone has developed several important techniques and published several books on statistical methods. At lunch I saw a group of some 20 persons in the private dining room at a table where R.A. Fisher sat. I judge we gave him an honorary degree. I had no part in any of this. I was not invited or consulted. It was not because I was an emeritus. Thurstone become an emeritus this July. I was away nearly all year. But that does not explain my not being in on this statistical gathering. The pang of not being invited is a feeling I have seldom experienced.

But twenty-five years ago, more or less, I was editor of the American Journal of the Statistical Association and also president of the American Statistical Association. Then, I think the nearest to an academic ambition I ever had was to be a social statistician, which is the most exact of the scientific activities of a scientist in the social field. Yet about 1912 or thereabouts, I recall definitely rejecting the idea of being nothing but a scientist and thus of restricting my intellectual, interests .... But then came the depression of the '30's, the War and there was competition for my interests. I became more and more interested in the significance of technological change for society. I spent lots of time on Recent Social Trends, a big undertaking. Then I gave up teaching statistics. But I envy those who stayed by statistics, and sometimes I think I wish I had.

Clearly this envy and this regret are strong emotions. But I wonder how much rationality there is to making this emotion the measure of my values, or the criterion of my action. My worship of statistics has a somewhat religious nature. If I wanted to worship, to be loyal, to be devoted, then statistics was the answer for me, my God. But a God only meets an emotional need, which has little to do with reason. I wonder would I have been content to have been only a very good statistician; and to be a good one, all one's effort and attention is needed. I doubt it. My work in technology and social change and social evolution give me much intellectual pleasure and many thrills. Yet I regret keenly that the march of statistics has passed me by. There was a vacant place at R. A. Fisher's table. (Ogburn Journal, 14th June, 1952).

[5] Burgess (1935a, p. 1) began

The purpose of this study is to assemble, present in tabular and graphic form, and interpret the materials now available through the census and other sources on the local communities and sectors of the city of Chicago. At the present time these data are available in raw and unanalysed form which makes then difficult to use for any specific practical purpose.'

These other sources included social history data on local communities collected by V. Palmer. The Social Science Research Committee at Chicago agreed to underwrite publication costs, and the research was seen as part of a programme of work involving members of the Committee on the history, demographic and socio-economic analysis of Chicago.

[6] This quote summarises Burgess' major research interest from 1930 to 1940 and shows how it relates to other research interests at Chicago and these are primarily quantitative. It reflects a wide base of interest, psychological and psychiatric as well as sociological. However, one must read this critically, in the sense that it is an application for funding, that an experienced proposal writer like Burgess will aim to include those elements he thinks will be well received and therefore may be including an 'overloading' of quantification background in order to secure funds in a climate which is more hospitable to quantified research. On the other hand, this represents a genuine interest for Burgess and reflects a concern with relating case study and statistics which has been central to Chicago research for twenty years. It reflects the interests of the Social Science Research Council as evident in the 1939 debate on the Polish Peasant and guidelines issued in the late 1930s and early 1940s, and had been a subject of debate in, for example, the American Sociological Review since 1936. Again, one might see Burgess as reflecting external concerns in his proposal, but these concerns were promoted by, among others, the Chicago sociologists (albeit from different sides). The 'canny' side of the proposal is perhaps reflected in Burgess' next paragraph which reflects the national/institutional interest in the area.

At the present time under the auspices of the Social Science Research Council a sub-committee on Predictive Methods in Social Adjustment is making a comparative study of methods of prediction now in use in the field of school success, vocational adjustment, marriage adjustment and criminal recidivism. The members of the sub-committee are Mr. Stouffer, chairman; L.S. Cottrell, Cornell University; E. Lowell Kelly, Purdue University and E.E. Richardson, U.S. Civil Service Commission with Paul Horst, psychologist, Proctor and Gamble, making the report. The report together with its recommendations will, in my judgement, give a great impetus to the improvement of present methods and to the rise of the level of research in this field.' (Burgess, 1941, p. 59)

This latter point, novel method, is an area of major concern for the Social Science Research Council as shown in its circular of 1945.

[7] Hammersely and Atkinson (1983) in assessing the unique contribution of ethnography, reflect the perspective adopted by the Chicagoans. Hammersley and Atkinson suggested that, unlike both sides of the 'positivist-naturalist' dispute, ethnography brings social science and its object closer together. Involvement in the field is a process which, if nothing else, leads to the challenging of the sociologists 'dangerously misleading preconceptions'. More importantly, ethnography, they argued, is valuable for its development and testing of theory. The need for this attempted reconceptualisation has, it is suggested here, arisen through the dichotomisation generated by the prevailing history of American sociological research. The Chicagoans did not address a phenomenological sociology but rather attempted the development of theory through a 'naturalistic' approach embedded in a 'positivistic paradigm', and utilising typification processes to help achieve explanatory power.

5 Chicagoans as atheoretical empirical researchers

The Myth

It is ironic that, although Chicago sociology is seen to dominate the development of the discipline in the United States for several decades (Martindale, 1976), it is commonly held that the Chicagoans produced little of theoretical import, at least for contemporary sociology. Chicago's oral tradition (Huber 1973a; Fisher and Strauss, 1978; Rock, 1979) may have given the impression of a lack of theoretical development and accounts of Chicago sociology tend to propound a myth which emphasises the empirical nature of the work done at Chicago. The Chicagoans are portrayed as concerned only with describing the world, particularly Chicago, irrespective of, or even in reaction to, theoretical concerns.

> The Chicago School of Sociology, motivated by the journalist's campaigning and documentary concerns was the example par excellence of determined and detailed empirical social research. (Taylor, Walton and Young, 1973, p.110)

In the period prior to the second world war, the Chicagoans' theoretical contributions are usually seen as restricted to the field of urban sociology. While being characterised as pioneers in this realm, the output of the 'Chicago School' is seen as rather limited and restricted to models of the growth of cities (Easthope, 1974; Giner, 1972; Rock, 1979). It is this role as urban sociologists which is among the more enduring aspects of the myth of the Chicagoans' atheoreticism. There are still a number of commentators who see the Chicagoans as engaged principally in the pursuit of urban sociology and who refer to the 'Chicago School of Urban Sociology', (Oliven, 1978; Philpott, 1978; Agocs, 1979; Caldarovic 1979; Choldin, 1980; Haussermann and Kramer-Badoni, 1980).

In the period following the war, the empirical activity of the Chicagoans is again highlighted and theory is seen as a secondary consequence. This post war period is usually seen in terms of the development of deviance studies, with 'labelling theory' as the major theortical contribution.

> The term 'Chicago School' has been used to designate a whole group of sociologists working at Chicago during this period [1920s and early 1930s]. Their major interest was in the city, and in the work of men like Robert Park and Louis Wirth they laid the foundations of what was to become the special field of urban sociology. They emphasised field work, that is, going out and collecting data rather than sitting in a study and spinning out theories. As Park kept advising his students: 'Get your hands dirty with research !' The Chicago sociologists also had a special affinity for social phenomena that were deviant or far-out in some way. Thus they produced a string of monographs in various colourful corners of urban life, such as the world of skid row or of crime. The Chicago School was also the beginning of what was later to be called the sociology of disorganization or of deviance. (Berger, P. L. and Berger, B., 1976, p. 48)

In consequence the Chicagoans tend to be viewed as peripheral to the development of theoretical sociology in the United States. The Chicagoans are seen as more and more anachronistic in their concern for empirical detail at the expense of developing rigorous theoretical propositions (Madge, 1963, p. 110; Brake, 1980, p. 30). In the event, they are seen as more or less taken by surprise, and therefore excluded from, the 'grand theoretical' or 'middle range theoretical' developments embodied in structural functionalism. In short, the Chicagoans are portrayed in terms of a desire to collect 'facts' irrespective of theoretical concerns, (Rex, 1973).

This chapter examines the work of the Chicagoans to assess their contribution to theoretical development. First, an assessment is made of the extent to which the empirical work at Chicago was developed at the expense of theory. This is followed by an assessment of the degree to which the Chicagoans were urban sociologists. The theoretical work of the Chicagoans as a whole is considered both in terms of the conceptual development and the contribution the Chicagoans made to substantive sub-

110

disciplines within sociology. The final section considers the theoretical work of the Chicagoans in the general context of the development of sociological theory in the United States.

The empirical approach of the Chicagoans

From its beginnings, the department of sociology at Chicago was in the vanguard of attempts to develop empirical research in sociology. Opposed to the general theoretical conjecture which had informed nineteenth century sociology, the turn of the century saw the beginnings of an attempt to merge social surveying with sociological theory. While not alone in this endeavour, the Chicago sociologists were very much involved in the call for empirical investigation as a basis for theoretical development.

The concern with the city of Chicago

The city of Chicago was rapidly expanding during the period from 1890 to 1920 and became a focal point for a considerable number of exploratory studies. This has led to a view that the Chicagoans, notably Park with his journalistic background, were concerned primarily with describing facets of the city of Chicago rather than developing a theoretical sociology. The implication is that the Chicagoans more closely resembled demographers than theoretical sociologists.

Thus Rock wrote

> Park exhorted his students to chronicle the myriad phenomena that were developing in the Chicago of the 1920's and 1930's. For a time at least, Chicago sociology was virtually identical with the sociology of Chicago. It was nursed as a cartographic exercise, studying Little Sicily, the Jewish ghetto, Polonia, the Gold Coast, the slums, Hobohemia, rooming house districts and the gangs of the city. (Rock, 1979, p. 92).

The concern with the city of Chicago as a subject for empirical investigation pre-dated Park. Small argued that the Chicagoans should make the most of their surroundings for research purposes and insisted that sociology could and should be greatly developed through empirical study. Henderson and Talbot were involved in and encouraged empirical enquiry as part of their concern with social issues.

The empirical approach at Chicago began as early as the last few years of the nineteenth century (Dunn, 1895; Clark, 1897; Bushnell, 1901; Gillette, 1901; Riley, 1904; Fleming, 1905; Rhoades, 1906) but became more systematic after the Polish

Peasant study, researched in the ealier part of the decade, was published in 1918 (Thomas and Znaniecki, 1918). Although not an active empirical researcher himself, Small came more and more to advocate direct observational study (Dibble 1972).

Two early graduate students tenured by the department, Vincent and Thomas, were schooled in this 'empirical' environment. Thomas did considerable 'legwork' for Henderson while Vincent provided an impetus to empirical study and also co-authoured the 'laboratory manual' with Small which was probably the earliest text to outline an approach to empirical sociology (Small and Vincent, 1894). Following Vincent's departure in 1908 to take the post of President of the University of Minnesota, and with Thomas becoming more and more involved in the Polish Peasant study and the start of a shift away from applied to pure research, there was a lull in the output of theses on aspects of Chicago. Nonetheless, Small, influenced by German sociology, continued to advocate direct empirical work and encouraged Thomas and later, through Thomas, Park to set about a more detailed and systematic analysis of the city of Chicago, which was substantially influenced by the emergent German urban sociology of the early part of the century (Smith, 1979).

On his arrival at the university, Park took up the cue and for fifteen years actively encouraged students to undertake empirical research, much of it in the city of Chicago. In 1915 he wrote an article entitled 'The City: Suggestions for the Investigation of Human Behavior in the City Environment' (Park, 1915) which outlined areas for investigation and suggested procedures for action. This article, (reprinted twice in different compendiums with some revisions) is seen by many commentators as the start of the intense period of empirical activity at Chicago during the 'golden era'.

The 'golden era' studies

The famous studies of the 'golden era', such as Anderson (1923), Shonle (1926), Thrasher (1926), Cressey (1929), Landesco (1929), Shaw et al. (1929) and Zorbaugh (1929), are noted for their lack of overt concern with theoretical issues. These studies, which have tended to attract most attention, have been the ones which provide documentary descriptions of little known or researched social phenomena and serve as social historical texts. For that reason they have been more durable while not necessarily representing the theoretical concerns of the Chicagoans. Neither Cressey's, Zorbaugh's, Shaw's nor Anderson's work were doctoral dissertations.

It has been suggested that an interest in an area was all that was required in the 1920s, that no formal hypotheses, representative samples, control groups or rigid data collection methods were necessary in planning research. Tentative general-

isations were made but these were purely 'concept identification' and the location of social processes in an exploratory
way was all that was involved. The process was a 'gaining of
insights', it was not theoretical, rather it constituted the
preliminary stages of science. The period was

> not a time of theorising. Rather it concentrated on col-
> lecting facts, grouping them under concepts, and/or identi-
> fying relationships among them. These facts, concepts and
> relationships might be compared to building blocks; the
> construction of theories was to come later.... Thomas rec-
> ognized the need for developing theories ... Wirth seemed
> opposed to theory construction. The time had come to theor-
> ize, but Chicago sociologists seemed reluctant to take this
> step. (Cavan, 1983, p. 416). [1]

This reflects a general view of the 'golden era' as lacking
theoretical orientation. Bierstedt (1981, p. xi), for example,
regarded Park as having had a great influence over his students
but that he 'exhibited little interest in sociological theory'.
An often cited quote from Park is used to support this view.

> You have been told to go grubbing in the library, thereby
> accumulating a mass of notes and a liberal coating of
> grime. You have been told to choose problems wherever you
> can find musty stacks of routine records based on trivial
> schedules prepared by tired bureaucrats and filled out by
> reluctant applicants for aid or fussy do-gooders or indif-
> ferent clerks. This is called "getting your hands dirty
> with real research". Those who counsel you are wise and
> honorable; the reasons they offer are of great value. But
> one more thing is needful: first hand observation. Go and
> sit in the lounges of the luxury hotels and on the door-
> steps of the flophouses; sit on the Gold Coast settees and
> on the slum shakedowns; sit in the Orchestra Hall and in
> the Star and Garter Burlesk. In short, gentlemen, go get
> the seat of your pants dirty in **real** research. (Park,
> 1920).

This quote is usually annotated to Park telling his students
to 'get their hands dirty with research', (e.g. Berger and
Berger, 1976). The implication is that Park extolled the vir-
tues of empirical data collection at the expense of theoretical
endeavours. This actually misrepresents what Park said. Park
was not simply calling for empirical data instead of theoretical conjecture but was demanding a combination of direct empirical and theoretical work, and suggesting that documentary
sources are of themselves insufficient without some first-hand
experience of the social world.

The retrospective views and the research work of other Chicagoans in fact confirm the importance of theorising during the
'golden era'. Ogburn, for example, endorsed Bierstedt's view
that Park had a great influence over his students but offered a
very different view of Park's theoretical contribution.

> I saw little of [Park] and almost never was in a conversa-
> tion or discussion with him; and yet I admired his contri-
> butions to sociology, which were ... a contribution of
> concepts, well thought out, and well selected as to impor-
> tance. I cannot recall any research he ever did, yet his
> concepts were a real contribution and have been adopted
> widely by sociologists.(Ogburn journal, 4th April 1955)

Cottrell (1972) remarked that there was a lot of German
sociological theory, for example, infused into Chicago, which
is reflected in the content of the Park and Burgess text
(1921). Dollard (1972) went further and inverted Cavan's recollections altogether. 'My notion about sociology was that it was
wildly theoretical and verbal and philosophical but through
Ogburn I saw that something could be gathered which was very
tangible'. Hayner (1972) pointed to the mix of theory and
empirical data that Park offered. 'At the time we thought we
were getting too much philosophy from Park, but in retrospect
that is what we needed. We needed his ability to have concrete
experiences and then generalize significantly from that experience.'

These recollections indicate a concern at Chicago for both
empirical enquiry and theoretical development. The promotion of
'inductive theorising' through the attempts to generalise
empirical observation certainly involved elements of what Cavan
called 'concept identification', but also amounted to more than
the construction of building blocks [2].

The recollections of the Chicagoans are borne out by an
inspection of their work. While the empirical study may have
been prompted by an interest in an area, the students were
expected, and helped, to locate their data in a general theoretical framework, and indeed, even the famous studies of the
period were far less bereft of theory than some commentators
suggested (Madge, 1963). Indeed, the survey of Ph.D. theses
(see Appendix 6) shows that eighty six per cent were directly
concerned with specific theoretical issues. Some of these,
particularly the work of Young (1924), Simpson (1926), Blumer
(1928), Neumeyer (1929), Brown (1930) and Stonequist (1930),
were directed entirely to an analysis of theoretical constructs.

Why the view that such research was atheoretical should have
grown up is not easy to pin down, other than to suggest that a
selective reading of research work may have been responsible.

The myth, then, becomes self-perpetuating. Theoretical concerns are not seen as central to Chicago sociology and thus the theoretical contribution is ignored. The style in which most of the work published in the University of Chicago Press Sociological Series is written may also have contributed to the view that theory was of little importance to the Chicagoans. The tendency was for them to present their sociological enquiry in 'ordinary language', which possibly led to an underestimation of their theoretical content. The utilisation of a simple documentary style and the extensive incorporation of subject's verbal and written comments, possibly serves to deflect the reader from the social theoretical content.

Further, it may be that, in a period of rapid development of sociological conceptualisation, some of the pioneering empirical studies of the 'golden era' which were researched in the 1920s were not as 'polished' theoretically as they might have been when finally published in the Sociological Series of the University of Chicago Press in the 1930s.

Whilst attempting to infuse empirical observation into sociological research, the Chicagoans were not, however, unconcerned with sociological theory. The nature of the theoretical contribution of the Chicagoans is examined in the next sections.

Urban sociology at Chicago

The 'Chicago School' is seen as providing the major traditional approach to urban sociology (Evers, 1975; McGrath and Geruson, 1977; Dotter, 1980) and its evident concern with empirical study of the city of Chicago has meant that, in assessing the theoretical impact of the 'Chicago School', many commentators refer only to those theoretical contributions which relate to urban sociology. Of these, the zonal model (Burgess, 1925) has achieved notoreity. This 'ideal typical' model is usually regarded as an interesting but essentially limited or naive model of city growth (Rex, 1973; Slattery, 1985). The implication is that Chicago sociologists did lots of empirical work on the city but were unable to combine it into any systematic theory (Madge, 1963).

Two issues arise here, the first concerns the extent to which the Chicagoans were urban sociologists, the second, the extent to which their research in the area developed theory.

It is usually assumed that the 'Chicago School' was heavily involved in urban sociology and essentially founded the sub-discipline in the United States. Lofland, however, has investigated the supposition that Chicago sociologists concentrated on urban sociology, and concludes to the contrary that 'the heritage of Chicago, then, is the virtual absence of a specifically urban sociology' (Lofland, 1983, p. 505). Her analysis intended to show that Chicago sociology was concerned with the private rather than the public realm. She illustrated this contention by grouping the two hundred and twenty one Ph.D. and M.A. theses awarded degrees at Chicago between 1915 and 1935 in terms of their focus of attention. Only five, she asserted, could be said to do with the public realm 'by any stretch of the imagination'. These she listed as Hayner (1923), Russell (1931), Cressey (1929), Anderson (1925) and Weinberg (1935). The latter three, she suggested, could just as easily be regarded as social problem theses. Lofland's classification is contentious. She relies totally on titles not content and provides a classification system which is not mutually exclusive, and asserts that only 'public' studies (as she defines them) should be taken to be indicative of urban sociology. Her analysis, however, does point a questioning finger at those who would circumscribe Chicago activities in terms of urban sociology.

The sample survey of theses reveals that ten (24%) were specifically investigations of some aspect of the city of Chicago or its immediate environs (see Appendix 6). Similarly, only one fifth (18%) of the regular presentations to the Society for Social Research were about Chicago. Up to 1930 a quarter of talks (27%) were on Chicago, after 1930 this dropped to ten per cent. Furthermore, discussions of Chicago were usually from visiting speakers. Only six per cent of the addresses given by the sociology faculty focussed on Chicago while forty one per cent of addresses from non-academic speakers were directed to Chicago (see Appendix 3).

The two elements of Chicago research work which are usually referred to as representing their theoretical contribution to urban sociology are Park's ecological perspective with its contingent concept of natural areas bounded by transportation and other barriers within which distinct actions developed (Turner, 1967; Tiryakian, 1979a; Dotter, 1980; Komorowski, 1978) and Burgess' concentric zone thesis. The clearest manifestation of the theories of human ecology is still often taken to be the concentric zone theory. Thus, for example, Easthope (1974, p. 66) suggested that the main work done at Chicago was in the field of human ecology and that it was codified in the concentric zone thesis.

> Three research workers developed this concept [of concentric zone]: Thrasher, Zorbaugh and Shaw. Each of these may be said to have brought out in greater detail and given empirical evidence for, theoretical concepts developed by Park and Burgess.

Burgess 'systematised ecological communities into concentric zones, each with its unique culture' (Cavan, 1983, p. 412) and these zones provided the means to social mobility, (Cottrell, et al., 1973). Mowrer (1927) identified family types for the zones, Frazier (1931) studied the zonal differences for black family life in Chicago and Shaw and McKay (1931) showed decline in juvenile crime through the zonal belt.

While acknowledged as early contributions to urban sociology both the ecological approach and the zone thesis have subsequently tended to be viewed as simplistic models of the internal structure and growth of the city. Neither are seen as having any substantial impact on the development of urban sociological theory (Firey, 1945; Madge, 1963; Rex, 1973; Easthope, 1974; Slattery, 1985). Some commentators go further and imply that the Chicagoans did a disservice to the development of urban sociology. For example, Haussermann and Kramer-Badoni (1980) argued that the central 'urban ecological model' of the Chicagoans dissects reality into a multitude of variables, yet despite them, is analytically weak, as is evidenced by its concepts of urbanism and urban density. In short, they saw the urban sociology of the 'Chicago School' as 'positivistic' and indifferent to history and meaning.

Conversely, Chicago urban sociology is seen as involving a pioneering approach which, for the first time, saw the city as an independent variable (Oliven, 1978; Dotter, 1980). Wirth's role is sometimes singled out because he was the first to formulate a sociological and socio-psychological theory of urbanism in which the city was an explanatory variable, and thus overcame the biological perspective present in the ecological approach (Vergati, 1976; Oliven, 1978). This work paralleled Redfield's anthropological thesis of the folk-urban continuum. Others, however, have suggested that this concept of urbanism fails to adequately relate the urban way of life to capitalist industrialisation (Gans, 1968; Williams, 1973; Castells, 1977).

Conceptual development

Besides developing concepts intrinsic to the development of the field of urban sociology, the Chicagoans also developed a number of other significant and enduring concepts in fields as diverse as the sociology of race, deviance, the family and technology and culture. Central to most of these developments was the concept of disorganization.

Social disorganization

It has been suggested (Carey, 1975) that the the work of the Chicagoans was underpinned by a 'social disorganisation paradigm', particularly evident in the period from around 1910 until 1930. Whether this really represents a 'Kuhnian paradigm' is debatable (Harvey, 1982; Martins, 1972; Eckburg and Hill, 1979) but it was a substantive underlying organising principle resembling a paradigm; although it was itself subsumed within a more general functionalist-interactionist orientation.

Social disorganisation was central to the sociological endeavour at Chicago and had been ever since its development in the **Polish Peasant** which was the first attempt to elaborate the Chicagoans general theoretical perspective. Thomas was the focus through which the diverse elements of the perspective came together, and, in collaboration with Znaniecki, the empirically based analysis of the adjustment of Polish rural emigres to American urban life was produced.

The thesis of social disorganisation was important as an orientation for early interactionist work. Social disorganisation explains stability in terms of consistent attitudes and values inculcated by individuals which will both satisfy personal desires and provide outlets for action. However, there was nothing immutable about this stability. Indeed, on one level, as societies constantly changed, they were always disorganised to a certain extent. On another level, individuals, although constrained by social norms which shape the personality, were able to transcend the prevalent norms as and when they obstructed progress to a more comprehensive state of organisation. Temperament therefore played a part in the accommodation of the individual to the social mileu. This 'temperament' was embodied in Thomas's 'wishes'. These wishes (initially response, recognition, security and new experience) were identified by Thomas as the motive force behind human action and moulded attitudes of individuals [3].

This approach thus made social psychology an integral part of sociology. The legacy of Thomas's social psychological component is far-reaching. Thomas had dispensed with the organic view of individuals as products of a given environment who merely reacted to stimuli. He had provided a place in social action for conscious reflection. He had provided a breakthrough that transcended the assumptions of nineteenth century American sociology. Thomas had severely challenged the idea of basic or immutable forces as determinants of social action. He had not entirely dispensed with the idea, his 'wishes' hark back, but their very name implies something indeterminable. Thomas stood at the crossroads of the challenge to immutable forces, the incorporation of conscious reflection shook the very foundation of the old preconception of original forces. He had, in effect, reasserted the 'ability of man to affect his own destiny'.

Although Thomas was forced to resign from the Chicago faculty in 1918, he remained a member of the Society for Social Research and his activities were reported in the Bulletin. His theoretical influence persisted and perhaps grew stronger during the 1920s. Carey's interviewees reflect the importance of Thomas

> His [Thomas's] spirit was quite pervasive around the place. The way to get at life and the problems and the knowledge you need to analyse what people were doing and how they behaved and so on, was to do what Thomas did. (Cottrell, 1972)

> The four wishes were being taught but that was felt to be too instinctual by most sociologists at the time although Thomas's legacy was still around, and of course, his **Polish Peasant**, we all had to read it.... Going over to empiricism and that was partly due to Thomas too. (Dollard, 1972)

> Thomas' social psychology was alive in my father's social psychology courses [1928], he took that course over from Thomas and carried on that tradition with much the same method and frequent reference to Thomas. In the seminar Blumer had, we had to read a number of theoretical statements from the **Polish Peasant**. Yes we were quite aware of Thomas and we picked up his favourite expressions. One of them is 'a thing is real if it is real in its consequences'... The 'definition of the situation', we couldn't have gotten along without that. Thomas's contribution was there in the spirit of the investigation, concepts that he contributed and his whole outlook in social psychology. (Faris, 1972)

Park certainly made no attempt to undermine the Thomasian perspective. The sample survey of theses shows that Thomas was cited in the bibliography of 50 per cent of theses. This tended to be concentrated in the period up to 1939, Thomas being cited in fourteen (64%) of the twenty two theses up to that date and only seven (35%) of the twenty theses in the sample submitted from 1940.

Social disorganisation was an integral and explicit part of the theoretical development of the vast majority of those theses which could be described as having produced a developed theoretical perspective. For example, Anderson (1923) utilised the general theoretical perspective of social disorganisation in his study of hobohemia, Thrasher (1926) adopted it as the basis for explaining the zonal variations in gangs, Zorbaugh (1929) investigated social disorganisation as it related to the 'interstitial areas' of cities', and Cressey (1929) used the thesis in his study of taxi-dance halls. Indeed, the famous studies of the 1920s can all be seen as empirical analyses of the theoretical orientation grounded in the thesis of social disorganisation. Cavan's **Suicide** (1926), Mowrer's **Family Dis-**

organisation (1924), Wirth's Ghetto (1926), Hiller's Strike (1924), and Reckless' Vice in Chicago (1925) all explicitly refer to the concept of social disorganisation, taking the essential nature of the concept for granted. In fact, rather than being an empirical validation of the zonal model, the mapping method so widely used at Chicago in the 1920s was central to the assessment of indicators of social disorganisation. The concentric zone thesis itself depended upon the concept of social disorganisation.

The theoretical ideas developed by Thomas were widely known and used throughout the discipline. The social disorganisation thesis and its associated concepts of 'definition of the situation' and 'social becoming' were among the few established and long lived concepts to emerge from the early part of the century. There are references to the 'definition of the situation' in the papers of the Society for Social Research in the 1930s which indicate a widespread familiarity with the concept and the Social Science Research Council sponsored conference on the Polish Peasant, 1939, took the concept for granted, it required no explanation.

Indicative of the centrality of the concept of disorganization is its inclusion in a list of major sociological concepts suggested by Nisbett (1962, p. 67).

> My interest in sociology as an art form was stimulated recently by some reflections on ideas that are by common assent the most distinctive that sociology has contributed to modern thought. Let me mention these: mass society, alienation, anomie, rationalization, community, disorganization ... all of them have had lasting effect upon both the theoretical and empirical character of sociology.

Within the framework of social disorganization, the Chicagoans were instrumental in several major conceptual and theoretical developments.

Race relations cycle

Probably the most significant and enduring impact of theorising at Chicago was in the field of the sociology of race. Concepts such as marginality and acculturation became developed into one of the major theories to emerge from the sociological work of the department, namely the assimilation theory which became popularised as the race relations cycle.

Park advanced the idea of a four stage process of interaction, drawn largely from his research into, and experience of, immigrants and of black-white relationships. The stages identified by Park were competition, conflict, accommodation and assimilation. This four stage process was originally labelled the 'race relations cycle' because it grew out of the work Park had done in that field at Tuskegee. This cycle was outlined in his Introduction to Steiner (1917) and was to become increasingly refined through the work of students, notably, Young (1924), Wirth (1926) and Brown (1930). Park's students increasingly concentrated on race and collective behaviour. Apart from anything else, the development of race studies at Chicago under Park's guidance clearly belies the impression that the Chicagoans were mere urban ecologists. Park, arguably, had far more impact on race studies than on any other area of sociology (Matthews, 1977, p. 157).

The Chicagoans developed the area of race continuously from 1915 to 1950 under the guidance of Park and then Wirth, examining the sociology of race in relation to various ethnic minorities and through various orientations from sociological through social psychological to psychoanalytic (Reuter, 1919; Detweiler, 1922; Young, 1924; Brown, 1930; Stonequist, 1930; Frazier, 1931; Doyle, 1934; Cox, 1938; Daniel, 1940; Strong, 1940; Alexander, 1942; Parrish, 1944; Walker, 1945; Hill, 1946; Faw, 1948; Janowitz, 1948; Turner, 1948; Cothram, 1949; Hale, 1949; Marcson, 1950; Star, 1950; Reitzes, 1950; Quinn, 1950; Lewis, 1951; Haimowitz, 1951; Edwards, 1952). Wirth (1948) noted that of his three areas of substantive interest

> my main love is the field of race relations and minority problems. I have published a number of things in this field including a number of articles in the Journal, a little monograph for the Social Science Research Council on "Problems of Minorities in War Time," a chapter in Linton's book on "The Science of Man in the World Crisis" entitled "The Problem of Minority Groups", which some of my friends think is one of the best things in the field, probably because it attempts to establish a typology of minorities. In this connection I co-operated with the Myrdal projects and published with Herbert Goldhamer a monograph in that series on miscegenation. I am, as you may know, the President of the American Council on Race Relations and the Chairman of our University Committee on Education, Training and Research in Race Relations. [4]

By 1930 the race relations cycle had become firmly entrenched in Chicago sociology and beyond, and was a taken-for-granted theory in the analysis of the interaction of diverse cultures. By the 1950s it had become extended into a general theory of interaction of groups. Wirth noted that

> Correlative to social organization is the study of social interaction in all of its phases which deals with such processes as contact and isolation; competition; conflict;

accommodation, and assimilation. (Wirth, 1948).

In their textbook on sociology, Ogburn and Nimkoff (1960, p. 111) made this generalised race relations cycle compatible with the structural functionalist approach. The theory persisted in American sociology generally until the 1960s (e.g. Gordon, 1964). Martindale (1960, p. 256) noted

> To this day there are persons who do not feel they have covered the basic subject matter of sociology until they have discussed competition, conflict, accommodation and assimilation.

Arguably, the assimilation perspective of the 'Chicago School' has dominated North American studies of urban ethnic settlement (Agocs, 1979). The notions of 'marginal man' and social distance (Bogardus), became taken-for-granted in sociology in the United States and were used into the 1970s (Martin and Franklin, 1973, p. 48; Ferrarotti, 1977).

Social change and cultural lag

Ogburn was interested in social change and the influence of technology on social change. Central to his approach was the notion of culture. For Ogburn (1937) 'culture cut the chains that tied sociology to biology'. Culture was a holistic notion, being the whole product of social interaction, manifested in the society's controlling mechanism. Sociological enquiry, for Ogburn, was directed to the effect culture had on individuals. He advocated the study of culture as a whole, that is an analysis of 'western civilizations' as cultural wholes as ethnologists had done for 'primitive' cultures. Of the study of particular facets of modern civilization, Ogburn saw the study of the city as most closely approximating a cultural approach. Ogburn and other culturologists (D. Thomas, White) extended this in an attempt to interrelate different aspects of modern society into an analysis of the cultural whole. A cultural emphasis led to the analysis of the effect of different factors on social change. Such factors were the impact of inventions, diffusion of cultural traits, the nature of culture contacts, social attitudes and resistance towards change, and the stock of knowledge.

Ogburn considerably developed the sociological analysis of technology. He saw the immutable forces of technology subsuming the individual in the sense that social evolution would take place irrespective of any individual historical figure, although accepting that the nuances of evolution are mediated by human activity. Ogburn thus tended to look for explanations of social disorganisation at a less individual and a more cultural level. He thus resolved the Thomasian context into the four stage process of invention, accommodation, diffusion and adjustment. Ogburn's general theory of change had its particular referent, the cultural lag hypothesis, (Ogburn, 1922). The interrelatedness of culture, the primary effects of inventions in producing change and the adaptive character of non-material culture 'led directly to Ogburn's famous concept of cultural lag' (Gough, 1942). Ogburn argued that social change lead to strain because there was a delay or lag in the assimilation of mechanical invention and scientific discovery by social organisations, philosophies and popular habits. Culture is forced to adjust to technological change, but there is a period of disorganization.

Ogburn's work on culture and social change, although begun before moving to Chicago, became widely known in the interwar years and 'Ogburn's ideas were familiar to sociologists who had never read any of his books' (Gough, 1942, p. 1). The American Journal of Sociology devoted one issue to the analysis of social change for a number of years and Ogburn wrote or edited books on social change throughout the twenties and thirties (Ogburn, 1922, 1927, 1934). His emphasis shifted to a closer study of the impact of technology (Ogburn, 1933, 1934b, 1937, Ogburn and Nimkoff, 1955) and in conjunction with Dorothy Thomas (Ogburn and Thomas, 1922) raised issues about the nature of scientific change and discovery which were developed by Merton (1973) and White (1969) and are still an issue in current discussions of sociology of science (Brannigan, 1981).

Deviance and labelling theory

The Chicago ecological tradition was a major source of theoretical schema for the development of deviance studies (Taylor, Walton and Young, 1973, p. 111). Park (1929, p. 36) noted that 'it is assumed that people living in natural areas of the same general type and subject to the same social conditions will display, on the whole, the same characteristics'.

This ecological approach to deviance was developed at Chicago during the 1920s, and Sutherland went on to develop deviancy theory to include elements of social processes as well as structure, thus including differential association along with differential social organisation (Dotter, 1978). Sutherland's association theory suggested that criminal activity is produced primarily through exposure to others having criminal attitudes and engaged in criminal activities. That is, deviant acts are learned and individuals are liable to engage in deviant activity if they are exposed to an overabundance of criminal activities as compared to non-criminal associations. The soundness of this thesis was debated into the 1970s (Vold, 1958; Cressey, 1962; Sutherland and Cressey, 1966; Box, 1971)

The predominant emphasis, then, amongst the early Chicago informed social disorganisation theorists of deviancy was on the 'normlessness' of delinquent areas. Later subcultural theorists (Cohen, 1955; Cloward and Ohlin 1960) influenced by Merton, used the concept of disorganization in a different way. They posited an anomie thesis which suggested that while cultural goals were widely diffused and internalised there was no corresponding achievement frame.

The more recent and well known work in the field of deviancy by researchers associated with the 'Chicago School', notably Becker, Lemert, Matza, and Polsky has its roots in the social disorganisation theories of the early Chicagoans. They attempted a fairly radical development of a social, rather than biological, theory of deviance by proposing the relative nature of deviant activity. This was expressed through the articulation of the deviant's viewpoint within a functionalist perspective (Celinski, 1974). Labelling theory grew out of Sutherland's work, in part as a critique of its limitations in respect of taking the view of the other. The role of the 'Chicago School' in the field of deviancy studies is widely accepted, and represents the 'classical environmental analysis of deviant behavior' (Caldarovic, 1979).

Other areas of theoretical and empirical study

As has also already been indicated, Burgess's personality research was of more note to him than his concentric zone thesis, but his real and enduring interest was with the sociology of the family. Burgess' family studies changed the face of American sociology of the family to the view that the family was 'a closely interacting group of people playing different roles' (Cavan, 1983, p. 412-413). Cottrell (1933) further developed the study of the family, working closely with Burgess.

Following his own work on the Chicago Real Estate Board, Hughes (1928), engaged in and encouraged a further generation of sociologists to investigate the sociology of work (Hughes, 1958), of organisations (Hall, 1944; Smith, 1949) and of professions (Hughes, 1970). Very little research had been attempted in this field, especially in the United States, until Hughes sparked off interest at Chicago on his return to the University in 1938. Of three identifiable 'paradigms' in the sociological study of professions (Ritzer, 1978) the 'process paradigm' flows out of Hughes' work in the 'Chicago School'. Only very recently has the process paradigm began to wane in importance as the study of professions has moved more towards the analysis of power relationships.

The Chicagoans' ecological perspective on organisational change, arguably, represents the most significant development in contemporary organisational research (Burns, 1980). The

Chicago model of ecological, economic and cultural organisation provides a novel examination of the relationship between organisations and environment through its concentration on natural history within a social disorganisation framework. While these innovations in organisational study were, possibly, inadequately formalised they have continued in the work of contemporary theorists.

Park also prompted the development of a substantial research tradition in the field of collective behaviour and mass society, which was developed in the work of Edwards (1927) and more recently by Shibutani (Witzgall, 1978). Park's own doctoral thesis was 'The Crowd and the Public', (Park 1972) an interest he retained throughout his life. Park provided one of the classic definitions of collective behaviour (Blake, 1978) and, by conceptualising the crowd as an object rather than a set of collective processes generated a perspective which has persisted through the work of succeeding writers.

One final area developed at Chicago was the sociology of knowledge. This was largely contained in the work of Wirth and Shils, and the doctoral candidates they supervised (Whitridge, 1946; Duncan, 1948). This is explored in more detail below as it raises issues of an alternative theoretical approach to the prevailing perspective on sociology in the United States in the 1930s and 1940s.

Summary of the theoretical contribution of the Chicagoans

Thomas provided the basis for a general theoretical orientation which underpinned much of Chicago sociological work. The Chicagoans developed the social disorganisation thesis in various ways, gradually discarding the psychologistic elements such as the 'wishes' and developing a more rigorous, although not entirely homogeneous, interactionist theory in particular areas. Park and many of his students developed the area of race relations, Burgess's students concentrated on the family and Ogburn's on social change and psychoanalysis. Wirth, Hughes and Stouffer encouraged a further generation to develop these areas and a more focussed empirical testing of specific theories evolved. These later generations developed the sociology of work, of organisations, of deviance, of mass society and the sociology of knowledge.

On a more general level, the Chicagoans avidly engaged in the debate that revolved around Freudianism. Indeed, there was probably a greater, and to some extent more clear cut division in the department over the efficacy of Freud's theories for sociology than there was about the value of quantitative techniques.

I know my father thought some of Burgess' interests were

shallow and ridiculous, he thought some of the others were quite good though.... My father did not care at all for psychoanalysis or Freud and Burgess did. My father would make quite critical comments about Freudian concepts in his class but would not mention Burgess or attribute them to him.... Ogburn had been analysed and was a fairly convinced Freudian.... (Faris, 1972)

Ogburn's students became less and less the journalistic Parkian oriented students and more and more the quantitative orientation. But Burgess sort of straddled that... He studied statistics and attended meetings of the psychoanalytic institute uptown to get hold of the Freud business.... I got quite interested in psychiatric theories and started quite an intensive bit of reading in the writings of Freud. In fact I read all of them, all his published works... The only thing we had on Freud was an attack, a target of antagonism. Louis Wirth who was a little more my senior, but still one of the younger members of the faculty, actually I got to be quite a Freudian, I had quite a Freudian phase, he really viciously attacked me as a person who was not properly orientated to the sociological problems. (Cottrell, 1972)

Blumer, Park and Faris were opposed to it [Freudianism]. Burgess was a very diplomatic sort of chap. He didn't confront any of his colleagues. But if he found a student with an interest he would encourage it.... (Dollard, 1972)

However, this disagreement did not lead to the fragmentation of the department, as the sociology developed at Chicago had an interactionist base that, in practice, cut across psychoanalytic concerns. The tendency to view Chicago sociology as essentially empirical and therefore as atheoretical reflects a confusion of first hand empiricism with 'abstracted empiricism'. On the contrary, Chicago sociology was involved in the development of a plethora of sociological theories in numerous areas and reflected the cumulative theoretical style which came to be known as middle range theorising (Merton, 1948).

Chicago theorising and sociology in the United States

The view that Chicago sociology was essentially concerned with empirical data collection, or the view that its theoretical work was confined to the pioneering stage of urban sociology, are both indicative of an idea that somehow Chicago stood outside the general development of American sociological theory. The emphasis on the empirical concerns of the Chicagoans in

126

presentations of their work tends to act to separate them from the sociological mainstream. While the Chicagoans were in the vanguard of the shift from 'armchair theorising' to 'inductive theorising' they were not alone in this endeavour nor, indeed, were they the sole pioneers in empirical data collection.

The social survey movement, based on ameliorist concerns of British social surveyors in the nineteenth century, was well established in the United States by the time the Chicagoans adopted an empirical base for sociological theorising during the 'golden era'. (Furner, 1975; Schwendinger and Schwendinger, 1974). Following in the footsteps of the Booth survey of London, a survey movement sprang up in the United States. The Pittsburg Survey (1909-1914) was followed by the establishment of a survey department within the Sage Foundation and by 1928 its director reported 154 general surveys and 2621 specialist surveys. These were not sociological surveys, much of the survey tendency 'took its own course, diverging early from academic sociology and finding a close partnership with organised welfare activities' (Faris, 1967, p. 8).

Nonetheless, as Burgess wrote in 1916 while at Ohio State University, the example of the the Belleville and Lawrence surveys directed by F. W. Blackmar at the University of Kansas was indicative of the increasing involvement of sociologists in social surveys. The social survey of a community is 'the scientific study of its conditions and needs for the purpose of presenting a constructive program for social advance' (Burgess, 1916)

Park's course at Chicago on the social survey (from 1915 to 1921) provided the critical framework in which empirical work was developed. His critique of the social survey was not only that it tended to overemphasise statistical data and reformist concerns but that, in so doing, it also distanced itself from sociological theorising. In this, he reaffirmed the stance of Small and Thomas and reflected the growing tendency towards 'inductive theorising' in American sociology.

Besides the empirical work done at Chicago, other sociologists were engaging empirical data in their attempt to develop sociological theorising. Notable was the work at Columbia under the directorship of Giddings which included Ogburn's early research; developments at the University of Southern California; as well as the research done at Michigan (Cooley, 1930; Rice, 1931). Indeed, Lapiere (1964) recalled that 'one man' departments all over the country were springing up with the aim of developing a credible empirical base for sociological theory. As Chicago sociologists became more and more concerned with empirically based study rather than 'armchair theorising', they reflected the emerging tendency in American sociology as a whole.

The epistemological basis of 'standard American sociology'.

While the Chicagoans were among the pioneers in the development of a sociological theorising grounded in empirical data, they were far from unique in this endeavour. Their empirical data collection orientation should not be viewed, in itself, as indicative of a separation of 'Chicago sociology' from the direction of mainstream sociological theorising. Further, it is necessary to address the extent to which Chicago sociologists developed a distinctive 'interpretive' or 'phenomenological' approach [5]. The following sections attempt to set out the approach to sociology in the United States which emerged out of the 1920s and prevailed into the 1960s (following Mullins (1973), this will be called standard American sociology) and to assess the extent to which the epistemological perspectives at Chicago differed from it.

The cumulative-falsificationist model

Over the course of the twentieth century, American sociology has emerged as an empirically grounded endeavour, adopting, in the main, what may be described as a falsificationist model of the production and validation of sociological knowledge [6]. In conjunction with such a model, there has been a tendency to accept the idea of the cumulative development of theory (Social Science Research Council, 1939; Merton, 1945; Mills, 1959; Willer, 1967).

Arguably, American sociology has also been dominated (if not exhausted) by two general theoretical perspectives, 'interactionism' and 'functionalism'. While not entirley compatible these two perspectives overlap and do not constitute the theoretical base of two distinct traditions. Rather they concur on many elements of the sociological process. Both are essentially nomothetic, both are anti-behaviourist, both focus on group processes, both are empirical and non-critical. The one approach assess the function served within a social process by a particular phenomenon, the other assesses the interactive process in order to see the way action is mediated by social processes. Clearly they are interrelated, to some extent the opposite sides of the same coin.

The prevalent model of sociological knowledge in American sociology emphasised cumulative theory, falsificationism, and nomological concerns incorporating meaning adequacy (Harvey, P., 1982). The tension that existed concerned the extent to which the problems of establishing adequacy at the level of meaning should inhibit nomological concerns. The Conference on the Polish Peasant, 1938, reflected these concerns and acted as an indication of the pervasiveness of the prevalent model. No alternative, 'anti-positivistic' model emerged from it; despite the existence of an embryonic critique in the work of Blumer and of Wirth.

The conference on the Polish Peasant was an important, well-documented and widely known debate; even if the participants were not 'representative' of the entire gamut of American sociology. A 'centralist' approach to sociology emerged from it despite some scepticism over the nomothetic possibilites voiced by some of the Chicagoans. The discussion on the Polish Peasant clearly indicates how the main institutionalised perspective in sociology saw the nature of the discipline. While the analysis of the conference that follows shows the points of debate, it also reveals a strong committment to a more or less agreed view of the nature and aims of sociology. Chicago does not stand outside the general approach.

The Conference on The Polish Peasant. This was called by the Committee on Appraisal of Social Research of the Social Science Research Council, in New York, on December 10th 1938. The main contributors of those present were three Chicago professors, Herbert Blumer, Louis Wirth, Samuel Stouffer in addition to G.W. Allport, Read Bain, Max Lerner, W.I. Thomas and W.W. Waller.

The debate followed Blumer's written critique of the Polish Peasant. Initially the debate was directed to the efficacy of personal documents as a device for testing theoretical assertion. In developing his written submission Blumer pointed to the premises underlying the Polish Peasant. These were, first, the need of a plan of research suited to a complicated changing society that may be applied to any society undergoing transition, and, second, the declaration that the understanding of human life necessitates the grasping of the subjective factor. Thus any sociological study should involve both the external factors (social values) and the internal factors (attitudes).

Given the above, Blumer argued that two things were necessary. First, to develop a guiding theoretical scheme which will set hypotheses, that is, provide a framework for interpretation and analysis. Blumer reckoned that in the Polish Peasant all the theories are developed in 'intrinsic relation to these basic concepts of attitude and value'. Second, the scheme needs source data that will reveal the 'subjective factor in human experience and which, at the same time, will meet the usual requirements for scientific data, viz., that one can always go back to these data and that other workers may have access to them' (Social Science Research Council, 1939, p. 108). The resulting debate thus tended to turn attention from the particular problems of personal documents as evidence to address the problem of proof, causal attribution and objectivity in sociology given the 'need of recognizing and considering the subjective factor in human experience'.

129

The conference spent considerable effort looking at the implications of Blumer's critique for the human document as data,
and in so doing broached the nature of scientific enquiry, of
society and of alternative approaches to sociology. Throughout,
however, certain elements were taken for granted. Most notable
was the primacy of inductive theorising. Interestingly, however, there was also a constant concern to ensure that sociology adopted approaches which do not regress to atheoretical fact
collection any more than it should to accept non-empirical
abstract theorising. In short, the idea that sociology should
progress in terms of a cumulative development of theory grounded in empirical data, in a manner which Popper was to codify in
the terms of a natural science debate as 'falsificationism',
underwrote the discussion.
The concern was with how different types of approach could
provide 'objective', that is 'reliable', data. The accepted
approach closely resembled what Merton (1948) came to call
middle range theorising [7]. Indeed, prefacing this, Lerner
noted

> Here we have the empirical data, here we have the abstrac-
> tion into which we are attempting to fit them. Modify the
> abstraction to fit the data and go and collect more data to
> fit the new abstraction; there is a constant interaction
> between them. (Social Science Research Council, 1939, p.
> 177).

The debate was concerned with the realist position which is
central to the **Polish Peasant**'s methodological note, that the
subjective factor be incorporated into social analysis. The
concern of the conference when assessing human documents was
that while they provide some 'attitudinal' insights, they may
not be 'objective' in as much as they may prove to be inadequate for consistent inductive inferential or testing purposes.
There were differing views on the degree to which human
documents could be treated as reliable, 'objective', or self
evident facts in the sense of data in the physical and biological sciences. This assumed that the model of science rested on
a factual base. Human documents, Bain contended, were non-
specific instances, reflecting a whole culture and could not be
seen as data in the sense of data in the natural sciences.
Blumer and Wirth defended the principle that documents, although specific instances, may provide abstracted data. They
argued that the document can be used as a specific instance
through an abstractive process which indicates what aspect of
the document is being considered through an application of a
prior conceptual scheme. Wirth suggested that, for example,
'Thomas does this by saying that this is a case of restlessness
or new experience. He says, 'Now I am focusing on those ele-

ments in the human document which to me incorporate this particular motive or this particular attitude' (Social Science Research Council, 1939, p. 119).

Wirth and Blumer argued that no data is as simply abstract as the ideal model of the physical sciences pretends, and that in the social sciences, one must incorporate meaning. However, these points are subverted by the underlying falsificationist objectivist position.

At no time during the discussion was there any suggestion that data has meaning only in terms of its theoretical base, (thus the approach resembled what Lakatos (1970) refers to as naive falsificationism), nor that the culturological frame raises problems of a hermeneutic nature. On the other hand, the realist position was rarely threatened and only Stouffer and Bain had any reservations about the necessity to include the subjective factor; and that only in terms of the possibility of some valid sociology having put aside the subjective aspect. Stouffer, in asking whether the taken-for-granted subjective factor really is so vital, pointed to the prediction studies of Glueck, Burgess and Vold which are 'very important for social action' and which provide 'fairly valid conclusions and generalizations' but are independent of the 'meaning of any of this activity to the individual'.

Nonetheless, there was agreement on the view that social science does involve, for whatever reasons, problems different to the natural sciences, and that these problems must somehow be overcome if sociology is to enhance its objectivist, falsificationist, scientific credibility. There was a general concern that sociology should avoid a 'nihilistic' attitude, given that social scientific research can only be seen as plausible not definitively validated, and that no laws (or approximations to laws) as directive of action can be drawn up at anything but a trivial level.

Bain summed up the cumulative-falsificationist orientation to science and its application to social science.

Those grand generalizations always get tested by being broken up into a great number of simple problems. What we call 'progress' in all the natural sciences, among which I would include the social sciences, has come about through the development of the art of stating simple or unequivocal propositions, or hypotheses, which are capable of empirical test. When enough such propositions have been tested and retested and all of them are logically consistent with the grand generalization, it may be said to be verified. The empirical verification of no one single hypothesis relevant to the general theory of organic evolution can be said to be adequate proof of it, but when thousands of such simple single hypotheses have been verified, and they all hang together - none of them are clearly negative cases - we eventually come to accept the general theory of organic evolution as an actual valid scientific fact. (Social Science Research Council, 1939, p. 161).

One aspect of the debate is an overall desire for a synthesis of grand abstraction and scientifically precise empiricism, a view that methodological monism is not particularly desirable, and that eclecticism should be further developed rather than discouraged. This is reflected in Thomas' own reappraisal of the Polish Peasant in which he commented that he would put methodological considerations out of view if doing a similar study and restated his view that a mixture of approaches is most suitable, i.e. life histories and statistics, including factor analysis.

In an appended summary to the transcript, Bain (the transcript editor) indicated what he saw were the main divisions among the conferencees, and which reflected differences in American sociology. There was disagreement over the nature of social phenomena, methods by which they can be studied, the possibility of laws and of the testing of generalizations. Bain suggested two opposing views of validation which he saw revolving around the issue of the possibility of social laws. On the one hand the view that social laws were impossible given that they could not grasp 'values'. The alternative view, accepting the possibility of social laws emphasizes the idea that 'laws are possible because there is considerable uniformity and permanence in the occurrence of observed and observable social phenomena, whether they be called 'objective' or 'subjective''.

Bain then identified four theoretical positions expressed at the conference, first, illuminative insight, second, organising concepts, third, logico-systematic analysis and fourth, delimited empirical research. The last is opposite to illuminative insight, it is reductionist and demands framing propositions for testing, therefore requires relatively simple problems, few controlled variables, accessible and permanent data which are uniform and repeatable.

It is the most highly abstract way of dealing with concrete, i.e., experienceable, reality. It stresses verification by repetition, prediction, application, external and internal logical consistency. It is based on the probability calculus, it is actuarial or statistical. It advocates the development of precision instruments for use in observation, recording or manipulation, as the indispensable prerequisites for sound scientific work in any field. It holds that the history of science is the history of scientific technology.... The general methods and point of view is the same for all science, though necessarily the parti-

132

cular methods, techniques and technological devices used will vary greatly with the data being studied... All scientific data are abstractions... It is out of the cumulative findings of such simple, particular, highly abstracted empirical researches that the material for valid general scientific theories must come. It is by such research only that 'causal validity' can be ascertained and upon it, at long last, that all 'meaningful validity' must depend. (Social Science Research Council, 1939, p. 201).

Bain concluded that none of the Conference participants saw any of these positions as adequate alone, all agreed that some kind of synthetic position was required.

However the trend is towards the type of research called 'delimited empirical'; logico-systematic analysis is increasingly dependent upon such research; organizing concepts tend to grow out of such research and to be tested by it in the general manner described. This is a continuous process. The specific researches make imperative the revision of organizing concepts and general theories, and such revision by logic-systematic analysis sets new problems for further empirical research which requires the development of new or improved precision procedures which depend upon the invention of new or improvement of old technological devices of observation, recording and manipulation along with new or improved methodological skills and procedures. (Social Science Research Council, 1939, p. 202).

Thus Bain clearly laid out the cumulative-falsificationist model which had emerged as prevalent in American sociology. Ironically, this 'delimited empirical' approach with its reductionist emphasis actually provided the potential for a division in American sociology. Its failure to take into account the theory laden nature of observation, meaning adequacy, the nature of historical evidence or the cultural frame which Bain referred to provided the basis for a fundamental critique of the falsificationist approach to sociological research. This critique existed in embryonic form at Chicago in the position advocated by Wirth, Blumer and even in the 'culturological' approach of Chicago's major quantitative practitioner, Ogburn. Nonetheless, as will be examined below, the Chicagoans tended to remain within the prevailing tradition rather than engage it in a radical way.

While the Polish Peasant conference was a major event in American Sociology and illustrative of the development of a consensus orientation towards sociology, it is, of course, not a definitive statement. However, similar issues were raised and discussed within very similar constraints when, for example, the American Sociological Review was inaugurated and the issue of operationalisation engaged (Lundberg, 1936; Waller, 1936). Similarly the earlier discussions about the relative efficacy of case study and statistics were contained within a framework of debate which took for granted the essentially nomothetic concerns of the cumulative theoretical approach [8].

The Chicagoans' general theoretical and epistemological orientation.

The codification of the nature of sociological theory encapsulated in Merton's call for middle range theorising had been an ongoing practice in American sociology since the 1920s. Merton's work merely served to formalise and clarify elements of confusion in the prevailing cumulative theoretical tendency. Chicago sociology was not at variance with prevailing tendencies, as was illustrated in the analysis of the Polish Peasant conference. While Stouffer was more inclined towards a view sympathetic to attributing causes in the social world, Blumer and Wirth were more sceptical although, like the other speakers at the conference, they endorsed a cumulative-falsificationist approach.

Chicago sociologists had, since Thomas, adopted a variant of the cumulative-falsificationist approach. In terms of Merton's categorisation of theory, the Chicagoans, in practice, reflected his concerns. Thus, methodological debate was not set apart from theoretical development. The Chicagoans were eclectic in their methods (see chapters three and four) and for them methodology was an integral part of theory.

Similarly, while concerned to clarify concepts, notably disorganisation, prejudice, marginality, and interaction, the Chicagoans did not consider these clarifications an end in themselves, but merely an adjunct to the development of theory. Such theory, as has already been discussed, was developed through empirical observation, rather than 'armchair speculation'. However, it was not 'post-factum' theorising (Merton, 1948), as studies were both underpinned by a general theoretical orientation (social disorganisation with its associated demand for a consideration of attitudes and values) and located within particular theoretical discussions. The mere collection of facts did not constitute sociology for the Chicagoans (Burgess, 1944a).

The adoption of a cumulative-falsificationist model for sociology effectively undermined the long-term division between nonimalists and realists (Lewis and Smith, 1981). In the wake of the Polish Peasant debate, Burgess readdressed this division and enquired as to the suitability of physical and biological scientific models for the study of the social world. The realist position, for Burgess, implied that society is a reality to be studied through social processes such as communication, collective representation or social control; in short society is seen as organic and existing in the 'interaction and inter-communication of its members' as in Comte's social consensus, Durkheim's collective representation, Simmel's social forms of interaction, Weber's ideal types, Sumner's folkways and mores, Small's group, Cooley's sympathetic introspection and Park's collective behaviour. Nominalists, on the other hand, Burgess argued, concentrated on individual physiological and mental processes, such as Tarde's imitation, Giddings' consciousness of kind and Allport's denial of 'group' and 'institution' as analytic concepts.

In reviewing the nominalist-realist debate, Burgess noted that while realism emerged victorious, the nominalist position retained some credibility. Burgess' position was that while, in the past, the nominalist-realist issue had been contentious the debate had moved onto a new plane in which a synthesis (domin-ated by the realist position) engaged in a more subtle debate. The synthesis suggested that while study of society required that

> the distinctly social aspects of human behavior cannot be studied adequately by the analysis of mental processes within individuals but requires examination of the social processes involved in their interaction.... there actually are aspects of human behavior which may be studied under a conception of society as an aggregate of independent indi-viduals, and other aspects which can only be adequately defined and examined by the opposing conception of society as a reality of which its members are products. (Burgess, 1944a, p. 2).

He argued that, in view of this, there was a convergence between the nominalist and realist positions in practice which belied their epistemological distance. In effect, he argued that the nature of the attempted scientific study was charac-terised by the two essential guiding criteria of falsification-ist 'scientific method', namely, the formulation of working hypotheses, and the 'objective use of an objective method of verification or disproof of the hypotheses that can be repeated by other[s]' (Burgess, 1944a, p. 8) [9].

Burgess's review of the realist-nominalist debate dispensed with the stale dichotomisation and effectively illustrated the synthesis achieved by the concern to establish a sound object-ive science grounded in a cumulative-falsificationist pragmatic model which tended to be adopted at Chicago as elsewhere. This is evident in the research work of the Chicagoans and emerged from the Polish Peasant conference where (publicly at least) there was, in principal, a nomological consensus amongst the participants at the conference.

Chicago alternatives to the prevailing model.

The Chicago sociologists, notably Blumer and Wirth, had, as part of their theoretical repertoire, the basis for an alternative to the prevailing model. Indeed, Blumer is often seen as fundamentally opposed to the tendency towards a 'scientific sociology', while Wirth is seen as providing a radical alternative based on a German sociology of knowledge tradition (Burgess, 1944a). The debate on the **Polish Peasant** (Social Science Research Council, 1939) had clearly indicated the root of this opposition. However, as has been suggested above, while Wirth and Blumer provided the grounding for a non-falsificationist position during the debate, they subsumed these concerns under the standard approach.

Blumer and symbolic interactionism

Blumer was openly sceptical of the possibility of causal laws. The value of the **Polish Peasant** for him, then, was its focus on understanding. The fact that it appears in his critique not to be capable (methodologically) of acheiving the control over society that it wanted does not bother Blumer. He suggested that understanding may provide a better resource for control than a nomothetic sociology. Blumer accepted that his position located social research between 'scientific laws' and 'literary insight' and saw no short term resolution of that situation.

Blumer was not alone in advancing the scepticism about the possible 'objectivity' of the social sciences as they stand. He was supported in the debate by Lerner who questioned

> the whole comparison that I have found so often being made between the natural sciences and the social sciences. I think one of the things we have suffered from has been that sense of inferiority that comes from our not being able to turn ourselves into natural scientists. I think we ought to recognize that and also recognize that there are attainable social generalizations that are worth making, and then to talk about research in terms of getting at those relatively attainable generalizations. (Social Science Research Council, 1939, p. 144).

Although there is little evidence of it in the Polish Peasant conference, Blumer is often regarded as a major figure in the development of a 'qualitative' or 'interpretive' sociology (Filstead, 1970; Denzin, 1970; Butters, 1973). The development of symbolic interactionism formalised his position and its adoption by some of the Chicagoans is seen as indicative of the 'Chicago School's' continued exclusion from mainstream development of sociological theory. Indeed, while symbolic interactionism provided a basis for an alternative to the prevailing falsificationist orientation that pervaded American sociology, no such fully articulated alternative emerged from the 'Chicago School'. Chicago was not the home of a critical ethnography, indeed, it was more the centre of a synthetic sociology, utilising eclectic approaches and a non-critical methodology, and reflecting mainstream American sociology (Thomas, 1983b).

So, although, the emergence of a strong symbolic interactionist approach at Chicago orchestrated by Blumer is sometimes seen as indicative of a radical shift in the Chicago tradition away from the nomothetic-falsificationist concerns of the earlier interactionists and of the enduring approach advocated by Burgess, towards an ethnographically based phenomenological perspective, this overstates the division in American sociology prior to 1960. An analysis of the symbolic interactionists at Chicago from 1930s onwards shows that they did not form a separate approach from the general developments at Chicago, nor were they phenomenologists. Further, there was no clear attempt at methodic prescriptions until at least the late 1950s, and then as much for pragmatic reasons (the nature of the researched groups) as out of methodological preference. The methodological debate (even as late as the 1960s) did not detach participant observation from the general methodological concerns of middle range theorising. In fact, Blumer never laid the groundwork for a 'truly' phenomenological critique of positivism, always resisting any charges of radical subjectivism. It was Goffman, if anyone, who provided the route to an alternative conceptualisation of the sociological enterprise which was developed at Berkeley as 'late symbolic interactionism' and emerged (eventually) in ethnomethodology (Scott, 1968).

The approach and orientation of those sociologists at Chicago who adopted the label of symbolic interactionist, or to whom such a label has retrospectively been applied, did not divorce themselves from the mainstream of interactionism at Chicago. There is, at no point, a shift indicative of a large movement towards a peculiarly symbolic interactionist perspective. Symbolic interactionism grew out of the general perspective and orientation at Chicago in line with similar debates in American sociology. The Polish Peasant conference is illustrative of the essential tension in the discipline but also reveals that no fully articulated and programmatic alternative was in evidence. Sociology as science and the nature of both science and sociology was under, and has remained under, scrutiny. Blumer's reservations were but a single articulation of what may be seen to be a post war 'qualitative style', however, he did not represent a 'Chicago School' position, nor was he leader of a set of sociologists who developed anything like a phenomenological critique or research practice.

In many respects, Blumer was out on a limb at Chicago. Janowitz (1980) argued that Blumer's theoretical position was distinct from the general perspective at Chicago and this is reflected in the social distance he tended to maintain from other faculty and graduates. 'I was fairly close with Herb Blumer although he was quite remote and distant, not too friendly with anybody' (Cottrell, 1972).

However, Blumer did not develop a position which detached him entirely from the prevailing sociological approach. This is evident in his own research at Chicago. An example of the approach is provided in a letter of application for funding to continue his study (with H.W. Dunham) on cataonic dementia praecox, written to Wirth as chairman of the Social Science Research Committee at Chicago, June 13, 1936. He outlined work to date, which very much reflects the general concerns of the Chicagoans. These concerns related to the environmental factors affecting action, social interaction, personality traits, attitudes and values. Blumer (1936a) noted that the catatonic dementia praecox boys in the study were excluded from childhood associations with delinquent boys at that point when delinquent acts are planned and that there was 'definite proof' that the catatonic boys were not delinquent despite being open to the same environmental stimuli as the delinquent boys. The result was a negative value placed on delinquency by the catatonic boys. Such boys tended to be conformist, timid, self conscious, attached to home and anxious. Such anxiety occasionally erupted into psychotic behaviour.

Blumer intended to develop the research along two lines, the first a deeper investigation of personal experiences of the catatonic boys, and compare these with similar boys in other areas of the city. Second, to

> construct a testing device in the form of a questionnaire built around the differences in traits of behavior existing between the catatonic boys and the delinquent boys. I hope to make this device into such a form that it will be possible to isolate out the two types from one another with ease.... (Blumer, 1936a)

Blumer wanted to check his feeling that it is the discrepancy between the 'psychological tempo of the community' and the 'personality disposition of the catatonic' which leads to psychotic outbreaks.

In much the same way, later symbolic interactionists, for example Becker, Geer, and Stauss, did not adopt a position opposed to the prevailing nomothetic-falsificationist model.

138

Even into the 1960s, the work of these noted symbolic interactionists, who are generally assumed to have taken their cue from Blumer, failed to adopt an approach at variance with the mainstream. Indeed, the contribution to the methodological debate in the 1960s by Becker and others was less inclined towards an anti-nomothetic position than Blumer. Becker (1958), Geer (1964), Becker and Geer (1957, 1957a, 1960) and Glaser and Strauss (1967) may have preferred and attempted to legitimate a 'qualitative' approach, yet they offered no fully developed 'phenomenologically' based alternative.

Becker (1958) and Geer (1964) provide a clear illustration of the methodological and general theoretical orientation of the 'later Chicagoans', and indicates the essentially nomological nature of their endeavour. The 'qualitative style' was the 'loyal opposition' (Mullins, 1973) in the 1950s and 1960s to variable analysis techniques in as much as it offered no critique of the cumulative-falsificationist epistemology of structural functionalism. Indeed, Becker and Geer (1957), were concerned to legitimate participant observation as a 'valid' data collection process and to show that participant observation could and should be a systematic technique. Becker and Geer argued that participant observation is not simply an exploratory tool of social research, and that it can generate and test theory and thereby conform to the taken-for-granted standards of middle-range theorising.

For Becker, participant observation was typically concerned both to discover hypotheses and to test them. The problem for Becker was that given the vast amount of 'rich' but varied data, how does one analyse it systematically and present conclusions convincingly ?

Becker reasserted the cumulative model view of the development of sociological knowledge by suggesting that participant observation research was sequential and analytically inductive. He pointed to three distinct stages of the fieldwork and a final analytic stage once the fieldwork was completed. The stages were, first, the selection and definition of problems, concepts and indices; second, the checking of the frequency and distribution of phenomena; third, the construction of social system models; and fourth, the post fieldwork stage of final analysis and presentation of results.

This four stage process rested upon a falsificationist model of knowledge production. Becker suggested that, after constructing a model specifying the relationships among various elements the model is successively refined by searching for negative cases, thus accommodating the 'Popperian principles' of conjecture and refutation at the level of individual testable statements. Becker suggested that

While a processural model may be shown to be defective by a

negative instance which crops up unexpectedly in the course of the fieldwork, the observer may infer what kinds of evidence would be likely to support or to refute his model and may make an intensive search for such evidence. (Becker 1958, p. 408).

The final post-fieldwork stage is systematic and involves checking and rebuilding models with as many safeguards as the data will allow, notably by cross classifying all items so that checks can be made as complete as possible. This approach can, Becker suggested,

profit from the observation of Lazarsfeld and Barton that the "analysis of 'quasi-statistical data' can probably be made more systematic than it has been in the past, if the logical structure of quantitative research at least is kept in mind to give general warnings and directions to the qualitative observer." (Becker, 1958, p. 409)

There is little in Becker (1958) to challenge the prevailing model. The identification of necessary and sufficient conditions reflected the nomothetic approach. The reductionism inherent in isolating basic phenomena and the attempts to build up and elaborate existing sociological theory with its taken-for-granted social system framework also reflected the concerns of middle range theorising. Becker made no attempt to critique the epistemological underpinnings of prevailing scientific sociology nor took into account Blumer's (1956) reservation.

In an account of ongoing fieldwork practice (published in Hammond (1964), but written around 1960) Geer reaffirmed Becker (1958). She reframed Becker's sequential model in terms of the generation and testing of working hypotheses and their combination into compound propositions. Reflecting Becker, she saw the first operation as consisting of the testing of 'crude yes-or-no propositions', the second stage as 'seeking negative cases' or setting out 'deliberately to accumulate positive ones'. One disconfirming instance, she argued, forces modification. A simplistic falsificationist model is reaffirmed, such that confirmation of 'what is' is accomplished by eliminating 'what is not'. The third stage is elaborated, by Geer, into a proto-path analytic model, following the suggestions of George Polya (1954).

Despite concluding that the first days in the field may transform a study out of recognition, Geer (1964) merely reflected Becker's earlier comments, and did not propose an interpretive ethnography with distinct epistemological possibilities. She persisted with the advocacy of a value free or neutral observational research. The researcher should not contaminate the research environment by appearing to take sides.

Yet Geer considered problems of interpretive methodology, when, for example, she referred to the problem of empathy. However, the critical potential was not developed and the discussion framed in terms of confronting prejudices.

Mullins' (1973) reference to symbolic interactionism in the post-war period as 'loyal opposition' is most apposite, given the gradual ascendency of the functionalist element of the functionalist-interactionist heritage in the 1950s through structural functionalism. That Mullin's 'loyal opposition' did not develop the radical anti-nomothetic critique it might have is probably due to the retention of a pragmatic base rooted in 'Kantian idealism' (Rock, 1979). Even later interactionist developments (Goffmann, 1959; Scott, 1968), and the emergence of ethnomethodology, were unconcerned to either develop a phenomenological orientation or engage the idealist base which informed American sociology. Ethnomethodology, in fact, attempted to synthesise Schutz and Parsons in its radical reformulation of participant informed symbolic interactionism (Filmer et al., 1972).

Wirth and the German Sociological Tradition

Wirth, like Blumer, advanced a potentially divisive view of sociological research. He drew on two elements of a German sociological tradition and used them to raise fundamental questions about the prevailing nomothetic cumulative-falsificationist model. Essentially, he called into question the possibility of sociological explanation and the possibility of non-ideological social science.

He adopted Weber's concept of 'verstehen' as a framework for reconsidering the complex interrelationship between 'value' and 'attitude'. During the Polish Peasant debate Wirth introduced Weber's distinction between meaning and causal adequacy, by actually reading a lengthy section from Weber (1947). However, rather than confront the epistemological problems of a hermeneutic nature which underpin the understanding-explanation controversy the idea of meaning adequacy was corrupted, by Wirth, and he relabelled 'adequacy' as 'validity'.

For Wirth the importance of the 'verstehen' approach was that it helped to differentiate between 'insight which reveals meaning' and 'causal explanation'. In terms of the Polish Peasant debate, Wirth argued that Thomas's scheme could not be derived from the material itself because that would imply that facts speak for themselves, whereas 'We know facts do not speak for themselves.'. (Social Science Research Council, 1939, p. 122). However, if attitudes and values were clearly defined we could verify whether a particular attitude or value was to be found in a document. But no simple definition exists, and this Wirth suggested was because there is a mistaken assumption that

141

values are objective. The mistake, he claimed, is not that values are subjective but that one can ascribe 'objectivity' to sociological data at all.

Wirth, in developing a critique based on Weber, appeared to be on the verge of questioning the fundamental taken-for-granted view of falsificationist science. However, this was not the case.

> I think we all agree that science is invariant relationship, but this cannot be determined from the observation of a single case. The continuous corroboration by inspection of single cases after single cases adds to the security of the generalizations by proving that the relationship as first observed was not the result of factors other than those specified. That is what I think we mean by proof. Single cases can be used (a) to illustrate the plausibility of a hypothesis before it has been tested by a series of observations in a number of cases. They also can be used (b) to illustrate the operation of a relationship already incorporated in a proved generalization. Regarding the security of judgement of documents, I see no insuperable difficulties if definitions are always unambiguous and exhaustive. (Social Science Research Council, 1939, p 123).

In effect, then, the adoption of a verstehen informed approach was essentially a means towards explanation.

Burgess (1944a), similarly, discussed the distinction between nomothetic and idiographic research, but addressed it in terms of explanatory potential. Thus methods were assessed as to whether they were explanatory or merely exploratory.

> Applicable to personal documents are two methods of interpretation (1) nomothetic or the comparative study of documents in order to arrive at generalizations and (2) idiographic, or the appreciation of the individual case in all its individuality and completeness. Allport asserts that prediction can be made upon the basis of the ideiographic [sic] study of a single case, a claim that has been challenged by others. (Burgess, 1944a, pp. 14-15).

This is an effective denial of the concept of idiographic understanding in the sense of rejecting causal/explanatory laws. In Burgess's paper, idiographic becomes restricted to the Weberian sense of meaning and causal adequacy. For him, the problem became one of methodic problems of control of the researcher (i.e. reliability) when using life histories and attempting 'sympathy, empathy, recipathy, insight and intuition', (Burgess, 1944a, p. 15). This perspective lay at the heart of the adoption of a Weberian approach by American sociologists.

Nonetheless, in his work in the sociology of knowledge, Wirth, along with Shils, were, potentially, developing another route towards a critique of nomothetic sociology. The work in the sociology of knowledge, heavily influenced by German theorising, was seen as radically different. Burgess (1944a, p. 10) divided conceptualisation into two camps, a traditional approach from Comte to the present which, he suggested, devises conceptual schemes for analysis of social change, social structure or social function and a sociology of knowledge approach, based primarily in Germany and centering on the theories of Max Scheler and Karl Mannheim, which 'stresses the importance of studying society through an understanding of past, current and emerging ideologies ... the relativity of conceptual systems'.

Wirth was a notable scholar of German sociology (Ogburn 1936), enhanced by his year in that country on a Guggenheim Fellowship in 1930. Along with Shils, who was well aquainted with the work of Mannheim, (Minutes of the Society for Social Research, 5.3.1934), he translated 'Ideology and Utopia' and 'The Sociology of Knowledge' into English, providing an introduction to locate the texts in an Anglo-Saxon context.

For Burgess

> the outstanding value of the sociology of knowledge for social research inheres in its function of manifesting the intimate interaction and interdependence of social life and social science. The understanding of this relation is essential to the investigator in grasping the nature and limitations of research and in appreciating the conditions which permit and handicap activity. (Burgess, 1944a, p. 11-12).

Wirth's development of a sociology of knowledge approach revolved around the notion of ideal type and reflected the concerns developed by Parsons (1937, 1951). Functionalism adapted ideal typification in a non-hermeneutic way and reflected the long term concerns of American sociology with German social philosophy which had underpinned much social theorising at Chicago as well as elsewhere (Dibble, 1972; Rock, 1979). Wirth and Parsons more explicitly developed this continental influence. Wirth was more radical in the sense of pursuing the 'relativistic nature of knowledge' and of 'ideology' (which Burgess acknowledged), while Parsons was more concerned with a synthesis (including Durkheim) and dissipated some of Mannheim's central concerns by utilising the more familiar concepts of value and norm (and hence central value system) instead of ideology. Parsons, in adapting to an American setting, thus watered down the critique implicit in the concerns of the German sociology of knowledge approach.

Wirth's development of the approach, as evident in his contributions to the Polish Peasant conference, made no attempt to engage the dissipation of the critical element of the German sociology of knowledge approach apparent in Parson's development of functionalism. The result was limited and uncritical, essentially pointing only to the interrelationship of research and mileu and questioning the possibility of an absolute objectivity.

Any potential for an alternative critical approach encapsulated in the sociology of knowledge orientation was defused by events. The rise of McCarthyism created a context in which any radical sociology was difficult to sustain. More specifically, the premature death of Wirth in 1951 effectively saw the end of any chance of a radical alternative, based on a 'German philosophy of knowledge' approach, being developed at Chicago [10].

The critique of the prevailing cumulative-falsificationist model that can be identified in the work of Blumer and Wirth did not materialise into a fully articulated alternative practised by the Chicagoans. Rather, elements of symbolic interactionism and the sociology of knowledge approach tended to be absorbed in the prevailing model. There was no alternative 'Chicago' approach, Chicago remained mainstream, epistemologically and methodologically, very much a part of the emerging cumulative-falsificationist theorising which came to dominate standard American sociology.

Arguably, only a few small scale alternatives to the prevailing nomothetic approach existed in the United States. These included the development of phenomenology at Buffalo and at the New School of Social Research (Spiegelberg, 1976), besides the work of individuals critical of the prevailing tendency such as Mills and those early social critics who fell under the umbrella of the 'New Sociology' (Horowitz, 1964). Added to these, could be those sociologists who adopted a policy of retrenchment to social problems, encapsulated in the publication of the journal of the same name.

Conclusion

Chicago sociology, I have argued, was neither atheoretical empiricism nor was it restricted to urban sociology. Certainly the Chicagoans promoted empirical work but always alongside theoretical development [11]. Park's scepticism of statistics (explored in detail in chapter four above) was not evidence of an epistemological disagreement with the nomothetic base of interactionist sociology. Rather, it was a concern that aggregates were unable to adequately incorporate the subjective factor into nomothetic analysis. Wirth, (1944, p.4) noted of Park, that

Objectivity in the realm of the social ... was to be achieved not primarily by collecting facts and ignoring values but by overtly examining values and especially by becoming conscious of those values that we take for granted.

Park saw social science as a natural science up to a point, that is, its methods were a good starting point but that 'one would soon enough encounter the values, morals, and preferences of men before which the methods of natural science would prove inadequate'. He thought that society was not a closed system and that it should not be seen as either an 'artefact' or 'as a system of mechanical forces', rather, society was a set of reciprocal claims and expectations and mutual understandings. This methodological orientation was intrinsic to the theoretical development of sociology at Chicago and in the United States in general.

As has been shown, the Chicagoans worked at various levels of theoretical concern. Over time, there was a tendency to move from general holistic views of the social world to specific testing of theories, thus reflecting the direction being taken by the sociological profession in its attempt to legitimate sociology as science. The **Polish Peasant** study, and the synthesis embodied in it by Thomas, constituted the initial break with the 'armchair theorising' of the past (as in the work of Sumner, Ross, Tarde). Thomas's theoretical orientation encapsulated in the 'social disorganisation paradigm', became resolved into general theories of change and interaction and much of the work done revolved around those theories and particular developments of them.

Later generations of Chicagoans became more concerned with particular issues and methodological confrontation. However, 'abstracted empiricism' (Mills, 1959) was certainly no part of Chicago sociology up to 1950. That element of the Chicago mythology which suggests that the 'School' was atheoretical is not borne out though the Chicagoans did have strong empirical concerns. They developed theory at various levels through an explicit inductive approach. Chicago sociology of the 1920s and 1930s was self consciously an attempt to 'objectively develop theory'. It was, as Park would have it, 'big picture' sociology, based upon general theoretical perspectives evolving out of a context for study synthesised and bequeathed to the Chicagoans by Thomas.

Chicago was not operating in isolation in the generation of theoretical concepts, nor was its major theoretical orientation, social disorganisation, a concept restricted to Chicago. Chicagoans provided conceptual frameworks and freely embraced concepts developed elsewhere. Chicago was not characterised by doctrinal debates (Rock, 1979).

What was important, as Burgess (1944a) argued, (pre-dating C.Wright Mills and Robert Merton), was to combine data collection and abstract theorising. He suggested that the work of Thomas, Park and their students were examples of such sociology and that the operationalism of Lundberg was in danger of assuming that the operational definition be equivalent to the conceptual definition, thereby jeopardising theoretical development.

Empiricism was important to the Chicagoans but was not an end in itself. From the first, empirical observation was ordered and categorised and inductive theorising was developed, notably through attempts at typification which gradually became more sophisticated as American sociology adapted Weberian ideal types to its own needs. Indeed if any one aspect of the work done by the Chicagoans can be said to be indicative of their approach it is the penchant for typification that probably has the largest claim. The reports of research presented to the Society for Social Research by both internal and external speakers contain numerous references to various attempts at typifying interactive processes, subject groups and functional objects. Many of the dissertations written by students throughout the period 1915 to 1950 contain a classificatory scheme as an important element of theoretical development.

Burgess, reflecting developing perspectives throughout the discipline, was instrumental in the encouragement of ideal typification at Chicago. By the 1940s Burgess argued that it was the only appropriate methodic development for dealing with personal documents. His view of ideal typification which he says is derived from Simmel, Tonnies and Weber is a process of 'abstracting from concrete cases a characteristic ... accentualizing it and defining it clearly unambiguously and uncomplicatedly by other characteristics' (Burgess, 1944a, pp. 15-16).

Burgess admired the role of ideal typification in Weber, Simmel and Sorokin but was concerned that ideal typical constructions may not be actually represented by concrete phenomena. Burgess wanted abstraction to mirror 'reality', His concern was that ideal typification should be more than approximation to reality as this leads to the the problem of degree of approximation. Thus, Burgess effectively detached ideal typification from verstehen and construed it as a procedure for eliciting definitive explanatory concepts. Following the developing practice in the United States, Burgess, suggested that ideal typifications provided the endpoints of scales (which more closely represented the variations of concrete, normally distributed, phenomena). This provided him with a link to statistical analysis. He also noted the ineffectiveness of critiques of ideal typification from 'statistically minded students' who argued that gradation of scales with peaking in the centre undermines ideal typical dichotomisation. Burgess maintained that such a view was fallacious because the end-points are still clearly conceptually sound. Burgess, like the contributors to the conference on the Polish Peasant, redefined ideal typification to correspond with nomothetic, measurement concerns and 'utilised' it to incorporate personal documents into quantitative work.

The Chicagoans were far from atheoretical empiricists divorced from the development of sociological theory in the United States. It was not until the late fifties that any distinction between the orientation of the Chicagoans of the twenties and prevailing structural functionalist perspectives could be identified. In 1939, for example, Parsons wrote to Wirth thanking him for his review of The Structure of Social Action and noted that the synthesis contained in the book, although directed to Durkheim, Weber and Pareto, also incorporated the theoretical position of Dewey, Mead, the 'cultural anthropologists' and 'I think, your own colleagues' (Parsons, 1939).

Blumer, similarly, suggested that a concern with structure only emerged as a dominant orientation in recent times.

> I think the fundamental premise in the case of Park and Thomas and the associates there at Chicago is just that of recognizing that a human group consists of people who are living. Oddly enough this is not the picture which underlies the dominant imagery in the field of sociology today. They think of a society or group as something that is there in the form of a regularized structure in which people are placed. And they act on the basis of the influence of the structure on them. This is a complete inversion of what is involved and I would say the antithesis of the premise that underlay the work of Park and Thomas. (Blumer, 1980b, p. 261)

Nonetheless, this development of a structural, or systems, approach, towards looking at people as if they were products of social factors, did not suddenly occur around the fifties, as is often assumed. Rather, as has been illustrated above, it emerged throughout the preceding quarter of a century and the University of Chicago played its part in this change [12]. Retrospective accounts which focus only on a narrow output of sociological work from the 1920s at Chicago and compare it with sociological practice in the late 1950s and early 1960s are misleading in detaching the Chicagoans from the evolution of sociological theory in the United States.

Notes

[1] Cavan's choice of Thomas and Wirth as indicative of the staff at Chicago is strange. Thomas had left in 1918 and Wirth was a graduate student himself until 1926, the year Cavan received her doctorate, and merely an instructor from 1926 to 1929 (before moving to Tulane University).

Further, Cavan's suggestion that Wirth was opposed to theory construction is surprising. Wirth was particularly interested in theoretical developments in sociology and was himself concerned with the sociology of knowledge. As part of this endeavour he circulated the department with a memorandum, part of which pointed to the traditional theoretical concerns of sociology.

As a general discipline sociology seeks to understand what is true of human behaviour by virtue of the fact that man everywhere leads a group life.... The anlysis of personality and collective behavior falls into a branch of sociology known as social psychology. The analysis of social institutions and of social structures and the processes of social interaction through which these structures come into being and change constitutes the field of social organisation. The environmental factors, resources and the technology conditioning populations, communities and social life generally, and the extent to which their relationships between man and man are, among other factors, influenced by the habitat, constitute human ecology. (Wirth, 1938)

This hardly seems to indicate a lack of concern with theoretical enterprises, even if it was written, in all probability, some time after Cavan was acquainted with Wirth. Nonetheless, Cavan would presumably have been aquainted with Wirth's own thesis, which, although providing an extensive historical analysis of the development of the ghetto, further developed and refined Park's race relations cycle.

Wirth (1948) reflecting on his involvement in sociology at Chicago summed up the approach to theory and practice adopted at Chicago.

Insofar as we wish to be a science we must seek to establish valid generalizations. Hence, we are concerned with a description of unique instances only insofar as they can be used for the establishment of generalized descriptions and more abstract general propositions. We should try to carry our findings to as precise a point of measuration as the data and out techniques allow. I do not, however, agree with those who believe that measurement is the only criter-

ion of science. The propositions at which we arrive should
have predictive value, but here again quantification is not
a necessary element in prediction....   ●
In my work in theory, especially through my years of teaching it to graduate students, I have tried to emphasize that
theory is an aspect of everything that they do and not a
body of knowledge separate from research and practice.

[2] Some disatisfaction on the part of students may have arisen
as a result of Park's rather forceful promotion of research
topics. Robert Faris (1972) noted that he wanted to 'do my
own thesis and not have one handed to me by Park' while
Hayner admitted to the influence of Park when deciding on
research projects.

The 'hotel life' thesis came really from Park, he was
pushing studies down in the Loop district and that appealed
to me... Park had wanted me to study the slum but I didn't
want to study the slums. There was another girl who was
more interested in slums. So I said, 'you can have it'.
(Hayner, 1972)

[3] Commentators have suggested that this drew upon, or was
consistent with, Durkheim's anomie thesis. There is a line
of argument (Farberman, 1979; Tiryakian, 1979a) that suggest a kind of continuum from the 'Durkheimian School' to
the Park-Burgess 'Chicago School'. Farberman (1979) contended that

What Park wanted to discover were the physical, social and
psychological mechanisms through which society tamed its
members. In attempting to delineate the social mechanisms
of control, [Park] leaned heavily on Durkheim's conception
of collective representation and Cooley's notion of the
primary group; for the physical mechanism, he drew on the
perspective of ecology: for the psychological mechanism, on
Thomas and Znaniecki's view of personal evolution as well
as Sigmund Freud and Alfred Adler's notion of sublimation
and compensation (Farberman, 1979, p. 12)

Park and Burgess adopted the idea of the 'corporate
existence of the social group', as something more than 'the
sum of the parts' as 'the fundamental fact of social control' from Durkheim. The group is 'fundamental in forming
the social nature and ideals of the individual'. Farbermann
implied this to mean that Park saw the individual as
'largely determined by forces and processes over which he
had but faint awareness and little control'. Thus Park saw
manipulation for control purposes as possible because the

individual has to fit into a pre-existing world. Drawing on Thomas and Znaniecki, Park cited personal disorganisation as pointing to an inevitable and constant struggle for personal self-expression. This struggle arises out of the basic motivational forces of the psyche, as summarised in Thomas' four wishes.

[4] In 1935 a Divisional Seminar in Race and Culture Contacts had been established at Chicago, meeting weekly under the direction of Blumer, Park, Redfield and Wirth and 'had the co-operation of about thirty graduate students from various parts of the University' (Wirth 1935). The following reported to the Seminar in 1935: Wirth, Redfield, Blumer, Lohman, Pierson, V. E. Daniel, M. Sprengling, A. Baker and Warner of Chicago, plus J. H. Johnson (Virginia), Park (Fisk), Tomasic (Rockefeller Foundation), Mitchell (Washington D.C), Hansen (Miami), Malinowski (LSE), Reuter (Iowa), J. Merlant of the United States Military Academy and P. Nash of the Klamath Reservation, Oregon.

[5] No attempt is made here to define the terms 'interpretive', 'phenomenological' or 'positivistic' as they are not used as a basis for comparison but merely indicative of the type of general contrast implied by some commentators when comparing, for example, 'Chicago sociology' with the structural-functionalism of the Columbia sociologists, (Bogdan and Taylor, 1975)

[6] The use of the term falsificationism here is indicative of the kind of approach that predominated in American sociology throughout the period of this study. This is not intended to represent an assertion about the nature of sociological enquiry in terms of a discussion as to whether American sociology is characterised by inductivism or hypothetico-deductivism, both of these are subsumed within the term falsificationism, especially as characterised by Lakatos (1970). Lakatos defined, in effect, three levels of falsificationism, naive, sophisticated and the refined version of sophisticated falsificationism to be found in his own methodology of scientific research programmes. The use of the term here is not meant to refer to any one of these in particular, but to embody the central tenets of falsificationism, viz. conjecture and refutation, cumulative progress through empirical validation of theoretical, falsifiable statements, and the acceptance of the impossibility of deductive or inductive proof. The niceties of the debate as to how science progresses, which underpins Lakatos' distinctions of types of falsificationism is not germane to the use of the label here. As has been shown else-

where (Chalmers, 1978) all falsificationist models ignore, in the last resort, the value laden nature of observation; see science as ultimately self-legitimating through its own protocols; and divorce scientific knowledge production from the wider scientific mileu. It is this critique combined with the general characteristics of falsificationism that makes the term appropriate as a descriptor of American sociological endeavours in the period under consideration.

[7] Merton codified the cumulative theory approach in various articles in the 1940s, which became the basis for the middle range theorising perspective so important to structural functionalism. The reference to middle range theory throughout the book is directly to Merton's formulation, although it is argued that such a formulation reflected sociological practice to which the Chicagoans subscribed.

Merton (1948) noted the continuity of theory and cited various instances including some integral to Chicago, notably the 'conflicting self' or 'marginal man'. He pointed to developments in this sphere of theorising but suggested that the central problem of conflicting roles 'has yet to be materially clarified and advanced beyond the point reached decades ago. Thomas and Znaniecki (1918) long since indicated that conflicts between social roles can be reduced by conventionalization and by role-segmentation.' (Merton, 1948, p. 515)

Merton (1945, 1948, 1949) in laying out the basis of middle range theorising attempted to forge a clear link between empirical research and social theory. Rather than 'the social theorist high in the empyrean of pure ideas' being replaced by the researcher 'equipped with questionnaire and pencil and hot on the chase of the isolated and meaningless statistic', he saw the interaction of theory and empirical research with empirical data informing theory and vice versa. In practice, however, he maintained that there were still those sociologists who did not link theory with research. Merton (1949) reflected Bain's contribution to the Polish Peasant debate of a decade earlier (Social Science Research Council, 1939) when he identified six approaches to theorising: methodology, general sociological orientation, analysis of concepts, 'post factum' interpretation, empirical generalisation and sociological laws. Methodology, he argued has nothing to do with substantive theorising. Conceptual analysis, Merton argued, is indispensable if confined to clarification of key concepts. However, to think of conceptual manipulation and definition in itself as theorising is spurious. Applying conceptual schemes in a 'post factum' and (heiniously) ad hoc manner to data, similarly does sociological theorising a disservice. Indeed, Merton scathingly attacked approaches which collected data and then subjected them to interpretive comment. He regarded such approaches as having the logical structure of clinical enquiry because they do not test pre-designed hypotheses. This applied to both statistical and case-study data. The result is a merely plausible explanation. General orientations merely indicate the approach, such that Durkheim's orientation was that social facts should be sought in the facts that preceeded it, and Znan-iecki and Sorokin (amongst others) invoked a 'humanistic coefficient' as orienting principle. They are non-empirical generic orientations and must be specified in terms of empirical generalisations. In isolation such generalizations are nothing more than summaries of observed uniformities in observational data. It is the combination of concept clarification, orientation, empirical generalisation within a theoretical frame that provides sociological theory. At the extreme this manifests itself as sociological laws. While this status is rarely achieved, Merton argued that it is possible to work towards it through the cumulative development of theory. Middle range theorising provides that possibility. Merton saw 'middle range theory' as the pragmatic answer to the continuing development of sociology which, he admitted must 'ultimately meet the canons of scientific method'. In this respect, Chicago sociologists would not have disagreed.

[8] Cooley is a possible exception. 'It was more and more borne in upon me that I could never really see the social life of man unless I understood the processes of mind with which it was indissoluably bound up. I saw that there was a gap between the ideas of structure and function I had so far been working on and the actual motives and behavior of men, which left the former somewhat hanging in the air...' (Cooley, 1930, p. 30). Referring to his work in the first decade of the century.

[9] Methodologically, this 'standard' view required the invention of an instrument for the study of particular phenomena and the question arose as to whether such an instrument existed. Given the role of the reflective consciousness 'an instrument is needed which provides the investigator access to the inner life of the person and to the web of intercommunications between persons.' (Burgess, 1944a, p.9). Burgess argued that the life history, like the microscope in biology, was an important element in study of the particular as it gets 'beneath the surface of the externally observable' (Burgess, 1944a, p. 9). Nonethless, for sociology to develop objective theory an objective record of

behaviour is needed, according to Burgess, therefore 'the perfection of the interview and its recording are of signal importance for sociological research.' (Burgess, 1944a, p.10).

[10] In addition, Shils was not an official member of the sociology department staff from 1948 to 1957. He taught part of the year during this period but was attached to the Committee on Social Thought. However, the extent to which Wirth may have developed a critical (neo-Marxist) alternative despite the prevailing tendency is difficult to judge. Parsons, with whom Shils was to work, killed off the critical potential by anaesthetising ideology instead using 'values', 'central value system' etc., (Centre for Contemporary Cultural Studies, 1978).

[11] Wirth (1938), in proposing specialised sociology training in the department suggested four quarterly courses, social psychology, social organisation, population and ecology and methods of investigation. Such a curriculum 'does not contain any reference to what is known as sociological theory; this is deliberate because it should be infused into every course we give and should not be separated out into a special course'. On another occasion Wirth indicated the Department's position on the interrelationship between theory amd method when proposing the core elements of a Master's programme which made no provision for a separate methodology course, arguing that methodology should be integral to all components of the course.

[12] Blumer noted that the structural approach 'was already beginning to emerge', interestingly enough, in Chicago right at the university there, back in the late '20s. It was well-represented by a very, very able, almost colossal figure in his own right, namely Thurstone - L.L. Thurstone - the psychologist, with his work on attitude studies, that [work] having an enormous influence on the work of Stouffer inside our department.' (Blumer, 1980b, p. 265)

6 G H Mead and the Chicagoans

The myth

Chicago sociology is frequently seen as owing much to the influence of George Herbert Mead. Indeed, along with the view that Chicago sociology is 'qualitative', the importance of Mead is the most enduring myth about the 'Chicago School'.

At its extreme, this myth is stated in terms of the centrality of Mead to all the work done in the 'Chicago School'. Thus, for example, Ciacci (1972) argued that German idealism, pragmatism and evolutionism were combined in Mead's work and became part of the 'Chicago School'. Mead's ideas showed up in the work of Thomas, Park, Burgess, Wirth and R.E.L. Faris and later in the work of Blumer and Hughes, and can also be seen in the preoccupations of Peter Berger and Alfred Schutz.

A less all embracing and more widespread view is that despite the diverse origins of interactionism, Mead was the 'founding father' of symbolic interactionism. This can be found in statements of two central figures within the tradition, Herbert Blumer and Manford Kuhn.

> A view of human society as symbolic interaction has been followed more than it has been formulated. Partial, usually fragmentary, statements of it are to be found in the writings of a number of eminent scholars ... Charles Horton Cooley, W.I. Thomas, Robert E. Park, E.W. Burgess, Florian Znaniecki, Ellsworth Faris, James Mickel Williams ... William James, John Dewey and George Herbert Mead. None of

these scholars, in my judgement, has presented a systematic statement of the nature of human group life from the standpoint of symbolic interaction. Mead stands out among all of them in laying bare the fundamental premises of the approach, yet he did little to develop its methodological implications for sociological study. (Blumer, 1962, p. 179)

The year 1937 lies virtually in the middle of a four-year period which saw the publication of Mind, Self and Society, Movements of Thought in the the Nineteenth Century, and The Philosophy of the Act. It would represent the greatest naivete to suggest that thus the year 1937 represented the introduction of symbolic interactionism. We are all aware of the long development: from James, Baldwin and Cooley to Thomas, Faris, Dewey, Blumer and Young.... Nor is it the fact that Mead represents the fullest development of the orientation that makes so significant the posthumous publication of his works. Mead's ideas had been known for a very long time. He had taught University of Chicago students from 1893 to 1931. His notions were bruited about in classes and seminars wherever there were professors conducting them who had studied at the University of Chicago.... No the significance of the publication of Mead's books is that it ended what must be termed the long era of the "oral tradition", the era in which most of the germinating ideas had been passed about by word of mouth. (Kuhn, 1964, p. 61)

Mead has thus been acknowledged by most commentators on interactionism and symbolic interactionism as the main 'founding father' of that intellectual orientation (Deutscher, 1973, p.325; Mullins, 1973; Fisher and Strauss, 1978, p. 483). He is assumed to be provider of the general theoretic orientation which later became encapsulated in the symbolic interactionist approach propounded by Blumer. (Faris, 1945; Young and Freeman, 1966; Petras, 1966; Meltzer and Petras, 1970; Warshay, 1971; Ritzer, 1975a; Kando, 1977; Littlejohn, 1977; Lauer and Handel, 1977; Lindesmith, Strauss and Denzin, 1977)
The identification of Mead with the roots of symbolic interactionism (Huber 1973a, 1974; Schmitt, 1974; Stone et al., 1974) has led to him being given considerable prominence within the 'Chicago School'. His relationship with the Chicagoans and the assumption about his central role in the genesis of a symbolic interactionist perspective are analysed below.

Mead's direct involvement with the Department of Sociology at Chicago

The extent to which Mead was an important figure in the 'Chicago School' has, however, come under closer scrutiny recently, despite Fisher and Strauss's (1978) assertion of the fruitlessness of such analysis [1]. Mead's direct impact on the Chicagoans is not as clear cut as it once was assumed to be, either in terms of his pedagogic input nor the assimilation of his ideas.

Mead is usually assumed to have had a very important role in the development of Chicago sociology not least because of the direct teaching link he had with the Department of Sociology. This link, however, is not as strong as is often popularly supposed (Goddijn, 1972a; Mullins, 1973).

Mead taught a course in 'advanced social psychology' in the Department of Philosophy (until 1931) which was an available option for sociology students. Despite the taken-for-granted view that his course was dynamic and highly regarded (Mullins, 1973), it seems that Mead, although brilliant, was a difficult lecturer (Carter, 1972). His style was unengaging, he tended to 'think out loud' (Faris, 1967), rarely provided opportunities for questions (Carey, 1975) and was generally unavailable for informal discussion with students.

Furthermore, an analysis of class enrolments, suggests that relatively few sociology students took his course (Lewis and Smith, 1981). This has been disputed by Kuklick (1984) who calculated that '72.2% of the recipients of Ph.D.s from 1910 to 1924 had studied with Mead'. Further, she claimed that when Faris was appointed to the Department in 1919 he taught a social psychology course which was heavily reliant on Mead's views and acted as a surrogate for Mead. This appears to be unsupported by Carter's (1972) recollections, though. 'Cooley was their [the sociology faculty's] God - Faris quoted Cooley all the time'.

Apart from his formal teaching, Mead seems to have had little direct involvement with sociology staff or students. Unlike some faculty in other departments, Mead, surprisingly for someone supposedly so central, was not a member of the Society for Social Research. He appears to have addressed the Society on just one occasion. This was an address in 1929 which was attended by over fifty members. In the four years after Mead's death only one session was given over to discussing Mead's philosophy. This session was the occasion of an address by Morris from the philosophy department on the nature of the 'significant symbol'. It is also notable that Morris edited the posthumous publication of Mead's work, rather than any of the sociologists, on whom Mead was supposed to have had such an enormous impact. It is, perhaps, rather glib to suggest that Mead was so taken-for-granted that first hand exposure to his ideas were not necessary for the Chicagoans (Kuklick, 1984). Park and the other sociologists, along with Thurstone, Gosnell and Lasswell, whose ideas were also well known, all regularly addressed the Society for Social Research, of which they were members.

Mead's theoretical impact on the early Chicagoans

Mead is assumed to have had a direct impact on the theoretical developments in the Department of Sociology at Chicago during his lifetime (Faris, 1967). In the introduction to the 1964 edition of Mead's collected papers, Strauss (1964) noted that despite Mead's early influence on the philosophy department, the sociologists did not begin to notice him until the 1920s and even then Thomas and Park drew little directly from Mead. Mead was not even included in the readings in the Park-Burgess text of 1921 although he had published a number of papers by this time. The vast majority of students and staff in the sociology department at Chicago appeared not to utilise Mead's social psychological perspective directly during his lifetime. Lewis and Smith (1981) have analysed citations in a selection of theses, articles and books and shown that Mead was not frequently mentioned. Kuklick (1984) has disputed the relevance of this arguing that to attempt to assess Mead's impact by counting formal citations in theses, texts and articles is spurious because his ideas were so widespread that they were taken for granted. She cited Nels Anderson who apparently recalled that 'he did not seek personal exposure to Mead be-cause he was "getting Mead second hand enough for my needs"' (Kuklick, 1984, p. 1436). Nonetheless, the sample survey of doctoral theses at Chicago (Appendix 6) shows that there were hardly any sutained reference to Mead's ideas, twelve (29%) of the forty two theses examined in detail cited Mead but only four actually used Meadian concepts, and three of the four were submitted after 1940. Both Thomas and Cooley are cited far more frequently than Mead. Cooley is referred to in twenty of the sample (48%), thirteen (65%) of these were submitted before 1940. Thomas is cited in half the sample, two thirds of these prior to 1940.

Lewis and Smith (1981) argued that Mead had little direct influence, except on a small group of graduate students. And this influence only emerged after 1920, at a time when enrol-ments in Mead's classes were declining. This, they claimed, can only be attributed to the role played by Ellsworth Faris and later by Herbert Blumer, both of whom were somewhat at variance with the theoretical perspectives of the rest of the depart-ment.

Ellsworth Faris was in many ways distinct from the other

faculty members in being a social psychologist interested in personality and was a sharp critic of both the local projects and also of the instinct hypothesis of psychologists which (in one form or another) seemed to be retained by the Chicagoans around the 1920s (Small's interests had become Thomas's wishes). Faris was 'a little remote, a loner' (Cavan, 1972) and it was he who provided the basis for Blumer's development of social psychology which was originally out of the mainstream of the work in the department (Janowitz, 1980).

Mead as 'founding father' of symbolic interactionism

While Mead may be seen as somewhat peripheral to the activities of the 'Chicago School' of his day, he is nonethless usually seen as the central founding father for the symbolic interactionism that emerged in the later developments at Chicago and spread, or were developed elsewhere, such as at Iowa (Petras and Meltzer, 1973; Carabana and Espinosa, 1978). If this is the case then it suggests that there is a dual tradition at Chicago, an early Thomas-Park tradition and a later Mead-Blumer tradition. Fisher and Strauss (1979) have attempted to put the position of Mead into perspective [2] by suggesting that there was a dichotomous tradition at Chicago. On the one hand is the interactionism of Thomas and Park and, on the other, symbolic interactionism developed by Blumer and based on Mead.

> There would, then, seem to be at least two interactionist traditions, each grounded in a different intellectual history .... While some interactionists owe little or nothing to a Meadian perspective, the work of others is rooted in both Mead and what is nowadays called the Chicago-style perspective, which derives in fact, mainly from Thomas and Park. A younger generation, coming more lately to interactionism and in a period after the Chicago Department of Sociology had radically changed in character, seem to divide - some moving toward Meadian interactionism, others doing work in accordance with the spirit of Chicago-style sociology. Still others draw on both sources of interactionism. (Fisher and Strauss, 1978, p. 458).

Whether there was two traditions, as Fisher and Strauss contend, with some overlap so that the role of Mead has been taken to be intrinsic to both, while really only germane to the later development, needs to be examined. Crucial to any divergence in the sociological tradition at Chicago would be the role of Elsworth Faris. Strauss (1964), Kuklick (1984) and Faris, R.E.L. (1967), emphasised the importance of Ellsworth Faris on the emergence of Mead and suggest that during the 1940s Mead entered the mainstream of sociological thought at Chicago and elsewhere and became the social psychologist for sociologists.

There is some evidence that Faris offered an alternative to the pragmatic view of social psychology central to the department. For example the Society for Social Research devoted three sessions (25th February, 10th March and 27th April, 1927) to 'Problems in social psychology' at which Park and Faris presented their views. Park saw social psychology as a subject concerning the individual and the community. He asked what is the role in communication of 'the sympathetic participation of one person in the feeling of another?' An individual admits that another has claims on him or her when one places him or herself in the position of the other and finds it appeals to his or her feelings. Social psychologists are also interested in the natural history of the conventionalisation of appetites. Material relating to this may most profitably be gleaned from ethnology with a view to answering the main question of the relation of community to human nature.

Faris, on the other hand, argued that community needs to be considered from four standpoints: spatial grouping, associations, social movements and the Zeitgeist. On one side there are elements of the community, on the other the impulsive individual. Personality develops out of this interaction and communication is a process of this interaction. Personalities are classifiable into two broad classes, the modal and the extremes.

In his 'Of Psychological Elements' (1936), Faris demolished the lingering remnants of the instinct theory of social psychology, which L.L. Bernard (1924) had substantially weakened. Faris attacked notions such as 'interests' (Small) and 'wishes' (Thomas) as being vestiges of old and unsound motivational doctrines. The long running disagreement over these notions, he maintained, arose because it was impossible to agree on something that did not exist. He turned round the idea that society is the construct of individuals and argued that society produces personalities and these 'will be found, not in the individual self at all, but in the collective life of the people' (Faris, 1936, p. 167).

However, this did not constitute a break with the Thomas inspired tradition at Chicago. All it served to do was to clear away the archaic clutter of residual motivations from a theoretical orientation already well grounded in the development of the social self which was already prominent at Chicago through Cooley's work and particularly in evidence amongst the sociologists. Park had been instrumental in popularising Cooley's concept of 'looking glass self'. In reviewing the posthumous publication of Mind, Self and Society, Faris (1936a) confirmed the primacy of the social at Chicago by suggesting that the title belied the author's intention and argument and suggested that 'Society, Self and Mind' would have been more fitting.

It would seem unlikely, then, that two separate traditions with distinct roots and adopting different theoretical perspectives and methodologies developed at Chicago in the 1930s. There was, though, no uniformity of approach in the sense of a single practice devoted to a narrow theoretical base. The discussion in the previous chapter, however, indicates that Chicago developed a sociology in accord with the predominant view of the discipline in America. This sociology was at root nomothetic, falsificationist and directed to a cumulative growth of knowledge model. Interactionism was not at variance with this perspective but embedded in it.

The role of Mead in this development is paradoxical. He, and those sociologists like Faris and Blumer who regarded Mead as their theoretical mentor, were to some extent peripheral to the central sociological enterprise; yet Mead served as a focus for a sharpening up of the rather loose general theoretical perspective which pervaded (and indeed continued to pervade) Chicago sociology. Taking on board Mead more systematically, if not adopting his perspective entirely, engendered a more cutting analysis of certain aspects which had been inadequately analysed in the development of a sociological perspective. Examples of this are: Faris' critique of residual instincts; Wirth's and Blumer's analysis of the construction of meaning and the nature of the self; their combined critique of the 'naive' notion of scientific method expounded in the conference on the Polish Peasant.

So, I would suggest that Blumer's development of Mead was somewhat peripheral to the mainstream of Chicago sociology. It did not either constitute an alternative tradition distinct from the Thomas-Park heritage, nor did it engage, as has been shown in chapter five, with the prevailing approach to American sociology of which Chicago sociology was an integral part. Arguably, then, Mead did not have a major impact on Park and Thomas, and Faris used his ideas selectively in order to sharpen up some areas of sociological theorising at Chicago. Nonetheless, Blumer has extensively argued that Mead provided the underpinnings of what Blumer came to call symbolic interactionism. Although this was not a distinct theoretical strand at Chicago, it clearly became an important rallying position for some sociologists in the 1950s and 1960s. Thus Mead could be seen as having a direct theoretical impact on a branch of sociology that has its roots at Chicago. However, the assumed role of Mead in this Blumerian endeavour has also been questioned by critics who argue that the links made between Blumerian Chicago sociology and Meadian social psychology are extremely tenuous and constitute a complete misreading of Mead. Blumer is singled out as responsible for creating a myth which legitimates his own approach to symbolic interactionism by asserting the correctness of his own interpretation of Meadian constructs. In short, it has been argued that there are epistemological, theoretical and methodological divergences between Blumer and Mead and that the assumed role of Mead in the development of 'Chicago symbolic interactionism' is also misleading.

Differences between Mead and Blumer: the recent debate

Over the last twenty years a debate as to the Meadian underpinnings of (Blumerian) symbolic interactionism has simmered. The attribution of the genesis, of what Blumer came to label symbolic interactionism, to Mead conceals, it is argued, fundamental differences in Blumer's and Mead's approaches. Since Bales (1966) reply to Blumer (1966) concerning the nature of operationalisation which incidentally questioned Blumer's appropriation of Mead's perspective, several acrimonious exchanges have taken place between Blumer and sceptics. The problem with this kind of argument is that of a 'correct' exegetical analysis of the compared theorists (Cook, 1977). Thus, no attempt is made here to determine 'what Mead really said'. The debate will be outlined below and its significance and relevance to the examination of the work of the Chicagoans as a whole assessed.

Blumer is accused of differing from, or distorting Mead in a variety of ways. These may be grouped under the headings of epistemological incompatibility, theoretical divergence and methodological incompatibility. These, however, should not be seen as mutually exclusive.

Epistemological incompatibility

Lewis and Smith (1981) argued that pragmatism as a philosophy was not a unified approach and that Mead like Peirce was a realist while James and the other pragmatists were essentially nominalists. Blumer, and the Chicagoans, they argued, derived their pragmatism from James and Dewey and thus espoused a nominalist perspective. Thus, they argued, not only did Mead have far less contact with the Chicago staff and students than is commonly supposed, his epistemological orientation set him apart from his contemporaries and was even alien to the theoretical perspective he is supposed to have generated. Lincourt and Hare (1973) also recognise this distinction among pragmatists and associate Mead with a 'continuous tradition on selfhood' made up from Peirce, Royce and Wright which anticipate contemporary symbolic interactionism.

Bales (1966) ignored the nominalist-realist debate and simply accused Blumer of being a philosophical idealist, unlike Mead, who was a 'pragmatist and social behaviorist' [3]. McPhail and Rexroat (1979) similarly argued that Mead was a consistent pragmatist who rejected realism and idealism. For him, reality is presumed but science orders observed events through 'convergent responses which establish objective facts'. Like Lewis and Smith, they suggested Blumer derived his pragmatism from James and Dewey rather than Peirce and Mead, and tended to vacillate between idealism and realism. Sometimes he presented reality as depending upon how it is perceived, at other times he insists that reality 'talks back' and does not 'bend to our conceptions of it'. For Mead, objectivity is consensual, for Blumer, it is contingent upon a perceptual event. Thus Blumer's claimed pragmatist stance 'bears no resemblance to Mead's position'.

Blumer, in reply, has repeatedly asserted that Mead's ontological position is the same as his own, namely that there is a real world but that it does not have a basic intrinsic makeup but changes as humans reconstruct their perceptions of it. This is neither idealist nor realist.

Theoretical divergence

Bales (1966), Stewart (1975), Lewis (1976), and Stryker (1977) have all pointed to theoretical differences between Blumer's symbolic interactionism and Mead's social behaviourism. Such differences are to do with, first, the centrality of 'self'; second, the relationship of the 'I' and the 'Me'; and, third, the universality of significant symbols.

On the first point of difference Blumer emphasised the active moment of the self (Carabana and Espinosa, 1978) and this is regarded as at variance with Mead. Mead placed social interaction at the centre of analysis rather than mind, or self, or society and that starting with any one of these three elements as fundamental was a dead end because the other two could not be derived from it. Blumer ignored this warning and, according to Bales (1966) seemed to start with the self, and in this sense he was not a social behaviourist like Mead. For Mead, the self arises out of human interaction and, thus, is an 'interposed process between stimulus and response'. Blumer saw the self as fundamental and thus argued for ascertaining the meaning that objects have for the social actor. He was opposed to an external 'objective' view of actors and actions. Mead, Bales argued, adopted both perspectives. Indeed, one could hardly conceive that social interaction, out of which emerge mind, self and society, is merely what the participant defines it to be.

Blumer, however, maintained that Mead did see the self as central. For Mead, human action is action that is built up through interaction and that objects come into being only in relation to the self. That the self is formed through interaction, Blumer argued, is irrelevant to the assertion that the self is central.

On the second point of difference, the relationship between the 'I' and the 'Me', Bales (1966, p. 545) argued that whereas 'Mead distinguishes between the "I" (the process) and the "Me" (the object or structure) - both aspects of the self. Blumer prefers to emphasize the "I"; he says that the self is a process and that that those who say it is a structure are mistaken'. Stone and Farberman (1967, p. 410) agreed with Bales' interpretation of the "I" and the "Me".

> The "I" is transforming; the "Me" transformed. As Mead put it, "the me is a me which was an I at an earlier time," and not the other way around". As Louis Wirth used to emphasize: "In the beginning was the act!" Clearly, only as a result of action can we transform unformulated experience into formulated knowledge. We must socialize, formulate or universalize experience to maintain the human dialogue that is human life. In this way, the unique, relative and percipient "I" emerges as the universal, structured and communally organized "me".

Blumer, in response to Bales and, later, to Stone and Farberman, reasserted that Mead definitely saw the self as a process and not as a structure, that the 'I' and the 'Me' were not process and structure respectively.

> The "I" and the "Me" Bales has introduced into the discussion were regarded by Mead as aspects of an ongoing process - the "Me" setting the stage for the response of the "I", with the expression of the "I" calling in turn for control and direction by the "Me". To say that one (the "I") is process and the other (the "Me") is structure is nonsense; both were treated by Mead as aspects of action. Mead saw the "self" not as a combination of the "I" and the "Me" but as an interaction between them. (Blumer, 1966b, p. 547).

On the third point of theoretical difference, Stone and Farberman (1967, p. 409) argued that Blumer had not penetrated to the core of Mead's thought as he failed to present 'a firm grasp and explicated statement of the significant symbol as a universal - its meaning fundamentally established, transformed and re-established in an on-going conversation'. They pointed to the dichotomy which fundamentally divided Blumer and Bales. For Bales, people are beings who selectively apprehend and sustain a unique perspective of the universe. This was rejected by Blumer, in favour of a view which saw people as acting interactively to test apprehensions and attitudes.

> Now we presume that Mead's great contribution is the demonstration that this dilemma is false: the production of a

significant symbol everywhere and always is a particular
production which mobilizes shared perspectives by its very
universality. (Stone and Farberman, 1967, p. 410).

For some problems, they contended, the focus of attention is
the particular act; for others, it is the universal. The stance
of the observer is the universal stance, for this requires a
grasp of the world in terms of generalizations. Blumer, for the
most part, explicitly accepted this position, but often drifted
towards a 'subjective nominalism' similar to 'Cooley's sympathetic introspection'. Mead's critique of Cooley, they argued,
led him to assert that permanence and structure is anchored in
universal symbolism, that explanation is not effected by concentrating on process rather than structure but that the 'explanation of one cannot be accomplished without the explanation
of the other'.
    In replying to Stone and Farberman, Blumer (1967) denied the
dichotomisation which he is supposed to have set up to distinguish between himself and Bales. Blumer referred to the original article in which he outlined that group life consists of
fitting together participants' actions through a process of
adaption of developing acts so as to grasp each others perspectives. In so doing, participants use universal significant
symbols. These universals do not however imply common action
but are the basis for articulated action. Irrespective of any
explication of universal symbols, Blumerian symbolic interactionism assumes the universality of social symbols.

Methodological incompatibility

McPhail and Rexroat (1979) suggested that Mead is not the
forefather of Blumerian symbolic interactionism, nor is Blumer's theory and methodological perspective a contemporary
extension and manifestation of the 'Meadian tradition'. They
argued that there is a divergence in the methodological perspective of Mead and Blumer which rests upon divergent ontological assumptions. Mead's emphasis on systematic observation
and experimental investigation is quite different from Blumer's
naturalistic methodology, and Mead's theoretical ideas are not
facilitated by Blumer's naturalistic enquiry, nor does this
latter complement Mead's methodological perspective. Blumer's
emphasis on sensitizing concepts was contrary to Mead's more
definitive approach. Even if Mead regarded scientific laws as
provisional, they acted as benchmarks against which exceptions
can be noted and acknowledged as contradictions to be explained. All theories and beliefs are sources of hypotheses to
confront contradictions.
    Similarly, McPhail and Rexroat regarded Blumer's concentra-
tion on observation techniques as indicative of an attempt to

derive the essential nature of objects to the exclusion of the 'reconstruction of observed fact'. This concern of Blumer's, with phenomenological essences at the expense of empirical evidence, they argued was in contrast to Mead who essentially saw scientific enquiry as problem solving. They further argued that Mead treated hypotheses as tentative solutions grounded theoretically and subject to empirical test and that he thought experiments constituted the method of modern science, as essential procedures for generating knowledge. Mead emphasised exact definition of the problem and careful techniques of data gathering and execution of the experiment along with the obligation of experimenter to specify replication procedures. Whereas Blumer, they suggested, derived hypotheses inductively and atheoretically from empirical instances and rejected hypothesis testing because it seldom 'genuinely epitomizes the model or theory from which it is deduced'; neglects the search for negative cases; and is limited to the particular empirical circumstances of the test.

McPhail and Rexroat argued that Blumer is wrong to assume an implicit and separate methodology in Mead vis a vis the social sciences. For Mead, the psychological laboratory, as with the physical laboratory, serves to 'render specific, exact and hence formally universal the instruments and behavior of untechnical conduct'. Blumer's demand for investigation which is naturalistic, i.e. directed 'to the given empirical world in its natural ongoing character', as opposed to 'a simulation of such a world'; is seen by McPhail and Rexroat as opposed to Mead who 'chastizes critics of experimental research'.

Blumer's reply (1980) was to state that his views of social reality and of naturalistic research had been distorted and that through their efforts to reduce Mead's thought to a narrow scheme of how human social study should be examined, McPhail and Rexroat had misrepresented Mead's view of scientific method and of social behaviour. This misrepresentation, he suggested, is to

> justify and promote a special mode of scientific enquiry that relies on controlled experiments or on observation closely akin to to those made in controlled experiments. [Cottrell, L.S., (1971), O'Toole and Dubin (1968), and Smith, L. (1971)] But they also regard themselves as followers of George Herbert Mead. They are, thus, forced to interpret Mead in such a way as to support their methodological orientation. They seek to do this in two ways. First, they try to interpret Mead's thought on "scientific method" in such a way as to uphold their methodological preference. Second, they endeavor to depict Mead's "social behaviorism" in such a manner as to fit their experimental or near-experimental commitment. (Blumer, 1980, p. 415).

Blumer argued that his emphasis on sensitizing concepts was not at variance with Mead, who saw no definitive concepts in social science and thus saw no possibility of the rigorous testing carried on in physical science. The sensitizing concepts provided a way to grasp the empirical reality and a basis for discovering more analytic concepts. It was not, as suggested in chapter five, an attempt at uncovering phenomenological essences.

An examination of the recent debate in relation to the work of the Chicagoans.

The debate outlined above clearly raises severe doubts about the way Blumer interpreted Mead. The overall view of Blumer's critics is to suggest that Mead is not the intellectual progenitor of (Blumerian) symbolic interactionism. Blumer, of course, vehemently denies the divergence between his perspective and Mead's. Part of the problem may lie in the type of comparison made, any critique of the 'purity' of a line of thought is bound to show discrepancies as the tenets are developed or utilised in diverse fields. This also, of course, applies in reverse as the disciple may adopt an attitude of unassailable insight. Part of the problem in this kind of debate is the 'presentist' reconstruction of a philosophical tradition in terms of particular and selective views about current manifestations.

Rather than reconsider this exegetical debate in terms of the adequacy of Blumer's interpretation, the core features will be examined in terms of their relation to the work of the Chicagoans as a whole. Whatever the accuracy of Blumer's interpretation, it was the basis for a development of the general symbolic interactionist approach initially developed at Chicago. Even if some of Blumer's ideas were peripheral to the general thrust of Chicago sociology (Janowitz, 1980), he was still an integral part of the 'Chicago School' and developed his ideas within that general framework of research. It is all very well to retrospectively accuse Blumer of misrepresenting Mead, what is at issue, however, is, given a non-dichotomous view of the development of Chicago sociology, just how important was Mead's theoretical influence ?

The debate has generated three areas in which Mead is seen as being at variance with the 'Chicago approach'. Mead is regarded as having a fundamentally different epistemological basis. The Chicagoans are seen as ignoring or subverting Mead's central theories. The research practice of the Chicagoans is seen as substantially different from that which Mead advocated.

The epistemological difference between Mead and the Chicagoans

General philosophical labels which pertain to epistemological and/or ontological perspectives, such as realist, nominalist, behaviourist, and pragmatist are, if applied loosely, liable to obscure rather than reveal differences and may serve to provide an artificial way of distinguishing perspectives. Bales and McPhail and Rexroat claim that Blumer is not a true pragmatist as was Mead, certainly not in any consistent manner. Bales referred to Blumer as an idealist and McPhail and Rexroat accused Blumer of vacillating between realism and idealism. Similarly, Mead is regarded as a social behaviourist while Blumer is not. These ill-defined categories, however, do not aid an analysis of substantive differences.

Lewis and Smith clearly define and utilise what they regard as the central dichotomy of the historical period under study, namely nominalism versus realism, to illustrate the divergence between Blumer and Mead. Heritage (1981) has suggested that to evaluate Mead's contribution in terms of an ancient dichotomy which has been philosophically discredited is to ignore the relationships that cut across this arbitrary and ultimately illusory divide. Similarly, Denzin (1984) and Kuklick (1984) accuse Lewis and Smith of 'presentism'. Coser (1971), more pragmatically, maintained that there is no need to draw too sharp a distinction between the inputs of Mead and nominalist pragmatists, such as Cooley, to symbolic interactionism. Such differences that existed were of style not content.

Farberman, in his analysis of the 'complex paradigm' of the Chicago School of urban ecology, redrew the battle lines, suggesting that the Chicagoans were

> partially at odds with the newly emergent brand of American social psychology propounded by Mead and Cooley.... [who] insisted that the initial building blocks of self-identities were warm, intimate face-to-face relationships and with this contention, laid down an axiomatic challenge to the urban sociologists. (Farberman, 1979, p. 16).

The nominalist-realist dichotomy suggested by Lewis and Smith also founders on the presumption that the Chicagoans could be distinguished in terms of their allegiance to one perspective or the other, and the generalisation that they were inclined towards nominalism. Burgess (1944a) quite clearly espoused a realist approach, which on general epistemological grounds would not have divorced him from Mead. Yet the picture is complicated because Burgess did not directly reflect Meadian concerns, his work rarely referred to Mead or to Mead's widely known (at least post 1935) theoretical terms (such as significant other). Similarly, to simply suggest that Park was a nominalist and therefore epistemologically at variance with Mead is inadequate as a basis for denying Mead's impact. While the Chicagoans were aware of the nominalist-realist distinction they did not consider themselves bound to one or other perspective. For the Chicagoans, pragmatism in general provided the categories for an analysis of the social world and they did not tend to distinguish clearly the genesis of such categories, as Park noted in referring to the style of work adopted at Chicago in the 1920s.

> This approach became a logical scheme for a disinterested investigation of the origin and function of social institutions as they everywhere existed, and was in substance an application to society and social life of the pragmatic point of view which Dewey and Mead had already popularized in the department of philosophy. Implicit in this point of view ... is the conception of the relativity of the moral order and the functional character of social institutions generally. (Park, 1939, p.1)

Park, in discussing the nature of social psychology, referred to the notion of adopting the role of the other which he saw as a pragmatic notion derived from Cooley and Mead (Bulletin for Society for Social Research, December, 1927). To regard Park and the Chicagoans as nominalists and essentially non-Meadian necessitates dismissing Park's own assessment of the development of his and his contemporaries' work.

In his extensive analysis of interactionism, Rock (1979) did not distinguish various strands of pragmatic influence on symbolic interactionism. Rather he argued that symbolic interactionism has its epistemological roots in the German philosophical tradition, from Kant through to Simmel. American pragmatism assimilated much of this tradition and symbolic interactionism grew out of a fusion of the early interactionists (Park and Thomas) and the psychology of Dewey, Cooley and Mead.

The tendency in the debate on the role of Mead as progenitor of symbolic interaction to retrospectively reconstruct an epistemological divide between the Chicagoans and Mead can, it seems, be quite reasonably disputed as 'presentism' given the eclectic way that the Chicagoans absorbed and developed pragmatic categories. It is inadequate to deny Mead's importance on the basis of these retrospective divisions.

The theoretical divergence between Mead and the Chicagoans

It would seem, then, that Mead was a general influence on the Chicagoans, but merely one of a number of different and relatively undifferentiated influences. As a pragmatist he was part of the general fund of ideas the Chicagoans drew on. His particular theories were, however, selectively appropriated by the Chicagoans. Above, it was suggested that there is little evidence that Mead's theories were adopted or developed extensively by Chicago sociologists during his lifetime. Subsequent development of his social psychological theories by Blumer and other symbolic interactionists of the 'Chicago School' have been criticised for their misrepresentation. What is important in assessing Mead's theoretical impact is to assess the way the Chicagoans used ideas which were central to Mead's theories.

In terms of the important concept of 'self', for example, the development of the idea by the Chicagoans does not rely entirely on Mead's view. The self was an important concept for pragmatists (and formalists) in general.

> Pragmatism and formalism have both raised the self of the observer to a position of special prominence. Not only was the self a source and synthesis of all viable knowledge, it constituted the elemental unit of sociological analysis. It was thus simultaneously an intellectual subject and an intellectual object. The self is taken to be a social construct, emerging from language, which lends order to all interaction. It is man made conscious of himself as a social process, and its basis is a reflexive turning-back of mind on itself. Reflexivity is made possible by the social forms and it advances the evolution of those forms. It is in the self that a fundamental grammar or logic of the forms is allowed to unfold. All social phenomena stem from that logic so that a socially formed mind and the processes of society display a unity. (Rock, 1979, p. 102)

Rock (1979, p. 166), however, suggested that the central concept of 'self' as developed by Mead expressly excluded much of the complex, unobservable phenomena and processes that later symbolic interactionists included.

> In its original formulation, the interactionist model of the self offered a limited but useful description of the relations between mind, body and society. It was useful because it referred to observable and communal processes which shaped mind. It permitted a synthesis of the different phases of social and individual processes into one master scheme. The model was limited because it did not pretend to embrace private, subjective experience. It was not comprehensive or phenomenological. Rather it adhered to the behaviourist principles which Mead had advanced... In its phenomenologically revised form, the self has also lost much of the practical utility which it once enjoyed. It has become a somewhat mysterious process whose problematic

qualities are little appreciated by the revisionist interactionists. (Rock, 1979, p. 147)

This does not mean to say, however, that later symbolic
interactionists have disassociated themselves from the pragmatic, and notably Meadian, heritage in any definitive way. The
core of the symbolic interactionist perspective, Rock argued,
is as it was developed by Cooley, refined by Mead, expounded in
sociological terms by Faris, and developed by Blumer. Essentially, symbolic interactionism

> conceives the self to be the lens through which the world
> is refracted. It is the medium which realises the logic of
> social forms. Fundamentally, however, the self emerges from
> the forms. It is made possible only by the activities and
> responses of others acting in an organised manner. A self
> without others is inconceivable. Its doings and shapes must
> be understood as a special mirroring and incorporation of
> the social process in which it is embedded. Because lan-
> guage and society are taken to be historically and analy-
> tically prior to mind, interactionism does not proceed by
> deducing social phenomena from consciousness. Neither does
> it assume that individuals are 'given' and therefore un-
> problematic. It is the self which arises in sociation, not
> sociation from the self. (Rock, 1979, p. 146)

From this point of view, then, other areas of theoretical
difference between Mead and Blumer may be recast. There is, for
example, no problem of theoretical disjunction in relation to
the nature of objects, of the relation between structure and
process or of the construction of universals. The dispute about
the structural nature of the 'me' and its relation to the 'I',
Rock obfuscates through his analysis of Mead's constructs which
he sees as complex and deliberately problematic. However, the
mystification accorded the concept by later symbolic interactionists has not negated the essential Meadian interactive process between the 'I' the 'Me'.
What this suggests is, again, that the exegetical analysis
misses the point. Rather than deny Mead's importance on such
grounds, which entirely ignores the Chicagoans own view of the
extent to which they (individually) appropriated Mead's theories, a more salient critique of Mead's theoretical importance
can be offered in terms of the centrality of his theories
generally. Ideas subsequently attributed to Mead such as the
'self' were part of a general fund of pragmatic ideas upon
which the Chicagoans drew. Mead offered a particular development of the theory of the self which was part of the adaptive
process undertaken by the Chicago sociologists in recasting
philosophical constructs for purposes of sociological research.

This adaptation permits a relatively easy dismissal of the concurrence of Mead and, say, Blumer on purely exegetical grounds. What such a critique ignores, however, is the spirit of the adoption of Meadian constructs. They were, then, part of general development of pragmatic ideas and the real confusion has come about as the result of Blumer, and others, asserting their primacy, and critics pointing out the discrepancies in the interpretation of Mead. Essentially, there is little to suggest that Mead's theories were generic to the development of Chicago sociology. Rather, Mead, like Cooley, Dewey and James provided ideas the Chicagoans selectively drew upon and merged with other non-pragmatic theoretical perspectives.

The methodic difference between Meadian prescriptions and Chicago practice.

The third area of concern is that the sociological and psychological work produced by the Chicagoans, particularly that of the later generation symbolic interactionists, does not match the sort of work that Mead or a Meadian would prefer. Considerable sociological work has been done by symbolic interactionists assuming that their epistemology is rooted in Mead. Whether or not it is what Mead would have preferred seems to be a matter of conjecture, and the discussion is of importance only in terms of providing a legitimating 'founding father' for a particular methodic orientation. Rock suggested that the fusion of formalism and pragmatism that underpins symbolic interactionism and which sees the self as central, is essentially served by participant observation because it inserts the self of the sociologist into the research setting.

The Chicagoans, as illustrated in chapters three and four, were methodologically eclectic. Up to the 1950s there was no commitment to any particular method. The development of a tendency towards participant observation by some later 'Chicago' symbolic interactionists may be regarded as the result of Mead's influence irrespective of the apparent marginality of Mead (Platt 1982a). On the other hand, the development of participant observation may be seen as either a pragmatic development given that much of the research was in deviant areas, or as the result of a concern to study the social world of the subject group from the inside, irrespective of Mead's thesis about the nature of the self.

Whether Mead demanded 'experimental' type research or not is clearly a contentious point. In practice, the Chicagoans did not abandon the essential tenets of nomothetic research and it was only the later development of symbolic interactionism into a more radical analysis of the scientific method and the nature of social interaction ostensibly based on Mead, which has created confusion about the relationship between Mead's concerns and the work of Chicago sociologists.

Much of the development of this proto-phenomenologically informed perspective was effected away from Chicago, notably by Blumer himself, Goffman and the emergent ethnomethodologists at Berkeley. Indeed, the embryonic anti-positivist relativism evident in Blumer's later perspective which became mixed with Schutzian phenomenology in the emergence of ethnomethodology was quite at variance with the Chicago orientation.

Conclusion

One must ask why Mead is seen as so important, and thus accredited the role of principal theoretician of, at least the later, 'Chicago School', when indeed, most of the Chicagoans exhibited little of his overall theoretical position ?

Those who invoked Mead either used his social psychology as a convenient framework without incorporating the wider presuppositions of his position or simply slotted some of his ideas into a Park-Thomas framework (Fisher and Strauss, 1979). The essential elements of that framework owe little directly to Mead, rather they are the product of the German tradition fused with a general pragmatic critique of early American sociology. Thus Dewey, Cooley and James had as much impact on the development of the Chicago sociological approach as did Mead. For most of the Chicago interactionists, no single strand of pragmatism caught their attention or led to a factional division within the Department. Indeed, the analysis of doctoral dissertations shows that Mead's theories are referred to and used only rarely (certainly up to 1940) whereas Cooley is often cited as the provider of social psychological theories and categories. This is not at all surprising if Mead's theory of the self was, in many respects, anticipated by other pragmatists such as Wright, Peirce and Royce (Lincourt and Hare, 1973). Mead's emergence as a major figure (and Cooley's relative 'decline') [4] only occurs after 1935 (following the departure of Park) in the wake of the publication of Mind, Self and Society (Mead 1934).

The reason for the widespread view that Mead provided the philosophical underpinnings of the 'Chicago School' are two-fold. First, the uncritical acceptance of the symbolic interactionist reconstruction of their intellectual history which has come to dominate histories of the 'Chicago School' [5]. Second, the tendency for intellectual history to concentrate on the 'great man' approach and therefore need to identify 'founding fathers' (Lewis and Smith, 1981; Harvey, 1983, 1986) [6]. This contention is reflected, for example, in Bogdan and Taylor's (1975, p. 14) introductory text to phenomenological sociology.

Symbolic interactionism stems from the works of John Dewey, Charles Horton Cooley, Robert Park, W.I. Thomas and George Herbert Mead, among others. Although interactionists continue to differ among themselves as to the meaning and importance of various concepts related to symbolic interactionism, Mead's formulation in Mind, Self and Society represents the most comprehensive and least controversial presentation of the perspective to date.

The legitimacy of the Mead-Blumer line of symbolic interactionism is attested to by numerous writers. Yet, the establishment of this tradition appears to owe much to the role of Blumer, himself, in the development of Chicago sociology and the determined advocacy of his own brand of interactionism. In order to legitimate his perspective he argued forcefully that he provided the most faithful development of Meadian constructs and, by degrees, has been taken by historians of symbolic interactionism to imply that Mead encapsulated the core of Chicago sociology. Thus, for example, Meltzer et al. (1975, p. 55) state 'Blumer has elaborated the best known variety of interactionism - an approach we call the Chicago School. This approach continues the classical, Meadian tradition'.

Through the assertion of a 'pure' heritage derived from Mead, Blumer and subsequent historians (especially those sympathetic to Blumerian symbolic interactionism) have generated a taken-for-granted view of the centrality of Mead. Once established, this myth generates its own momentum and, in the case of the development of symbolic interactionism, a tradition of work evolves which takes this mythical element as 'true'.

In short, the attempt to legitimate symbolic interactionism has given Mead a role in the 'Chicago School' he did not have. This role is not merely the product of Blumer's own accentuation of Mead it is also a result of the other elements of the 'Chicago myths' spelled out above. Blumer cannot, however, be entirely vindicated from responsibility. He has suggested that his is the purest form of interactionism and implied that its progenitor was Mead and that Mead gave a new dimension to pragmatism. It has become assumed that Mead took up and developed 'Chicago pragmatism' and that it is through Mead that sociology incorporated pragmatic epistemological presuppositions (Rucker, 1969). Despite close links between Mead and Dewey, both academically and personally, Blumer has, it seems, attempted to set Mead apart.

Blumer relates that Mead would sometimes point with a bit of sarcasm to the profuseness of Dewey's output and to his attendent tendency to write sloppily and with lack of precision. (Coser, 1971, p. 355)

On the contrary, during their association at Chicago, 'Mead was content to play second fiddle to Dewey's resounding first violin' (Coser, 1971, p. 355). Indeed, there appears to be little support for any view that Mead was cynical of Dewey's philosophy. For example, in an address to the Society for Social Research at Chicago, Mead referred to Dewey in the following glowing terms.

> His statement of ends in terms of their means reached American life as no earlier philosophy had. In the pro-
> foundest sense John Dewey is the philosopher of America. (Minutes of the Society for Social Research, 7th November 1929)

Besides Blumer's insistence on the significance of Mead, there are other reasons for the prominent position attributed to Mead in the practice of sociology at Chicago. Mead is seen, by some, as the only major theoretician at the time in the social sphere and it became taken-for-granted that symbolic interactionism was rooted in Meadian social psychology. This interpretation gained credibility as structural functionalism became important because 'it is hardly a subject of dispute that modern role theory from Linton and Parsons to Newcomb and Merton has been enriched by freely borrowing from Mead' (Coser, 1975, p. 340). Functionalists have frequently taken 'bits and pieces from the interactionists' armamentarium' especially constructs like 'the significant other' or 'role taking' which eventually transformed Mead's dynamic development of the self into a static notion fitting the structural functionalist ideas of 'status', 'role' and 'reference groups' (Strauss, 1964, p. xii).

Finally, as the later generations were more affected by a narrowing of methodological focus and developed the sociology of deviance, so too there was a tendency towards adoption of Meadian constructs particularly in terms of adopting the role of the other. As suggested above, there was a shift away from the overt moralising of criminological studies towards an attitude of enquiry that demanded the deviant perspective be engaged sympathetically (Becker 1967).

Notes

[1] Most treatments of interactionism as a school of sociological thought or a general intellectual position designate George Herbert Mead as one of its founding fathers. The ambiguous character of such terms as 'Chicago School', 'interactionism' or 'symbolic interactionism', makes it difficult - and perhaps fruitless - to argue with such

claims. Mead's importance as an intellectual figure and his association with the theory of 'interaction' is well established. (Fisher and Strauss, 1979, p. 483)

[2] This follows an earlier comment by Strauss who noted that there were several streams of faculty influence in the Department, some of whom gave more prominence to Mead. For illustration Strauss offered an autobiographical note.

Before I went to Chicago as a graduate student in 1939, I had been directed to the writings of Dewey, Thomas and Park by Floyd House, who had been a student of Park in the early twenties. House never mentioned Mead, that I can recollect. But within a week of my arrival at Chicago, I was studying Mead's Mind, Self and Society, directed to it by Herbert Blumer. (Strauss, 1964, p. xi)

[3] This accusation of philosophic idealism has been extended to all symbolic interactionists (Carabana and Espinosa, 1978).

[4] Arguably Cooley's influence did not decline, but shifted. He had a considerable effect on the quantitative approach developed by Lazarsfeld and Stouffer in the 1940s and 1950s particularly in relation to Cooley's ideas on small groups and reference group behaviour (Goddijn, 1972a).

[5] This lack of critique of the reconstructed heritage is confounded by its being heavily dependent on the posthumous publications, especially Mind, Self and Society. As Faris (1936a) pointed out, for various technical reasons, Mead did not teach the fundamentals of his theory of social psychology after the early 1920s. Thus the notes which went to make up the text of Mind, Seld and Society were an inadequate basis for an exposition of Mead's theories. For an examination of Mead's contribution which does not rely on the posthumous publications, see Joas (1985).

[6] Lewis and Smith (1981) only develop their analysis up to 1935 and make no attempt to account for Mead's posthumous influence and why he has been accepted as founding father of symbolic interactionism given his marginality. They make no attempt to explain how Blumer adapted Mead and thereby influenced an important mid-century tradition within American sociology (Harvey, 1983). This tradition owes a lot to Blumer's work, ideas and institutional role. He developed the core concepts of the symbolic interactionist position from Mead, whether accurately or otherwise. Mead was seen as the progenitor of a tradition.

7 Chicago dominance

The myth

It is commonly assumed that the Department of Sociology at
Chicago was the foremost sociology department in the United
States until well into the 1930s. Chicago, it is argued, domin-
ated American sociology for about forty years.

> Established in 1892, the University of Chicago department
> of sociology dominated general sociology and sociological
> theory until the 1930s... Other departments, such as that
> of Columbia, initially chaired by Franklin Giddens [sic],
> were not able seriously to challenge Chicago's preeminence
> during this period. (Coser, 1976, p. 146)

It does seem that Chicago was a major force during the first
quarter of the twentieth century, as will be outlined below.
However, this central position inevitably came to an end as the
discipline of sociology became ever more popular and ever more
fragmented. The myth that surrounds Chicago in respect of its
dominant position is about its loss of prestige. After the mid-
1930s, the 'Chicago School' is presumed to have declined rapidly (Goddijn, 1972b; Mullins, 1973; Martindale, 1976; Coser,
1978; Tiryakian, 1979a). There are a number of views that have
emerged about the 'decline' of Chicago, which is usually dated
at around 1935, the time of the 'coup' in the American Sociological Society which 'excluded' Chicago candidates from executive posts.

One view is that Chicago had become autocratic and domineering and had developed an unjustified and unacceptable stranglehold on the discipline. This grip was epitomised in its control of the American Sociological Society and the American Journal of Sociology which was the Society's official organ. A corrolory of this, and to some extent the first two views, was that Chicago was holding back the development of sociology in the United States.

A second view is that Chicago represented an 'old fashioned' approach to sociology which is evidenced in its failure to keep in touch with developments. Such developments are linked to the 'scientizing' of sociology. Chicago is seen as representing a 'soft' ethnographic approach to sociology which was unable to fend off the sustained attacks of more rigorous scientific methods. Its indifference to quantitative methods is indicative of this anti-scientism. The state of sociological enquiry had moved on from exploratory study to scientific explanation, and Chicago, it is assumed, while having provided some interesting accounts of social situations, was unable to make the jump to scientific analysis.

A third, and similar view, suggests that Chicago failed to grasp the significance of, or was indifferent to, the development of new theoretical developments, particularly those which crytalised as structural functionalism.

A fourth, and related, view was that Chicago was parochial and continued to be preoccupied with local concerns at a time when sociology was moving on to national issues, and through this parochialism adopted an insular approach to the discipline.

A fifth view was that, by the mid 1930s, the research impetus at Chicago had gone. This is accounted for primarily in terms of the loss of Park . His retirement in the mid 1930s saw the end of the dynamic era of empirical research at Chicago, for it had been heavily dependent on Park's own charisma and drive (Matthews, 1977; Bulmer 1984).

Chicago's role in American sociology until 1930.

The Department of Sociology and Anthropology at the University of Chicago, established in 1892, was the first such department in the United States. It was closely followed by the Department of Sociology at Columbia. A number of other departments appeared before the first world war, but these tended to be 'one man departments' and the 'one real center of sociology in the United States' was Chicago (Lapiere, 1964).

In many ways the 'undoubted preeminence of Chicago' (Bulmer, 1984, p. 208) was as much a matter of dominance by default as it was a deliberate policy to establish a leading sociology department. Chicago had relatively little competition as a graduate sociology school, most other sociology departments that existed were undergraduate colleges which offered little encouragement for research. Yale had very little post-graduate work in sociology; and there was no sociology department at Harvard until 1930. By the early 1920s, Columbia was the only serious rival to Chicago but was about to start its own slide into a period of ineffectiveness that was to last into the 1930s. During that time Ogburn, disenchanted with research opportunities at Columbia, had moved to Chicago. McIver (1968) recalled that in 1929, the department was in a 'parlous state' amd the 'reputation of the department had fallen', it did 'not attract able students' and leadership in the discipline 'had passed to other institutions, notably the flourishing sociology department at the University of Chicago'.

The University of Chicago's influence on the discipline, then, was very much a function of its having established and sustained a small but well organised and dynamic department. Small, Vincent, Thomas, Burgess, Park and Faris, although con-tributing to the academic environment at Chicago in different ways, were all committed to empirical sociological enquiry. This involvement in, and promotion of, first hand engagement with the social world led to a recognition that Chicago University was 'the place to study sociology. We had no doubt about the superiority of the department.... This feeling was shared by the faculty' (Cavan, 1983, p. 408). The 'students of the 1920s knew that their approach was "something special" and that they were perceived to be leaders in social analysis' (Thomas, 1983a, p. 389). There was something novel in the sociological approach at Chicago in the period around 1910-15, 'it was sociological and opposed to the moralistic, social problem orientation of the past' (Park, 1939). A reputation had, then, been established by 1915 which identified Chicago as one of the most innovative and prestigous places for sociological research (Bartlett, 1972; Blumer, 1972). Chicago was at the forefront of 'the beginning of a new epoch in sociology' which justified 'the designation of the year 1915 as symbolic of the debut of sociology as an empirical science.' (Wirth, 1947, p. 274)

This feeling was backed up by the expanding output of publi-cations from the department, headed by the monumental and enduring Polish Peasant, (Thomas and Znaniecki, 1918) and the widely read compendium of articles on research in the urban environment entitled The City (Park & Burgess, 1925). Chicago sociologists produced some influential text books in those early years, notably Small and Vincent (1894), Thomas (1909), and Park and Burgess (1921). The development of the University of Chicago Press (supported by generous grants to aid publica-tion) allowed much of the work done by staff and students in the department to be published and thus to become widely available (Tiryakian, 1979a). The growth of the city of Chicago, which the Chicagoans used as a 'natural laboratory', gave the 'Chicago School' an impetus which led to its considerable impact (Goddijn, 1972b; Bulmer, 1984).

The impact of Chicago was felt in other respects, too. These owed much to Small's organisational skills (Faris, 1967). Small helped to found the American Sociological Society in 1905 and was president in 1912 and 1913. Other faculty members were prominent in the Society, indeed, Henderson was the 'only member of the early faculty of the department never to be elected president' (Faris, 1967, pp. 12-13). Chicago, along with Michigan, also tended to dominate the midwest regional association.

Small also founded the American Journal of Sociology in 1895, and edited it until 1925. It was the only sociology journal in the United States until the 1920s and was the official organ of the American Sociological Society for forty years. However, the journal, despite having a Chicago-based editorial board, published a wide variety of contributions, and was not simply the mouthpiece of the Chicagoans.

As more and more undergraduate departments started teaching sociology in the first decade of the twentieth century, so there was increasing pressure for a clear indication of what should be included in an introductory sociology course. The American Sociological Society undertook a survey of introductory teaching and, in 1911, appointed a committee of ten university professors to suggest appropriate subject matter for a fundamental course in sociology. The members of this committee were Jerome Dowd of Oaklahoma who was chairman, Charles Cooley (Michigan), James Dealey (Brown), Charles Ellwood (Missouri), H. P. Fairchild (Yale), Franklin Giddings, (Columbia), Edward Hayes (Illinois), Edward Ross (Wisconsin), Albion Small (Chicago) and Ulysses Weatherly (Indiana). The committee drew on the responses from the three hundred and ninety six institutions who had been surveyed. There was general agreement amongst the committee as to content. Broadly it consisted of three areas, first 'the socius', (the nature of 'man', hereditary and environmental factors in the constitution of the social self); second, 'social organization' (group formation, class and caste, institutional development and democracy); third, 'social process' (evolution, competition, the development of the family and the state). Although different emphases were placed on these three broad areas, none of the committee deviated greatly from the essential nature of the content. However, Giddings and Small argued strongly for a practical rather than simply theoretical orientation to sociology.

Perhaps I do not attach quite so much importance to the

selection and arrangement of topics for a fundamental
course in sociology as some of my fellow-teachers do. I
have come to think that the essential thing is to develop
painstaking habits of sociological study. Many topics are
available, but whatever ones be chosen the pupil must be
required to attempt certain simple exercises and complete
them in a workmanlike manner. (Giddings, 1911, pp. 628-629)

Small (1911, p. 635) endorsed this view and, along with Columbia, Chicago paved the way for a more practical and empirical
approach to sociology in undergraduate courses. This was reflected in the teaching of ex-Chicago graduates who moved into
the profession. The Department at Chicago produced many more
qualified graduate students in the period up to 1935 than any
other university [1]. These graduates became widely appointed
to posts in sociology departments, and an informal network was
created with the influential Society for Social Research at
Chicago as its focus. Barnhardt (1972), for example, recalled
that Small encouraged him to go into teaching and had recommended him to three different institutions who had contacted Small
for advice on appointments. These graduates served to promote,
not only empirical enquiry, but also the reputation of the
University of Chicago Department of Sociology (Anderson, 1983).
'I went to Vanderbilt and took courses in sociology under
Walter Reckless and Ernest Kreuger. They were ardent Chicago,
in fact they were called by the faculty at Vanderbilt, "mis-
sionaries from Chicago"' (Cottrell, 1972). This 'missionary'
zeal has passed into folklore.

It is my impression, one that I cannot document, that most
of the men who came out of the Chicago department during
this time were fairly passive disciples of the 'Chicago
School' - mostly trained in the ideas of Park, if not by
him, and that they went out to spread the good word with a
strong sense of mission. (Lapiere, 1964)

There appears to have been a strong feeling for Chicago amongst
its graduates, although this should not be overstated. Cavan
(1983) for example, says that she felt no obligation to Chicago, that she was neither aware of, nor engaged in, any 'missionary zeal' to promote Chicago sociology wherever she went.
After the 1920s her contacts with Chicago were sporadic and she
did not feel obliged to return to renew her 'Chicago spirit'.
    While I think it would be unwise to suggest that the Univer-
sity of Chicago controlled American sociology up to the 1930s,
it was certainly an extremely influential force. Other universities had the opportunities that Chicago had in terms of
research, developing teaching and producing graduate students,
involvement in the organisation of sociology, and so on. But it

was the University of Chicago alone who, at least during the 1920s and early 1930s, was a major force in all these fields. Chicago stood out amongst the group of leading universities and had a disproportionate influence upon the development of the social sciences in the United States and, indeed, probably ranked as the leading centre of sociology in the world up to 1930. This, arguably, was due to the research environment and 'collective intellectual endeavour' that was matched nowhere else (Bulmer, 1984).

The question, then, is what happened to this dominance ? Did Chicago fade out because it lost its organisational pre-eminence? Or, did it sit back on its laurels and allow sociology to develop a more scientific bent without it? Did it ignore developments in theory and methodology ? Did it fail to engage the substantive issues of the Depression Era ? Or, did its research environment dissipate ?

The 'coup' and the organisational decline of Chicago

In 1935 the American Sociological Society voted to establish its own independent journal, the American Sociological Review. Prior to 1936, the American Journal of Sociology printed by the University of Chicago Press and with an editorial board consisting of Chicago sociologists, had been the official organ of the society. This decision to establish the American Sociological Review is often seen as a move by sociologists in America to free themselves from the dominance of Chicago.

> The hegemony of the University of Chicago over the field stimulated resentment among sociology departments in other centers. This resentment tended to center on the fact that the official journal of the American Sociological Society, the American Journal of Sociology, had always been owned by the University of Chicago and edited by a member of its faculty. (Matthews, 1977, pp. 181-182)

Matthews described the so-called 'coup' as a 'palace revolt' which signalled that other centres 'were emerging strongly enough to challenge Chicago's long held role of leadership', notably Columbia and Harvard.

The attack on Chicago's organisational dominace is, however, viewed in a variety of ways. Martindale (1960), reflected the most popular view of the significance of the coup when he described it in terms of a methodological confrontation in which 'positivist' quantifiers confronted the conservative humanism of Chicago. Thus the coup is taken as symbolic of the final victory of 'hard' quantitative sociology over the 'soft' sociology epitomised by the 'Chicago School'. Faris (1967) saw the coup in terms of an activist group challenging the Chicago value neutral approach. Kuklick (1973) saw it as merely the tip of the iceberg that was forming around structural functionalism, from which Chicago supposedly absented itself or was excluded. The coup is therefore seen as indicative of the recognition of the anachronistic nature of Chicago sociology. Martindale (1976, p. 141), for example, taking his cue from Faris (1967), wrote

> Forces were in motion that would transform the character of American sociology. As its unquestioned center of dominance, the Chicago department had to either assume leadership in the transformation or be thrust aside. It did not possess the charismatic leader who could assume the role.... A new epoch was dawning [following the coup] that would see the point of gravity in sociology shift decisively toward quantitative methodology and toward theoretical collectivism. The capitals of sociological culture in America were relocating from the Midwest to the coasts.

Some commentators go further and argue that the period of Chicago dominance hindered the development of a scientific sociology and the coup symbolised the maturing of the discipline in the United States with the emergence of a more scientific approach, embodied in structural functionalism.

> The first dominant school of thought, the Chicago School, crystallized around World War I and continued until the early thirties. The second dominating school, the functionalists, succeeded the Chicago School in the forties and fifties after a period of interregnum. (Wiley, 1979)

Reflecting on the period up to 1935 Coser noted

> The end of the Chicago dominance may conveniently be dated as 1935, when the American Sociological Society, previously largely, but not wholly dominated by the Chicago department or Chicago-trained scholars, decided in a minor coup d'etat to establish its own journal, The American Sociological Review, thus severing the long time formal and informal links of the discipline to the Univeristy of Chicago department. Two years later the appearance of Talcott Parsons' The Structure of Social Action heralded the emergence of a theoretical orientation considerably at variance with that developed at the University of Chicago. This new orientation was largely to dominate American sociology for the next quarter of a century. Having gradually become institutionalized and largely professionalized in the years [up to 1935], having passed through a period of incubation

during the years of Chicago dominance, sociology could
embark on its mature career. (Coser, 1978, p. 318).

Thus, the suggestion is made that Chicago dominated and in so
doing somehow hindered the development of American sociology.
It is suggested that the empirical concerns of the Chicagoans,
combined with their pre-eminence within the discipline up to
1930, inhibited the development of a unifying 'paradigm' for
sociology (Tiryakian, 1979a). Such a 'paradigm', it is argued,
only became established in the 1940s following the pioneering
work of Parsons, and became concretised in the emerging structural functionalist perspective.

> While formulating his basic paradigm in the 1930s, [Par-
> sons] was a "voice in the wilderness" at a time when Ameri-
> can sociology was predominantly empirical, atheoretical and
> positivistic; Parsons' central notion of "action", synthe-
> sising elements from four major European figures, was, in a
> sense, not that much of a radical departure from the native
> American tradition of pragmatism and voluntarism found in
> Mead, Park, Thomas and Cooley. However, whereas these men
> had had illuminating insights, Parsons was to insist on a
> general theory of action. (Tiryakian, 1979a, p. 228)

Such a perspective entirely misconstrues prior sociological
endeavours, ignores the inter-disciplinary approaches adopted
at many universities and their encouragement through the Social
Science Research Council. It gives the impression that sociology only came theoretically of age in the post-Parsonian era,
and that structural functionalism alone, and for the first
time, conjoined theory and research. 'The collaboration of
Parsons the theorist with Sam Stouffer the empirical researcher, and the similar pairing of Merton with Lazarsfeld, seemed
ample proof that the new paradigm could integrate sociological
analysis and research' (Tiryakian, 1979a, p. 229).
A particularly insidious connotation of the above is that
only with the overthrow of the Chicago dominance of sociology
as epitomised in the coup within the American Sociological
Society, could a theoretical sociology emerge in America.

The nature of the coup

Lengermann (1979), in a re-examination of the coup, argued that
the coup was not about method or theory. Opposition to Chicago
was 'bound together, not by a theoretical viewpoint, but by an
organizational ideology of antielitism' (Lengermann, 1979, p.
194). Indeed, the main contention of the anti-Chicago group at
the time was the threat to career chances from the 'patronage'
of Chicago in a time of increasing pressure on jobs, due to the

depression [2]. Other sociology departments 'began to chafe under the dominance of the Chicago group... and definite steps were taken to increase leadership in the American Sociological Society from non-Chicago sociologists.' (Cavan, 1983, p. 418).

At the meeting which established the American Sociological Review, organisational changes in the American Sociological Society were also voted in and all but one Chicago supporter (Dorothy Thomas) failed to be elected to executive or committee posts. However, Lengermann argued that the meeting of itself did not constitute the 'rebellion' against Chicago, rather it was the cumulation of a five year sustained opposition to the Chicago base which began with Ogburn's election to the presidency of the society in 1928. This election, arguably, brought to a head the concern of the anti-Chicago group that Chicago had a too dominant role. The Bulletin of the Society for Social Research (February 1933) noted that seventy four members of the Society had been registered at the American Sociological Society's Annual Conference in Cincinnatti (December 1932).

The December 1935 issue of the Bulletin for the Society for Social Research announced the following members to give papers at the annual conference of the American Sociological Society that December: Nels Anderson, J.O. Babcock, Read Bain, E.W. Burgess, L.S. Cottrell, C.S. Hughes, C.S. Johnson, E.S. Johnson, H. Mowrer, R.E. Park, F.F. Stephan, W.W. Waller, H. Zorbaugh with E. Eubank, J. Dollard, L. Wirth as well as Park and Bain presiding at sectional meetings. In addition R. Faris, J.H. Kolb, S. Stouffer, C.S. Johnson, E.B. Reuter, F.M. Thrasher, and C.C. Zimmerman were to act as discussants.

The Chicagoans were aware of the undercurrents of dissatisfaction with the national association, but did not ascribe it to their own pre-eminence. For example, in the discussion of the American Sociological Society Conference of 1932

> most of the reporters paid more attention to the undercurrents felt in the national society than to the papers read at the formal meetings. Many seemed to feel that there were more or less serious tensions in the organisation which were giving rise to preliminary millings about which may follow through some sort of social movement which in turn may eventuate in new institutional structures within or without the mother structure. (Minutes of the Society for Social Research, 9th January 1933)

The tension that followed Ogburn's election was not a function of Chicago providing the President of the Society. Chicago had, of course, provided the president of the society before, but the rebels had not been so organised before nor had the Chicago base been so firm. Ogburn was not only a Chicagoan, but was also a quantifier and was supported by other quantifiers.

The result was a gradual build up of combatants that had Chicago and the quantifiers on one side and, on the other, a diffuse group with no obvious identifiable theoretical or methodological or institutional links whom Lengermann described as 'association men', supported by a wider (and in the last resort crucial) group whose links were geographic (from the East and Southwest). This group were 'agitated and divided by theoretical issues' and acted spontaneously in their discontent with Chicago's influence. The two sides were acting politically and over five years each side came to the ascendency in turn. It was only when the opponents managed to manoeuvre into a position when they could motivate the large band of general sympathisers that they effected the 'defeat' of the Chicago group.

An examination of the two camps reinforces the political rather than theoretic or methodological nature of the division. On the Chicago side were the Chicago faculty, W.I. Thomas, a group of Chicago graduate students from the 1930s and some earlier graduates and members of the Midwestern and Southern regional associations. In addition Stuart Rice, S. A. Chapin, Dorothy Thomas, Kimball Young and George Lundberg among other quantifiers strongly supported Chicago.

The other side was effectively lead by L.L. Bernard, a graduate of Chicago in 1910 who had been a professorial lecturer for two quarters at Chicago in 1927 but failed to get a full time post at the University. He was supported by J. Davis of Yale, W.P. Meroney of Baylor (M. A. Chicago, 1922), Newell Sims of Oberlin and Harold Phelps of Pittsburgh. These were the collaborating group that organized the opposition in an overt and direct way.

They were in turn supported more or less strongly by C. North, (Chicago doctorate, 1908), M.C. Elmer (a Chicago doctorate, 1914), Earle Eubank (Chicago doctorate, 1915), W.C. Smith (Chicago doctorate, 1920), Floyd House (Chicago doctorate, 1924 and assistant professor at Chicago in 1925 and 1926), Howard P. Becker (a Chicago doctorate, 1930), Willard Waller (MA, Chicago, 1925, and author of a reply to Lundberg supporting Blumer's position in the first issue of the American Sociological Review), O.D. Duncan (a quantifier who later obtained a doctorate from Chicago, 1949, and was appointed an assistant professor in 1950), Read Bain, M. Parmelee, F.H. Hankins, J. Bossard, M. Davie, C. Dittmer, S. Kingsbury, J. Lord, H. Miller, J.J. Rhyne, E.A. Ross, M.M. Willey, and J.M. Williams. In addition the membership of the Eastern, Southwestern and Ohio regional societies supported the anti-Chicago group.

This oppositional group, then, included a number of ex-Chicagoans as well as current members of the Society for Social Research (see Appendix 3). The division was not, therefore, simply the Chicago network versus the non-Chicagoans. It seems likely that the members of the anti-Chicago group were motivated by a number of different things, chief amongst them being the 'geographic factor' and the 'quantitative factor'.

In the event each side legitimated their position, in one way or another, by suggesting that they, rather than the opposition, adopted a scientific attitude. Those who supported the Chicagoans adopted two different approaches. The quantifiers argued that operationalisation and/or measurement were central to a scientific sociology, while the Chicagoans themselves, in the main, espoused a value free scientism. Bernard, on the other hand, argued that his opponents were a 'group of men who are dominated by a viewpoint that is almost wholly unscientific' (Quoted in Lengermann, 1979, p. 190, footnote 9).

In view of the taken-for-granted views about Chicago's lack of involvement in quantitative social research (chapter four) it is ironic that a major reason for its defeat in 1935 was its alignment with the quantifiers in the American Sociological Society.

The significance of the coup

The coup, then, was essentially political. Did it, however, have any other significance than an overdue rearrangement of administrative responsibilites within the discipline ? Was it symbolic of Chicago's failure to grasp the new developments within the discipline ? To the contrary, Park (1936), reflecting on the coup, saw sociology as a rather narrow endeavour. For him, Chicago, rather than inhibiting the development of the discipline, was the focus through which such a broadening could be effected. He recognised that the University of Chicago had 'been put on the spot by the recent attacks upon it and is more or less forced to make itself the protagonist of academic freedom'. This, Park argued, it could do in a variety of ways, some already initiated. Principally, it should 'not use the academic rostrum for the purpose of making political speeches but to use the freedom and detachment which University life offers to investigate the problems that agitate the public'. In which respect, he was heartened by the lead given by Burgess in his 'presidential address in which he raised and sought to answer the question "What contribution can sociology make to social planning ?" '

Park also approved of the broadening of the compass of the Institutes of the Society for Social Research and urged that the American Journal of Sociology (which he saw as needing to attract a new readership) adopt a broader approach in view of an increasingly sophisticated public. The time, he argued, was ripe for a review of fundamental points of view and a reorganisation of research on a broader front. 'The questions that are agitating the public now are fundamentally political. I am convinced that the issues raised can be studied objectively and

186

that we may lift the whole level of sociological thinking by attempting to define and investigate these problems rather than merely discuss them.'

Others, however, see the loss of official recognition for the American Journal of Sociology as the beginning of the end of the 'Chicago School'. It is regarded as the point at which Chicago sociology went into decline. (Odum 1951; Madge, 1963; Faris, 1967; Goddijn, 1972b; Bernard, 1973; Kuklick, 1973; Martindale, 1976; Coser, 1976, 1978; de Bernart, 1982). Matthews (1977, p. 179), for example, argued that after 1935, the Chicago department's ascendancy rapidly waned. This was due to forces outside Chicago, notably

> an increasing concern with the scientific status of the field, reflected in a preoccupation with methodology; the rise of other sociology departments as centers of research and graduate instruction; the absorption of major European sociological theories; and changing concepts of the proper role of the sociologist in relation to the society he studied.

That Chicago was unable to cope with these changes, Matthews attributes primarily to Park's influence and legacy. This legacy was one which was incompatible with the new direction in which American sociology was going.

Chicago's neglect of methodological and theoretical developments

Matthews claimed that the

> analysis of complex situations in terms of the subjective perceptions of actors pushed Park and the 'Chicago school' away from statistics. More intensely as he grew older and the demand for statistics grew, Park came to despise it as 'parlour magic'.... This aversion to statistics, however, meant that as sociological research became more quantitative in the late twenties, the development isolated Park himself as an exotic. (Matthews, 1977, p. 179-180).

This isolation of Park, Matthews sees as also an isolation of Chicago, given Park's enormous charasmatic dominance over the Chicagoans.

However, methodology was becoming more self conscious at Chicago in the 1930s. This was in conjunction with a changing appreciation of the notion of objective science. Explanation of an external reality via classification procedures derived from direct but unverifiable and unsystematic observation was no longer deemed adequate. Instead, the twin gods of validity and reliabilty were being invoked.

The Chicagoans were not of an accord with Park's view. As discussed in chapter four, the Chicagoans were fully involved in methodological innovation up to the 1950s. Besides the work of the faculty, a cursory glance at the Ph.D. theses produced between 1930 and 1950 shows a heavy concern with correlation and prediction studies and with attempts to isolate causal factors, (Appendix 5). A considerable amount of effort was directed towards testing prediction instruments and measuring devices, as epitomised in Reiss (1950) 'The Accuracy, Efficiency, and Validity of a Prediction Instrument' and Star (1950) 'Interracial Tension in Two Areas of Chicago: An Exploratory Approach to the Measurement of Interracial Tension'. In this respect the Chicagoans were responding fully to the initiatives coming from the Committee on University Social Science Research Organizations in 1929, 1936 and 1944. [3]

While Chicago tended not to have the acknowledged personnel in the rapidly expanding quantitative field in the post war period, it was not slow in importing the required expertise and adopting the new techniques.

The rise of other major centres, notably Harvard and Columbia, [4] Matthews argued, was the result of the adoption of either a methodic or theoretic orientation which was alien to the Park inspired 'Chicago School'. Columbia developed a 'highly rationalized, efficient and large scale organization of research' which lacked 'personal inspiration' and was 'easily reproducible and multiplied'. This contrasted sharply with the individualistic research at Chicago which relied heavily on the 'inspiration of a great teacher and the personal flair of the researcher'. Harvard, whose prominence owed much to Parsons' system theories, drew on the European theory at the expense of the traditional American pragmatists. While Park had been aware of these 'great continental masters', their ideas never penetrated 'beyond the horizon of Park's intellectual spectrum' [5]. What is more, Matthews (1977, p. 179) argues that

> Without Thomas or Park to provide a dominant personal force and inspiration, the deficiencies of Chicago's theories and methods became more apparent. [6]

As we have seen, in chapter five, the Chicagaoans were very much involved in theoretical developments. Through the work of Blumer and Wirth, in particular, Chicago was integrally involved in the assimilation of European perspectives. Blumer had spent a sabbatical year in France on a Social Science Research Council Fellowship in 1932 with the aim of discovering the theoretical perspectives dominant in that country and Wirth was very much influenced by Weber and the German sociology of knowledge approach. Both Blumer and Wirth were very well versed in European sociology (Ogburn, 1930). Blumer and Wirth provided the basis for what could have amounted to alternatives to the prevailing functionalist-interactionist approach. [7] That the department lost their services around 1950 left a gap which was not easily or quickly filled.

Although Park might not have been inclined towards co-operative research, this was not reflected by the Chicagoans at large. Among its recommendations, the Ogg Report (1928) proposed that research be more effectively organised, that it should follow the pattern of broad social science research as evident at Chicago, Columbia and North Carolina. Several departments at Chicago were involved in interdepartmental organizations, including the social sciences through the Local Community Research Committee. Park, as was suggested in chapter three, tended to be somewhat remote from the Committee. Burgess, and later Ogburn and Wirth, however, were very much involved with the Local Community Research Committee, the Social Science Research Committee that succeeded it, and the Social Science Research Council, of which Burgess was Chairman from 1945 to 1946.

Matthews' account of the decline of the 'Chicago School', then, is integrally related to the surpassing of the ideas of Park. However, the Chicagoans were, as has been examined above, far from constrained by Park's ideas. For example, in his journal Ogburn recalled

> I was glad to speak [at the dedication of the Robert E. Park Hall at Fiske University] for five minutes in tribute to my former colleague at the University of Chicago, Robert Park... He had great influence, distinguished students who did excellent research, and a considerable following.... All the other members of the Department of Sociology were students and followers of Park except Faris. Two or three times in these early months [of 1927] we began conversations, but they never went well. I don't know why. I think I got the idea rightly or wrongly that [Park] was trying to tell me what was what, and I did not recognize anything new in what he said. I thought also perhaps wrongly that he would like to have had me one of his followers.... I am sure I am too sensitive about being anyone's follower, especially if that person in any way tries to dominate me. I usually don't mind an egotist or how much he displays his egotism, so long as it is not accompanied by a love of power, especially a power to be exercised over me. (Ogburn journal, 4th & 5th April 1955)

Park influenced a lot of research at Chicago in the 1920s, but to restrict the notion of the 'Chicago School' to this limited sphere of operations is to exclude a considerable amount of the work undertaken in the Department of Sociology at Chicago. The Chicagoans did not stand still but, as has been shown, engaged widely in the debates and the activities which Matthews indicated transcended their traditional approach.

That the Chicagoans had moved ahead of Park's rather out of date conception is illustrated by the special meeting of the University of Chicago Social Science Research Committee on Friday and Saturday, the 1st and 2nd of December 1939, to commemorate the first decade of the Social Science Research Building. A large number of invited social researchers from the United States and Canada attended this prestigious occasion. The Friday morning session was addressed by C.E. Merriam on 'Urbanism' and H. Bruere on 'The Social Sciences in the Service of Society'. The Saturday morning session, chaired by L.J. Henderson of Harvard was, on a survey of research and was addressed by Ogburn on 'Social Trends' and by Thurstone on 'Factor Analysis as a Scientific Method'. The latter was discussed by W. Line of Toronto University and E.L. Thorndike of Columbia. The luncheon speaker was Beardsley Ruml (of the Social Science Research Council) who commented on the prospects for social science research. The afternoons of both days were given over to round table sessions on 'generalization in the social sciences', 'integration of the social sciences', 'quantification' and 'social science and social action'.

Those very features Matthews had indicated were overtaking Park, were, then, assimilated by the Chicagoans. If the 'Chicago School' suffered a decline, it has to be explained in terms other than the loss of Park and the failure to keep up to date methodologically and theoretically.

The introspection of the 'Chicago School'

Chapters three and four have suggested that, methodologically, the Chicagoans were eclectic and involved in the development of both quantitative and qualitative techniques, and that this involvement continued into the 1950s (and beyond). Similarly, the Chicagoans were extensively involved in theoretical developments, going far beyond urban sociology, as we saw in chapter five. In line with changes in the discipline, the Chicagoans tended less towards holistic theorising and more towards sustained analysis of specific areas of study. General concepts, however, such as 'social disorganisation' and 'definition of the situation' remained central to American sociology throughout the first half of the century.

Nonetheless, the decline of the 'Chicago School' is sometimes framed in terms of Chicago's parochialism. Chicago is seen as losing touch, through its introspective attitude which was dominated by complacency and conservatism. They could not let go of their study of Chicago and tended to ignore more substantive areas of research, and were indifferent to academic and organisational developments in the discipline outside Chicago.

The Chicagoans, I would suggest, were not insular. They were very much a part of sociology on a national level through their involvement in formal organisations notably the American Sociological Society and the Social Science Research Council. In addition, the American Journal of Sociology remained a major sociological journal and continued to be edited and published at Chicago. The Summer Institutes of the Society for Social Research continued to develop a broader perspective. The Society had constantly appealed for such broadening.

> The Summer institute has become one of the most interesting and valuable events of the year for sociologists and students of sociology at the University of Chicago and neighboring schools. Its purpose is to serve as a clearing house for current research projects. Here students and faculty members bring their hypotheses, data, and conclusions and submit them to the shafts of friendly criticism from some 75 or 100 fellow research workers.... Moreover, if any members, especially at schools other than the University of Chicago, know of fellow instructors or graduate students whose research could profitably be brought before the Institute, a prompt note about it would be appreciated.
> The plan this year is to have a still larger number of research reports from other graduate departments than in the past. Increased contact with points of view in other universities and with points of view in departments closely allied with Sociology at the University of Chicago should be stimulating. (Bulletin of the Society for Social Research, June 1929, p. 1)

This expansionist attitude was repeated in 1930. 'Reports are not limited to members, however. If members know of others who are doing research work falling within the scope of the institute, a word about it will be appreciated' and went further in 1931 with the Institute being the most ambitious to date with the three Mid-West universities co-operating with a central theme of regionalism. In November 1932 the Bulletin carried an article on page 1 which noted that

> Your officers and executive committee are in agreement that these tendencies [of growth] should be, or are, in the direction of greater inclusiveness of membership and of participation. The Society desires both persons who are engaged in research among all of the social sciences (and not in sociology merely); and who are members of institu-

tions throughout the north central region (and not only at the University of Chicago).... Information concerning interesting research undertakings in other social fields and in other institutions which might profitably be brought to the attention of members is therefore solicited.

This broadening of interest and appeal is reflected in the doubling of the number of non-sociology staff at the university who addressed the society over the period 1924 to 1935 and the increase from six to thirty one per cent in talks on philosophy and other social sciences over the same period, (see Appendix 3).

The Society for Social Research had applied for membership of the American Sociological Society as a regional chapter in 1934 and, even after the coup, continued with this affiliation. In 1937, H.A Phelps, Secretary of the American Sociological Society wrote to Bernhard Hormann, Secretary of the Society for Social Research at Chicago to ask for advice on, and consent to, the formation of a Conference of Secretaries of regional societies, (Phelps, 1937).

Besides the formal involvements of the Chicagoans the informal network of relationships with graduate students working in the discipline, and communications with other academics on issues ranging from tenure recommendations to academic discussion all continued uninterrupted.

The Chicagoans had fairly close academic links with other major sociology departments, through both visiting lectureships and personal contact and correspondence. During the thirties, for example, Burgess taught at Columbia and Park at Harvard. Visiting lecturers at Chicago included Talcott Parsons (see Appendix 1) and Wirth communicated extensively with Parsons, particularly in relation to Parsons' The Structure of Social Action which Wirth reviewed. Parsons also sent Wirth a preview of his address to the American Sociological Society of 1937 entitled 'The Role of Ideas in Social Action' (Parsons 1937a). Wirth also had a long standing friendship with Robert Lynd, who would have liked Wirth to join him at Columbia (Lynd, 1941b), and with Howard Odum of North Carolina. Wirth was also on first name terms with Robert Merton and Paul Lazarsfeld and was instrumental in the invitation extended to the latter to teach at Chicago in 1949.

The Chicagoans were also very much involved in Government sponsored research, notably Works Program Administration (WPA) and Federal Employment Relief Agency (FERA) projects. Blumer, for example, worked on narcoticism and Sutherland worked on probation and parole as well as studying men living in Chicago shelters in conjunction with H.J. Locke. Hauser was granted two years leave of absence (1934-5) to work on FERA projects and Ogburn was heavily involved in government sponsored research throughout the thirties. Such activities prompted the following comment in the Bulletin of the Society for Social Research (December 1934, p. 3)

DEMAND FOR SOCIOLOGISTS
It appears that it is a good rule, if a sociologist is unaccounted for in these days of the New Deal, to look for him either in Washington or somewhere on the staff of the F.E.R.A. Conservatively estimated, about 10% of the Society members are occupied in this manner. The following are in Washington: P.M. Hauser, C.S. Newcomb, E.J. Webster, S.A. Stouffer, F.F. Stephan, J.O. Babcock, E.D. Tetrau, H.G. Woolbert.

Park shied away from political doctrine (Blumer, 1972) and his continuing detachment from this new perspective on the relationship between the sociologist and society is clearly reflected by his letter to Wirth (Park, 1941). In it Park referred to a petition he had been asked to sign. He wrote that he was usually 'allergic to pressure groups' but in this case supported 'the President and the policy of the Government in this crisis'. He was 'in favor of militarism' but was 'not interested in the defeat of Germany, nor the destruction of the Nazi regime, in order to preserve the English Empire, much less to preserve the existing regime in Russia. I am interested, however, insofar as such a defeat will discourage international crime and aid in the creation or restoration of international order'.

The academic climate of the thirties was unfriendly to Park's determinedly detached, apolitical approach to research. The number of sociologists working in public agencies increased, and many came to consider their role as that of manipulative elite, consultants to a powerful state rather than an active, rational public. As they became involved in the practical problems of the depression era and the challenge of Fascism from abroad, an open committment to social engineering and political involvement replaced the Parkian image of the concerned scholar as detached observer and midwife to attitude change. (Matthews, 1977, p. 183)

While Park may have been disinclined to breach his apoliticism, this was not the case with the other members of the department. Wirth was concerned with the political implications of sociological enquiry and specifically the defeat of Nazism (Wirth, 1941); and Ogburn too, considered the sociologist's role to be more than the detached observer (Ogburn, 1942). In a scathing attack on popular folk lore, customs and norms, presented as a retrospective on the peculiarities of mid-twentieth century Americans, Ogburn abandoned the 'objective reporting of attitude' for a thinly disguised ridicule of popular ignorance. For example, he noted that

> The adults sometimes had a childish faith in experts. The opinions of a Negro boxing champion named Joe Louis were eagerly sought on political matters, especially as to whom to vote for in a presidential election. The connection between the strength that could deliver a knockout blow to an opponent's chin and wisdom in political matters seems not to have been questioned. (Ogburn, undated, pp. 2-3)

Similarly, writing around 1952 on McCarthyism, Ogburn again directed attention against the folly of popular misconceptions and their dangers, in a manner that reflected the new role of the sociologist.

> Granting the need of stamping out communism, it hardly seems necessary to turn our political institutions upside down in order to do it....
> However, as a slogan [communism] has very broad appeal to a people whose warlike patterns are activated and who want to fight an enemy, at home if not abroad. The leader of such an emotional drive may well become a hero to many who respond with extreme devotion.
> This extreme devotion helps to explain why followers are not alienated by McCarthy's gross behavior. (Ogburn, 1952, p. 1-8)

Throughout his career, Ogburn had been concerned with major social and political issues, from his early research for the 'President's Mediation Commission' on the strike in the lumber-jack industry (Ogburn, 1917), through his involvement as Director of Research on the Presidents' Research Committee on Social Trends (1933), and his subsequent social trends research which was directed towards the problems of the depression era and war years. Indeed, his 'detached' enquiries and observations on the second world war and the cold war with Russia that followed resulted in him being labelled alternately 'pro-Nazi' and 'pro-Soviet', the latter during the McCarthy era. Burgess, too, had been involved with national policy initiatives through his work on the Wickersham Committee and he was chairman of the Family and Parent Education sub-committee of the White House Conference, (Burgess, 1934).

However, during the 1920s, such involvements were individual endeavours and 'the thrust of concern was to get out and study the world, not get involved in these controversial issues of public policy' (Blumer, 1972, section 2, p. 7). It was during the 'New Deal' that things began to change, though, and when Ogburn edited 'American Society in Wartime' (1943) the majority of the Chicago faculty contributed, including Faris and Park who were, at that time, emeritus professors.

The substantive research interests of the Chicagoans were, therefore, rather broader than the myth would suggest. The study of the city of Chicago was at its height in the 1920s, although, of course, even then the Chicagoans did not spend all their research time in this way. In many respects, the study of the city of Chicago was pragmatic. The rapidly developing city was a superb and convenient microcosm of social life and change in America and funding for its study was available for researchers. This, of itself, did not make the Chicagoans parochial and insular, for, as we have seen, the sociologists were encouraged to adopt a 'big picture' approach to sociological enquiry, even when it was of a small area or aspect of the city of Chicago. Furthermore, as we have also seen, many of the staff had commitments beyond the narrow confines of the University, notably through government sponsored research. A stubborn parochialism was, then, not the cause of Chicago's 'decline' in the 1940s.

The loss of research ethos

There is, arguably, another key to all this. Chicago's own somewaht surprising dominance earlier in the century, given the relatively small size of the department, and its apparent loss of prestige in the 1940s and 1950s could be explained in terms of the dissipation of its research environment. The secret of Chicago's success was possibly that

> The dense, highly integrated, local network of teachers and graduate students centered around common problems, which was characteristic of Chicago sociology in the 1920s, had few parallels at the time or since. (Bulmer, 1984, p. 1)

Chicago sociology flourished in a research environment stimulated by an inter-disciplinary approach to the social world. In effect, the dynamism of the research collectivity, at a time in which sociology was emerging from its infancy, was central to the impact that Chicago made on the discipline. Park's influence on the research ethos has been emphasised (Faris, 1967; Matthews, 1977; Raushenbush, 1979; Bulmer, 1984) and it seems that for a decade or so he was a crucial motivator of graduate students. The research he encouraged was frequently directed to the city of Chicago, following the earlier suggestion of Small and Thomas. It was not, however, in any other sense a programmatic research policy.

Matthews (1977) has suggested that theoetical development at Chicago was somewhat limited and that with Park's going and the end of a period of intense and primarily empirical research, the theoretical weaknesses of Chicago sociology began to appear. For Bulmer (1984, p. 203), the going of Park did not expose theoretical weaknesses but was important in the dissipation of the research ethos.

> With his departure, the department began to falter, lacking the stimulus derived from the intellectual integration he provided. No one else could supply the compelling overview, the insistent movement between the particular and the general, the curious and penetrating questioning, the devotion to students, which he did.

Blumer and Hughes see Park's departure, and the loss of research ethos that followed it, in a more practical light. They suggested that Park worked hard to developed students in the 1920s although some of them were not particularly bright. 'He took these people and he brought out of them whatever he could find there.' (Hughes, 1980, p. 267)

> Park had an extraordinary amount of patience in working with someone who had an interest and, consequently, Park would take individuals who - most of them men... - who were really very mediocre ... but in working with them, he would just continuously draw out, lay out new lines along which to proceed, just leading these individuals more and more into a depthlike kind of knowledge of the area in which they were working. And some of the better monographs which came out, frankly, were of this sort. (Blumer, 1980b, p. 268)

Park's lack of involvement in the Department in the 1930s and his final departure in the middle of the decade undoubtedly affected the environment. It is debateable, though, whether the loss of one person could have had as profound an effect as some of the commentators suggest. A more fatal blow to the ethos and development of research at Chicago arguably occurred later, in the early 1950s, when the core of the Chicago faculty was uprooted. Chicago's dominance had, of course, gone by 1950, but the loss of Ogburn, Wirth, Burgess and Blumer within a two year period at the start of the decade signalled the end of an era and a loss of ambience. Chicago was no longer 'the place to be' for a sociologist. The environment epitomised by the enthusiastic meetings and Institutes of the Society for Social Research was gone.

The unique research experience that was located at Chicago and seemed to radiate out from it in the 1920s was an important factor in the rise to prominence of the 'Chicago School'. Once the momentum had begun to slow down then Chicago gradually lost its domiance. The loss of Park was probably associated with this gradual loss of momentum, but so too was the staleness of the subject matter. Chicago sociology, at least to the outsider, was very much the sociology of Chicago and this gradually lost its uniqueness and appeal, especially as national issues became more and more the concern of sociologists. The combination of factors that came together to make the 'Chicago School' such an outstanding research department gradually lost their significance or disappeared. Chicago shifted from being a dominant to a leading sociology department. The loss of research ethos was important in this shift, but it was by no means the sole reason for the change. Indeed, the loss of research ethos reflected more substantive structural changes in the discipline.

Structural factors leading to Chicago's decline

Rather than the loss of organisational prominence, or the loss of any one faculty member, or the parochialism of the Department or any theoretical or methodological insufficiencies, I would suggest that Chicago's decline was the result of structural changes. Structural changes in sociology inevitably brought about a lessening of the dominance of any one department or group of departments. The rapid expansion of sociology, the increase in specialisation within sociology and the consequent narrowing in focus of research areas and realms of competence made it impossible for one department to dominate the whole discipline, even if it had been a possibility earlier when sociology was seen in more holistic terms.

This change is perhaps best reflected in the changing nature of social scientific research in the United States between 1920 and 1950, as epitomised in the changes in funded social science research and the role and nature of the Social Science Research Council. In the period up to 1930, Chicago University was one of half a dozen universities well endowed with research monies and having a research environment which allowed them to play a major part in the development of social scientific research. Chicago played a large part in this group, without, however, being an oppressive force. Chicago led by example. The Local Community Research Committee at Chicago (which later became the Social Science Research Committee) was probably the first university based organisation to adopt the concerns of the Social Science Research Council at a local level (Bulmer, 1980), and this Chicago approach came to be emulated by other institutions. Research in the social sciences at Chicago was becoming well established and encouraged by the end of the twenties.

Ogg's (1928) report to the American Council of Learned Societies singled out the University of Chicago as one of the most research oriented universities in the United States in respect of the social sciences and humanities [8]. The flexible teaching arrangements, easily obtainable sabbaticals, the recognition of research professorships with small teaching loads and the use of research as the prime basis for judging promotion and salary increases, contributed towards the research environment at Chicago. [9]

By the standards of the time, the University of Chicago had, in 1928, exceptionally large, although limited term, research funding. The social sciences had an enormous budget of $143,000, of which about one hundred thousand dollars was administered by the Local Community Research Committee. A considerable amount of this money came from the Laura Spellman Rockefeller Memorial Foundation. An additional fund of $100,000 spread over five years, was also available for publication of material in all fields. However, Chicago had not always been so well endowed and this represented a considerable advance over the previous five years as, in 1922, Chicago University did not indicate that they were in receipt of regular funds through which research in any departments could be financed. (Bulletin of American Association of University Professors, 1922, (Vol 8), p. 32). As an indication of its financial standing, and rapid improvement, between 1924 and 1927, the University of Chicago raised around twenty million dollars in endowments. Nonetheless, despite the relatively healthy environment, and the ability of some sociologists to tap the research funds, sociologists, as noted in chapter two, were not the sole, or even the major, beneficiaries of the money administered by the Local Community Research Committee. Nor was Chicago alone in its support of research. Columbia, Harvard, North Carolina, Yale and California all actively supported social science research.

President Butler of Columbia University noted, 'at Columbia the spirit of research is everywhere active and persistent' (Butler, 1925, p. 38) and considerable research was taking place in the social sciences while the Columbia University Press offered a ready outlet for research work. The appointment of five new professors in 1926 principally for research work (including one in statistics and one in economics) further stimulated research. In 1925 the Columbia University Council had created a Council for Research in the Social Sciences with the duty of furthering co-operative research. In its first year it administered in excess of one hundred thousand dollars derived partly from the University and partly from the Laura Spellman Rockefeller Memorial Foundation. In addition, the University received numerous large gifts, and there was an emergency fund for research purposes ($40,000) appropriated annually by the president.

Research at Harvard, too, was deemed to be of the highest importance from 1910 onwards, and facilities were greatly improved, with financial support being increased from an 'insignificant figure to several hundred thousand dollars' per year. The development of the Widener Memorial Library into one of the finest in the world, and the reduction of teaching burdens from 1927, helped research endeavours. In addition the Milton Fund amounting to one million dollars provided an annual sum of fifty thousand dollars for research of which (in 1927) the social sciences and humanities received about a third, although very little went directly to the promotion of sociological research. However, there were additional funds for research in the social sciences and humanities, most important was the fifty thousand dollar grant for five years from the Laura Spellman Rockefeller Memorial Foundation for the work of the Bureau of International Research.

The University of North Carolina similarly gave a great deal of support, from relatively meagre funds, to research in the social sciences. Apart from an annual grant of twenty five thousand dollars from the Graduate School and the Smith Fund available to all departments, the University's Institute for Research in Social Science administered a research fund of sixty five thousand dollars annually, granted by the Laura Spellman Rockefeller Memorial Foundation for five years. The University of North Carolina was the motor force behind the series of southern university social science conferences that began in 1925. Highly motivated towards research it created a research atmosphere in the social sciences and attempted to stimulate research in various ways including the publication of an extensive annual review of research in progress, the launching of local surveys in rural social economics, making liberal provision for publication through the Univeristy of North Carolina Press, and the editorship of Social Forces besides the establishment of the Institute.

Yale University was also gradually developing a research ethos in the social sciences, this was helped by the establishment of both the Sterling Memorial Library in the late 1920s, and the Institute of Psychology in 1924 which was grant aided by the Laura Spellman Rockefeller Memorial Fund. About forty thousand dollars per annum were available for research in the humanities and social sciences, mainly income from the Sterling bequest.

The University of California, later to be a major contributor to sociological research was, in 1927, beginning to establish itself as a research centre. About half of The Searles Fund ($10,000 per annum) was available for research in the social sciences and humanities. In addition the Laura Spelman Rockefeller Memorial Foundation provided a grant in 1927 to support a research institute of child welfare for a period of six years.

On the fringes of this group were several others including Cornell University, the University of Illinois, Stanford University, and the University of Cincinnati. All of these had small amounts of money established for social science research or were otherwise promoting such research [10].

In terms of research funding and encouragement, then, the University of Chicago was not alone but part of small group of institutions. However, little of this social scientific research funding enabled sociological research. Sociology, was after all, a new subject and in traditional universities had limited opportunities to establish itself and gain access to funding (Bulmer, 1984). In this respect Chicago had an edge over other centres. This edge, however, was to gradually disappear. The development of the Social Science Research Council; the accompanying clearer specification of research endeavours; the developing status of sociology; the closer relationship of funding allocations to the professionalisation and 'scientising' of the discipline; all tended to reduce the advantage enjoyed, initially, by Chicago.

From the late 1920s onwards, sociology in the United States was very much shaped by the fifteen universities who constituted the core of the Social Science Research Council. The fifteen universities were California, Chicago, Columbia, Harvard, McGill, Michigan, Minnesota, North Carolina, Northwestern, Pennsylvania, Stanford, Texas, Virginia, Wisconsin and Yale. They tended to be the major beneficiaries of research funding and attracted the more able graduate level students.

The Social Science Research Council had been founded in 1923 because there was an imperative need for an agency with a concern for the common research interests of all social scientists. The disciplinary societies were weak and narrow minded, colleges and universities were more concerned with teaching than research in social science [11]. The lack of any other body with a similar interest in the over-all research problems of the social sciences demanded its creation. 'The one goal of the Council since its beginning, of course, has been the advancement of research in the social sciences by any effective available means.' (Burgess, 1944b)

This co-operative auspices made it easier for the universities involved to attract research funds from foundations such as the Rockefeller Foundation and the Laura Spellman Rockefeller Memorial Foundation. Further, government initiatives in the social sciences were also directed to these institutions. This was facilitated by the establishment of the Committee on University Social Science Research Organisations of the Social Science Research Council. The aim of this committee was to exchange information on the problems of social science research

and the administration of research in the universities. It held
an annual conference to which representatives of research foundations, government and non-academic research organisations
were invited. The Rockefeller Foundation, which was the principal provider of research funds for the social sciences, had
hoped that such a committee of the Social Science Research
Council would facilitate co-operation among the various universities it financed, and establish lines of communication for
sharing experiences and for co-operative ventures. Such a body,
it hoped, could also record and evaluate research. Besides the
annual conference the committee visited research centres to
collect first hand information on work in progress.

Through this committee, the Social Science Research Council
formulated its approach. In 1929 it adopted seven objectives:
improving research organizations; developing personnel; improving and expanding materials; improving research methods
[12]; facilitating dissemination of materials, methods and
results; facilitating research projects; and enhancing public
appreciation of social sciences. Following the 1936 recommendations of the Committee on Review of Council Policy these
became the four categories for the appointment of committees on
research planning and appraisal, on research agencies and institutions, on research personnel and on research materials.

The situation was reviewed again in 1944 and the following
criteria for supporting research were made: advance of scientific methods; inventing or improving research instruments;
repetitive study; interdisciplinary experimental studies; appraisal of research methods; studies integrating methods from
different disciplines; and pilot studies in new fields. This
firmly put the onus on methodological analysis and large scale
research enterprises. Columbia University, through its considerable involvement in research on the Second World War and the
consequent establishment of the Bureau of Applied Social Research, stole a march on many other institutions, especially
Chicago, who were not undertaking specific large scale research
on the war (Wirth, 1949) [13].

Changes in research organisation were being made too. For
some time the organisation and goals of the Social Science
Research Council had been under review and by 1945 the structure was seen to be a decade out of date. Previously, funding
from the Rockefeller foundation had been concentrated on a
group of fifteen universities. This changed after 1945 and
Chicago University's influence, like most of the universities
in the group, diminished.

Following recommendations made in 1945 the organisation of
the Social Science Research Council was changed, with the
Committee on University Social Science Research Organisations
giving way to the Committee on Organisation for Research in the
Social Sciences, in 1946. This new committee was formed because

the annual conferences were rather limited, the original fifteen universities constituted a dated grouping because other universities with no formal social science organisations had started doing social research, and new research organisations outside the universities had come into being. The new committee was therefore not restricted to universities.

In a review of this new organisation, Wirth (1949) noted that the conferences were concerned with getting further financing rather than with the substantive problems of the social sciences or the technical problems of developing research organisations. However, the Committee

> was the one real bridge that allowed for co-operation that was established in the first two decades of the the Social Science Research Council's operations. Through the informal discussions among the members present at these conferences much was learned about the successful and unsuccessful experience.

The reorganised committee still placed social science research in the universities at the forefront, argued that such research had become team research with technical backup and that this made research organisation important although it was no substitute for ideas. And while the Committee recommended that each organisation establish a committee, in effect equivalent to the Social Science Research Committee at Chicago [14], the maturation of social science research now made it impossible for any University to dominate.

This maturation of social science research was matched by the extensive development of the discipline of sociology, itself. In less than fifty years sociology had moved from a rather general and schematic holistic discipline to a fragmented multitude of sub-disciplines. The range of sociology was vast, published sociological work was growing at an exponential rate and the number of sociologists and sociology departments was burgeoning rapidly. Many more sociologists were vying for recognition, large numbers of sociology departments were challenging for research monies and universities were establishing social research units. Increasing specialism and the search for new fields meant that sociologists with broad interests, especially those associated with bygone eras were eclipsed. Reflecting on this, Ogburn wrote, at the time of his retirement from Chicago

> I put much time and effort on social action in the community, state and nation. I saw I could not do this and maintain my scientific research work. So when I went to Columbia in 1919, my urge to help make the world a better place to live in, was transferred to helping make the social

sciences more scientific; and so for 20 years there was much scientific organizational work. But looking at the records of all this, it all seems dead and gone. I helped found the Social Science Research Council, served for years as chairman of its most important committee, the Problems and Policy Committee, and then was for three years chairman of the Council. Now when I happen to go up to the S.S.R.C. headquarters in New York Central Building, I am practically unknown and my work forgotten. They never send me any communications, and I don't know what is going on. (Ogburn journal, 13th September 1952).

It is, therefore, debatable the extent to which Chicago influence diminished as a result of the coup. Arguably, Chicago experienced a natural 'decline' given the structural changes in the discipline. By the late 1930s there would appear to be little chance for any one sociology department to dominate the discipline. A high level of research involvement, publication and methodological and theoretical innovation may serve to mark out a department as a centre of excellence, but for any one school to achieve a pre-eminent position after the 1930s would be extremely difficult while sociology continued to expand. I would suggest that Chicago's 'decline' was not so much a rejection of the Chicago contribution as an accommodation by Chicago of structural changes. The coup was the embodiment of this accommodation at a formal administrative level. It was not, however, indicative of the discarding of 'Chicago sociology'.

The extent of Chicago's decline

The Chicagoans were not isolated or rejected, even if the substantive work of some of them was forgotten in the post war period. Their inclusion in the elitist Sociological Research Association [15] along with many of the members of the American Sociological Society who had voted against the Chicago nominees in 1935, points to the continued involvement and prominence of the Chicagoans in the discipline nationally. Furthermore, a year after the coup, the Chicagoans were back in executive positions in the American Sociological Society, with Ellsworth Faris as President and E.W. Burgess on the Executive Committee. Charles Johnson of Fisk, and a close friend of Park and member of the Society for Social Research was Vice President. Three of the remaining four ex-presidents who were members of the executive committee and half the six elected members were also members of the Society for Social Research.

After 1935, and even in its 'doldrum period' in the 1950s, Chicago never dropped out of the circle of half a dozen most influential sociology departments which included Columbia, Michigan, California, Carolina and Harvard. Chicago remained part of the privileged group that tended to benefit most from the Social Science Research Council and, despite the 'setbacks' of the coup, it remained centrally involved in national and regional societies. The speakers at The Annual Institutes of the Society for Social Research continued to be drawn from a wide spectrum within the discipline.

Indeed, there is little to suggest that such prestige did anything other than wane following the spectacular rise of Columbia in the immediate post World War Two era. This rise itself followed almost two decades in which the department at Columbia was nearly closed down and its impact on the discipline was negligible. Columbia did not fill any void left by Chicago in the 1940s, rather it was providing a 'shallow training' for sociologists, (Lynd, 1941b) [16]. It was not until Paul Lazarsfeld was appointed and the Bureau of Applied Social Research became established after the second world war that Columbia University got the impetus that made it the leading, although not dominant, sociological research institution, (Coleman, 1980).

The waning of Chicago, irrespective of the advances made elsewhere, was inevitable given the expansion and diversification of sociology in the United States. What is surprising is that Chicago University exerted such a strong organisational influence for so long, especially as, up to 1935, it had never been a large department in terms of tenured staff. Chicago's impact was bound to decrease as more and more institutions developed sociology departments and sociological research programmes. Structural changes in the discipline meant that Chicago's dominance would never be recovered, and that no single department would again dominate sociology in the United States to the same degree that Chicago had in the 1920s.

Conclusion

During the 1950s Chicago was less innovative than some of the rival departments, but this was more a function of the simultaneous loss of key personnel in 1951-52 than of the cumulation of a downward spiral. Ogburn and Burgess retired in 1952, (as did Thurstone). The War had inhibited the recruitment of new faculty or the elevation or development of existing faculty to take over. The death of Wirth in 1951 could not be planned for. Stouffer moved to Columbia University via the War Department and Shils' involvement with the department between 1948 and 1958 was limited due to his leave of absence on government service and his involvement on the Committee for Social Thought. Blumer moved to California in 1952.

Chicago was bereft of key personnel who might have developed the quantitative techniques that came to dominate in the 1950s. That is not to say that Chicago had nobody to develop this area, and indeed, much fine work was done by Duncan, (before his surprising departure to Arizona, where he faded out of the limelight, (Coleman, 1980)). Goodman and Hauser also made important contributions, but without the same recognition afforded the work done at Columbia and Michigan. The restructuring of the Department at Chicago through the recruitment of quantifiers like Blau came rather late and, according to some sources (Janowitz, 1980), failed to establish a credible environment through which pioneering quantification might have prospered.

It is, furthermore, misleading to equate any decline in the role of Chicago University with a decline in ethnographic research.

> I don't think there ever was a decline in the amount of ethnographic research... I started doing research in 1946, 47, 48, doing ethnographic research, and I've done it ever since. And lots of other people were doing it, at the same time I was. And it's true that, that as survey research became more important, people, especially in the Eastern part of the United States that the notion that it was dominating sociology, that was sort of a parochial kind of view that people at Harvard and Columbia essentially had. And I never saw any evidence of it myself, because, you know, we were just going right on doing what we were doing, and there were lots of us. In fact, I noticed some years ago that there was a very interesting phenomena... I took the list of [McIver] prize winning books and .... out of, I think, perhaps I'd say ten or fifteen, I think one or two were done with the use of those quantitative techniques. So in fact, quantitative techniques were not as dominant as people thought. (Becker, 1979, pp. 15-17)

The post World War Two era was also supposed to have been the point at which Chicago's ethnographic orientation became most developed. It was in 1952, however, that Blumer moved to Berkeley and neither Geer, Vidich nor Glaser were tenured at Chicago in the 1950s. Howard S. Becker was an instructor in 1951 and 1952 following his award of a doctorate in 1951. His next official link with the Department was in the late 1950s through his work on the project sponsored by Community Studies Incorporated of Kansas City, Missouri [17]. Strauss was an assistant professor, too, for five years 1954-1958 inclusive, before moving away from a department that was becoming increasingly dominated by quantitative interests. Retrospective accounts suggest that the tradition that Becker and associates developed at Chicago at this time was the end of a longer tradition of ethnographic work. On the contrary, however, such work was in many senses the beginning. It represented an attempt at a novel validation of participant observation which was later to lead to a questioning of value neutrality (Becker, 1967).

In the event, the coup which is supposed to have undermined the influence of the Chicago School on the theoretical and methodological development of sociology, actually serves to show that the 'Chicago School' was not a homogeneous and united grouping of practitioners standing at a distance from prevailing theoretic and methodic tendencies. On the contrary, what seems to be an improbable alliance between quantifiers and Chicagoans is only improbable if the two groups are seen as exhibiting irreconcilable theoretical or epistemological differences. The argument developed throughout this book undermines such an assumption. The quantifiers may be seen as a committed theory group (Lengermann, 1979) advocating radical positivism, with an interdisciplinary sub-group at Chicago. The Chicagoans as a whole, however, were not so cohesive. What they had, and what was instrumental in their dominant position, was a flourishing research environment. It was the dissipation of this environment, rather than any complacency or failure to address new developments in sociology, that led to the waning of the Chicagoans. A waning that seemed inevitable given the rapid development of sociology in the United States and associated structural changes.

Notes

[1] For example, Chicago produced 113 Ph.Ds up to 1935 while Columbia, the second largest produced only 50 in sociology. Between 1954 and 1968 the situation had changed with Chicago producing 163, Columbia 172, and Harvard 120 and Berkeley 84.

[2] The question of patronage, however, was perhaps not quite as overriding a concern as it was projected. Certainly Chicago faculty were regularly consulted with a view to recommending staff, but there was no attempt to infiltrate their own graduates into departments. They wrote openly and in a non-partisan way when requests were made for suggestions and opinions. A reply from Ogburn (1930) to Hankins (who in 1935 was to vote against Chicago in the coup) is worth quoting at length

Dear Hankins:
In answer to your letter of the 15th about a man for Sociology at Smith, how would Bernard do ? He is much interest-

ed in the history of sociology. I think he is a little hard
to get along with. You know him, of course, quite well.
House at Virginia is much interested in social theory and
the history of social doctrines. He was thought very highly
of here by Small and many others. Another very good man,
who is an instructor here now, is Herbert Blumer. He has a
fine critical head, is very much interested in social
theory, knows French sociology particularly well and German
sociology also pretty well. He reads both languages quite
fluently. He is a very good teacher. His interests are a
good deal like those of Cooley perhaps. Our plan, I think,
is to keep him on here at Chicago, though he might be
willing to go away. Another possibility is Louie Wirth at
Tulane. He has a very keen mind. He is a Jew, however. At
the present time he is in Germany and is especially well
versed in European sociology. I think very highly of Wirth
also. Another man worth considering is Dawson at Montreal
who is one of the best men turned out here for some time.
He is the head of the department and might be a little hard
to pry loose. I think Malcolm Willey is one of the finest
young men we have in sociology. He is probably the best
teacher of any of these and has really extraordinary abili-
ties along these lines. I believe he was a student of yours
at one time. I think Willey is an unusually promising man.
Let me know if I can write more fully about any of these
men, or if none of them are suitable I can try some others.
Abel at Columbia might be worth considering also. I don't
envy your problem of finding a good man. Good men are now
wanted by Michigan, Minnesota, Illinois, and Oberlin.
With cordial good wishes, I remain,
Sincerely yours,
William F. Ogburn.

Bernard, House and Willey all voted against Chicago in 1935

[3] See, for example the following Ph.Ds: Cottrell (1933), Lang
(1936), Cox (1938), Reeden (1939), Dunham (1941), Devinney
(1941), Campisi (1947), Bowerman (1948), Turner (1948),
Shanas (1949), Lunday, (1949), Nelson (1949).

[4] See note 1.

[5] In the late 1930s and 1940s, Parkian concepts appeared to
be rather limited. Blumer (1980b), Hughes (1980) and Matthews (1977) all point to the distortion of his social
ecological approach by later generations who concentrated
on spatio-statistical studies in 'psychological behaviorism', led to the ecological approach being fiercely attacked (Alihan, 1938). Park accepted the criticism of his

approach on the whole with the exception of 'some malicious
interpretations' (Matthews, 1977). Ironically, by the mid
fifties, the ecological approach was going through a revi-
val (Schnore, 1958).

[6] For Matthews, Park's going is seen as the final passing of
an holistic perspective at Chicago. However, it is quite
likely that Park would have 'retreated' into a specialist
field at Chicago as he did at Fisk. Race studies had always
been his major concern (Barnhardt, 1972; Blumer, 1972;
Matthews, 1977), and this he developed in two ways, according to a letter written to Wirth in 1938 (Park, 1938). Park
was concerned with the investigation of the moral and
personal social world which, in terms of his own research,
involved the investigation of 'two types of 'world' the
Bohemia of the Lower North Side in Chicago where Park House
is located, and Cedar Street, in Nashville Tennessee. The
first is an area like Greenwich Village; the other is an
underworld, such as every metropolitan city supports. But
it is an underworld of Negroes. I am interested in explor-
ing these underworlds, which are characteristically cultural and racial melting pots, in every part of the world'.
    His method of investigation, reflecting his increasing
intolerance of statistical study as he grew older, was
mainly based upon 'life histories of a generally psychoanalytic bias' which were designed to 'throw light on the
nature of the intimate and relatively closed moral and
personal order to which the individual person is most
responsive, and they throw light also upon the processes of
acculturation which take place within the limits of such a
minor cultural unit'. (Park, 1938)

[7] In the United States in the 1930s and 1940s Weberian and
Marxist perspectives were taken up directly, although the
life of these as autonomous roots to analysing the social
world were curtailed as structural functionalism muted the
phenomenological potential of the Weberian approach and
McCarthyism inhibited the growth of Marxist perspectives.

[8] The report concluded that, in the humanities in general, a
lot of research was going on but that it was of poor quality, being badly planned, poorly executed and barren of
significant results. Methods of investigation, it maintained, were imperfectly developed, with, in general, too
much concern with applied research. The report noted a
tendency for specialisation to destroy co-operation, but
noted the exceptions of both Chicago and Columbia where co-
operative efforts in the social sciences were evident.
    The report made the following suggestions. First, that

research should be more directed to 'pure learning'. Second, that research and learning should be more closely related. Third, that graduate work should be better organised. Fourth, that increased attention be paid to research methodology. Fifth, that research be more effectively organised, that it should follow the pattern of broad social science research as evident at Chicago, Columbia and North Carolina. Sixth, that systematic periodic surveys of research projects be undertaken, either through the publication of 'research in progress' as in the case of North Carolina and Minnesota, or through the annual publication of faculty research, as in the case of Columbia, Cornell, Chicago, Michigan and Virginia. Seventh, the university system should develop specialisation and division of labour.

[9] Only a lack of special provision for attendance at conferences and inadequate clerical assistance were pointed to as factors that Chicago might improve upon.

[10] The following Universities were listed as having very little or no specific provision for research in the social sciences: Indiana University, University of Nebraska, Princeton University, Washington University, State University of Iowa, Johns Hopkins University, University of Kansas ($250 in 1925-6) Michigan, Minnesota ($1000 in 1927) Missouri, Northwestern University, Ohio State University, University of Pennsylvania ($3151 in 1926) University of Wisconsin ($7500 in 1927), Clark University.

[11] This feeling that universities and colleges devoted too much time to teaching was not a universally held view. In a newspaper report with the headline 'Book Writing Professors are Scored by Speaker at Meeting of Sociologists', (Anon, 1913) a student at the American Sociology Society conference was reported to have been concerned that lecturers spent too much time writing for their own benefit and too little engaged in teaching.

[12] The Committee on Scientific Methods of the Social Science Research Council undertook a thorough study of research methods in the latter part of the 1920s. Two Chicago University faculty were members of this committee of eight, L.L. Thurstone from the Psychology Department and Edward Sapir, an anthropologist in the Department of Sociology. The rest of the committee were Horace Secrist (Northwestern University) as chairman, A.N Holcombe, W.I. King, Mary Van Kleeck, R.M. MacIver and F.J. Teggart.

[13] Poffenberger, Chairman of the P&P Committee of the Social Science Research Council, circulated members in April 1944, on research methods, notably concerning the opportunity, afforded by the war, of monitoring attitude scaling techniques.

Techniques for the measurement of attitudes and opinions have been used for years as laboratory devices by psychologists and sociologists. More recently their use has been widely extended and their popularity greatly increased with their adoption for opinion polls and for surveys of attitudes by government bureaus and by several branches of the armed forces. Specialised procedures for administration and statistical treatment are employed by the various groups and champions have arisen to defend one or another of the favoured techniques.... P & P have authorised an enquiry into the feasibility of a thorough appraisal of attitude measurement in the armed forces and government bureaus... The methods of great potential and value are certain to be widely employed for a variety of purposes in the next few years. Therein lies the real danger that their utility will be heavily oversold and that inadequate techniques will flourish. Indeed, there is a reason to expect an attitude measuring boom after this war similar to the mental test boom that followed the last war. Something may be done now by the Council in order to make the outcome in this instance less unfortunate. P & P is now considering such a critical survey which would include suggestions for further research into methods of construction, administration and validation of all such measuring instruments. In undertaking such a survey the Council would be making a contribution in the field which is common to all the social sciences for one can easily forsee applications in every one of our disciplines.

[14] The Committee proposed that each university have an organisation which took responsibility for acceptance and expenditure of all research funds and to represent the university in relations with external funding bodies. The organisation should appraise the research needs of the social sciences; furnish counsel and guidance in the planning and design, prosecution and appraisal of research projects; discover and foster research talents and interests of university staff and to provide facilities for carrying on research; report such interests and needs to the general university administration; facilitate communication between research workers between and within institutions; provide a continuous record of research in progress, completed and planned and to facilitate publication. (Social Science

Research Council, Committee on Organisation for Research in the Social Sciences Report, 1946.)

[15] The establishment of the Sociological Research Association following the coup was not the product of a Chicago separatist movement, but was, and remained for many years, an elitist conclave of sociologists including (by 1940) Burgess (president in 1942), Ogburn, Thomas, Wirth, Blumer Merton, Parsons, Lazarsfeld, Stouffer, and Bain.

The first president (1936) was F. Stuart Chapin (University of Minnesota), the secretary-treasurer was E. B. Reuter (University of Iowa) and the remainder of the initial Executive Committee were Donald Young, Robert MacIver and Stuart Rice. The first annual meeting to take place in conjunction with the December annual meeting of the American Sociological Society was to be addressed by Dorothy Thomas and Thorsten Sellin with Warren Thomson, F. H. Hankins, G. B. Vold and W. I. Thomas as discussants. A Further session analysing Lundberg's paper 'The Thoughtways of Contemporary Sociology' was to be lead by Herbert Blumer along with Read Bain and Samuel Stouffer. The membership clearly cut across 'factional' lines. As Park (1939) noted, the Association was not concerned with factional divisions but rather with research practice. In correspondence between Chapin (1936a, 1936b) and Wirth (1936a) the fear was expressed that the meeting of the Association may be gate-crashed by Society members opposed to the small selective nature of the group, then numbering about fifty.

[16] Lynd was also concerned that this was a national problem, and that sociology was not highly thought of in government circles. He wrote to Wirth. 'Having done "Knowledge for What ?" I'm inclined to say: "Enough, let's get to work and stop talking", But this creeping extension of "the sociology of this and that" is dangerous from the p[oin]t of view of what students are trained to do. The predicament of our dep[artmen]t is not unique, and the shallowness of the training of young sociologists is recognized in Wash[ington].' (Lynd, 1941a).

[17] Howard S. Becker received his doctorate at Chicago in 1951 and was an instructor in the Department in 1951 and 1952. He does not appear again on the Official Publications until 1959, when he is listed as assistant professor (at Kansas). This listing is repeated in 1960 and 1961. Prior to 1959, Becker undertook field work on the study of a state medical school, sponsored by Community Studies, Incorporated, of Kansas City, Missouri. A project directed by Everett C.

Hughes. Blanche Geer was Becker's field work partner on the project and Anselm Strauss was a member of the research team.

8 Schools and metascience

Introduction

In chapters three to seven a number of myths about the 'Chicago School' of sociology were examined. These myths occur both in introductory textbooks and in more advanced discussions of sociological theory. Commentators resort to taken-for-granted ideas about the 'Chicago School'. It is frequently seen as concerned with reform, as adopting ethnographic techniques with little concern for theoretical issues, and as having been dependent on the ideas of George Herbert Mead. Generally, the Chicagoans are portrayed as having dominated sociology in the United States up to the mid thirties, before their isolationism and intransigence in the face of the growth of a more scientific approach to sociology led to a rapid decline in their influence.

Most of the discussions quoted to illustrate the myths about the 'Chicago School' are relatively brief and superficial accounts, rather than detailed historical case studies. These, as suggested in chapter one, adopt a rather casual approach to the concept of school. However, there are others who have used the 'Chicago School' as a critical case in the devlopment of theories about the growth of sociological knowledge (Mullins, 1973; Tiryakian, 1979a, 1979b) or who have adopted a metascientific concept of 'school' when examining the history of the Chicagoans (Bulmer, 1984). Interestingly, with perhaps the rare exception of Bulmer, these more developed metascientific accounts lean heavily and selectively on secondary sources for their historical detail (Harvey, 1985).

Views of the 'Chicago School' are well established in the history of sociology, as can be seen by the large number of casual references to their work. The 'Chicago School', I have suggested, is surrounded by myths. This book has examined a number of the major ones, and has shown that most taken-for-granted views of Chicago sociology are misleading.There is a considerable amount of recent research, besides my own, examining elements of the taken-for-granted views of Chicago sociology, most of which have been referred to in this book. Perhaps more direct first hand investigation and a wider dissemination of the results of these investigations will lead to a revised view of the 'Chicago School'. Maybe, such close scrutiny will reveal the superficial nature of the constructions of a 'Chicago School' (Kurtz, 1984) and result in the notion of a 'Chicago School' being abandoned altogether.

This, then, raises interesting questions about the efficacy of a 'school' approach to the history of an academic discipline. Do all schools evaporate under close inspection ? Are schools inevitably liable to be the harbingers of myths ? Or is there something intrinsic and vital for the history of social science in having research seen as located within a social network ?

As indicated in chapter one, a number of different metascientific concepts are in use, ranging from 'school' to 'invisible college'. The efficacy of a 'schools' aproach to the understanding of the development of social scientific knowledge should, I suggest, be located within a general assessment of the role of metascientific units in the history and sociology of knowledge.

The potential of a unit approach

If one is to use a metascientific unit such as 'school', 'research unit' or 'network' then clear definitions of the concepts are necessary. Taken-for-granted views of the constituents of a school, its activities, orientations and theoretical endeavours, must be suspended. A critical engagement with the historical evidence is essential. One must avoid adopting prevailing myths about historical entities uncritically.

The key to the efficacy of a unit approach is that the criteria which serve to identify units should be consistent with theoretical ideas about how knowledge grows. Membership, citations and so on are merely indicators of interactive units rather than frames for assessing the process of science production. Much of the confusion about the 'Chicago School', I would contend, comes from a lack of any clear idea of the processes involved in the development of sociological knowledge. Even those who adopt a clear metascientific orientation, tend to rely heavily on a framework which derives from Kuhn's notion of paradigm and reworkings of the concept of 'paradigm group'. However, this kind of analysis has tended to drift further and further away from the mechanism of crisis and transformation that Kuhn argued underlay the growth of knowledge. The tendency has been to argue that the mechanism takes place within social units, to then identify the units, and presuppose that being able to fit individuals to prescribed roles is sufficient to explain the development of sociological knowledge (e.g. Mullins, 1973; Tiryakian, 1979a, 1979b).

This approach is historicist, in selectively reconstructing schools to fit favoured models, and also ignores the critical process in knowledge transformation. I would thus suggest that a unit approach would have more potential if, instead of concentrating on ideas, personnel or institutional groupings, the unit was viewed in terms of its knowledge transformative processes. One way to do this would be to focus on the processes of critique within a unit and how the critique is carried out, institutionalised and legitimated. There would be no need, then, to attempt to construct barriers around an intellectual enclave, either in terms of personnel or subject matter. The dynamic and changing nature of the enterprise would be the focus of investigation, rather than the underlying presuppositions, genesis and history of an idea, or gelling together of a group of practitioners.

The tendency towards an internalist perspective evident in unit approaches would also be avoided. Unit approaches tend to construct the school or emerging unit as internally consistent, and as providing a set of internal justificatory and legitimating criteria. Apart from the problems of cross-fertilisation of ideas, this internalistic orientation disengages the unit from both the wider discipline in which it is located and also the social mileu. The investigation of a school or unit is thus usually in terms of how it develops a new sub-area rather than how it engages with the discipline and acts to transform the stock of scientific knowledge.

The 'Chicago School', for example, constituted a metascientific unit in as much as it incorporated an open, and accessible, critical process which was integral to the work of practitioners both directly involved in work, of various sorts, at Chicago and of others in communication with those based at Chicago. The Chicagoans extensive involvement in American sociology (chapter seven) made the 'Chicago School' one of the focii through which developments in sociological knowledge in the United States were directed. This critical process at Chicago was institutionalised, as Park (1939) suggested, in the Society for Social Research. As the discussions throughout the book have indicated (especially chapters two to four), the

215

society acted as a supportive association of sociologists af-
filiated, in one way or another, to Chicago. The aim of the
society, as set out in its constitution, was to disseminate
knowledge and act as a clearing house of ideas. The accessibil-
ity of the society, its summer institutes, communication network, frequent discussion meetings, and regular bulletin all
served to advance this aim.

A unit thesis which investigates the processes by which
knowledge is developed and evaluated would provide a basis for
rational selection and interpretation of unit indicators. It
would also discourage reliance on secondary sources and thereby, perhaps, avoid the retelling and perpetuation of myths.

Conclusion: units, myths and metascience

In general, when referring to units, notably to 'schools', most
commentators adopt the term quite loosely and it is usually
directed to a number of interrelated ends. First, school is
used as a categorising device in an attempt to provide a root
through the diversity of the history of sociology, be it at a
theoretical, substantive or methodological level. Second, this
mapping of history has been used as a means for marking out
territory by representatives of different theoretical approaches. Third, the school is used as an exemplar of a particular
approach to sociology, particularly directed at the colonis-
ation of a sub-discipline. None of these are directly concerned
with a metascientific enquiry which would critically engage
these categorical and demarcation processes.

The problem that arises in these non-metascientific usages is
that a large degree of over-generalisation takes place with
secondary accounts piling on each other and leading to mytholo-
gisation. This is in part a result of the reliance on memory
and oral tradition by sociologists engaged in writing about the
history of sociology, and a lack of detailed research to check
what they presume they know. This book, in the first instance,
has illustrated how such a process has occurred in the case of
the 'Chicago School of Sociology' by focussing on five myths
about the work of those sociologists in, or associated with,
the Department of Sociology at Chicago.

The designation of the 'School', motivated by the various
concerns of commentators, has drawn on and reinforced the
myths, while such myths also provide suitable handles for
historians and sociologists of sociology to grasp. The analysis
of the myths has suggested some of these interrelations, for
example the legitimating role of Mead in the history of symbolic interactionism, the establishment of an historical tradition
of participant observation research, the exemplary nature of
early Chicago urban sociology, and the dichotomisation of Amer-

ican sociology into 'qualitative' and 'quantitative' traditions as a framework for locating the development of the discipline.

Myth generation is both a function of the process of constructing history and of prevailing conceptualisations of the areas of knowledge to which the history relates. There is an interrelationship between historical accounts and taken-for-granted contemporary conceptualisations such that, for example, in constructing the history of the 'Chicago School' current ideas about the nature of sociology inform the historical reconstruction of its component parts and, conversely, historical accounts, written for whatever purposes, provide case data that inform a general conceptualisation of the history of sociology.

The examination of the myths of the 'Chicago School' suggested why specific myths might have arisen. In more general terms, however, the implication has been that myth construction is an almost inevitable consequence of the development of academic disciplines and their historical reconstruction. Such reconstruction has tended to be a presentist or 'Whig interpretation' (Butterfield, 1931) of the history of the contribution of significant figures ('great man' history) or of the progress of influential ideas ('great ideas' history). Sociologists and historians of science have, however, come increasingly to question the historical reconstruction of a discipline in these terms.

The debate in the philosophy of science, stemming from the Popper-Kuhn engagement and taken up by Lakatos, among others, has, in two ways, generated a critique of historiography of science. First, it has raised questions about the relationship between history and the rationality of science. Second, the concern to specify the community framework of scientific knowledge production has undermined both the sweeping construction of ideational traditions and the naive idealistic assumption of history as the work of individuals.

Arguably, the 'unit' approach to the history of sociology overcomes many of the problems of the 'great man' and 'great ideas' perspectives (Mullins, 1973; Tiryakian, 1979a). This view, as has been suggested, is grounded in the paradigmatic view of the development of science deriving from Kuhn (1962) which has brought a reassessment of traditional notions of the 'progress of science'. However, in practice unit approaches are problemmatic as their attempts to force historical events into preformed categories leads to internal inconsistencies, a distortion of the historical evidence and an abandonment of the Kuhnian paradigm thesis which purports to underpin the model (Harvey, 1985). Furthermore, adopting a frame of reference located so squarely in the philosophy of science debate means that an essentially internalistic perspective is adopted. This fails to provide any mediation of science and society and of past and present (Chalmers, 1978; Feyerabend, 1975a, 1975b). Kuhn and Lakatos, and the models based on them, are all 'historicist' in that their models appropriate history selectively in order to establish the credibility of their frame [1]. This approach thus inhibits detailed empirical investigation.

While providing a basis for a critique of the 'great man' and 'great ideas' approaches to the history of academic disciplines, most 'unit' approaches do not provide a satisfactory alternative because they, too, tend to lead to distortions of the knowledge production process. A unit approach is not, of itself, immune to the construction of myth.

In the case of the historical reportage of the 'Chicago School of Sociology', the unit approach has accentuated the development of myths and has fed through to affect the very nature of the sociological enterprise and thus of what constitutes sociological knowledge. This, then, suggests that the usage of terms such as 'Chicago School' are of limited value and should be approached critically when undertaking metascientific work or examining the history of science. This is particularly clear when a 'school' appears to have a number of overlapping designations, as in the case of the 'Chicago School'.

The critical examination of the myths of the 'Chicago School' suggested an alternative characterisation of the work and impact of the Chicagoans to that popularly held. The 'School' was an integral part of American sociology, developing as the discipline developed. It was early concerned with social reform but not in isolation from theoretical understanding, and rapidly moved away from reformist concerns as the discipline attempted to establish a more overt scientific basis. This shift coincided with the institutionalisation of the knowledge transformative processes in the Society for Social Research. The Chicagoans were concerned with empirical data collection and tended towards methodological eclecticism. However, they did not neglect theory and developed theoretical concerns in line with the general development of the discipline and drew on a number of different traditions, particularly pragmatism, of which Mead was but one source. Chicago sociology had been prominent in America throughout the first half of the twentieth century and was particularly dominant administratively in the discipline for a number of years. Its decline, when it came, was not becasue Chicago was out of touch, or retained a dogmatic attatchment to an outmoded approach to sociological work, but more likely because it lost key personnel and with them a unique research environment. Structural changes in the discipline due to the rapid expansion of sociology in universities from 1930 meant that it could never regain its former dominance.

The detailed analysis of the history of the 'Chicago School' highlights some severe problems for the unit approach. However, this, of itself, does not mean that a unit approach is an unsuitable way to proceed. It may well be preferable to the simplistic cumulative theses usually embodied in the 'great man' and 'great ideas' approaches. The issue is not so much the focus of attention of the history, and thus of the metascientific enquiry, as the process of engagement with the historical material. Identifying the unit is merely the beginning rather than the climax of such metascientific enquiry.

In constructing a unit, decisions have to be made about the way it is circumscribed. The identification of the unit is of major importance because it clearly colours the way in which the historical evidence is approached. Linking people together into research units requires some thesis about the criteria for knowledge production. The problem, for unit approaches is, then, the determination of the criteria.

I would suggest that rather than build a stage by stage model to accommodate a revised Kuhnian thesis (Mullins, 1973) or to tightly define roles within an ideal type community in order to accommodate a research programme thesis (Tiryakian, 1979a), a metascientific unit analysis should concern itself with the processes by which cross-fertilisation of ideas through critique is managed. The focus should be on the way in which the body of sociological knowledge, to which members apply themselves, is transformed through critique [2]. There is no requirement to concentrate on reconstructing groupings of ideas or people and thus, rather than adopt 'conventional' or taken-for-granted categories, a critical engagement with the historical evidence is encouraged. The unit is seen as dynamically interacting with established knowledge rather than as the harbinger of a segregated orthodoxy or the cultish development of a heresy.

In this sense the unit is a community circumscribed in terms of an institutional affiliation and a communicative network for the transmission and critique of ideas. Such a network may be restricted to direct interpersonal relations, or based on more formal structures such as conferences and institutes, and may or may not be supported by one or more journals. In the long run, a periodical would appear to be important in sustaining the coherence and momentum of a critical unit. It is not necessary, however, that the journal be 'wholly controlled' by the unit, but rather that it re-present the processes of critique. The work of the unit may or may not be directed to a specific subject matter or involve elaborations of a core theory. The dynamic of the school may then be perceived in Kuhnian terms as dependent on puzzle-solving within a wider discipline or sub-discipline (Martins, 1972), with occasional revolutions transforming the paradigm; or in Lakatosian terms, as the cross-fertilisation of researchers working in different research programmes located within a school (or possibly even across school boundaries).

Essentially, then, the focus of attention is on the supportive association of researchers (which must be able to attract
or generate research monies and have the facilities to undertake research) which acts constructively to criticize the research endeavours of its members. The emphasis is on study of
the development of knowledge through critique, rather than the
pursuit of presuppositions, core ideas, subject boundaries or
groupings of practitioners in, and for, themselves. The case
study of the 'Chicago School' provides an initial exploration
of this approach. Assessment of its fruitfulness requires further research. However, such research must be based on primary
sources rather than trading on myth.

Notes

[1] This reflects the situation in the philosophy of science
    where historical material is used as a basis for supporting
    a given thesis about the generation of scientific know-
    ledge. See, for example, Holton (1973), Howson (1976). This
    is also evident in the development of the sociology of
    science, for example, Barnes (1972), Mulkay (1972). It
    would seem, however, that when it comes to their own sub-
    ject area, sociologists tend to be less scrupulous in
    examining the historical evidence and presume to know the
    subject.

[2] This is not to imply that all knowledge derives from crit-
    ique within metascientific units. All I am suggesting is
    that an approach that concentrates on metascientific units,
    which I think may well be a valuable approach, should
    investigate the knowledge transformative processes rather
    than be overly concerned about the constituents of inter-
    active networks.

Appendices

Appendix 1

Personnel in the Department of Sociology and Anthropology
at the University of Chicago 1892-1963 *

Table 1a
Sociology Faculty   1892-1906 [1]

	1892	93	94	95	96	97	98	99	1900	01	02	03	04	05	06
Small A.W	1	1	1	1	1	1	1	1	1	1	1	1	1	1	1
Henderson C.R	3	3	3	3	3	3	2	2	2	2	2	2	1	1	1
Talbot M	4	4	3	3	3	3	3	3	3	3	3	3	[2]		
Thomas W.I	0	0	7	4	4	4	4	3	3	3	3	3	3	3	3
Vincent G		9	7	4	4	4	4	3	3	3	3	2	2	2	2
Zeublin C [3]			5	5	5	5	5	5	2	2	2	2	2		
Bentley A.F				8											
Raymond J.H									3	3	3	3	3	3	3
Taylor G.												5	5	5	
Woodhead H													0	0	
Bedford S.W														0	0
	1892	93	94	95	96	97	98	99	1900	01	02	03	04	05	06

Table 1b
Sociology Faculty   1907–1920

	1907	08	09	10	11	12	13	14	15	16	17	18	19	20
Small A.W	1	1	1	1	1	1	1	1	1	1	1	1	1	1
Henderson C.R	1	1	1	1	1	1	1	1	[4]					
Thomas W.I	3	3	2	2	2	2	2	2	2	2	[5]			
Vincent G	2	2	[6]											
Raymond J.H	3	3												
Woodhead H		7	7	7	7	7	7							
Bedford S.W	0			4	4	4	4	4	4	3	3	3	3	3
Burgess E.W				0	0					4	4	4	4	4
Sutherland E.H					0	0								
Handman M.S					8									
Abbott E. [7]							6	7	6	7	6	6	6	6
Rainwater C							9	9	9					
Park R.E [8]								5	5	5	5	5	5	5
Znaniecki F											6	6	6	
Faris E														4

1907 08 09 10 11 12 13 14 15 16 17 18 19 20

Table 1c
Sociology Faculty   1921–1936

	1921	22	23	24	25	26	27	28	29	30	31	32	33	34	35	36
Small A.W	1	1	1	1	1											
Bedford S.W	3	3	3	3	3											
Burgess E.W	3	3	3	3	3	3	3	2	2	2	2	2	2	2	2	2
Park R.E	5	5	2	2	2	2	2	2	2	2	2	2	2	2	E2	E2
Faris E	4	4	4	4	4	1	1	1	1	1	1	1	1	1	1	1
House F.N		9		9	4	4										
Simpson E.N		9		9		7	7		8							
Shaw C [9]				9											9	9
Wirth L						7	7	7		7	4	3	3	3	3	3
Blumer H						9	9	7	7	7	4	3	3	3	3	3
Ogburn W.E							2	2	2	2	2	2	2	2	2	2
Webster E.J									7							
Cressey P.F									7	7						
Stouffer S.A [10]									7	7					2	2
Sutherland E.H									2	2	2	2	2			
Rice S.A											2					
Cottrell L.S											7	7	7			
Davis M.M											5	5	5		5	5
Hauser P													7	7	7	7
Johnson E.S													7	7	7	7
De Vinney L.C													0	0	0	
Lohman J.D													0			
Warner W.L [11]															3	3

1921 22 23 24 25 26 27 28 29 30 31 32 33 34 35 36

Table 1d
Sociology   Faculty   1937-50

	1937	38	39	40	41	42	43	44	45	46	47	48	49	50
Burgess E.W	2	2	2	2	2	2	2	2	2	2	1	1	1	1
Park R.E	E2	E2	E2	E2	E2	E2	E2							
Faris E [12]	1	1	1	E2	E2	E2	E2	E2	E2	E2	E2	E2	E2	E2
Shaw C	9	9	9	9	9	9	6	6	6	6	6	6	6	6
Wirth L	3	3	3	2	2	2	2	2	2	2	2	2	2	2
Blumer H	3	3	3	3	3	3	3	3	3	3	2	2	2	2
Ogburn W.E	2	2	2	1	1	1	1	1	1	1	2	2	2	2
Stouffer S.A	2	2	2	2	2	2	2	2						
Davis M.M	5													
Hauser P	7										2	2	2	2
Johnson E.S	4	4		4	4									
De Vinney L.C	0			7	7									
Lohman J.D				7	7	7	4	4	4		6	6	6	6
Warner W.L	3	3	3	3	2	2	2	2	2	2	2	2	2	2
Shils E.A [13]	0			7	7	7	7	7	4	3	3			
Hughes E.C		4	4	4	4	4	5	5	5	5	5	5	5	4
Bonner H			0				6	6	6	6				
Winch R.F [14]						0	7	7	7	7				
Whyte W.F						0	0	9	4	4	3	3		
Gilfillan S.C								9						
Williams J.J								0			7	7	7	3
Swanson G.E								0	0		7			
Goldhamer M											3	3	3	3
Horton D												9	9	9
Duncan O.D											9			
Reiss A.J												7	7	4
Roy D.F												7	7	7
Shibutani T.												7	7	7
Junker B.												7	7	7
Smith H.L												7	7	7
Kitagawa E.R												7	7	7
Solomon											7			
Goodman L														4
Moore D.G														4
Becker H.S														0
	1937	38	39	40	41	42	43	44	45	46	47	48	49	50

Table 1e
Sociology Faculty 1951-1963

	1951	52	53	54	55	56	57	58	59	60	61	62	63
Burgess E.W	1	E1	E1	E2	E2	E2	E2	E2	E2	E2	E2	E2	E2
Wirth L	2												
Blumer H	2												
Ogburn W.F	2	E2	E2	E2	E2	E2	E2	E2	E2				
Hughes E.C	2	2	2	1	1	1	2	2	2	2	2		
Hauser P	2	2	2	2	2	2	1	1	1	1	1	1	1
Warner W.L	2	2	2	2	2	2	2	2	2				
Shaw C	6	6	6	6	6	6	6						
Lohman J.D	6	6	6	6	6	6							
Shils E								2	2	2	2	2	2
Reiss A.J	4												
Goodman L	4	4	4	3	3	2	2	2	2	2	2	2	2
Horton D	4	4	4	4	4	4	4						
Duncan O.D [15]	4	4	4	4	4	4	4				2	2	
Williams J.J	9												
Moore D.G		2	2	2	3								
Kitagawa E.R [15]	4	4	4	4									
Foot N		4	4	4	4	4							
Willensky H	0	4	4										
Bradbury W		4	4	3	3	3	3	3					
Loeb M.B		4	4										
Becker H.S		7	7										
Reisman D				4	4	4	4	4					
Bogue D				5	5	5	5	5	4	4	4	4	4
Blau P				4	4	4	4	4	4	3	3	3	3
Strauss A				4	4	4	4	4					
Katz E					4	4	4	4	4	4	4	2	2
Rossi P						4	4	2	2	2			
Barton A.H							4						
Coleman J.S							4	4	4				
Davis J.A								4	4	4	4	4	3
Wohl R								3					
Anderson C.A									2	2	2	2	2
MacRae D									4	4	4	4	3
Whyte H										4	4	4	4
Dibble V.K										7	7	7	
Halsey A.M										3	3		
Sawyer J											4	4	4
Zald M											7	4	4
Janowitz M												2	2
Warkov S												4	4
Street D.P													4
Caplovitz D													4
Levine D													4
Crain R.L													4
Anderson O													3
Blauner R													3

	1951	52	53	54	55	56	57	58	59	60	61	62	63

Key to Tables 1, 4, 6 & 8

1 Head of Department
2 Professor (inc. Distinguished Service Professor)
3 Associate Professor
4 Assistant Professor
5 Professorial Lecturer
6 Lecturer
7 Instructor
8 Docent
9 Assistant, Assistant Graduate Scholar, Associate or Research Associate
0 Fellow (only those included who became full members of staff of the Department of Sociology. Table 2 provides a full list of fellows)
E Emiritus Professor
R Retired

* Source: The Official Publications of the University of Chicago. These are issued annually and the information in these tables are collated from these publication.

Notes to Table 1

[1] Research assistants who did some teaching but whose careers in the Department of Sociology at Chicago did not develop are not included in Table 1. These are listed in Table 3 up to 1932. Fellows of the Department are listed in Table 2.

[2] Talbot was associate professor of Sanitary Science before moving to the newly created Department of Household Administration in 1904

[3] Zeublin did a lot of his teaching in the Extension Division (Diner, 1980, p. 526). The courses he taught, according to the Official Publications of the University of Chicago were Elements and Structure of Society, Municipal Sociology and Structure of English Society.

[4] Henderson was (associate) Professor of Divinity until 1904 before his appointment as head of the Department of Ecclesiastical Sociology. This became the Department of Practical Sociology in 1915.

[5] All mention of Thomas were erased from the Official Publications for 1917 prior to publication in the wake of the court case which lead to Thomas' enforced resignation, despite aquittal.

[6] Diner (1980, p. 526) noted that Vincent became Dean of the junior college in 1900 and Dean of the Faculty of Arts, Literature and Science in 1907.

[7] Abbott taught part time. In 1908 she was the assistant director of the newly created School of Civics and Philanthropy. This became the School of Social Science Administration in 1920 at which time Abbott gave up her connection with the Sociology

226

Department.

[8] There is some difference among sources over the date of Park's inclusion in the Deptartment of Sociology. Diner (1980) says that Park taught a course on 'The Negro' in Autumn of 1913. Matthews (1977) concurs. Raushenbush (1979) says that this was an address and that the first course given by Park was in June 1914. (He was originally located in the Divinity Department before being trans- ferred to Sociology). Park actually wrote to Washington, June 1914, that ne had twice as many students as last year. The Official Publications do not list Park on the Sociology faculty in 1914, nor is there mention of a course by him in that year. In 1913 he is recorded as a professorial lecturer for the autumn. In 1915 he only taught in spring and summer quarters and in 1916 only during the summer quarter.

[9] Shaw was an associate member of the Department from 1935 to 1942.

[10] Stouffer was granted leave of absence for Government Service 1944 and 1945.

[11] Warner is listed as 'Sociology and Anthropology Professor' in each year of his tenure except 1936, 1937, 1952, 1953

[12] Faris was emeritus professor until 1953

[13] Shils was granted leave of absence for Government Service 1943 and 1944.

[14] Winch was granted leave of absence for Government Service in 1943 and for military sevice in 1944 and 1945.

[15] These staff were also associate staff, see Table 6.

Table 2
Fellows of the Department of Sociology (and Anthropology)
1892-1952 [1]

Years	Name	Years	Name
1892, 1893	W. I. Thomas *	1895, 1896	P. Monroe
1895, 1896	J. D. Forrest	1896	H. A. Millis
1896	A. T. Freeman	1896	D. P. Barrows
1897	C. A. Ellwood	1897, 1898	A. W. Dunn
1897, 1900	A. Hewes	1897	G. R. Sikes
1898	C. J. Bushnell	1898	A. D. Sorenson
1898, 1909	E. K. Eyerly	1898, 1900	R. G. Kimble
1900	B. F. Stacey	1900, 1902	E. Mumford
1900	H. B. Woolston	1901	R. C. Adams
1901	E. C. Hayes	1901	V. O'Brien
1901, 1903	T. J. Riley	1902	R. Morris
1903-05	E. Woods	1903	J. Dowd
1904	H. E. Fleming	1904, 1905	H. Woodhead *
1905-07	S. E. Bedford *	1906	L. Gray
1906	C. C. North	1907	V. E. Helleberg
1907, 1908	J. B. Obenchain	1907	G. A. Stephens
1907	A. H. Barron	1907-09	L. L. Bernard
1908, 1909	F. Fenton	1909	A. R. Mead
1909	R. B. McCord	1909	E. F. Colburn
1909, 1910	E. S. Bogardus	1909	W. L. Chenery
1910, 1911	A. M. Durand	1910	D. I. Pope
1911, 1912	E. H. Sutherland *	1911	A. H. Woodworth
1911, 1912	R. F. Clark	1912	S. A. Queen
1912	W. T. Cross	1913, 1913	R. W. Foley
1913	V. W. Brooder	1913	P. E. Coleman
1913, 1914	E. E. Eubank	1913	R. M. Leavell
1914	M. G. Bacon	1914	A. B. Lemstromm
1914, 1915	E. B. Reuter	1915, 1916	R. W. Stone
1916, 1917	H. E. Jensen	1916, 1917	E. D. Sanderson
1917	F. Thrasher	1918, 1919	W. B. Bodenhafer
1918, 1919	F. O. Daniel	1918, 1919	J. Horak
1918, 1919	A. C. Zumbrunnen	1920	R. W. Nelson
1920	K. Sato	1920	L. M. Spaeth
1920	G. S. Rossouw	1921	V. M. Ames
1921	K. E. Barnhart	1921	E. R. Mowrer
1922	A. E. Earl	1922, 1923	J. H. Meuller
1922	E. H. Shideler	1923	M. H. Neumeyer
1924, 1925	D. E. Proctor	1924	M. W. Roper
1924	T. C. Wang	1925	O. E. Kessling
1925	R. Fox	1925	G. E. Breece
1926, 1927	C. D. Gower	1926, 1927	E. T. Thompson
1926, 1927	E. L. Remelin	1926, 1927	W. T. Watson
1926, 1927	C. C. Wu	1928, 1929	C. D. Clark
1928-9,34-6	C. H. Schettler	1928	P. H. Nesbit
1928, 1929	E. V. Stonequist	1930, 1931	R. E. Faris
1930, 1931	C. C. Van Vechten	1930-1932	H. P. Hayes
1932	C. H. Young	1932	E. S. Johnson
1933	F. E. Merrill	1933-35, 37	L. C. De Vinney *
1933	J. D. Lohman *	1933, 1934	R. D. Pierson
1934	T. W. Gardlund	1935, 1936	R. O. Lang
1935, 1936	F. E. LaViolette	1936	C. W. Hart

Table 2 (continued)

1936	C. N.	Elliot	1937	E. A.	Shils *
1937	B. L.	Hormann	1937, 1938	L. M.	Spencer
1938	W. A.	Hillman	1938, 1939	H. D.	Duncan
1938	O.	Hall	1939	A. J.	Jaffe
1939, 1940	F. E.	Moore	1939	S.	Provus
1940	P.	Wallin	1940	H.	Bonner *
1940	I. V.	Toabe	1941, 1942	E.	Shanas +
1941, 1942	W. F.	Whyte *	1941	R. F.	Winch *
1941	A. M.	Rose	1941	R.	Freedman
1941	S. F.	Miyamoto	1942	R. E.	Clark
1942	F.	Marcelo	1942	N.	DeCampos
1942	R. B.	Reed	1942	E.	Rosenthal
1943	G. W.	Breese	1943, 1944	L. A.	Sussmann
1943, 1944	W. M.	DePoister	1943	N.	Keyfitz
1943	H. J.	Walker	1943	J. C.	Falardeau
1943	F. B.	Lindstrom	1943	M. L.	Mc.Donald
1944	J. J.	Williams *	1944, 1945	G. E.	Swanson *
1944	H. M.	Hughes	1944, 1945	J. R.	Burnet
1944	D. E.	Wray	1945	A.	Bender
1945-1947	B. N.	Meltzer	1945, 1946	D. M.	Okada
1945, 1947	M. S.	Schwartz	1945	O. E.	Westbrooke
1946, 1947	E. H.	Bernert	1946, 1947	E.	Gross
1946	B.	Ong	1946	A. W.	Rose
1946	A. C.	White	1947	E. V.	Eggers
1947, 1948	C. R.	Walgreen	1947	T. C.	Cothran
1948	W. H.	Hale	1948	Y.	Kimura
1948, 1949	E. R.	Kitagawa *+	1948, 1950	S. C.	Lee
1948	A. J.	Reiss *	1948	N.	Rogoff
1948	J.	Rosestein	1948, 1949	L. J.	Shapiro
1949	M. J.	Carr	1949	H.	Finestone
1949, 1950	D.	Gold	1949	F. P.	Grow
1949	L.	Huang	1949	L.	Zakuta
1950	H. S.	Becker *	1950	E. R.	Brown
1950	R. A.	Atkins	1950	S. M.	Dornbuch
1950	D. C.	Lortie	1950	W. A.	Westley
1951	J. E. J.	Brazeau	1951	F.	Davis
1951, 1952	L.	Kriesberg +	1951	D. M.	Lilienthal
1951	H. L.	Wilensky *	1952	M.	Blough
1952	L.	Breen	1952	S.	Cassidy
1952	B.	Goldstein	1952	K.	Lang
1952	D.	Matthews	1952	M.	Whacks
1952	T.	Yazaki			

Note to Table 2

[1] These fellows are included in Table 1 only if their careers developed beyond 'assistant' in the sociology department at Chicago. Those included in Table 1 are marked by an asterisk. Those fellows who became Associate staff are marked with a '+' and are included in Table 6.

Table 3
Assistants in the Department of Sociology (and Anthropology)
1922-1932 [1]

1922, 1923	W. F. Byron	1924	C. W. Strow
1922-1925	H. B. Sell	1924	F. L. McCluer
1922-1924	E. T. Kreuger	1924, 1925	J. H. Mueller
1922, 1923	F. M. Thrasher	1925	C. R. Shaw *
1922	R. W. Nelson	1925	J. A. Quinn
1922, 1923	S. C. Kincheloe	1926, 1927	H. Blumer
1923, 1925	E. N. Simpson *	1925, 1926	R. Shonle
1923, 1925	F. N. House *	1932	R. G. Newcomb
1923	E. Buchan		

Note to Table 3

[1] These assistants are included in Table 1 only if their careers
developed beyond 'assistant' in the sociology department at
Chicago. Those included in Table 1 are marked by an asterisk. The
Official Publications only listed assistants up to 1932.

Table 4
Anthropology Staff in the Department of Sociology
and Anthropology up to 1929

Starr F.	: Assistant Professor 1892-94; Associate Professor 1895-1922; Associate Prof. Retired 1923-28
West G.M	: Docent 1892-94
Miller M.L	: Assistant 1899-1900
Dorsey G.A	: Assistant Professor 1905-1914
Cole F.C	: Associate Professor 1924-1928
Sapir E	: Associate Professor 1926-1927; Professor 1928
Wallis W.D	: Professor 1927
Redfield R	: Instructor 1927-1928
Spier L	: Professor 1928

Table 5
Extension Staff 1892 - 1934

Bemis E.W	Associate Lecturer 1892 to 1894
Fulcomer D	Lecturer in 1893
Howerth I [1]	Associate 1894, Instructor 1898 to 1900, Assistant Professor 1901 to 1910
MacLean	Assistant Professor 1921 to 1934
McDowell M	Resident Head of the University Settlement 1892 to 1934

Note to Table 5

[1] Diner (1980) maintained that all Howerth's teaching was in the
Extension Division and in its special section for school teachers. The Official Publications do not make this clear after 1900.

Table 6
Associate Members (from 1948)

	1948	49	50	51	52	53	54	55	56	57	58	59	60	61	62	63
Population Research & Training Centre																
Kittagawa E [1]								9	9	4	4	3	3	3	3	3
Cuzzort R									7							
Duncan O.D											3	3	3			
Taeuber E															4	4
National Opinion Research Centre																
Hart C.W [2]			2	2	2	2	2	2	2	2	2	2	2	R2	R2	R2
Starr S.A			9		9	9	9	3	3	3	3	3	3			
Marks E.S							3	3	3							
Elinson J							3	3								
Shanas E											3	3	3	3	3	3
Kriesberg L												3	3	3		
Rossi P [2]														2	2	2
Feldman J														3	3	3
Johnstone J.W															3	3
Miller N																3
Farm Study Centre																
Litwak E							9	9	9							
Community Studies Inc. Kansas City, Miss.																
Becker H.S												4	4	4		
Industrial Relations Centre																
Nelson C			9	9	4	4	4	3								
Breen L							4	4								
Frankfurt School																
Horkheimer P							2	2	2	2	2					
Other Associates or Research Associates who did not develop career at Chicago up to 1963																
Meltzer B.N			9	9												
Rosenthal			9	9												
Farber B					4	4										
Wohl R							9	9	3	3						
Zeisler H							2	2	2	2	2	2	2	2	2	2
Ohlin L.E							9	9	9							
Mayershon R										4	4	4				
James R.M													4	4		
Moore J.W													4	4		
Ennis P.H													4	4	4	4
	1948	49	50	51	52	53	54	55	56	57	58	59	60	61	62	63

Notes to Table 6

[1] Kittagawa was linked to the Chicago Community Inventory in 1955 and 1956

[2] Director of The National Opinion Research Centre.

Table 7
Staff in Other Departments Listed in the Official Publications
of the Department of Sociology

Puttkamer E.	Professor of Law 1933-53 (1933 instructor)
Rheinstein N.	Professor of Comparative Law 1943-53
Kincheloe S.	Professor of Religion 1947-55
Sherman M.	Professor of Educational Psychology 1948-1951
Campbell D.	Associate Professor in Paychology 1951-53
Barton A. H.	Associate Professor in Law and Sociology 1953-54
Strodbeck F.	Associate Professor in Law and Sociology, 1954-63

Table 8
Visiting Lecturers [1]

Year	Visiting Lecturer	Institution	Position	
1895	E.A Ross	Leyland Stanford Univ.	2	
1896	L. Ward	Smithsonian Institute	4	
1915	J.H Raymond	New York City College	4	
1916	E.L Holton	Kansas State Agricultural College	2	
1917	G.E Howard	Nebraska Univ.	1	
1918	E.C Hayes	Univ. of Illinois	1	
1919	E.C Hayes	Univ. of Illinois	1	
1920	C.A Ellwood	Univ. of Missouri	1	
1920	W.B Bodenhofer	Univ. of Washington	2	
1920	W.S Thompson	Cornell Univ	3	
1922	L.L Benard	Univ. of Minnesota	2	
1923	L.L Benard	Univ. of Minnesota	2	
1924	L.L Benard	Univ. of Minnesota	2	
1925	R. McKenzie	Univ. of Washington	3	
1927	E.E Eubank	Univ. of Cincinnati	2	
1927	L.L Bernard	Tulane Univ.	5	*
1928	F.N House	Univ. of Virginia	2	
1929	L. Wirth	Tulane Univ	3	
1929	K. Young	Univ. of Wisconsin	3	
1929	R. McKenzie	Univ. of Washington	2	
1930	R. McKenzie	Univ. of Washington	2	**
1930	E.F Young	Univ. of California	2	
1930	T.C McCormick	Univ. of Oaklahoma	2	
1931	E.N Simpson	Univ. of Virginia	2	
1931	E.C Hughes	McGill University	2	
1937	T. Parsons	Harvard Univ.	4	
1939	H.J Locke	Indiana Univ.	4	
1941	O. Hall	Brown Univ.	7	
1947	S. Kimball	Univ. of Michigan	3	
1947	S Reimer	Univ. of Wisconsin	3	
1949	P. Lazarsfeld	Columbia Univ.	2	
1959	K.M Kapatia	Univ. Of Bombay	4	
1960	J.D Short	Washington State College	3	
1960	S. Eisenstadt	Hebrew University	2	
1961	J.D Short	Washington State College	3	
1961	A.L Stinchcombe	Johns Hopkins University	4	

Note to Table 8
[1] Source: Official Publications. Visiting lecturers taught in the
    Summer quarter except: * spring and summer, ** autumn and winter.

Appendix 2 [1]

The Local Community Research Committee publications 1923-1929

A. Books and monographs published under the auspicies of the Local Community Research Committee fall into various headings :

1. University of Chicago Social Services Series

    Abbott, E., 1926
    Breckinridge, S.P., 1924
    Breckinridge, S.P., 1927

2. Social Service Monographs (numbered)

    Beeley, A., 1927 (No.1)
    Breckinridge, 1928 (No.3)
    Hathway, M., 1928 (No.4)
    Hughes, E.A. & Stuenkel, 1929 (No.8)
    Ladewick, E., 1929, (No. 7)
    Nims, E., 1928 (No.2) [2]

3. Materials for the Study of Business

    Baker, N.F., 1927
    Montgomery, R.E., 1927
    Schultz, H., 1928
    Warne, C.E., 1926
    Wolf, H.D., 1927

4. Social Science Studies (numbered)

  Studies in geography:
    Duddy, E.A., 1929 (No.15)
    Fryxell, F.M., 1927 (No.5)
    Goode, J.P., 1926 (No.3)

  Studies in politics:
    Beyle, H.C., 1928 (No. 10)
    Gosnell, H.F., 1927 (No.4)
    Johnson, C.O., 1928 (No.11)
    Merriam, C.E., & Gosnell, H.F., 1924 (No.1)
    White, L.D., 1927 (No.9)
    White, L.D., 1929 (No.14)
    Wooddy, C.H., 1926, (No.2)

  Studies on the census:
    Jeter, H.R., 1927, (No.7)

  Studies in history:
    Beckner, E.R., 1929 (No. 13)

  Studies in sociology:
    Palmer, V., 1928, (No.12)

Studies on welfare:
  Chicago Civic Agencies, 1927 (No.6)

Studies in economics:
  Houghteling, L., 1927 (No.8)
  Staley, E.A., in press [1929] (No.16)

5. University of Chicago Sociological Series

  Mowrer, E.R., 1927
  Wirth, L., 1928
  Zorbaugh, H.W., 1929

6. University of Chicago Studies in Urban Sociology

  Park R.E and Burgess, E.W., 1925
  Thrasher, F.M., 1927

7. Studies in the Packing Industry [3] .

  Rhoades, E.L., 1929a
  Rhoades, E.L., 1929b
  Rhoades, E.L., 1929c

In addition the following publications were not included under a
series banner:

  Abbott, E., 1924
  Region of Chicago Base Map, 1926

All the above were published by University of Chicago Press

The following were published elsewhere:

  Williams, D., & Skinner, M.E., (undated)
  Millis, S., (undated)
  Park, R.E., contribution to Gee, ed, (in Press)
  Bruce A.A. et al, 1928
  White, L.D., 1925

B. Journal Articles

In addition there are a large number of journal articles listed.

Sociologists with articles in the list are:

E.W. Burgess (8 articles)
F.E. Frazier (2 articles)

Other major publishers:

S.E. Leland (7 articles all in National Real Estate Journal)
L.L. Thurstone (13 articles)

Location of articles:

Africa
American Economic Review
American Elevator and Grain Trade
American Journal of Psychiatry
American Journal of Psychology
American Journal of Sociology 3 [4]
Annals of American Academy of Politics and Social Science 2
Annals of American Sociological Society
Distribution and Warehousing
Educational Record 2
International Journal of Ethics
Journal of Abnormal and Social Psychology
Journal of Educational Psychology
Journal of Experimental Psychology 2
Journal of General Psychology
Journal of the American Statistical Association 3
National Real Estate Journal 7
Proceedings of the National Conference of Social Work 2
Psychological Review 3
Religious Education
Social Forces 3
Social Service Review 2

Of the list of research studies completed but not published as of 1929, seventeen could be described as sociological which is less than those on welfare or political science. From the titles and personnel the following breakdown: [5]

23 economics
18 welfare
17 sociology
9 politics
6 union/labour relations
2 anthropology
1 history
1 psychology
1 census/population trends

Sociology research in progress: (1929)

Conway, MA, 1926   McGill, MA 1927
Cressey, MA, 1929   Reckless, Ph.D, 1925
Glick, MA, 1928   Scott, MA, 1929
Hayner, Ph.D., 1923   Stephan, MA, 1926
Lieffer MA, 1928

plus work referred to as follows:

Ireland, W.R.P., The Study of the Process of Americanization among Polish Young People in a Settlement Neigborhood.
Ogburn, W.F., Fertility According to Occupations and Social Classes.
Ogburn, W.F., Ranking of Different Influences in the Last Presidential Election
Ogburn, W.F., Variability in Birth Rates in Different Civilizations
Shaw, Clifford, Juvenile Delinquency
Stephan, F.F., Public Recreations in Chicago
Tibbits, R.C., Immigrant Groups in Chicago
Tibbits, R.C., Social Forces and Trends in Settlement Neigborhoods.

Local Community Research Committee matched fund agencies: 1923-1929

Official sources:
   City of Chicago
   Smithsonian Institution
   U.S. Children's Bureau

Foundations and institutes:
   Wiebolt Foundation
   Rosenwald Foundation
   Commonwealth Fund
   Helen Critenden Memorial
   Institute of Economics
   Chicago Historical Society
   American Institute of Criminal Law and Criminology

Clubs:
   City Club of Chicago
   Commonwealth Club
   Union League Club
   Chicago Woman's Club
   Rotary Club
   National League of Women Voters

Special Interest Groups:
    Chicago Real Estate Board
    Chicago Heart Association
    Chicago Urban League
    Chicago Council of Social Agencies
    Chicago Foundlings Home
    Evangelical Orpahanage and Old People's Home
    Federation of Settlements
    Henry Booth Settlement House
    Child Guidance Centers
    Northwestern University Settlement
    Chicago Commons Association
    Chicago Immigrant Protective League
    American Home Economics Association
    Illinois Association for Criminal Justice
    Illinois State Federation of Labor
    Joint Service Bureau
    Scholarship Association For Jewish Children
    Association of Community Chests and Councils
    International Advertising Association
    Institute of Meat Packing
    Lower North Child Guidance Center

In addition various donations by individuals were made towards matched fund research.

Notes to Appendix 2

[1] Source : Smith & White, 1929.

[2] There is no record of Numbers 5 and 6.

[3] These were short monographs less than 35 pages.

[4] The contributers from the Local Community Research Committee to the American Journal of Sociology were Thurstone, Gosnell, and Douglas. None of these were sociologists.

[5] One study unclassified , viz. Brown, E., 'Chicago Typothetae'.

Appendix 3

The Society for Social Research at the University of Chicago

1. Constitution of the Society for Social Research.

The following is a copy of a document from the University of Chicago,
Regenstein Library, Special Collections Department, Wirth Paper. It
is undated but is probably the original consitution of the Society
with two amendments appended.

THE SOCIEIY FOR SOCIAL RESEARCH

The University of Chicago

Constitution

1. The name of this organization shall be the "The Society for
Social Research of the University of Chicago".

2. The purpose of the Society is to bring about the cooperation
of persons engaged in social research and social investigation.

3. In order to stimulate and promote efficiency in research and
investigation among its members, the Society will develop the
following activities:

a. The permanent registration of its members.

b. A clearing house of investigagtion and research, to assemble
bibliographies, to collect pamphlet literature, and to formulate
methods.

c. The organization of an advisory committee to provide service,
in the supervision of research, to the members of the Society,
and to promote the publications of standard works in research and
investigation.

4. Membership shall be open to graduate students in the Department of Sociology, and to other persons who have attained professional standards of research approved by the executive committee.

5. The initiation fee is one dollar. The payment of the initiation fee and the annual dues of one dollar shall entitle a
member to the services of the Society.

6. The secretary-treasurer of the Society shall, under the suggestion and direction of the executive committee, organize and
conduct the activities of the Society. He shall be appointed by
the executive committee.

7. The official year of the Society is October 1 to September 30,
inclusive.

8. The Executive Committee of the Society is composed of the

President, Vice-President and Secretary-Treasurer of the Society, and two other members appointed by the President.

9. Members shall be elected by the Executive Committee upon written application by the candidate upon the official blanks to be secured from the Secretary-Treasurer.

10. The regular meetings of the Execuitve Committee shall be held each Tuesday before the regular meeting of the Society.

11. The President of the Society shall be elected by the members, at the last meeting of the Summer Quarter.

12. The Trustees of the Society shall be composed of the members of the Execuitive Committee, with two additional members elected annually by the Society.

13. Amendments to the Constitution may be made by a two thirds vote of the members present and voting at a regular meeting, providing that the amendment shall have been submitted in writing at the previous regular meeting.

14. A quorum shall consist of one third of the resident members.

Amendment I.

The trustees of the Society shall be composed of the members of the Executive Committee. with the Dean of the Graduate School of Arts and Literature, who shall serve ex officio.

Minutes of the meting of the Exec. Comm. on Dec. 9. 1925, of the Society, Dec. 9, 1925, and of the society, Jan. 14, 1926, record the presentation and adoption of this amendment:

'Any individual eligible for membership in the Society may be elected to honary membership by the Executive Committee'.

A later Constitution, again undated incorporated the amendments, gave more power to act to the Executive Committee and made membership more open. The following is a copy of a document also located in the Wirth Papers.

THE SOCIETY FOR SOCIAL RESEARCH
The University of Chicago

CONSTITUTION

1. The name of this organization shall be the "The Society for Social Research of the University of Chicago".

2. The purpose of the Society is to bring about the co-operation of persons engaged in social research and social investigation. The Society will endeavor to develop such activities as will stimulate and promote efficiency in research and investigation among its members.

3. Membership shall be open to faculty mambers in the Social Sciences, graduate students in the Social Sciences who are engaged in a program of research approved by a member of the faculty, and to other persons who have attained professional standards of research approved by the Executive Committee.

4. Members shall be elected by the Executive Committee upon written application by the candidate upon the official blanks to be secured from the Secretary-Treasurer.

5. The Executive Committee shall be empowered to elect honary members.

6. The initiation fee is one dollar. The payment of the initiation fee and the annual dues of one dollar shall entitle a member to the services of the Society.

7. The following officers of the Society shall be elected by the members for a period of one year at the annual business meeting at the Summer Institute: the president, vice president, executive secretary, secretary treasurer, and two editors of the Bulletin.

8. The executive secretary of the Society shall, under the suggestion and direction of the executive committee, organize and conduct the activities of the Society.

9. The Executive Committee of the Society shall be composed of the six elective officers and two other members to be appointed by the president from the Social Science faculty for terms of two years which shall terminate in alternating years. The powers of the Executive Committee shall be those usually exercised by executive committees and in addition those specifically provided in this constitution.

10. Meetings of the Executive Committee shall be at the call of the president or executive secretary.

11 The official year of the Society is October 1 to September 30, inclusive.

12. There shall be an annual audit of the books of the Society under the direction of the Chairman of the Department of Sociology. This audit shall be reported at the annual business meeting of the Society at the Summer Institute.

13. Amendments to the Constitution may be made by a two thirds vote of the members present and voting at a regular meeting, providing that the amendment shall have been submitted in writing at the previous regular meeting and providing that announcement of the intention to propose amendments and to act upon amendments shall be made on the respective regular meeting notices sent to all resident members.

14. A quorum shall consist of fifteen members.

2. Members of the Society for Social Research up to 1935

The following list of members is compiled from various sources and may not be comprehensive. The sources used were
(1) a typed list headed 'Dues Received 1925-1926', those listed are indicated in column one of the table
(2) The Bulletin of the Society for Social Research of Dec 1926, those listed are noted in column 2
(3) The Bulletin of the Society for Social Research, Jan 1928 (col 3)
(4) A list of members from the files of the Society for Social Research, undated, but which, on the basis of the location of members was almost certainly drawn up in 1932 (col 4)
(5) A similar list, also undated, but again almost certainly from 1935 (col 5).
(6) Respondents to a questionnaire reported in the December 1934 issue of the Bulletin. Two hundred and thirty four letters were sent out (92) 44% returned with Society for Social Research membership dues, 12 discontinued membership, 7 returned as having been sent to the wrong address and 123 non-responses. Column 6 shows those respondents who indicated their research and whom the Bulletin included in its summary. On Nov 1st 1935 a further questionnaire sent to 239 members, 97 (45.6%) replied and paid, 5 to pay in Dec., 7 discontinued, 3 incorrect address, 127 non responses. 56 of replies indicated research. A number of letters sent abroad: 5 China, 4 Hawaii, 3 Canada, 2 Japan, 1 Brazil, Czechoslovakia, France, Mexico, Russia, Switzerland. Column 7 shows those members of the Society who responded to the questionnaire and whose work was included in the summary of the responses in the Bulletin. Other members mentioned in the December 1935 issue of the Bulletin are indicated by an M. Columns 6 and 7 thus provide an indication of the 'active' members of the Society, in the mid 1930s.

The date in brackets is the date of joining the Society. Where no date is given, the individual was a member before 1925. Where the year only is given, this is the best estimate available for year of joining. Where the month and year is given this is accurate to within a month either way.

	Dues Paid 1925 1926	BSSR Dec 1926	BSSR Jan 1928	Memb List 1932	Memb List 1935	BSSR Mar 1935 Qu R	BSSR Dec 1935 QRM
A:							
B. Achtenberg (Oct 1935)					I		I
E.A. Ahrens (7.11.27)				0	0		
D. Allen ***				0			
C.O. Anderson (Mar 1933)				I	I		
N. Anderson	0	0	0	0	0		M
E.A. Aubrey	0	0	0	I	I		Ï
G.E. Axtelle (Oct 1935)					I		I
B:							
J.O. Babcock (Mar 1933)				I	0		0
R. Bain		0	0	0	0		M
A.J. Baker	I	IF	IF				
P. Baker (1.6.27)			0	0	0		
K.E. Barnhart	0	0	0	0	0		
H.M. Bartlett (6.5.27)		I					
H.P. Becker (1.6.27)		I	0				
A.L. Beeley		0	0	0	0	0	
L.L. Bernard (post 1926)		0	0	0			M
W.S. Bittner (1929)							
E.E. Black (1927) [Winston]		I	0	0			M
A. Blumenthal (Apr 1931)				0			M
H. Blumer	0	IF	IF	I			M
W.B. Bodenhafer	0	0	0	0	0		
E.S. Bogardus		0	0	0	0		
P. Booth (Oct 1933)				I	I		
G.E. Breece (14.1.26)	I	0	0	0			
L.G. Brown	I	0	0	0	0		
W.O. Brown (7.11.27)		I	0	0			
E. Buchan		0					
E.W Burgess	I	IF	IF	I	I		M
W. Burke (13.11.24)		I					
W.A. Butcher		0	0	0	0		
A.P. Butler (June 1930)							
H. Byrd (Jan 1931)							
A.M. Byrnes		0					
W.F. Byron	I	I	I	I	I		
C:							
W.P. Carter (14.1.26)	I	I	I				
J. Cavan	I	0	0	0			
H. Cayton (Mar 1933)				I	I		M
G.E. Chaffee	U	0	0	0	0		
H. Chao (Jan 1931)				0	0		
C.Y. Chen (Oct 1932)							
C.D. Clark (1929)				0	0		
H.I. Clarke	I	0	0	0	0		
M.B. Clinard (Dec 1934)					I		I
C.B. Cohen (Mar 1933)				I	I		
H.E. Cohen (Oct 1933)					0		0

	Dues Paid 1925 1926	BSSR Dec 1926	BSSR Jan 1928	Memb List 1932	Memb List 1935	BSSR Mar 1935 Qu R	BSSR Dec 1935 QRM
F.C. Cole	I	IF	IF	I			
J.A. Conner (Mar 1933)					0		0
F.A. Conrad		0	0	0	0		
L.A. Cook (8.4.26)	I	I	0	0	0		
L.C. Copeland (Oct 1935)							
B. Corman		I	I	I			
L.S. Cottrell (7.11.27)			I	I	0		M
O.C. Cox (Dec 1934)					I		
P.F. Cressey (9.12.25)	I	I	0	0	0		
P.G. Cressey	I	I	0	0	0	0	
E.B. Crook *				0	0	I	0

D:

	Dues Paid 1925 1926	BSSR Dec 1926	BSSR Jan 1928	Memb List 1932	Memb List 1935	BSSR Mar 1935 Qu R	BSSR Dec 1935 QRM
B. Dai (Jan 1931)				0	0		M
D.M. Dailey (Oct 1935)					I		I
V.E. Daniel ***				0	0		
W.A. Daniel	0	0	0	0	I		0
S. Dauchy		I	I	I	I		
C.R. Davidson ***				0	0		
A.J. Davis (22.4.26)	I	0	0	0			
R.N. Davis (Mar 1935)					0		0
M. Davis *				I	I	I	I
C.A. Dawson	0	0	0	0	0		M
C.L. Dedrick **					0		M
F.G. Detweiler		0		0			
L.C. DeVinney (1935)					I		
P.T. Diefenderfer (28.1.26) I	I	0	0	0			
J. Dollard (June 1930)				0			M
F. Donovan	I	I	I	I			
B. Doyle (Sep 1930)					0		
G. Dow (16.12.26)							
J.L. Duflot (1929)							
W.F. Dummer		I	I	I	I		I
H.W. Dunham (Mar 1935)							M

E:

	Dues Paid 1925 1926	BSSR Dec 1926	BSSR Jan 1928	Memb List 1932	Memb List 1935	BSSR Mar 1935 Qu R	BSSR Dec 1935 QRM
A.E. Earl		0					
Z.T. Egartner		I	I				
J.C. Ellickson				I			
T.E. Eliot ***				I	I		
J. Elmdorf (Jan 1931)							
J. Emory (14.1.26)	I	0	0	0	0		
E.E. Eubank (1927)				0	0	0	M

F:

	Dues Paid 1925 1926	BSSR Dec 1926	BSSR Jan 1928	Memb List 1932	Memb List 1935	BSSR Mar 1935 Qu R	BSSR Dec 1935 QRM
D.I. Fahs (June 1930)[Beck]				0			
E. Faris	I	IF	IF	I	I		0
R.E. Faris (June 1930)				0	0		M

	Dues Paid 1925 1926	BSSR Dec 1926	BSSR Jan 1928	Memb List 1932	Memb List 1935	BSSR Mar 1935 Qu R	BSSR Dec 1935 QRM
J.L. Frank	I	I		O			
F.E. Frazier (1927)			I		O		
A.A. Friedrich		O					
G:							
W.E. Gettys		I	I	O	O		M
R.L. Gibbs (June 1930)					I		M
S.C. Gilfillan (1929)				I	I	I	I
C. Glick (1927)			I	I	O		O
F. Goldeen (Apr 1931)				I			
H.F. Gosnell		IF	IF	I	I		M
L.R. Greene		I	I	I			
E.B. Groves		O	O	O	O		
C. Guignard (Jan 1931)							
H:							
S.T. Hajicek		I					
M.H. Hall (Apr 1931)							
L.M. Handsaker (May 1935)					O		M
E.B. Harper	O	O	O	O	O		
C.W. Hart (Oct 1935)					I		M
G. Hartmann	O	O	O	O			
P. Hauser (Jan 1931)				I	O		O
F.M. Hawley (Jan 1934)							
E.M. Haydon (Dec 1934)					I		
N.S. Hayner	O	O	O	O	O	O	O
C.W. Hayes		O	O	O	I		
H. Hayes (Sep 1930)				I			
W.H. Heinmiller ***				O			
C.E. Hendry (Mar 1933)					I		
A.P. Herman (Mar 1933)					I	O	I
E.P. Hershberger **					I		I
B.M. Hill (May 1935)							
E.T. Hiller	O	O	O	O	O	O	
E.V. Hines **					O		O
A.E. Holt (1927)			IF	I			
J. Horak	O	O					
B.L. Hormann (May 1935)					I		O
F.N. House	I	O	O	O	O		
H. Hoyt (1935)					O		
L. Hsu ***				O	O		
E.C. Hughes	I	I	O	O	O		M
C.R. Hutchinson (Mar 1933)							
T.G. Hutton (Mar 1933)					I		M
C.J. Hyming (Dec 1934)					I		
I:							
W. Ireland (14.1.26)	I	I	I	I	I		O

244

	Dues Paid 1925 1926	BSSR Dec 1926	BSSR Jan 1928	Memb List 1932	Memb List 1935	BSSR Mar 1935 Qu R	BSSR Dec 1935 QRM
J:							
J. Jacobs (Jan 1931)				I	I		
A.J. Jaffe (Oct 1935)							
A.B Jameson ***				0			
R. Jenkins (8.4.26)	I	0	0	0	0		
E.C. Jensen (Dec 1934)					I		
H.E. Jensen	0	0	0	0	0	0	
C.S. Johnson	0	0	0	0	0		M
E.S. Johnson (Sep 1930)				I	I		M
R.C. Jones *				I	I	I	I
W.H. Jones		0	0		0		
S. Jusama ***				0			
K:							
F.B. Karpf	0	0	0	0			0
M. Katow		0					
K. Kawabe		0	0	0	0		
T. Kawamuru (25.2.27)			I	0	0		
F.M. Keesing (June 1930)				0	0		
M.M. Keesing (June 1930)				0	0		
E. Kennedy (13.11.24)		I					
S.C. Kincheloe	I	I	I	I	I		
J.H. Kirk (Oct 1933)							
E.E. Klein (Mar 1933)					I		
M.D. Kneberg (Oct 1933)							
F.H. Knight (Mar 1933)					I		M
J.H. Kolb		0	0	0	0		M
R. Koshuk *				I	I	I	I
E.T. Kreuger		0	0	0	0		
A.F. Kuhlman	I	0	0	I			I
D.H. Kulp	0	0	0	0			
S. Kusama	0	0	0		0		
H. Kyrk (Dec 1934)					I		
L:							
M.M. Lam (Oct 1935)					I		I
J. Landesco		I	I	I	I		
R. Lang (Oct 1932)				I	I		I
F. LaViolette (Dec 1934)					I		M
H.D. Lasswell			IF	I	0		M
I.H. Latimer (Oct 1933)					I		
R.N. Latture (Mar 1933)					0		
O.R. Lavers		0	0				
G.K. Laves (1929)							
R.W. Leeper (Oct 1933)							
L.L. Leh		0	0				
M. Leiffer (9.12.25)	I	I	I	I	I	0	
P. Lejins (Dec 1934)					0	0	
A. Lepawsky **				I	I		M

	Dues Paid 1925 1926	BSSR Dec 1926	BSSR Jan 1928	Memb List 1932	Memb List 1935	BSSR Mar 1935 Qu R	BSSR Dec 1935 QRM
Y. Levin (1935)					I		
G.G. Leybourne (Oct 1935)					I		I
A. Lind (9.12.25)	I	I	O	O	O	O	
A.R. Lindesmith (Mar 1933)					I		I
H.J. Locke (Dec 1934)					I		M
J.D. Lohman (1935)					I		
D.M. Lorden (Mar 1933)				I		O	M
K.D. Lumpkin (Oct 1933)							

M:

	Dues Paid 1925 1926	BSSR Dec 1926	BSSR Jan 1928	Memb List 1932	Memb List 1935	BSSR Mar 1935 Qu R	BSSR Dec 1935 QRM
H. MacGill (9.12.25)	I	I	O	O	O		
M. McAfee (25.2.27)			O	O	O		
F.L. McCluer	O	O	O	O	O		
T.C. McCormick (1.6.27)			I				
H.E. McNeil ***				I	O		
H. McKay ***				I	I		
R.D. McKenzie	O	O	O	O	O	O	
O. Machotka **					O		M
P.C. Maurer (Dec 1934)					I		
B.H. Mautner (9.12.25)	I	O	O				
W.P. Meroney		O	O	O	O		
F.E. Merrill **				I	O		M
D.G. Monroe ***				O			
E.W. Montomery (1932)				O	O		M
M. Moore (Jan 1931)				O	O	O	
E.L. Morgan (1927)			O	O	O		
W. Morrison (8.4.26)	I	O					
V. Morrow		O					
E.R. Moses				I	O		
E.R. Mowrer	I	I	I	I	I		M
H.R. Mowrer	I	I	I	I	I		
J.H. Mueller	O	O	O	O	O		M
T.W. Mueller ***				O	I		
A.M Myhrman	O	O	O	O	O	O	O

N:

	Dues Paid 1925 1926	BSSR Dec 1926	BSSR Jan 1928	Memb List 1932	Memb List 1935	BSSR Mar 1935 Qu R	BSSR Dec 1935 QRM
R.E. Nelson (June 1930)				I	I		
M.H. Neumeyer	I	I	O	O	O		
C.S. Newcomb (8.4.26)	I	I	IF	I	O		M
R.G. Newcomb (7.11.27)			I	I	O		
C. Niemi		O					
K. Niles (Oct 1932)				I			
T.K. Noss (Jan 1934)					O		O

O:

	Dues Paid 1925 1926	BSSR Dec 1926	BSSR Jan 1928	Memb List 1932	Memb List 1935	BSSR Mar 1935 Qu R	BSSR Dec 1935 QRM
W.F. Ogburn (1927)			IF		I		M
M.D. Oyler (Oct 1931)					O	O	O

	Dues Paid 1925 1926	BSSR Dec 1926	BSSR Jan 1928	Memb List 1932	Memb List 1935	BSSR Mar 1935 Qu R	BSSR Dec 1935 QRM
P:							
V.M. Palmer	I	I	I				
R.E. Park	I	IF	IF	0	0		M
R.R. Pearson		I	I				
W. Pfeil **							M
D.R. Pierson **				I	0		M
M.H. Phelps (Oct 1931)				I			
M.L. Plumley (Oct 1933)					0		
R.A. Polson (June 1930)				0			
M.T. Price	0	0	0	0	0	0	0
D.E. Proctor (14.5.25)	I	0	0	I	0		M
Q:							
S.A. Queen	0	0	0	0	0	0	0
J.A. Quinn (14.5.25)	0	0	0	0	0		
R:							
S.C. Ratcliffe	0	0	0	0	0		
E.O. Rausch (7.11.27)			I		I		
W. Raushenbush		I					
I. Rausseau					I		
C. Razovsky	0	0	0				
W.C. Reckless		0	0	0	0		0
R. Redfield (30.10.24)	0	0	IF	I	I		
E. Redden (Dec 1934)					0		M
E. Remelin (16.12.26) [Whitridge]		0	0				
E.B. Reuter		0	0	0	0		M
S.A. Rice (Oct 1932)				I	0		
M.W. Roper	0	0	I	0	0	0	M
A.C. Rosander (Mar 1933)				I			
S.M Rosen (Mar 1933)					I		I
K.M. Rosenquist (7.11.27)			I	0	0		
F.B. Ross		0	0	0	0		
D. Russell		0	0	0	0		
S.K. Rychlinski (Mar 1933)							
W.S. Ryder	0	0	0	0	0		
G.S. Rossouw		0					
S:							
J.M. Sampson		I					
E. Sapir	I	IF	IF	0	0		
D.J. Saposs	0	0	0	0			
A.J. Saunders		0					
M.C. Schauffler (Mar 1933)				I	0	0	0
C.H. Schettler (Oct 1933)					I	0	I
H.B. Sell	0	0	I	I	I		M
L. Setterlund (Oct 1931)				I	0		0
A.L. Severson (Oct 1935)					0		M

	Dues Paid 1925 1926	BSSR Dec 1926	BSSR Jan 1928	Memb List 1932	Memb List 1935	BSSR Mar 1935 Qu R	BSSR Dec 1935 QRM
E. Shanas (Oct 1935)					I		
C.R. Shaw	I	I	I	I	I		I
M. Sheahan	I	I	I	I	I		
E.H. Sheidler	0	0	0	0			
E.A. Shils (Dec 1934)					I		M
R. Shonle	I	I	I	I	I	0	M
E.N. Simpson	I	IF	0	0	0		M
G.H. Simpson		0					
C.M. Skepper (Oct 1933)							
D. Slesinger **					0		M
C.W. Smith ***				0			
R.C. Smith (7.11.27)				0			
W.C. Smith	0	0	0	0		0	
A.W. Small	I						
L.S. Smythe (Mar 1935)					0		
H.M. Snyder	0	0	0	0			
J.F. Steiner		0	0	0	0		M
A.S Stephan	0			0	0		
A.S. Stepanian (June 1930)							
F.F. Stephan		I	0	0	0		M
W.B. Stone		0	0	0	0		
E.V. Stonequist (1929)				0	0		M
S.A. Stouffer (1.6.27)			I	0	I		M
C.W. Strow	0	0	0	0	0		0
H.A. Sturges	0	0	0	0			
K. Su (Jan 1931)				I			
T.E. Sullinger	0	0	0	0	0		
J.E. Sumner (25.2.27)			0	0	0		
E.H. Sutherland (1930)				I	0		M
C.D. Sylvester (Mar 1935)					I		I
J.N. Symons (Dec 1934)					I		M

T:

	Dues Paid 1925 1926	BSSR Dec 1926	BSSR Jan 1928	Memb List 1932	Memb List 1935	BSSR Mar 1935 Qu R	BSSR Dec 1935 QRM
N.S. Talbot (Mar 1935)							
H.B. Taylor **				I	I		I
J.B. Tegarden	0	0	0	0			
C.A. Thompson (1929)							
E. Thompson (11.1.27)			0		0	0	0
F.M. Thrasher	0	0	0	0	0	0	M
L.L Thurstone (Mar 1933)				I			
R.C. Tibbitts	I	I	I	0			M
I.V. Toabe (Oct 1935)					I		I
D.M. Trout	0	0	0				

V:

	Dues Paid 1925 1926	BSSR Dec 1926	BSSR Jan 1928	Memb List 1932	Memb List 1935	BSSR Mar 1935 Qu R	BSSR Dec 1935 QRM
C. Van Vechten (Apr 1931)				I	I		M
J.A. Vieg (Oct 1935)					I		I

	Dues Paid 1925 1926	BSSR Dec 1926	BSSR Jan 1928	Memb List 1932	Memb List 1935	BSSR Mar 1935 Qu R	BSSR Dec 1935 QRM
W:							
W. Waller	I	0	0	0	0		M
M. Walker	I	0	0				
T.C. Wang		0	0	0	0		
W. Watson (8.4.26)	I	0	I	0	0	0	
E.J. Webster (1929)				0	0		M
S.K. Weinberg (May 1935)							M
F.L. Weller (Jan 1934)					I		I
E.R. Whitridge					I		
C.W. Whitney		0					
L. Wirth (30.10.24)	I	IF	IF	I	I		M
A.E. Wood ***				0			
A.V. Wood		I	0	0	0		
L.F. Wood	0	0	0				
R.L. Woolbert (1929)				0	0		0
H.G. Woolbert *				0	0	0	M
M.N. Work	0	0	0	0	0	0	0
C.C. Wu (22.4.26)	I	I	I	0	0		
Y:							
C.Y. Yen (Mar 1933)				I	0		
H. Yokoyama		0					
C.H. Young (Oct 1931)							
E.F. Young	0	0	0	0	0		
K. Young	0	0	0	0	0		M
O.B. Ytrehus	I	I	I	I			
Z:							
C.C. Zimmerman	0	0	0	0	0		M
H.M. Zorbaugh	0	0	0	0	0		M
F.M. Zorbaugh			I	0	0		

Key:

I   In Residence or local
0   Out of town
F   Recorded as faculty member or as having address at faculty exchange
*   Membership date not located but likely between 1930-35 (and prob 1934)
** Membership date not located but likely to have been during 1935
*** No record of the date of joining could be located, these members just appeared on the 1932 list. It is likely they joined in that year.

3. Meetings of the Society for Social Research 1924-1935

The reports of 152 meetings of the SSR between 1924 and 1935 were analysed. Some of these meetings were business meetings and some were report backs on the American Sociological Society Conference. A total of 140 addresses were presented to the meetings of the Society on which information was available in the period 1924-1935.

Table 1
Year of address by speaker's auspices

Auspices	Years				
	1924-26	1927-29	1930-32	1933-35	All
Sociology Faculty	6 (17)	5 (19)	9 (24)	13 (36)	33 (24)
Sociology Students	13 (37)	3 (11)	5 (13)	2 (6)	23 (17)
Other U.C. Faculty	6 (17)	12 (44)	13 (34)	12 (33)	43 (32)
Non U.C. Faculty	6 (17)	3 (11)	5 (13)	6 (17)	20 (15)
Outside non-academics	4 (11)	4 (15)	6 (16)	3 (8)	17 (13)
Totals	35	27	38	36	136

Numbers in brackets are column percentages rounded to nearest whole number. Four missing values

Table 2
Year of address by members of the Society

Membership	Years				
	1924-26	1927-29	1930-32	1933-35	All
Members	25 (66)	12 (43)	17 (45)	20 (56)	74 (53)
Non Members	13 (34)	16 (57)	21 (55)	16 (44)	66 (47)
Totals	38	28	38	36	140

Numbers in brackets are column percentages to nearest whole number

Table 3
Year of address by major concern(s) of address

Major Concern(s)	Years				
	1924-26	1927-29	1930-32	1933-35	All
Theory	8 (22)	14 (52)	12 (32)	16 (44)	40 (29)
Methodology	15 (42)	13 (48)	12 (32)	15 (42)	45 (33)
Substantive Issues	15 (42)	4 (15)	17 (46)	15 (42)	51 (38)
Practical	13 (36)	1 (4)	5 (14)	1 (3)	19 (14)
Number of addresses	36	27	37	36	136

Numbers in brackets are percentages of all meetings in each three year period that were addressed by speakers and on which information is available, to nearest whole number. Note that as some addresses covered more than one area the column percentages do not sum to 100%.

Table 4
Year of address by discipline area of address

Discipline Area	Years				
	1924–26	1927–29	1930–32	1933–35	All
Sociology [1]	21 (58)	13 (48)	23 (62)	24 (67)	81 (60)
Welfare & Reform	12 (33)	1 (4)	3 (8)	0 (0)	16 (12)
Psychology	5 (14)	9 (33)	1 (3)	1 (3)	16 (12)
Other Soc. Sci. [2]	2 (6)	6 (22)	13 (35)	11 (31)	32 (24)
Number of addresses	36	27	37	36	136

Numbers in brackets are percentages of all meetings in each three year period to the nearest whole number. As some addresses covered more than one area the column percentages do not add up to 100%.

Table 5
Year of address by focus on a study of Chicago in address

Chicago	Years				
	1924–26	1927–29	1930–32	1933–35	All
Focus on Chicago	14 (39)	3 (11)	2 (5)	5 (14)	24 (18)
Not on Chicago	22 (61)	24 (89)	35 (95)	31 (86)	112 (82)
Number of addresses	36	27	37	36	136

Numbers in brackets are column percentages to nearest whole number

Table 6
Auspices by major area(s) of concern

Auspices All	Area of Concern			
	Theory	Method	Subst.	Practical
Sociology Faculty	13 (27)	15 (28)	17 (33)	1 (6)
Sociology Students	10 (21)	11 (20)	10 (20)	2 (11)
Other U.C. Faculty	17 (35)	17 (31)	11 (22)	4 (22)
Non–U.C. Faculty	6 (13)	7 (13)	9 (18)	2 (11)
Outside Non-academics	2 (4)	4 (7)	4 (8)	9 (50)
Total [3]	48	54	51	18

Table 6 (continued)

Auspices	Area of Concern Pre 1930			
	Theory	Method	Subst.	Practical
Sociology Faculty	5 (25)	5 (19)	5 (26)	0 (0)
Sociology Students	6 (30)	8 (30)	7 (37)	2 (17)
Other U.C. Faculty	6 (30)	9 (33)	4 (21)	3 (25)
Non-U.C. Faculty	1 (5)	3 (11)	2 (11)	2 (17)
Outside Non-academics	2 (10)	2 (7)	1 (5)	5 (42)
Total	20	27	19	12

Auspices	Area of Concern 1930-1935			
	Theory	Method	Subst.	Practical
Sociology Faculty	8 (29)	10 (37)	12 (38)	1 (17)
Sociology Students	4 (14)	3 (11)	3 (9)	0 (0)
Other U.C. Faculty	11 (39)	8 (30)	7 (22)	1 (17)
Non-U.C. Faculty	5 (18)	4 (15)	7 (22)	0 (0)
Outside Non-academics	0 (0)	2 (7)	3 (9)	4 (66)
Total	28	27	32	6

Numbers in brackets are column percentages to nearest whole number

Table 7
Auspices by discipline area

Auspices All	Discipline area			
	Soc.[1]	Welfare	Psych.	Soc Sci [2]
Sociology Faculty	31 (39)	0 (0)	0 (0)	1 (3)
Sociology Students	22 (28)	2 (14)	1 (7)	2 (6)
Other U.C. Faculty	11 (14)	3 (21)	9 (64)	22 (69)
Non-U.C. Faculty	12 (15)	2 (14)	3 (21)	2 (6)
Outside Non-academics	4 (5)	7 (50)	1 (7)	5 (16)
Total [4]	80	14	14	32

Auspices	Discipline area Pre 1930			
	Soc.[1]	Welfare	Psych.	Soc Sci[2]
Sociology Faculty	11 (33)	0 (0)	0 (0)	0 (0)
Sociology Students	15 (45)	2 (18)	1 (8)	2 (25)
Other U.C. Faculty	2 (6)	3 (27)	7 (58)	6 (75)
Non-U.C. Faculty	3 (9)	2 (18)	3 (25)	0 (0)
Outside Non-academics	2 (6)	4 (36)	1 (8)	0 (0)
Total	33	11	12	8

Table 7 (continued)

| Auspices | Discipline area 1930-1935 | | | |
	Sociol.	Welfare	Psych.	Soc Sci
Sociology Faculty	20 (43)	0 (0)	0 (0)	1 (4)
Sociology Students	7 (15)	0 (0)	0 (0)	0 (0)
Other U.C. Faculty	9 (19)	0 (0)	2 (100)	16 (67)
Non-U.C. Faculty	9 (19)	0 (0)	0 (0)	2 (8)
Outside Non-academics	2 (4)	3 (100)	0 (0)	5 (21)
Total	47	3	2	24

Numbers in brackets are column percentages to nearest whole number

Table 8

Auspices by focus on a study of Chicago in address

| Auspices | Focus on Chicago All | | |
	Yes	No	Total
Sociology Faculty	2 (6)	31 (94)	33
Sociology Students	7 (30)	16 (70)	23
Other U.C. Faculty	5 (12)	38 (88)	43
Non-U.C. Faculty	2 (10)	18 (90)	20
Non-academics	7 (41)	10 (59)	17

| Auspices | Focus on Chicago Pre 1930 | | | 1930-1935 | | |
	Yes	No	Total	Yes	No	Total
Sociology Faculty	1 (9)	10 (91)	11	1 (5)	21 (95)	22
Sociology Students	5 (31)	11 (69)	16	2 (29)	5 (71)	7
Other U.C. Faculty	3 (17)	15 (83)	18	2 (8)	23 (92)	27
Non-U.C. Faculty	2 (22)	7 (78)	9	0 (0)	11 (100)	11
Non-academics	5 (63)	3 (27)	8	2 (22)	7 (78)	9

Numbers in brackets are row percentages to nearest whole number

Table 9

Membership of the Society by major area(s) of concern

| Membership | Area of Concern All | | | |
	Theory	Method	Subst.	Practical
Members	29 (58)	36 (65)	34 (67)	6 (30)
Non-members	21 (42)	19 (35)	17 (33)	14 (70)
Total	50	55	51	20

Table 9 (continued)

| Membership | Area of Concern Pre 1930 | | | |
	Theory	Method	Subst.	Practical
Members	14 (64)	20 (71)	15 (79)	5 (36)
Non-members	8 (36)	8 (29)	4 (21)	9 (64)
Total	22	28	19	14

| Membership | Area of Concern 1930-1935 | | | |
	Theory	Method	Subst.	Practical
Members	15 (54)	16 (59)	19 (59)	1 (17)
Non-members	13 (46)	11 (41)	13 (41)	5 (83)
Total	28	27	32	6

Numbers in brackets are column percentages to nearest whole number

Table 10
Membership of Society by discipline area

| Membership | Discipline area All | | | |
	Soc.[1]	Welfare	Psych.	Soc Sci [2]
Members	60 (74)	5 (31)	5 (31)	9 (28)
Non-Members	21 (26)	11 (69)	11 (69)	23 (72)
Total	81	16	16	32

| Membership | Discipline area Pre 1930 | | | |
	Soc.[1]	Welfare	Psych.	Soc Sci[2]
Members	31 (91)	5 (38)	3 (21)	3 (38)
Non-Members	3 (9)	8 (62)	11 (79)	5 (62)
Total	34	13	14	8

| Membership | Discipline area 1930-1935 | | | |
	Sociol.	Welfare	Psych	Soc Sci
Members	29 (63)	0 (0)	2 (100)	6 (25)
Non-Members	17 (37)	3 (100)	0 (0)	18 (75)
Total	46	3	2	24

Numbers in brackets are column percentages to nearest whole number

Table 11
Membership by focus on a study of Chicago in address

Membership	Focus on Chicago All		
	Yes	No	Total
Members	14 (21)	54 (79)	68
Non-members	10 (15)	58 (85)	68

Membership	Focus on Chicago Pre 1930			1930-1935		
	Yes	No	Total	Yes	No	Total
Members	8 (31)	18 (69)	26	6 (14)	36 (86)	42
Non-members	9 (76)	28 (24)	37	1 (3)	30 (97)	31

Numbers in brackets are row percentages to nearest whole number

Notes to tables

[1] Sociology and population studies

[2] General social science, philosophy, anthropology, economics, politics and public administration

[3] These totals do not correspond exactly to those in Table 3 due to missing values in the auspices.

[4] These totals do not correspond exactly to those in Table 4 due to missing values in the auspices.

Appendix 4

Courses offered in sociology by the Department of Sociology and Anthropology [1]

Table 1
Courses offered 1913-1925

Course Number[2]	Date of Commencement [3]	Last Year Offered	Title	Lecturer
1 (201)	1913 [4]	1924 [5]	Introduction to the Study of Society [6]	Bedford 1914-19; Brown 1916; Burgess 1917-19; Unspecified 1920-24
2 (220)	1920	1924	Introduction to Social Psychology [7]	Faris 1920-24; Thomas 1914-1917; Unspecified 1918-19
3 (230)	1913	1924	Social Origins	Faris 1920-24
4 (240)	1923	1924	Social Evolution and Social Organization	Faris 1923-24
5	1913	1920	The Family [8]	Henderson 1914; Unspecified 1915; Burgess 1916-20
6 (260)	1914	1924	Modern Cities [9]	Bedford 1914-24
7 (270)	1916	1924	Social Pathology	Burgess 1917-24
11 (351)	1921	1924	The Family	Burgess 1921-24
14 (310)	1922	1924	Study of Society	Burgess 1922 & 1924; Park 1923
15	1913	1924	Elements of General Sociology	Small 1914-24
16	1914	1914	History of Sociology from the Beginning of 19th Cent.	Small 1914
16A (316)	1915	1924	History of Sociology from the Beginning of 19th Cent.	Small 1914-24; NG 1924 [10]
16B (317)	1915	1924	History of Sociology in the United States from 1865	Small 1914-24; NG 1916-23
17 (312)	1917	1924	Conflict of Classes in Modern Society	Small 1914-24

18	1913	Ethics of Sociology	1924	Small 1914-24 NAT [11]
19	1913	Development of Sociology in Germany Since 1870	1915	Small 1914-15 NAT
19A	1921	General Sociology	1923	Bodenhofer 1921 Bernard 1922-23
19B	1915	The Growth of Militarism in Germany	1915	Small 1915
20A (315)	1921	History of Social Thought	1924	Bodenhofer 1921 Bernard 1923-24
20B	1922	History of Sociology	1924	Bernard 1922 & 1924
21	1914	Social Forces in Modern Democracy: United States	1923	Small 1914-23 NAT
22 (311)	1924	Social Progress	1924	Bernard 1924
	1914	Social Forces in Modern Democracy: England	1923	Small 1914-23 NAT
23	1914	Social Forces in Modern Democracy: France and Germany	1923	Small 1914-21, 1923 NAT
27-29	1914	Seminar: Working Concepts of German Sociology	1915	Small 1914-15
	1916	Seminar: Problems in General Sociology	1918	Small 1916-18
(411-3)	1919	Seminar: The Marxian Philosophy of Science	1924	Small 1919-24
30 (320)	1914	Social Attitudes	1924	Thomas 1914-17 Unspecified 1919 Faris 1920-24
31	1913	Mental Development in the Race	1916	Thomas 1914-16 Faris 1920-24
(324)	1920	Social Control	1924	Thomas 1914
32	1914	The Psychology of Divergent Types	1914	Thomas 1915-16
	1915	Divergent Types	1916	Thomas 1917
(378)	1917	Theory of Disorganization	1924	Burgess 1920-24 NG 1918-24
33 (331)	1914	Prostitution	1916	Thomas 1914-16 Faris 1920-24
34 (358)	1920	Mind of Primitive Man	1924	Burgess 1920-24 NG 1922-24
	1920	Play and the Social Utilization of Leisure Time	1924	
35	1919	Immigration	1920	Abbott 1919-20
36	1915	The Survey [12]	1915	Park 1915-24

No.		Year	Year	Title	Sources
37	(326)	1915	1917	Crowd and Public [13]	NG 1921, 23, 24; Park 1915–24
38	(358)	1915	1924	The Newspaper	NG 1918–24; Park 1915–24
39	(328)	1920	1924	Social Communication	NG 1918 & 1920; Faris 1920–24; NAT
43	(334)	1914	1924	The Negro in America	Park 1914–24; NG 1917,20,24
43A		1917	1919	Research in the Field of Social Psychology	Park 1917–19
43B	(335)	1917	1919	Field Studies [14]	Park 1917–19
		1914	1924	The Negro in Africa	Unspecified 1914–19; NG 1916–20; Faris 1920–24; NAT
45	(332)	1913	1915	European Peasant	Thomas 1914–1915
		1916	1924	Race and Nationalities	Thomas 1916–17; Unspecified 1918; Park 1919–24; NG 1922
46		1914	1916	The Jew	Thomas 1914–16; Thomas 1917
		1917	1919	Research Course	Unspecified 1918–20; NAT
	(338)	1920	1924	Conflict and Fusion of Cultures	Faris 1920–24; NAT
47		1914	1916	The Oriental	Unspecified 1914–16
48	(369)	1920	1924	Social Forces	Park 1920–24; NG 1924
49		1913	1920	Social Politics	Unspecified 1914–16; NG 1916
50		1913	1917	Urban Communities	Abbott 1917–20; Unspecified 1914–17; NAT
		1918	1923	Municipal Sociology	Unspecified 1918; NAT

No.	orig. p.			Title	Contributors
51	(363)	1924	1924	Urban Sociology	Bedford 1919-23
51	(373)	1924	1913	Crime and Its Social Treatment	Bedford 1924; Henderson 1914; Unspecified 1915; Breckeridge 1916; Abbott 1917-20; Burgess 1917 & 1920-4
52		1920	1913	Evolution of Philanthropy	Henderson 1914; Unspecified 1915,17; Burgess 1916; Abbott 1918-20
53	(354)	1924	1914	Church and Society	Henderson 1914; Unspecified 1915-16; Hoben 1917-19; Matthews 1920-4 [15]
54		1918	1913	Problems and Methods of Church Expansion	Henderson 1914; Unspecified 1915-18; Faris 1919-20
54-56		1924	1923	Research Problems in Social Psychology	Unspecified 1914-17; NG 1914 & 1915
55		1916	1913	Contemporary Charities	Abbott 1918-20
56		1920	1917	Social Statistics [16]	Abbott 1914-20
57		1920	1914	Methods of Social Investigation [17]	Bedford 1914-15
57	(366)	1915	1913	Rural Communities	Holton 1916; Sanderson 1917
57		1924	1916	Rural Sociology	Bedford 1918-24
58		1920	1914	Organization and Administration of Charities	Unspec. 1914-5, 17-8; Burgess 1916; Young 1920; NO 1919 [18]
59		1924	1913	The Group of Industrials	Unspecified 1914-24; NAT
60		1916	1914	The Immigrant [19]	Thomas 1914-16
61	(375)	1924	1920	Causes and Prevention of Poverty	Burgess 1920-24; NAT
63		1918	1914	The Playground Movement	Rainwater 1914-16

64	1914	1916	Playground Direction	Unspecified 1917-18
				Rainwater 1914-16
65	1914	1916	Playground Administration	Rainwater 1914-16
68	1914	1914	Family Rehabilitation	Breckenridge
		1920	Research Course in Social Psychology	Faris, Pk, Bg 1920-3
				NG 1920 & 1921
				Park & Burgess 1924
73-75	1913		Seminar in Methods of Social Amelioration	Unspecified 1914-24
				NG 1916
76-8(466-9)	1920		Field Studies	Pk & Burgess 1920-3
				Faris & Burgess 1924
79	1921		Teaching of Sociology in Colleges	Pk, Faris, Bg 1921-3
				Faris & Burgess 1924

The following courses were listed in 1914 with a course number as indicated. They were courses in other departments which, from 1915 to 1924 these were only appended to the Official Publications of the Sociology and Anthropology Department as 'brought to the attention' of students. In some cases these same courses had been 'brought to the attention' of students prior to 1914. These courses are indicated

Sociology Course Number	Orig. Dept. & Number	Brought to Attention Pre 1914	Title (in Sociology Publications) [20]	Lecturer
4	PE 4	Yes	Labor Conditions and Problems	Not specified
8	PY 4	No	Social Psychology	Not specified
9	PE 9	Yes	Introduction to Statistics	Field
10	PS 10	Yes	Elements of Law	Freund
11	PY 7	No	Abnormal Psychology	Hayes
12	ED 7U	No	Psychopathic, Retarded and Mentally Deficient Children	Stevens
13	PT 14	No	Moral Education and Juvenile Delinquency	Hoben
35	PH	No	Evolution of Morality	Tufts
36	PH	No	Psychology of Religion	Ames
61	PE 18	Yes	Population and the Standard of Living and Eugenics	Field
61A	PE 24	Yes	Vital Statistics	Field
62	PE 40	Yes	Trade Unionism	Hoxie
69	HA 22	No	The Child and the State	Breckenridge
70	HA 21	No	The Economic Position of Women	Breckenridge

Key: ED Department of Education   PS Department of Political Science
     HA Department of Household Administration   PT Department of Practical Theology
     PE Department of Political Economy   PY Department of Psychology
     PH Department of Philosophy

Other course which did not appear on the listings in the Official Publications but were mentioned as
'brought to the attention' from time to time included :Political Economy no. 41, 'The State in Relation to
Labor', and no. 58 'Program of Social Reform' and in Social Science Administration course no. 10 'English
Philanthropy and Social Politics'.

Notes to Table 1

[1] Source: Official Publications of the University of Chicago. Course in the Department of Sociology and
    Anthropology which were specifically Anthropology are not included.

[2] All course were numbered. Courses with a given number were replaced from time to time, hence a several
    titles for the same course number. The whole system was revised in 1925 and those course retained given
    a new number, these numbers are recorded in square brackets.

[3] All dates refer to academic year commencing August

[4] Courses dated 1913 usually began before that date

[5] The course structure was revised in 1925 and a new numbering scheme devised. Courses noted as ending in
    1924 continue after that date if a new course number is indicated. See Table 2 for the period 1925-52

[6] This course is listed as 'elementary' in 1925, and probably was so before that date.

[7] Course 2 to 8 inclusive are listed as 'intermediate' in 1925

[8] See Course 11 in 1921

[9] See Course 50 in 1918 In 1915 this course subtitled 'Municipal Sociology'

[10] NG indicates that although the course was listed it was not apparantly given during these years. In
     some cases a lecturer is specified although the course was not taught. These are usually shown in the

261

listing of each course.

[11] NAT indicates that although the course is listed between 1914 and 1925 it was never actually taught as far as can be ascertained from the records

[12] This course was sometimes referred to as 'The Social Survey'

[13] This course was subtitled 'Introduction to Collective Behavior' from 1918-24

[14] See Courses 76-78 after 1919

[15] Matthews was in the Divinity School

[16] Social Science Administration course no. 20

[17] Social Science Administration course no. 21

[18] NO indicates that the course was not offered in these years (which lie between the firsat and last dates the course was listed)

[19] Social Science Administration course no. 6

[20] Course titles in the Official Publications of the sponsoring department vary slightly in some cases.

Table 2
Courses offered 1925-52

Course Number	Date of Commencement	Last Year Offered	Title	Lecturer [1]
110	1925	1931	Survey of Sociology and Anthropology	Unspecified 1925, 1927 Burgess & Wirth 1928 & 1931 Blumer, Webster & Cressey 1929 Blumer & Cressey 1930 NO 1926 [2]
201 [3]	1926	1952 [4]	Introduction to Sociology [5]	Unspecified 1926, 1951 Faris 1927-1930 Cottrell & Blumer 1932-34 Burgess & Blumer 1935 Blumer 1936-37 Hughes 1938-43 (with Locke 1939) (with Hall 1941) Hughes & Bonner 1945 Bonner 1944 & 1946 Swanson 1948 Shubutani 1949 & 1950 Becker 1952 NO 1946 NG 1930 [6]
202	1943	1952	Introduction to Field Studies	Hughes 1943-52 (unspec. 1948) (with Lohman,Burgess,Warner '44) (with Lohman 1944 & 1945) (with Roy 1950)
203	1936	1947	Introduction to Statistical Sociology	Stouffer 1936-41 Ogburn 1942 Burgess 1943
204	1948	1950	Introduction to Statistical Reasoning	Williams 1947 Williams 1948 & 1950 Kittagawa 1949

No.	Year	Title	Year	References
205	1945	Modern Social Problems	1951	Ogburn 1945-51 NO 1947
206	1948	Mathematics Essential to Elementary Stats.	1952	Williams 1950 Kittagawa 1951 Goodman 1950-52
210 [7]	1925	The Study of Society	1952	House 1925 Hoben 1926 Bernard 1927 Wirth 1928 Wirth & Burgess 1929, 1931-32 Burgess 1930, 1934, 1936-51 Burgess & Blumer 1933 & 1935 Hughes 1952
211	1938	Comparative Institutions	1946	Warner 1938-46 Whyte 1945
212	1945	The Informal Group	1945	Faris 1925-1938 (with Blumer 1933) McCormick 1930 Blumer 1939-46 (with Bonner 1945) Swanson 1948 Shibutani 1949 & 1950 Kornhauser 1951 Becker 1952
220	1925	Introduction to Social Psychology	1952	
221	1936	Contemporary Social Psychology	1941	Blumer 1937 NG 1938-41
225	1945	Minorities	1951	Wirth 1945, 1947-51 [8] NO 1946
226	1937	Crowd & Public: Intro. to Collective Behavior	1940	Park 1925-28, 1930-33 Young 1929 Blumer 1934-48, 1951 Blumer & Shibutani 1949 Shibutani 1950 Unspecified 1952 [9]
230	1925	Social Origins [10]	1940	Faris 1925-1931, 1933, 1935-38 Faris & Sutherland 1934

No.			Title	References
240	1925	1925	Social Education and Social Organisation	Blumer 1932 & 1939 / Unspecified 1940
	1926	1940	Social Evolution	Faris 1925 / Faris 1926-40
242	1947	1951	General Intro. to Human Relations of Ind. Soc	NG 1927-30, 1932-40 / Whyte 1947 & 1948 / Roy 1949 / Unspecified 1951 / NO 1950
244	1948	1951	Intro. to the Study of Popn. & Human Ecology	Hauser 1948-1950 / Duncan 1951
245	1950	1950	Intro. to Counselling & Interviewing Methods	Glick
251	1925	1950	The Family [11]	McKenzie & Burgess 1925 & 1930 / Burgess 1926-28, 1931, 1942-47 / Burgess, Young & Winters 1930 / Cottrell 1932 / Burgess & Cottrell 1933 & 1934 / Warner 1935-39 / Warner & Burgess 1940 & 1941 / Burgess & Reiss 1949 / Burgess, Warner & Reiss 1950-51
260	1925	1939	Modern Cities	Bedford 1925 / NG 1926-39
264	1926	1935	Growth & the City	Burgess 1926-32, 35-37 [12] / NG 1933-4, 1936-9
265	1940	1951	The City [13]	Wirth 1940-43, 1945-46 / Unspecified 1944 / Reiss 1948-51
266	1945	1945	Individual Study Project	NG 1944
270	1925	1951	Social Pathology	Wirth 1945 / Burgess 1925-47 / (with Sutherland 1932) / (with Locke 1939) / (with Shaw 1941) / Reiss 1948-51
271	1943	1951	Crime and Juvenile Delinquency	Shaw 1943-44, 1946-48

302	1936	1952	Advanced Social Psychology	Unspecified 1950-51 NO 1945 & 1949 Faris 1936 & 1938 [14] NO 1936 Blumer 1940-49, 1951 Blumer & Shibutani 1950 Unspecified 1952 NG 1938
	1943	1944	Advanced Field Studies:Personality	Unspecified 1943-44 NG 1943-44
	1945	1947	Thesis Seminar	Unspecified 1945 & 1947 NO 1946
303	1927	1930	Introduction to Statistics	Ogburn 1927-1929 Stouffer 1930
	1932	1935	Statistical Sociology	Rice 1932 Ogburn 1933-34 Stouffer 1935
304	1927	1931	Statistical Methods	Ogburn 1927-29 Stouffer 1930 NG 1931
	1932	1947	Methods of Quantitative Sociology	Ogburn 1932-36, 1942, 1944-45 Stouffer 1937-41 Williams 1947 NG 1943 & 1946
305	1948	1952	Statistical Methods of Research I	Williams 1948-49 Unspecified 1950 Goodman 1951-52
	1927	1930	Social Philosophy From Plato to Present	Ogburn 1927-29 Stouffer 1930
	1931	1936	Statistical Problems	Ogburn 1931-35 NG 1931 & 1936
	1937	1944	Measurement of Relationships	Ogburn 1937, 1939-41 Stouffer 1938 NG 1942-44
	1948	1952	Statistical Methods of Research II	Williams 1948 Kittagawa 1949

306	1932	Measurement in Social Politics	1934	Unspecified 1950 Goodman 1951 & 1952 Rice 1932 NG 1933 & 1934
	1936	Partial Correlation Analysis	1945	Ogburn 1936-7, 1939-42, 1945 NG 1938, 1943, 1944
307	1935	Sampling in Social Research [15]	1949	Stouffer 1935-38, 1940-41 Unspecified 1947 Williams 1948 & 1949 NO 1945 & 1946 NG 1939, 1942, 1944
308	1950	Statistical Methods of Research III	1952	Goodman 1950-52
	1935	Applications of Probability to Sociology	1935	Stouffer 1935
	1936	Quantitative Aspects of Social Problems	1944	Stouffer 1935-38 NG 1937, 1939-44
	1951	Statistical Inference III	1952	Unspecified 1951 Goodman 1952 [16]
309	1940	Methods of Sociological Research	1944	Burgess 1940-43 NG 1944
311	1952	Recent Advance Methods	1952	Goodman 1952
	1925	Theories of Social Progress	1925	House 1925
	1926	The Study of Social Change	1928	Hoben 1926 NG 1927 & 1928
311	1937	Modern European Sociology	1940	Parsons 1937 NG 1938-40 Mass 1951 [17]
312	1925	Conflict of Classes in Modern Society	1925	Unspecified 1925 NG 1925
313	1927	Sociology and the Social Sciences	1939	Ogburn 1927-1937 NG 1928, 1930-39
	1940	Statistical Problems in Governmental Research	1942	Stouffer 1940 NG 1941 & 1942
	1943	Methods of Government Research	1944	Unspecified 1943-44 NG 1943 & 1944
314	1925	Logic of the Social Sciences	1928	House 1925 Hoben 1926

No.			Title	References
315	1935	1952	The Sociology of Knowledge	NG 1927 & 1928; Wirth 1935-51; Unspecified 1952
	1925	1936	History of Social Thought	House 1925; Hoben 1926; Unspecified 1927; NG 1926, 1928-36; Unspecified 1944
	1944	1944	The Sociology of Art	NG 1944
316	1925	1928	History of Sociology from the Beginning C19th	House 1925; Hoben 1926 & 1928; Unspecified 1927
	1929	1932	European Sociology from Beginning of C19th	Wirth 1929, 1931-32; NG 1930
	1933	1940	European Sociology	Wirth & Blumer 1933-34; Wirth 1935-39; NG 1940
317	1925	1940	History of Sociology in the United States	House 1925; Hoben 1926 & 1928; Bernard 1927; Hoben & Wirth 1931; Wirth 1932, 1935-6, 1938-9; Blumer & Wirth 1933 & 1934; NG 1929, 1930, 1937, 1940
318	1935	1940	Modern German Sociology	Wirth 1935-36; NO 1937 & 1938; NG 1935-40
	1948	1952	Symbolic Behavior	Warner 1949-52 [18]; Warner & Henry 1948
319	1933	1944	Contemporary French Sociology [18b]	Blumer 1933-36, 1939, 1941; NO 1937 & 1938; NG 1933-4,1936, 1940-43
320	1925	1951	Social Attitudes	Faris 1925-1937 & 1939; Blumer 1941, 1943, 1947-49, 1951; Shibutani 1950; NO 1945 & 1946

No.			Title	References
321	1938	1942	Quantitative Studies in Soc. Psychology [19]	NG 1927,29-33,35-38,40,42,44 Stouffer 1938 & 1940
322	1940	1952	Introduction to the History of Sociology	NG 1939, 1941-2 Wirth 1940-51 [20] Unspecified 1952
323	1940	1952	History of Sociological Theory	Wirth 1940-41, 1943-51 [21] Unspecified 1952 NO 1942
324	1925	1941	Social Control	Faris 1925-37 Unspecified 1938-41 NG 1926,28-30,32,34,36,38-41
325	1950	1950	Human Nature and Personality	Hart 1950
	1951	1952	Public Opinion and Social Organization	Hart 1951-52
	1929	1934	Psychology of Social Groups	Faris 1929-34 NG 1930-34
	1941	1942	Cultural & Racial Contacts	Hughes 1941-42
	1943	1944	Racial and Cultural Relations in Wartime	Hughes 1943 NG 1943
327	1945	1951	Racial and Cultural Relations	Hughes 1945-49, 1951 NO 1950
	1935	1940	Reform and Revolution	Blumer 1935 & 1937 NG 1936, 1938-40
	1943	1951	The Psychology of Social Movements	Blumer 1943-5, 1947, 1949, 1951 Shibutani 1950 NO 1946 & 1948
328	1925	1934	Social Communication	Faris 1925-34 NG 1925-34
	1947	1947	Labor Arbitration	Blumer 1947
329	1951	1951	Collective Behavior in Industry	Blumer 1951
	1935	1947	Methods of Study of the Modern Community [22]	Warner 1935-9,1941-2,1944,1947 NO 1940, 1943, 1945, 1946
330	1936	1951	Social Organization of the Modern Community	Warner 1936-8,1940-4,1946-7,1951 Warner, Hollingshead, McGuire 48 Warner & Junker 1949-50 [23] NO 1939 & 1945
331	1925	1930	Mind Of Primitive Man	Faris 1925-30

No.	Year	Year	Title	References
	1932	1940	The Sociology of Preliterate Man	NG 1926-30 Faris 1932-40 NG 1933-40 Wirth 1942
332	1942	1944	Symbol Systems	Park 1925-30, 1933 Redfield 1931-32, 1934-35 Unspecified 1936-39 NG 1926,28,30,33,36-39 Hughes 1945-46, 1950 NO 1947-49
	1925	1939	Races and Nationalities	
333	1941	1950	Problems and Methods of Prediction	Burgess 1941, 44, 46, 48, 50 NG 1942 & 1943
334	1925	1939	Negro in America	Park 1925-1933 NG 1925, 1927, 1929-39
	1942	1944	Morale and Collective Behavior	Blumer 1942 & 1943 NG 1944
335	1925	1931	The Negro in Africa	Faris 1925, 1927-28 Blumer 1931 NG 1925 & 1928
	1932	1949	Folkways and Fashions	Blumer 1931-40, 1944,1949 NO 1945-48
336	1927	1942	Culture and Sociology	NG 1932-4, 1936, 1941-3 Ogburn 1927-1938, 1940, 1942 Unspecified 1939, 1941
	1943	1949	The Theory of Culture	NG 1928, 1930-2, 1937,39,41 Ogburn, 1944, 1946-49 NG 1943
	1950	1951	The Principles of Social Change	Ogburn 1950 Duncan 1951
337	1927	1945	Social Change	Ogburn 1927-35,1937-39,1943,1945 Unspecified 1936,38,40,42,44 [24] NO 1941
338	1925	1929	Conflict and Fusion of Cultures	NG 1928,30-2,34,38,40,42,44 Faris 1925-29
	1932	1951	Social Trends	NG 1925-29 Ogburn 1932-37,39,41,43,47,49,50

No.	Year	Year	Title	References
339	1929	1934	A Sociological Study of Mexico	Ogburn and Duncan 1951 NO 1946 & 1948 NG 1938,40,42,44 Simpson 1929 NG 1930-34
340	1942	1944	War and Social Change	Ogburn 1942-44
	1928	1948	Population and Society	Ogburn 1928,1930,1931-7,1939-46 Stouffer 1931, 1938 Hauser 1947 Vance 1948
341	1927	1934	Social Character of Populations	Ogburn 1927-34 NG 1927, 1929, 1932-34
	1940	1941	Primitive Economics	Wirth 1940 NG 1941
342	1947	1950	The Labor Force	Hauser 1947-50 Ogburn 1927-35
	1927	1935	Social Conditions and Economic Factors	NG 1927, 1929, 1931-35
	1936	1950	The Economic Factor in Modern Culture	Ogburn 1936-37,1939,1946-50 [25] NO 1941-45 NG 1936, 1938, 1940
343	1926	1944	Human Migrations	Park 1926-33 Unspecified 1934-5,1937-8,1940-4 Stouffer 1939 NO 1936 NG 1927,29,33-35,37-38,40-44
344	1947	1947	Statistical Data For Social Science Research	Hauser 1947
	1948	1951	Comparative Population Structure & Dynamics	Hauser 1948, 1950 & 1951 [26]
	1936	1936	Quantitative Problems in Population	Stouffer 1936
	1941	1941	Primitive Government	Warner 1941
344X	1948	1948	Cultural Dynamics	Horton 1948
345	1936	1944	Quantitative Studies in Popn. & Human Ecology	Stouffer 1936,37,39,41 [27] NG 1938,40,42-44
346	1943	1949	The Folk Society	Redfield 1943-49
	1936	1940	Dynamics of Population	Stouffer 1936 & 1939 [28] NO 1937 NG 1938, 1940

347	1951	1945	Human Problems in Industrial Organization	Whyte & Gardner 1945 & 1946 Whyte 1947 & 1948 Junker 1949 & 1950 Moore 1951
348	1950	1950	Counselling Methods & Interviewing Techniques	Glick 1950
	1951	1937	Sociology of the Professions	Parsons 1937 Hughes 1939,41,43-44,46-51 [29] NO 1945
349	1937	1934	Health Institutions & Services	NG 1938, 1940, 1942 Davis 1934-37 NG 1935
350	1951	1931	Social Institutions	Hughes 1931, 1938-49, 1951 Unspecified 1932-37 NO 1950 NG 1932-37
351	1947	1943	Family Systems	Warner 1943-44, 1946-47 [30] NO 1945
352	1945	1930	Family Case Studies	Burgess 1930-37, 1939, 1945 NG 1932-34,36-38,40-44
353	1942	1935	Quantitative Studies In The Family	Stouffer 1934, 1937, 1939 NG 1938, 1940-42
354	1944	1943	Psychological Studies of Industrial Scoiety	Kornhauser 1943 NG 1944
	1934	1925	Church and Society	Matthews 1925-27 [31] NG 1928-34
355	1946	1936	The Social Orientation of the Child	Warner 1936-1946 [32] Slessinger 1934 & 1935 NG 1936
	1936	1934	Legal Sociology	
356	1947	1946	Primitive Religion	Warner 1946 & 1947
	1938	1925	The Newspaper	Park 1925-1933 NG 1925, 1929-38
357	1949	1939	Voluntary Associations	Hughes 1939, 1941, 1943 Smith 1949 NO 1945-48 NG 1940, 1942, 1944
358	1939	1925	Play & the Social Utilisation of Leisure Time	Burgess 1925-37

No.			Subject	References
359	1940	1944	Quantitative Studies in Social Organisation	NG 1925, 1929-33, 1935-39 / Stouffer 1940
360	1939	1951	Social Organization	NG 1941-44 / Wirth 1939-41,13-46,49-51 / NO 1947 & 1948 / NG 1942
361	1925	1951	Human Ecology	Park, 1925-28, 1930-33 / McKenzie 1929 / Wirth 1940, 1944, 1946 / Burgess 1947-51 [33] / NO 1942 & 1945 / NG 1926-8,1931-2,1937-9,1941
362	1942 / 1938	1945 / 1939	Social Planning / Urban Civilization	Wirth 1942-45 / Wirth 1938 / NG 1939
363	1948 / 1925	1948 / 1928	Social Structure / Urban Sociology	Vance 1948 / Bedford 1925 / NG 1926-28
	1937	1939	Metropolitan Region	Wirth 1938
	1943	1952	Methods of (in) Cultural Anthropology	NG 1938 & 1939 / Redfield 1943-45, 1946-50, 1952 / Warner 1946 / Unspecified 1951
365	1925	1932	Rural Sociology	Bedford 1925 / McCormick 1930 / NG 1926-9, 1931-32
367	1947 / 1925	1947 / 1918	Rural Communities / The Industrial & Econ. Org. of the Community	Kimball 1947 / Hoben 1926 / NG 1925, 1927-8
368	1947 / 1925	1947 / 1940	Sociology of Housing / The Social Survey	Riemer 1947 / Park 1925-33 / NG 1925-8, 1930-40
369	1950 / 1951 / 1925	1950 / 1951 / 1932	Leadership in Communication / Leadership & Social Organization / Social Forces	Nelson 1950 / Nelson 1951 / Park 1925-32 / NG 1926, 1928, 1930-2

370	1933	1940	Theories of Criminality	Sutherland 1933 & 1934 NG 1935-40
371	1949	1951	Social Nature of Delinquency	Reiss 1949-51
	1933	1934	Methods and Theories of Punishment	Sutherland 1933 & 1934 NG 1933
	1935	1949	Criminality	Faris 1936-37 Burgess 1937, 1939, 1940, 1944 Shaw 1941-43, 1945, 1947-48 Unspecified 1949 NO 1938 & 1946 NG 1936
372	1927	1929	Statistics of Social Maladjustment	Ogburn 1927-29 NG 1927-29
	1932	1944	Criminal Law and Procedure	Puttkamer 1932-1941, 1943 [34] NO 1942 NG 1944
373	1925	1932	Crime & Its Social Treatment	Burgess 1925-1929 Burgess & Young 1930 Sutherland 1931 & 1932
	1937	1947	European Criminology	Burgess 1937 & 1947 NO 1945 & 1946 NG 1938-44
374	1930	1941	The Study of Organised Crime	Burgess 1930-32 Sutherland 1933-34 [35] Ogburn 1941 NG 1930-32, 1935-40
	1947	1952	Organised Crime and the Professional Criminal	Lohman 1947-48, 1950-51 NO 1949
375	1925	1940	Causes and Prevention of Poverty	Burgess 1925-1937 NG 1925-6, 1929-40
376	1929	1934	Present Day Mexico	Simpson 1929 NG 1930-34
377	1935	1944	Quantitative Criminology	Stouffer 1935, 37, 39, 41 [36] NG 1936, 38, 40, 42-44
377	1947	1951	Community Organizn. & Delinquency Prevention	Shaw 1947-51
378	1925	1944	Theory of Disorganisation	Burgess 1925-37 [37]

No.	Year	Year	Course Title	References
380	1951	1951	Social & Psychological Factors of Delinquency	NG 1925-44 Bettelheim 1951
	1935	1944	Field Studies in Delinquency	Shaw 1935-1942 [38] NG 1943 & 1944
381A	1947	1949	Theories of Personality	Goldhammer 1947-49
	1950	1951	Practicum in Social Psychology	Rosenthal & Shils 1950 Campbell 1951
381B	1950	1951	Practicum in Social Psychology	Rosenthal 1950 Campbell 1951
382	1947	1949	Communication & Consensus	Goldhammer 1947-49 [39]
384	1949	1950	The Slum Community	Lohman 1949 & 1950
386	1948	1949	The Development of Modern Communications	Horton 1948 & 1949
			Social Aspects of Mass Communications	Horton 1951
387	1951	1951	Culture and Social Change	Horton 1951
388	1949	1951	Theories of Criminal Causation	Lohman 1949 & 1951 NO 1950
389	1949	1949	Communication & Culture	Horton 1949
390	1937	1944	The Sociology of Max Weber	Wirth 1937 [40] NO 1942 & 1943 NG 1938-44
	1943	1951	The Individual in Society	Wirth and Havinghurst 1943-45 Wirth 1946 Wirth & Henry 1949-51 NO 1947
397	1949	1951	Criminal Careers	Shaw 1949-51
399	1941	1951	Methodology & Logic of Social Research	Blumer 1941,44-45,48-49,51 NG 1943 & 1944 [41]
401	1925	1940	Methods of Social Research	Park 1925-26, 1928-30 Park & Burgess 1931 Wirth 1932 & 1939 Blumer 1933-37 [42] NO 1927
402	1944	1951	Thesis Seminar	NG 1925,29,30,37,39 Blumer 1944,45,48,49,51 NO 1946, 1947 & 1950
403	1935	1940	Research in Sociological Theory	Wirth 1935-40 [43]

No.	Year	Year	Course	References
404	1941	1942	Individual Research Seminar	Unspecified 1941 & 1942 [44]
	1944	1951	Individual Research Seminar	Unspecified 1944-51 [45]
406	1940	1940	Research in Quantitative Sociology	Ogburn 1940 [46]
407	1929	1939	Research in Quantitative Sociology	Ogburn 1929-1939 [47] NG 1936 & 1938
410	1925	1934	Teaching of Sociology in Colleges	Faris, Park, Burgess 1925, 29-33 Faris & Burgess 1934 NO 1926-28 NG 1925, 1929-34
411	1946	1946	Contemporary Sociology	Wirth 1946
	1925	1925	The Marxian Philosophy of Science	Small 1925 [48]
412	1945	1946	Biological Backgrounds of General Sociology	Allie 1945 & 1946 [49]
	1949	1951	Social Adjustment in Old Age	Burgess & Havinghurst 1949-50 Havinghurst & Shanas 1951
415	1926	1934	Modern German Sociology	Park 1926 Wirth 1927-28, 1931-34 NG 1929-33
416	1947	1948	The Design of Experiments in the Study of H.B	Goodman 1947 & 1948
	1926	1934	Modern French Sociology	Faris 1926-34
	1949	1949	Research in Social Psychiatry	Goodman 1949
421	1926	1928	Research Course in Social Psychology	Park & Burgess 1925 NO 1927 Burgess 1926 Faris, Park & Burgess 1928 NG 1926
423	1929	1940	Human Nature	Faris 1929-1937 Blumer 1939 [50] NG 1929, 31, 37, 40
	1941	1951	Seminar in Human Nature	Blumer 1941,44,45,47,50,51 NO 1946, 1948, 1949
426	1925	1940	Research Problems in Social Psychology	NG 1942 & 1943 Faris 1925-6, 1928-38 Faris & Blumer 1939 [51] NO 1927
427	1948	1948	Methodology in Collective Behavior	Shibutani 1948
	1951	1951	Social Contagion & Crowd Behavior	Blumer 1951

No.	Years	Title	References
431	1940–1944	Seminar in the Professions	Hughes 1940; NG 1941-44
433	1948–1951	Seminar in Occupations & Professions	Hughes 1948-51 [52]
433	1929–1938	The Social Attitudes	Faris 1929-36, 1938 [53]; NO 1937; NG 1930,32,34,36
440	1939–1939	Seminar in the Social Attitudes	Blumer 1940; NG 1939, 1941-44
440	1935–1935	Special Research	Blumer 1935-38 [54]; NG 1931-34
441	1947–1948	Case Studies in Racial & Cultural Tension	Lohman 1947 & 1948
441	1930–1934	Special Research	Blumer 1930-34
441	1950–1952	Design of Research	Hauser 1950 & 1952; NO 1951
443	1950–1950	Sources of Data for Social Research	Hauser 1950
444	1948–1952	Quantitative Methods for Population Research	Hauser 1948; Duncan 1951 & 1952; NO 1949 & 1951
445	1948–1948	Seminar in the Analysis of Census Data	Hauser 1948
446	1948–1951	Seminar in Human Relations in Industry	Whyte 1948 [55]; Junker & Roy 1949-50; Unspecified 1951
450	1933–1939	Research in the Field of the Family	Burgess 1933-37; NG 1934, 1935, 1937-9
453	1947–1947	Seminar on Methods of Studying Institutions	Hughes 1947; Hauser & Hart 1949
453	1949–1951	Sample Surveys as Research Method	Hart 1950
455	1948–1948	Seminar: The Community & Social Institutions	Duncan, Hauser & Hart 1951
456	1948–1948	Seminar: The Individual in the Social System	Warner & McGuire 1948
459	1949–1951	Status Relations & Character Structure	Warner, Henry & Tryon 1948; Warner & Havinghurst 1949
460	1950–1950	Seminar in Status Relationships: S.M. & C.S.	Warner & Havinghurst 1950-51
460	1950–1951	Problems in Correctional Administration	Lohman 1950 & 1951
461	1925–1936	Local Community Studies	Burgess 1925-6, 1928-36; NO 1927; NG 1929-36

Soc. Course No.	Year First Listed	Last Year Listed	Title	
465	1932	1940	Field Studies in Criminology	Sutherland 1932-34
467	1925	1940	Field Studies	Park & Burgess 1925-6, 28-9 [56] NO 1927 Park 1931 Burgess & Wirth 1932-39 Burgess 1940 NG 1933-40
473	1931	1940	Clinical Sociology	Burgess 1931-37 [57] NG 1934-40
475	1947	1951	Seminar: Personal & Social Disorganization	Burgess 1947 & 1948 Reiss 1951 NO 1949 & 1950
476	1930	194	Research in Criminology	Sutherland 1930-34 [58] Burgess 1939, 1941, 1942 NG 1935-8, 1940, 1943-4
480	1948	1948	Seminar: Theories of Social Change	Ogburn 1948
483	1951	1951	Crime and Urban Community	Reiss 1951
485	1950	1950	Research in Public Opinion	Hart 1950
487	1951	1951	Research on Human Behavior in the City	Unspecified 1951
489	1951	1951	Seminar: Soc. Research in Mass Communications	Horton 1951
496	1949	1949	New Developments in Attitude Measurement	Lazarsfeld 1949

There were also a number of course listed which were taken from other departments and taught by staff from those departments

Soc. Course No.	Orig. Dept. & Number	Year First Listed	Last Year Listed	Title	
261	PY 261	1951	1951	Elementary Social Psychology	Unspecified 1951
311	ZO 211	1943	1945	Human Genetics	Stanskov 1943-45 [17]
311	ED 311B	1950	1951	Later Childhood and Adolescent Society	Tryon & Mass 1950 [59]
312A	ED 312A	1948	1952	Human Development in Infancy & Early Childhood	Koch & Cooper 1948-9[60] Koch 1950-52
312B	ED 312B	1948	1952	Human Development in Later Childhood & Adolescence	Havinghurst,Peck,Tryon 48

Course	Dept			Title	Lecturers
312C	ED 312C	1948	1952	Human Development in Adulthood & Old Age	Hav., Pe.,Try.,Haggard 49 Mass & Peck 1950 Mass, Hesse & Hav. 1951 Mass & Hesse 1952 [61]
316	ZO 416	1944	1944	Problems in the Biology of Social Insects	Hav,B'gess,W'thngtn 48-50 Hav, Burgess, Shanas 1951 Hav, Shanas Foot 52 [62]
316	ZO 416	1945	1945	Seminar in the Biology of Social Insects	Emerson 1944 Emerson 1945
317	AN 317	1943	1952	Social Status & Learning	Wirth & Hav. 1943-7 1951 Wirth 1950 [63] Havinghurst 1952
322	ED 322	1943	1951	Psychiatric Problems in Education	McGuire 1949 Sherman 1943-51
356	DV 362	1949	1951	Sociology of Religion	Kincheloe 1949-51
389A	PY 389A	1950	1950	Social Psychology	Rosenthal 1950
389B	PY 389B	1950	1950	Social Psychology	Campbell 1950
389C	PY 389C	1950	1950	Social Psychology	Campbell 1950
411	ZO 411	1944	1946	Animal Aggression	Allie 1944-46
482	PY 482A	1950	1950	Theory of Group Dynamics	Rosenthal 1950

Key: AN Department of Anthropology
DV School of Divinity
ED Department of Education
PY Department of Psychology
ZO Department of Zoology

Notes To Table 2

[1] Where the course is not given and no lecturer is specified, then no entry is usually made in the list of lecturers in this table. Where the course is apparently given but no lecturer is recorded in the Official Publications, then an entry of 'Unspecified' will be made.

[2] NO indicates that the course was not offered in these years (which lie between the firsat and last dates the course was listed)

[3] From 1926-1930 this was course number 101

[4] Courses with final dates of 1952 usually continued after that time, the survey only covered the period up to 1952.

[5] This course was entitled 'Introduction to the Study of Society' up to 1931 and 'Introduction to the Study of Sociology' from 1932 to 1937.

[6] NG indicates that although the course was listed it was not apparantly given during these years. In some cases a lecturer is specified although the course was not taught. These are usually shown in the listing of each course.

[7] Course number 310 from 1925-1943

[8] This course was not offered in 1946. From 1947 onwards it was number 369

[9] This course was numbered 326 before 1937. From 1934 it was entitled 'Collective Behavior'.

[10] This course was entitled 'Social Origins and Social Institutions' from 1937

[11] This course was number 351 until 1943

[12] This course numbered 364 after 1934

[13] This course was number 365 from 1940-42 and 1949-50

[14] In 1943 this course was renumbered 321.

[15] This course was entitled 'Sampling' in 1935

[16] This course was identical to Statistics 303, Business 323 and Economics 316

[17] Maas was in the Education department, this course was identical to Education 311B & Home Economics 336

[18] Course number 457 from 1948-49

[18b] This course entitled 'French Sociology' from 1939.

[19] This course referred to as 'Seminar in Quantitative Studies in Social Psychology' from 1940

[20] This course changed number to 323 in 1943

[21] This course changed number to 324 in 1943 and to number 424 in 1948.

[22] This course was entitled 'The Modern Community' before 1938.

[23] This course had a variety of names. From 1935-37 it was entitled 'Problems dof the Modern Community'; from 1942 to 1943 it was 'Comparative Study of the Social Organisation of Contemporary Communities' and from 1944 'Contemporary Communities'.

[24] This course was titled 'Technology and Social Change' from 1933. Course number 437 in 1948. Title changed to 'Technology, Social Change & Urbanisation' in 1951.

[25] This course changed number to 442 from 1948-50

[26] This course numbered 344 in 1948

[27] Changed number to 346 from 1943-44

[28] In 1936 this course was number 345

[29] From 1939 this course was titled 'Professions'

[30] The course is identical to Anthropology course 351.

[31] Matthews was in the Divinity Department

[32] This course was entitled 'The Social Orientation of Children' before 1939 and 'The Social Development of the Child' from 1943 onwards.

[33] It was numbered 362 in 1929 and 364 from 1943. In 1951 its title changed to 'Human Ecology and the Urban Community'

[34] Puttkamer was in the Law Department.

[35] The title of this course from 1933 was 'Organised Crime and Criminal Culture'

[36] This course was titled 'Quantitative problems In Social Disorganization' from 1939

[37] This course was titled 'Theory of Personal Disorganization' from 1934

[38] Courses 381 and 382 for the same period also had the same title

[39] This course titled 'Communication and Social Solidarity' in 1948

[40] This course was number 328 in 1944

[41] This course was number 402 from 1941-1943

[42] This course was number 402 from 1931 to 1940

[43] Courses 404 and 405 identical for these dates

[44] Courses 404, 405 and 406 identical for these dates

[45] Courses 405 and 406 identical for these dates, course 407 identical from 1946 to 1951

[46] Courses 407 & 408 identical for this date

[47] Courses 408 & 409 identical for this date

[48] Courses 411 & 412 identical for this date

[49] Allie was in the Zoology department

[50] Courses 424 & 425 identical for these dates

[51] Courses 427, 428 & 429 identical for these dates

[52] Course number changed to 448 in 1949. Course 450 identical in 1950

[53] Courses 434 & 435 identical for these dates

[54] Course 441 identical from 1935 to 1938. Courses 442 and 443 identical from 1935 to 1937

[55] Courses 447 & 448 identical in 1948, course 447 identical 1949-1951.

[56] Courses 466, 468 & 469 identical from 1925-29. Courses 468 & 469 identical from 1930-39. Courses 466 & 468 identical in 1940.

[57] Courses 474 & 475 identical for these dates.

[58] Number 478 in 1933. Courses 477 and 479 identical from 1933 to 1938 and from 1942 to 1944.

[59] Also identical to Home Economics 336

[60] Also identical to Home Economics 312A & Psychology 312A

[61] Also identical to Home Economics 312B & Psychology 312B

[62] Also identical to Home Economics 312C & Psychology 312C

[63] Also identical with Education 317

283

Appendix 5

Ph.D. Theses

Theses awarded the Ph.D. in the Department of Sociology (and Anthropology) at the University of Chicago from 1895 to 1952 [1]

Raymond, J. H., 1895, 'American Municipal Government'
Sanders, F. W., 1895, 'An Exposition in Outline of the Relation of Certain Economic Principles to Social Adjustment'
Thomas, W. I., 1896, 'On Differences of the Metabolism of the Sexes'
Vincent, G. E., 1896, 'Sociology and the Integration of Studies'
Miller, M. L., 1897, 'A Preliminary Study of the Peublos of Taos, New Mexico'
Clark, H. B., 1897, 'The Public Schools of Chicago: A Sociological Study'
Borows, D. P., 1897, 'The Ethnobotany of Coahuila Indians of Southern California'
Howerth, I. W., 1898, 'The Social Aim of Education'
Ellwood, C. A., 1899, 'Some Prolegomina of Social Psychology'
Gordon, W. C., 1899, 'The Social Ideals of Alfred Tennyson as Related to his Time'
Forrest, J. D., 1900, 'The Development of Industrial Organisations'
MacLean, A. M., 1900, 'The Acadian Element in the Population of Nova Scotia'
Gillette, J. M., 1901, 'The Culture Agencies of A Typical Manufacturing Group, South Chicago'
Bushnell, C. J., 1901, 'A Study of the Stock Yards Community at Chicago, as a Typical Example of the Bearing of Modern Industry upon Democracy, with Constructive Suggestions'
Hayes, E. C., 1902, 'The Sociologist's Object of Attention'
Hewes, A., 1903, 'The Part of Invention in the Social Process'
Cressey, F. G., 1903, 'The Church and The Young Man' [2]
Riley, T. J., 1904, 'A Study in the Higher Life of Chicago'
Adams, R. C., 1904, 'A Technique for Sociological Research'
Fleming, H. E., 1905, 'Some Phases of the Production and Consumption of Literature in Chicago'
Perkins, R. R., 1905, 'The Treatment of Juvenile Delinquents' [3]
Steelman, A. J., 1905, 'Charities for Children in the City of Mexico' [3]
Woods, E. B., 1905, 'Progress as a Sociological Concept'
Rhoades, M. C., 'A Case Study of the Delinquent Boys in the Juvenile Court in Chicago'
Mumford, E., 1906, 'The Beginning of Authority' [4]
Dyer, G. W., 1907, 'Democracy in the South Before the Civil War'
Woodhead, H., 1907, 'The Social Significance of the Physical Development of Cities'
North, C. C, 1908, 'The Influence of Modern Social Relations Upon Ethical Concepts'
MacPherson, H., 1910, 'Co-operative Credit Associations in the Province of Quebec'
Fenton, F., 1910, 'The Influence of Newspaper Presentations Upon the Growth of Crime and Other Anti- Social Activity'
Bernard, L. L., 1910, 'The Transistion to an Objective Standard of Control'
Reep, S. N., 1911, 'Social Policy of Chicago Churches'

Bogardus, E. S., 1911, 'The Relation of Fatigue to Industrial Accidents'

House, J. T., 1912, 'Purpose, the Variant of Theory'

Burgess, E. W., 1913, 'The Function of Socialization in Social Evolution'

Steiner, J. F., 1913, 'The Japanese in America' [5]

Sutherland, E. H., 1913, 'Unemployment and Public Employment Agencies'

Taft, J. J., 1913, 'The Woman Movement From the Point of View of Social Consciousness' [6]

Ware, N. J., 1913, 'An Instrumental Interpretation of Social Theory: 'L'Ordre Naturel Et Essentiel Des Societes Politiques' of Le Mercier de la Riviere, Physiocrat'. [7]

Elmer, M. C., 1914, 'Social Surveys of Urban Communities'

Coleman, G. T., 1914, 'The Transition From the Ideals of Personal Righteousness of the Seventeenth Century to the Modern Ideals of Social Science' [7]

Eubank, E. E., 1915, 'A Study of Family Desertion'

Handman, M., 1917, 'The Beginnings of the Social Philosophy of Karl Marx'

Stone, R. W., 1919, 'The Origin of the Survey Movement'

Reuter, E. B., 1919, 'The Mulatto in the United States: A Sociological and Psychological Study' [8]

Weynard, L. D., 1919 'A Study of Wage-Payment to Prisoners As A Penal Method' [7]

Queen, S. A., 1919, 'The Passing of the County Jail'

Kawabe, K., 1919, 'The Japanese Newspaper and its Relation to the Political Development of Modern Japan' [9]

Blachley, C. D., 1919, 'The Treatment of the Problem of Capital and Labor in Social Study Course in the Churches'

Smith, W. C., 1920, 'Conflict and Fusion of Cultures as Typified by the Ao Nagas of India' [10]

Jensen, H. E., 1920, 'The Rise of Religious Journalism in the United States'

Horak, J., 1920, 'The Assimilation of the Czechs in Chicago'

Carroll, M. R., 1920, 'The Attitude of the American Federation of Labor Toward Legislation and Politics'

Bodenhafer, W. B., 1920, 'The Comparative Role of the Group Concept in Ward's Dynamic Sociology and Contemporary Sociology'

Sanderson, D., 1921, 'The Rural Community: A Social Unit'

Ratcliffe, S. C., 1921, 'Pauper Law and Institutions in Illinois'

Rainwater, C. E., 1921, 'The Evolution of the Play Movement in the United States: Its Structure and Function'

McKenzie, R. D., 1921, 'The Neighborhood, A Study of Local Life in Columbus, Ohio'

Rossouw, G. S. H., 1922, 'Nationalism and Language'

Detweiler, F. G., 1922, 'The Negro Press in the United States'

Bickham, M. H., 1922, 'The Scientific Antecedents of the Sociology of August Comte'

Dawson, C. A., 1922, 'The Social Nature of Knowledge' [11]

Hayner, N. S., 1923, 'The Sociology of Hotel Life'

Young, E. F., 1924, 'Race Prejudice'

Price, M. T., 1924, 'Protestant Missions as Culture Contact'

Mowrer, E. R., 1924, 'Family Disorganization - An Introduction to a Sociological Analysis'

House, F. N., 1924, 'Industrial Morale: An Essay in the Sociology of Industrial Control'

Hiller, E. T., 1924, 'The Strike as Group Behavior: A Study in the Process and Technique of Control of the Striking Group'

Barnhart, K. E., 1924, 'The Evolution of Social Consciousness in Methodism'

Wang, T. C., 1925, 'The Youth Movement in China'

Roest, P. K., 1925, 'White Magic and its Theories'

Reckless, W. C., 1925, 'The Natural History of Vice Areas in Chicago'

Kreuger, E. T., 1925, 'Autobiographical Documents and Personality'

Karpf, F. B., 1925, 'American Social Psychology and its European Background'

Daniel, W. A., 1925, 'Negro Theological Seminary Survey'

Wirth, L., 1926, 'The Ghetto: A Study in Isolation'

Thrasher, F. M., 1926, 'The Gang: A Study of 1,313 Gangs in Chicago'

Simpson, E. N., 1926, 'Wishes: A Study in Social Psychology'

Shonle, R., 1926, 'Suicide - A Study of Personal Disorganization'

Janzen, C. C, 1926, 'A Social Study of the Mennonite Settlement in the Counties of Marion, McPherson, Harvey, Reno, and Butler, Kansas'

DeGraff, H. O., 1926, 'A Study of the Juvenile Court of Iowa with Special Reference to Des Moines'

White, L. A., 1927, 'Medicine Societies of the Southwest'

Shideler, E. H., 1927, 'The Chain Store: A Study of the Ecological Organization of a Modern City'

Wu, C. C., 1928, 'The Chinese in the United States'

McCluer, F. L., 1928, 'Living Conditions among Wage-earning Families in Forty-one Blocks in Chicago (1923)'

Redfield, R., 1928, 'A Plan for the Study of Tepozlan, Mexico'

Kawamura, T., 1928, 'The Class Conflict in Japan as Affected by the Expansion of Japanese Industry and Trade'

Hughes, E. C., 1928, 'A Study of a Secular Institution: The Chicago Real Estate Board'

Gower, C. D., 1928, 'The Supernatural Patron in Sicilian Life'

Mueller, J. H., 1928, 'The Automobile: A Sociological Study' [11]

Blumer, H., 1928, 'Method in Social Psychology'

Neumeyer, M. H., 1929, 'Conscience: A Socio-Psychological Study'

McCormick, T.C. , 1929, 'Rural Unrest: A Sociological Investigation of Rural Movements in the United States'

Kuhlman, A. F., 1929, 'Crime and Punishment in Missouri: A Study of the Social Forces in the Trial and Error Process of Penal Reform'

Kincheloe, S. C., 1929, 'The Prophet: A Study of the Sociology of Leadership'

Winston, E. B., 1930, 'A Statistical Study of Mental Disease'

Watson, W. T., 1930, 'Divsion of Labor: A Study in the Sociology and Social Psychology of Work Satisfaction'

Stouffer, S. A., 1930, 'An Experimental Comparison of Statistical Case Study: Methods of Attitude Research'

Stonequist, E. V., 1930, 'The Marginal Man: A Study in the Subjective Aspects of Cultural Conflict'

Rosenquist, C. M., 1930, 'A Sociological Study of the Swedes of Texas'

Cressey, P. F., 1930, 'The Succession of Cultural Groups in the City of Chicago'

Brown, W. O., 1930, 'Race Prejudice: A Sociological Study'

Becker, H. P., 1930, 'Ionia and Athens: Studies in Secularization'

Quinn, J. A., 1931, 'Sublimation - A Study of A Social Process'

Lind, A. W., 1931, 'Economic Succession and Racial Invasion in Hawaii'

Koshuk, R. P., 1931, 'A Comparative Study of Social Contracts Involving Play Material in Four Pre-School Groups'

Frazier, E. F., 1931, 'The Negro Family in Chicago'

Faris, R. E. L., 1931, 'An Ecological Study of Insanity in the City'

Russell, D., 1931, 'The Roadhouse: A Study of Commercialized Amusements In the Environs of Chicago' [11]

Dollard, J., 1931, 'The Changing Functions of the American Family'

Clark, C. D., 1931, 'News: A Sociological Study'

Thompson, E. T., 1932, 'The Plantation'

Strow, C. W., 1932, 'The Human Resources of a Community'

Palmer, V. M., 1932, 'The Primary Settlement Area as a Unit of Urban Growth and Organization'

Webster, E. J., 1932, 'Reform: A Sociological Study' [12]

Cottrell, L. S., 1933, 'The Reliability and Validity of A Marriage Study Schedule'

Blumenthal, A. B., 1933, 'A Sociological Study of a Small Town'

Yen, Y. C., 1934, 'Crime in Relation to Social Change in China'

Montgomery, E. W., 1934, 'The Urbanization of Rural Recreation'

Doyle, B., 1934, 'The Etiquette of Race Relations in the South'

Van Vechten, C. C., 1935, 'A Study of Success and Failure of One Thousand Delinquents Committed to a Boy's Republic'

Roper, M. W., 1935, 'The City and the Primary Group'

Lang, R. O., 1936, 'The Relation of Educational Status to Economic Status in the City of Chicago, by Census Tracts, 1934'

Joslyn, M. N., 1936, 'Profit Sharing For Old-Age Security: A Case Study with a General Approach' [12]

Reed, J. P., 1937, 'Kokutai: A Study of Certain Sacred and Secular Aspects of Japanese Nationalism'

Myhrman, A. M., 1937, 'The Swedish Nationality Movement in Finland'

Merrill, F. E., 1937, 'The Chicago Stock Exchange'

Moore, A. J., 1937, 'Citywide Internal Migration: An Analysis of the 1930 Population of Stockholm Born in Vastmanland County, Sweden'

Lindesmith, A. R., 1937, 'The Nature of Opiate Addiction'

Hughes, H. M., 1937, 'The Human Interest Story: A Study of Popular Literature'

Dai, B., 1937, 'Opium Addiction in Chicago'

Carter, W. P., 1937 'The Only Child in the Family: A Comparison with Other Order of Birth'

Schroeder, C. W., 1938, Divorce in a City of 100,000 Population'

Schettler, C., 1938, 'Problems of Personality Traits with Emphasis Upon the Problem of Mutability'

Lejins, P., 1938, 'The Concept of Imitation and Imitation as a Factor in Crime'

Hauser, P. M., 1938, 'Differential Fertility, Mortality and Net Reproduction'

Glick, C., 1938, 'The Chinese Migrant in Hawaii'

Cox, O. C., 1938, 'Factors Affecting the Marital Status of Negroes in the United States'

Reeden, E. A., 1939, 'Embezzelement: A Study of One Kind of Criminal Behavior with Prediction Tables Based on Fidelity Insurance Records'

Pierson, D. R., 1939, 'A Study of Racial and Cultural Adjustment in Bahia, Brazil'

Daniel, V. E., 1940, 'Ritual in Chicago's South Side Churches for Negroes'

Strong, S. M., 1940, 'The Social Type Method: Social Types in the Negro Community of Chicago'

287

Noss, T., 1940, 'Resistance to Social Innovations as Found in the Literature Regarding Innovations which have Proved Successful'

Hillman, W. A., 1940, 'Urbanization and the Organization of Welafare Activities in the Metroploitan Community of Chicago'

Schauffler, M., 1941, 'The Suburbs of Cleveland: A Field Study of the Metropolitan District Outside the Administrative Area of the City'

Johnson, E. S., 1941, 'The Evolution of the Chicago Central Business District'

Jaffe, A. J., 1941, 'Urbanization and Fertility'

Gittler, J. B., 1941, 'Society's Adjustment to a Mechanical and Social Invention: A Study in Social Change'

Dunham, H. W., 1941, 'The Character of the Interrelationship of Crime and Schizophrenia'

Devinney, L. C., 1941, 'Some Relationships Between Educational Achievement and Social Stratification'

Clinard, M. B., 1941, 'Crime and the Process of Urbanization: A Study of Culture Conflict'

Winch, R. F., 1942, 'Social Personality Characteristics of Courtship Revealed in Men'

Weinberg, S. K., 1942, 'Incest Behavior and Family Organization'

Wallin, P., 1942, 'The Characteristics of participants in a Social-Psychological Study'

Johns, E. D., 1942, 'Chicago's Newspapers and the News: A Study of Public Communication in a Metropolis'

Goldhammer, H., 1942, 'Some Factors Affecting Participation in Voluntary Associations'

Baur, E. J., 1942, 'Voluntary Control in the Advertising Industry'

Alexander, C. S., 1942, 'Antipathy and Prejudice: A Study of the Distinctions Between These Two Phenomena'

Whyte, W. F., 1943, 'Street Corner Society: The Social Structure of an Italian Slum'

Oyler, M. D., 1943, 'Fertility and Migration of Kentucky Population, 1920-1940, as Related to Communication, Income and Education'

Rose, C. B., 1943, 'Worker's Education, The Labor Movement, and the Intellectuals in the United States.

Symons, J. N., 1944, 'Utah Residence Types and Criminal Behavior'

Strauss, A. L., 1944, 'A Study of Three Psychological Factors Affecting the Choice of a Mate in Marriage'

Parrish, C. H., 1944, 'The Significance of Color in the Negro Community'

Hall, O., 1944, 'The Informal Organization of Medical Practice: Case Study of a Profession'

Wu, P. S., 1945, 'The Social Characteristics of Increasing, Stable and Decreasing Cities'

Weller, F., 1945, 'The Sect in Transition'

Walker, H. J., 1945, 'Changes in Race Accommodation in a Southern City'

Whitridge, E. R., 1946, 'Art in Chicago'

Sarna, J., 1946, 'The Social Categories of Friendship'

Rose, A. M., 1946, 'Living Arrangements of Unnattached Persons in American Cities'

LaViolette, F., 1946, 'Americans of Japanese Ancestry: A Study of Assimilation in the American Community'

Hill, M. C., 1946, 'The All-Negro Society'

Rose, A. W., 1947, 'A Socio-psychological Analysis of the Ambition Patterns of a Sample of Industrial Workers'

Miller, V., 1947, 'The Areal Distribution of Tax Delinquency in

Chicago and Its Relationship to Certain Housing and Social Characteristics'

Lee, R. H., 1947, 'Growth and Decline of Chinese Communities in the Rocky Mountain Region'

Freedman, R., 1947, 'Recent Migration to Chicago'

Ericksen, E. G., 1947, 'Protest Society: Social Irrationality in the Extraterritorial One-sex Company Town'

Dubin, R., 1947, 'The Grievance Process: A Study of Union-Management Relations'

Clark, R. E., 1947, 'The Relationship of Occupation and Various Psychoses'

Campisi, P. J., 1947, 'A Scale for the Measurement of Acculturation'

Breese, G. W., 1947, 'The Daytime Population of the Central Business District of Chicago'

Bendix, R., 1947, 'The Public Servant in a Democracy'

Swanson, G. E., 1948, 'Emotional Disturbance and Juvenile Delinquency'

Meltzer, B. N., 1948, 'Preprofessional Career and Early Publication as Factors in the Differential Productivity of Social Scientists'

Klapp, O., 1948, 'The Hero as a Social Type'

Janowitz, M., 1948, 'Mobility, Subjective Deprivation and Ethnic Hostility'

Cohen, L., 1948, 'Factors Associated with Home Ownwership in Twenty-two Metropolitan Districts, 1940'

Burnett, J., 1948, 'The Problem of Community Instability in East Central Alberta'

Bowerman, C. E., 1948, 'The Measurement of Areas of Adjustment in Marriage'

Duncan, H. D., 1948, 'Chicago as a Literary Center: Social Factors Influencing Chicago Literary Institutions from 1885 to 1920'

Turner, R. H., 1948, 'Some Factors in the Differential Position of Whites and Negroes in the Labor Force of the United States in 1940'

Shibutani, T., 1948, 'The Circulation of Rumors as a Form of Collective Behavior'

Rosenthal, E., 1948, 'The Jewish Population of Chicago, Illinois: Size and Distribution as Derived from Voter's Lists'

Ni, E. I-H., 1948, 'Social Characteristics of the Chinese Population: A Study of the Population Structure and Urbanism of a Metropolitan Community'

Milne, D. S., 1948, 'Juvenile Delinquency and Youth Services in Wartime California'

Faw, V. E., 1948, 'Vocational Interests of Chicago Negro and White High School Junior and Senior Boys'

Willkening, E. A., 1949, 'The Acceptance of Certain Agricultural Programs and Practices in a Piedmont Community of North Carolina'

Thomas, J. L., 1949, 'Some of the Factors Involved in the Breakdown of Catholic Marriage'

Shanas, E., 1949, 'The Personal Adjustment of Recipients of Old Age Assistance: With Special Consideration of the Methodology of Questionaire [sic] Studies of Older People'

Gross, E., 1949, 'Informal Relations and the Social Organization of Work in an Industrial Office'

Dee, W. L. J., 1949, 'The Social Effects of a Public Housing Project on the Immediate Community'

Sheldon, E., 1949, 'The Chicago Labor Force, 1910-1949'

Hale, W. H., 1949, 'The Career Development of the Negro Lawyer in Chicago'

Klassen, P., 1949, 'Internal Migration in Relation to Literacy and Language'

Lunday, G. A., 1949, 'A Study of Parole Prediction'

Clausen, J., 1949, 'Soldiers' Plans and the Prediction of the Post-Separation Activities of Veterans'

Cothran, T. C., 1949, 'Negro Stereotyped Conceptions of White People'

Stone, R. C., 1949, 'Vertical Mobility and Ideology: A Study of White Collar Workers'

Smith, H. L., 1949, 'The Sociological Study of Hospitals'

Nelson, C. W., 1949, 'Development and Evaluation of a Leadership Attitude Scale for Foremen'

Bonner, H., 1949, 'Paranoia and Paranoid Condition: A Social-Psychological Study of Paranoic Personality'

Duncan, O. D., 1949, 'An Examination of the Problem of Optimum City Size'

Wray, D., 1950, 'The Foreman and Managerial Functions'

Williams, J. J., 1950, 'The Professional Status of Women Physicians'

Reiss, A. J., 1950, 'The Accuracy, Efficiency, and Validity of a Prediction Instrument'

McKeown, J. E., 1950, 'The Dynamics of the Childhood Families of Small Highly Selected Groups of Male and Female Schizophrenics, Behavior Problems and Normals'

Killian, L. M., 1950, 'Southern White Laborers in Chicago's West Side'

Hormann, B. L., 1950, 'Extinction and Survival: A Study of the Reaction of Aboriginal Populations to European Expansion'

Dalton, M., 1950, 'A Study of Informal Organization among the Managers of an Industrial Union'

Ramsy, N. G., 1950, 'Recent Trends in Occupational Mobility'

Reitzes, D., 1950, 'Collective Factors in Race Relations'

Quinn, O. W., 1950, 'Racial Attitude and the Conforming Personality'

Marcson, S., 1950, 'The Prediction of Intermarriage'

Fitchett, E. H., 1950, 'The Free Negro in Charleston, South Carolina'

Mayer, A. J., 1950, 'Differentials in Length of Life, City of Chicago: 1880-1940'

Ikle, F. C., 1950, 'The Impact of War Upon the Spacing or Urban Population'

Lindstrom, F. B., 1950, 'The Military Mind and the Soldier Press'

Motz, A. B., 1950, 'Conceptions of Martial Roles in Transition'

Rowenstein, J., 1950, 'Small-Town Party Politics'

Ross, A. D., 1950, 'Ethnic Relations and Social Structure: A Study of the Invasion of French-Speaking Canadians into an English Canadian District'

Schmidt, J. F., 1950, 'Patterns of Poor Adjustment in Persons of Later Maturity'

Lu, Y-C., 1950, 'A Study of Dominant, Equalitarian and Submissive Roles in Marriage'

Lee, S-C., 1950, 'Social Implications of Farm Tenancy in China'

Henry, A. F., 1950, 'The Nature of the Relation Between Sucide and the Business Cycle'

Harlan, W. H., 1950, 'Isolation and Conduct in Later Life: Study of Four Hundred and Sixty Four Chicagoans of Ages Sixty to Ninety-Five'

Goldman, N., 1950, 'The Differential Selection of Juvenile Offenders for Court Appearance'

Calhoun, D. W., 1950, 'The Reception of Marxian Sociological Theory by American Academic Sociologists'

Bogart, L., 1950, 'The Comic Strips and their Adult Readers: A Study of Male Workers in a New York City Neighbourhood'

Star, S. A., 1950, 'Interracial Tension in Two Areas of Chicago: An Exploratory Approach to the Measurement of Interracial Tension'

Stafford, A. B., 1950, 'Trends of Invention in Material Culture: A Statistical Study of the Class-Wise Distribution of Inventive Effort in the United States as Determined by Patents Granted During the Period 1914-1945'

Pan, J-S, 1950, 'A Comparison of the Factors in the Personal Adjustment of Old People in the Protestant Church Homes for the Aged and the Old People Living Outside of Institutions'

Miyamoto, F., 1950, 'The Career of Intergroup Tensions: A Study of the Collective Adjustments of Evacuees to Crises at the Tule Lake Relocation Center'

King, C., 1951, 'Factors Making for Success or Failure in Marital Adjustment Among 466 Negro Couples in Southern City'

Schwartz, M., 1951, 'Social Interaction in A Disturbed Ward of a Mental Hospital'

Becker, H. S., 1951, 'Role and Career Problems of the Chicago Public-School Teacher'

Westley, W. A., 1951, 'The Police: A Sociological Study of Law, Custom and Morality'

Short, J. F., 1951, 'An Investigation of the Relation Between Crime and Business Cycles'

Lewis, H. G., 1951, 'The Social Life of the Negro in a Southern Piedmont Town'

Kitagawa, E. M., 1951, 'Differentials in Total and Marital Fertility, Chicago 1920-1940'

Hare, A. P., 1951, 'A Study of Interaction and Consensuses in Different Sized Discussion Groups'

Jacobson, A. B., 1951, 'A Study of Evaluations of Nisei as Workers by Caucasian Employment Agency Managers and Employers of Nisei' [12]

Haimowitz, M. L., 1951, 'The Development and Change of Ethnic Hostility'

Elkin, F., 1951, 'A Study of the Relationship between Popular Hero Type and Social Class'

Ireland, R., 1951, 'The Aging Industrial Worker: Retirement Plans and Preparation with Some Reference to the Meaning of Work'

Keyfitz, N., 1952, 'Urban Influence on Farm Family Size'

Blackiston, D., 1952, 'The Judge, the Defendant and Criminal Law Administration'

Edwards, G. F., 1952, 'Occupational Mobility of A Selected Group of Negro Male Professionals'

Benson, P., 1952, 'The Interests and Activities of Engaged and Married Couples in Relation to Their Adjustment'

Al-Tahir, A. J. A., 1952, 'The Arab Community in the Chicago Area: A Comparative Study of the Christian- Syrians and the Muslim Palestinians'

Roy, D., 1952, 'Restriction of Output by Machine Operator in a Piecework Machine Shop'

Reeder, L., 1952, 'Industrial Location in the Chicago Metropolitan Area with Special Reference to Population'

London, J., 1952, 'Decision Making in a Local Union: A Case Study'

Linn, E., 1952, 'The Correlation of Death Rates from Selected Causes with the Business Cycle, 1919-47'

Freidson, E., 1952, 'An Audience and Its Taste: A Study in Mass Communication'

Dornbush, S., 1952, 'The Family in the Labor Force: A Study of Supplementary Workers in U. S. 1940'

DePoister, M., 1952, 'Trends in Theological Beliefs Within Selected Denominations'

Buckman, R., 1952, 'Interaction Between Women's Clubs and Institutions'

Winget, J., 1952, 'Teacher Inter-School Mobility Aspirations: Elementary Teachers, Chicago Public School System 1947-48' [13]

Wilson, E. K., 1952, 'Community Participation in Policy Formation' [14]

Solomon, D. N., 1952 'Career Contingencies of Chicago Physicians'

Kimura, Y., 1952, 'A Comparative Study of Collective Adjustment of the Idei, The First Generation Japanese, In Hawaii and in the Mainland, U. S. Since Pearl Habor'

Notes to Appendix 5

[1] Sources: A mimeographed list provided by Professor M. Janowitz, University of Chicago, dated 1968. The collection of theses lodged in the Social Science Research Building at the University of Chicago. Faris (1967), who has a list of doctoral theses up to 1935. Files of the Regenstein Library, University of Chicago. Computer search, Dialog File 35, Ph.D theses in sociology 1900-1920. Not all sources concur. Where any differences occur these are noted, details from the original theses or the most likely version are recorded in the listing. Various other commentators refer to Chicago PhDs, but where these are not in any of the above source lists they are not included. For example, Mullins (1973, pp. 54-57) lists Chicago Ph.Ds who he included as symbolic interactionists, on this list is William Troyer (1942), but no other reference to this thesis could be located.

[2] This is the title on the computer printout, it does not appear on Janowitz's list, nor in Faris (1967) nor was it located in the Social Science Research Building. On the Regenstein Library file the title was 'The Church and Young Men'.

[3] These theses only appear on the computer printout and in none of the other sources. It is possible that these were Henderson's students. Henderson was made head of the Department of Ecclesiastical Sociology in 1904, later (1913) Practical Sociology. This still seemed to be under the general rubric of the Department of Sociology and Anthropology at the time, see the Official Publications of the University of Chicago, although subsequent classifications of the theses may have detatched them from the sociology output. Alternatively, they may just have been lost. Henderson died in 1914 and no further mention was made of Practical Sociology in the section of the Official Publications relating to the Sociology Department.

[4] This is missing from Janowitz's list, is entitled 'The Origins of Leadership' on the Regenstein list. A book by the author with this latter title was published by the University of Chicago Press in 1909.

[5] Janowitz's list, Faris (1967) and the computer printout have this

reference. However, the computer printout also lists 1915, 'The Japanese Invasion: A Study in the Psychology of Inter-Racial Contacts'. The Regenstein list has no reference to either title. A book. entitled 'The Japanese Invasion' by Steiner with an introduction by Park was published by A. C. McClung and Co., in 1917. Raushenbush (1979) noted that Steiner was a graduate from Washington who wrote a thesis on the Japanese on the Pacific Coast in 1913.

[6] This is not in any source except the computer printout. In 1916 a book with the same title was published by the University of Chicago Press, sponsored by the Committee on Publications in the Physical Sciences.

[7] The only reference for this is on the computer printout.

[8] The subtitle is missing from the Regenstein catalogue

[9] The title in the Regenstein catalogue is 'The Press and Politics in Japan'. A book with this title plus a subtitle: 'A Study of the Relation between the Newspaper and the Political Development of Modern Japan' was published in the Sociological Series of the University of Chicago Press in 1921.

[10] Not in the Regenstein file

[11] These theses are missing from Janowitz's list and Faris (1967) but are included in the Regenstein file.

[12] These are missing from Janowitz's list

[13] The subtitle is missing from Janowitz's list

[14] The title is missing from Janowitz's list

Appendix 6

Survey of 42 Ph.D. theses in Sociology at Chicago 1915-1950

The sample of 42, theses was drawn at random from Appendix 5. *

Table 1: Usage of Methods

The following table shows the extent to which different techniques were used in the theses. More than one technique may have been used in a thesis. Major usage refers to a technique upon which the author primarily relied. Supporting usage means that the technique(s) were adopted to provide back-up information. Minor usage means that the technique was used but played no substantial part in the final thesis.

	All theses (n=42)		
	Major	Support	Minor
Historical Analysis	10 (24)	9 (21)	6 (14)
Comparative Analysis	11 (26)	1 (2)	5 (12)
Literature Review	16 (38)	8 (19)	14 (33)
Life History	6 (14)	6 (14)	1 (2)
Participant Obs.	5 (12)	5 (12)	5 (12)
Document Analysis	13 (31)	2 (6)	6 (14)
Informal Interviews	11 (26)	4 (10)	3 (7)
Questionnaires	6 (14)	0 (0)	0 (0)
Scheduled Interviews	13 (31)	0 (0)	0 (0)

Method	Pre 1940 theses (n=22)			1940-1950 theses (n=20)		
	Major	Support	Minor	Major	Support	Minor
Historical Analysis	9 (41)	7 (32)	2 (9)	1 (5)	2 (2)	4 (20)
Comparative Analysis	8 (36)	1 (5)	3 (14)	3 (15)	0 (0)	2 (10)
Literature Review	12 (57)	4 (19)	3 (14)	4 (20)	4 (20)	11 (55)
Life History	6 (27)	3 (14)	0 (0)	0 (0)	3 (15)	1 (5)
Participant Obs.	0 (0)	1 (5)	4 (18)	5 (25)	4 (20)	1 (5)
Document Analysis	9 (41)	0 (0)	5 (23)	4 (20)	2 (10)	1 (5)
Informal Interviews	1 (5)	2 (9)	3 (14)	10 (50)	2 (10)	0 (0)
Questionnaires	2 (9)	0 (0)	0 (0)	4 (20)	0 (0)	0 (0)
Scheduled Interviews	0 (0)	0 (0)	0 (0)	13 (65)	0 (0)	0 (0)

Historical Analysis:

10 (24%) Used Historical analysis to determine categories, models or
   derive theories
 5 (12%) Used Historical Analysis to provide a descriptive setting
10 (24%) Concentrated on analysis in terms of 'natural history'
17 (40%) Did not use historical analysis.

Comparative Analysis:

11 (26%) Made a comparative analysis between two or more counties,
   states or regions
 6 (14%) Compared methods, cases etc.
25 (60%) Did not use comparative analysis

Literature Review:

14 (33%) Were based on sociological texts
 9 (21%) Were based on a mixture of sociology and psychology
   literature
12 (29%) Were based on non-sociological literature
 4 (10%) Used a variety of sources
 3 (7%) Made no use of a literature review and analysis

Life History:

12 (29%) Were collected from subjects
 1 (2%) Were based on case records
29 (69%) Did not use life histories

Participant Observation:

 2 (5%) Complete participant observation
 6 (14%) Partial participant observation
 7 (17%) Used casual observation, past personal involvement or other
   observers
27 (64%) Did not use participant observation in any sense

Document Analysis:

 5 (12%) Analysed newspapers
 5 (12%) Analysed published autobiographies
11 (26%) Used letters, case documents, hotel registers or a variety
   of such sources.
21 (50%) Made no use of document analysis

Informal Interviews:

11 (26%) Used a systematic approach to in depth interviews (6 were
   guided interviews)
 7 (17%) Used an unsystematic approach to in depth interviews
24 (57%) Did not use informal interviewing

Questionnaires:

 4 (10%) Were administered to students
 2 (5%) Were mailed to respondents
36 (85%) Made no use of questionnaires

Scheduled Interviews:

10 (24%) Used formal schedules
 2 (5%) Used flexible schedules
30 (71%) Made no use of scheduled interviewing

	All theses	Pre-1940	1940-1950
Table 2: Attitude analysis			
Made no attempt at att. analysis	25 (60%)	16 (73%)	9 (45%)
Attempted some form of a. a.	17 (40%)	6 (27%)	11 (55%)
Of the latter			
Constructed an attitude scale	6 (14%)	1 (5%)	5 (25%)
Used or adapted an existing scale	3 (7%)	1 (5%)	2 (10%)
Did not attempt to construct a scale of attitudes	8 (19%)	20 (90%)	13 (65%)
Table 3: Case Study			
Case study approach adopted	17 (40%)	13 (62%)	4 (20%)
No mention of case study approach	25 (60%)	9 (38%)	16 (80%)
Table 4: Discussion of Methods			
Extensive discussion	13 (31%)	6 (27%)	7 (35%)
Some discussion	19 (45%)	8 (36%)	11 (55%)
No discussion	10 (24%)	6 (27%)	2 (10%)
Table 5: Discussion of Methodology/Epistemology			
Extensive discussion	11 (26%)	9 (43%)	2 (18%)
Some discussion	10 (24%)	1 (5%)	9 (45%)
No discussion	21 (50%)	11 (52%)	9 (45%)
Table 6: Reformism			
Research directed to reform concerns	2 (5%)	1 (5%)	1 (5%)
Some mention of reform concerns	3 (7%)	3 (14%)	0 (0%)
Clearly opposed to reform concerns	9 (21%)	8 (36%)	1 (5%)
No mention of reform concerns	28 (67%)	10 (46%)	18 (90%)
Table 7: George Herbert Mead			
Mead's theories/approach utilised	4 (10%)	1 (5%)	3 (15%)
Mead mentioned but not utilised	8 (19%)	4 (18%)	4 (20%)
Mead not mentioned	30 (71%)	17 (77%)	13 (65%)

Table 8: Charles Horton Cooley

Cooley referenced	20 (48%)	13 (59%)	7 (35%)
Cooley not referenced	22 (52%)	9 (41%)	13 (65%)

Table 9: William Isaac Thomas

Thomas referenced	21 (50%)	15 (67%)	6 (30%)
Thomas not referenced	21 (50%)	7 (33%)	14 (70%)

Table 10: Park and Burgess (1921)

Major source text	10 (26%)	5 (28%)	5 (25%)
Referenced	8 (21%)	2 (11%)	6 (30%)
Not referenced	18 (53%)	11 (61%)	9 (45%)
Missing	4	4	

Table 11: Use of Official Statistics

Extensive use inference/description	5 (12%)	4 (18%)	1 (5%)
Some use	12 (29%)	8 (36%)	4 (20%)
No use of official statistics	25 (59%)	10 (46%)	15 (75%)

Table 12: Chicago references in bibliography

Up to 20% Chicago references	17 (47%)	12 (71%)	5 (26%)
20 to 40% Chicago references	16 (44%)	5 (29%)	11 (58%)
Over 40% Chicago references	3 (8%)	0 (0%)	3 (16%)
Missing	6	5	1

* Appendix 7 contains a review of sources.

A note on documentary sources

The primary documentary sources used in this book consisted of the following: published work of the Chicagoans and their contemporaries; Ph.D. theses produced at Chicago up to 1952; unpublished papers, research proposals, letters, minutes of meetings and other documents located in the personal papers of Chicagoans; the private journal of William Fielding Ogburn; minutes and papers of the Society for Social Research; transcripts of tape recordings of interviews conducted in 1972 by James Carey with twenty five surviving Chicagoans of the 1920s; copies of correspondence between Fred Matthews and Chicagoans written during the 1970s.

Apart from the published material and the Ph.D. theses, the source material is all located in the Special Collections Department of the University of Chicago Regenstein Library. The examination of the papers in the Special Collections Department provided a general profile against which other retrospective accounts could be compared. Such accounts included some recollections in Ogburn's journal, the reflections of Anderson, and Cavan amongst others in Urban Life, 11, (1983), Matthews' letters (including correspondence with N. Anderson, J. Bernard, and B. Hormann) and, more importantly, Carey's interviewees. Carey interviewed the following in 1972 as part of the research for his book Sociology and Public Affairs (1975): Barnhardt, Blumer, Cavan, Bartlett, Carter, Cottrell, Dollard, R. E. L. Faris, Hayner, Mrs. H. Jensen; G. B. Johnson, Karpf, Kincheloe, McCluer, McKay, E. Mowrer, H. Mowrer, Nelson, Neumeyer, Newcomb, Pederson, Reckless, Stephan, Stonequist, Thompson, and Winston. (Full references in bibliography, by contributor, dated 1972).

The range of personal papers located in the Special Collections Department is extensive. The papers of William Fielding Ogburn, Ernest Watson Burgess and Louis Wirth were examined in some detail. These collections are very large and a selective reading was necessary. The selection of material was aided by the Special Collections catalogue which outlined the contents of different files in the collection. In the case of the Burgess papers, however, the catalogue was of limited use as the collection (in 1980) was only partially sorted and it was necessary to resort to a pseudo random selection of file boxes.

The three collections provided a great deal of useful information and as different items were pieced together, a general picture of the Department of Sociology at the University of Chicago from the 1920s to 1950 emerged. This picture was reinforced and given more depth by the the extremely valuable and detailed accounts of meetings found in the papers of the Society for Social Research and by the overview of the research work of the members of the Society available in successive issues of the Bulletin of the Society.

The inspection of source documents was primarily directed to the period 1920 to 1950 as this emerged as the period in which there was the greatest conflict between the Chicagoans activities and the taken-for-granted views of their activities. Additional material on the research activities, social organization and wider context of the earlier period came from a number of well researched secondary sources including Bulmer 1980, 1981, 1981a; Burgess 1952; Carey, 1975; Coser 1978; Dibble, 1972; Diner, 1980; Faris, 1967; Furner,

1975; Hinkle and Hinkle, 1954; Martindale, 1976; Matthews, 1977; Odum, 1951; Raushenbush, 1979; Schwendinger & Schwendinger 1974; Smith & White, 1929; Wirth, 1947. Additional material on this period relating to research practices and theoretical developments came from published texts of the Chicagoans and Ph.D. theses (see references).

To augment the investigation of the development of sociological work at Chicago a sample of forty two Ph.D. theses were selected at random from the list of theses completed between 1915 and 1952 and examined in detail (see Appendix 6). This source proved exteremely useful and clearly showed the variety and trend of methodological approaches, typological procedures, theoretical orientations, epistemological underpinnings and extent of concern with reform. The progress and development of ideas in substantive areas (such as the sociology of race) were identifiable as a result of this analysis.

In reading primary sources one must be critical of both one's own interpretation and of the content of the material. First, such sources are not self-evident facts. Their sense and meaning are derived from their context and the researcher should be careful of avoiding dislocating text from its context. The context, of course, is, in part, created by the historian. Any documentary source must also be treated not as a static picture but part of a dynamic process. In short, one should not 'fix' any document with too rigid an interpretation, but should be constantly critical of the interpretation.

Second, the material itself may not be fully 'transparent'. For example, in the case of the Chicago material, minutes of meetings did not provide a verbatim report and may have concealed fundamental differences under a gloss of consensus. A precis of a speaker's presentation to a meeting, such as the Society for Social Research, may have tended to be complimentary irrespective of the quality of the contribution, and discussion sessions following such presentations seem to have been underreported. Applications for funding, too, tend to paint the institution in glowing colours and make the most of supporting evidence and on-going research whether or not it is particularly significant for the institution as a whole.

References

Abbott, E., 1926, **Historical Aspects of the Immigration Problem**: Select Documents. Chicago, University of Chicago Press.

Abbott,. E., 1924, **Immigration:** Select Documents and Case Records. Chicago: University of Chicago Press.

Agocs, C., 1979, 'Ethnic Groups in the Ecology of North American Cities', **Canadian Ethnic Studies**, 11, pp. 1-18.

Alexander, C. S., 1942, 'Antipathy and Prejudice: A Study of the Distinctions Between These Two Phenomena', Ph.D., University of Chicago.

Alihan, M. A., 1938, **Social Ecology:** A Critical Analysis. New York.

Anderson, N., 1923, **The Hobo:** The Sociology of the Homeless Man. Chicago, University of Chicago Press.

Anderson, N., 1925, 'The Hobo' M.A., University of Chicago.

Anderson, N., 1983, 'Stranger at the Gate: Reflections on the Chicago School of Sociology', **Urban Life**, 11, pp. 396-406

Anon, 1913, 'Book Writing Professors Are Scored By Speaker At Meeting of Sociologists'. Newspaper article, no auspices, undated but contents suggest 1913. Found in University of Chicago, Regenstein Library, Special Collections, Burgess Papers.

Arensberg, C. M. and Kimball, S. T., 1940, **Family and Community in Ireland**. Cambridge, Mass., Harvard, University Press.

Baker, N. F., 1927, **The Legal Aspects of Zoning**. Chicago, University of Chicago Press.

Bales, R.F. 1966 'Comment on Herbert Blumer's Paper', **American Journal of Sociology**, 71, pp. 545-7

Barnes, B., 1972, **The Sociology of Science**. Harmondsworth,

Penguin.

Barnhardt, K. E., 1972, Interview with James Carey; 1. 5. 1972. University of Chicago, Regenstein Library, Special Collections.

Barthes, R., 1967, **Elements of Semiology**. London, Cape.

Barthes, R., 1974, **Mythologies**. London, Cape.

Bartlett, H. M., 1972, Interview with James Carey; 13. 4. 1972. University of Chicago, Regenstein Library, Special Collections.

Becker, H. P., 1930, 'Ionia and Athens: Studies in Secularization', Ph.D., University of Chicago.

Becker, H. S., 1958, 'Problems of Inference and Proof in Participant Observation', **American Sociological Review**, 23, pp. 652-60

Becker, H. S., 1963, **Outsiders**: Studies in the Sociology of Deviance. New York, Free Press.

Becker, H. S., 1964, **The Other Side**: Perspectives on Deviance. New York, Free Press.

Becker, H. S., 1967, 'Whose Side Are We On', **Social Problems**, 14, pp. 239-47.

Becker, H. S., 1979, Draft transcript of an interview with Vic Lockwood. Ref. O.U., 0525. 2431

Becker, H. S. and Geer, B., 1957, 'Participant Observation and Interviewing', **Human Organization**, 16, pp. 28-32.

Becker, H. S. and Geer, B., 1957a, 'Participant Observation and Interviewing: A Rejoinder', **Human Organization**, 16, pp. 39-40.

Becker, H. S. and Geer, B., 1960, 'Participant Observation: The Analysis of Qualitative Data', in Adams, R. N. and Preiss, J. J., eds., 1960, **Human Organization Research**. Illinois, Dorsey Press.

Beckner, E. R., 1929, **A History of Labor Legislation in Illinois**. Chicago, University of Chicago Press.

Beeley, A., 1927, **The Bail System in Chicago**. Chicago, University of Chicago Press.

Bell, C., 1977, 'Reflections on the Banbury Restudy', in Bell and Newby, eds., 1977, **Doing Sociological Research**. London, Allen and Unwin, pp. 41-62.

Berger, P. L. and Berger, B., 1976, **Sociology**: A Biographical Approach. Harmondsworth, Penguin.

Bernard, J. 1973 'My Four Revolutions: An Autobiographical Account of the American Sociological Society', **American Journal of Sociology**, 78, pp. 773-92

Bernard, L. L., 1910, 'The Transistion to an Objective Standard of Control', Ph.D., University of Chicago.

Bernard, L. L., 1924, **Instinct**: A Study in Social Psychology

Bernard, L. L., 1930, 'Schools of Sociology', **Southwestern Political and Social Science Quarterly**, 11, pp. 117-34.

Bernard, L. L. and Bernard, J., 1943, **Origins of American**

Sociology: The Social Science Movement in the United States. New York, Crowell.

Besnard, P., ed, 1983, The Sociological Domain: The Durkheimians and the founding of French sociology. Cambridge, Cambridge University Press.

Beyle, H. C., 1928, Governmental Reporting in Chicago. University of Chicago Press.

Bierstedt, R., 1981, American Sociological Theory: A Critical History. New York, Academic Press.

Blake, J. A., 1978, 'The Structural Basis of Theory Production: Park, the Chicago School, and Collective Behavior', Quarterly Journal of Ideology, 2, pp. 2-19.

Blumenthal, A. B., 1929, Letter to E. W. Burgess, 20. 4. 1929. University of Chicago Regenstein Library Special Collections, Burgess Papers, Box 3, File 1.

Blumenthal, A. B., 1932, Letter to E. W. Burgess, 14. 9. 1932. University of Chicago Regenstein Library Special Collections, Burgess Papers, Box 3, File 1.

Blumenthal, A. B., 1932a, Small Town Stuff. Chicago, University of Chicago Press.

Blumenthal, A. B., 1933, 'A Sociological Study of a Small Town', Ph.D., University of Chicago.

Blumer, H., 1928, 'Method in Social Psychology', Ph.D., University of Chicago.

Blumer, H., 1931, 'Science Without Concepts', American Journal of Sociology, 36, pp. 515-33.

Blumer, H., 1936, 'Social Attitudes and Non-Symbolic Interaction', Journal of Educational Sociology, 9, pp. 515-23

Blumer, H., 1936a, Research funding application to Social Science Research Committee. University of Chicago Regenstein Library Special Collections, Ogburn Papers, Box 31.

Blumer, H., 1940, 'The Problem of the Concept in Social Psychology', American Journal of Sociology, 1945, pp. 707-19.

Blumer, H., 1954, 'What Is Wrong With Social Theory ?', American Sociological Review, 19, pp. 3-10.

Blumer, H., 1956, 'Sociological Analysis and the Variable', American Sociological Review, 21, pp. 683-90.

Blumer, H., 1962, 'Society as Symbolic Interaction', in Rose, A. M., ed., 1962, Human Behavior and Social Processes: An Interactionist Approach. Boston, Houghton Mifflin, pp. 179-92.

Blumer, H., 1966, 'Sociological Implications of the Thought of G. H. Mead', American Journal of Sociology, 71, pp. 535-44.

Blumer, H., 1966b 'Reply [to Bales]', American Journal of Sociology, 71, pp. 547-8

Blumer, H., 1967, 'Reply to Woelfel, Stone and Farberman', American Journal of Sociology, 72, pp. 411-2.

Blumer, H., 1969, Symbolic Interactionism: Perspective and Method. Englewood Cliffs, Prentice-Hall.

302

Blumer, H., 1972, Interview with James Carey; 22. 5. 1972. University of Chicago, Regenstein Library, Special Collections.

Blumer, H., 1973, 'A Note on Symbolic Interactionism', **American Sociological Review**, 38, pp. 797-8

Blumer, H., 1980, 'Mead and Blumer: The Convergent Methodological Perspectives of Social Behaviorism and Symbolic Interactionism', **American Sociological Review**, 45, p. 409

Blumer, H., 1980b, Contribution to 'Reminiscences of Classic Chicago: The Blumer-Hughes Talk' 1. 9. 1969', **Urban Life**, 9, pp. 254-281

Bogdan, R. and Taylor, S. J., 1975, **Introduction to Qualitative Research Methods:** A Phenomenological Approach to Social Research. London, Wiley.

Boudon, R., 1974, **The Logic of Sociological Explanation.** Harmondsworth, Penguin.

Bowerman, C. E., 1948, 'The Measurement of Areas of Adjustment in Marriage', Ph.D., University of Chicago.

Box, S., 1971, **Deviance, Reality and Society.** London, Holt, Rinehart and Winston.

Bracey, J., Meier, A. and Rudwick, E., 1973, 'The Black Sociologists: The First Half Century', in Ladner, J. A., ed., 1973, **The Death of White Sociology,** New York, Random House.

Brake, 1980, **The Sociology of Youth Culture:** Sex and Drugs and Rock 'n' Roll ? London, Routledge and Kegan Paul.

Brannigan, A., 1981, **The Social Basis of Scientific Discoveries.** Cambridge, Cambridge University Press.

Breckinridge, S. P., 1924, **Family Welfare Work in a Metropolitan Community:** Selected Case Records. Chicago, University of Chicago Press.

Breckinridge, S. P., 1927, **Public Welfare Administration in the United States:** Selected Documents. Chicago, University of Chicago Press.

Breckinridge, S. P., 1928, (Introduction to) **Medical Social Case Records:** Submitted in the 1927 Case Competition of the American Association of Hospital Social Workers. Social Service Monograph No. 3. Chicago, University of Chicago Press.

Brown, W. O., 1930, 'Race Prejudice: A Sociological Study', Ph.D., University of Chicago.

Bruce, A. A., Harno, A. J., Landesco, J. and Burgess, E. W., 1928, **Parole and the Indeterminate Sentence:** The Workings of the Indeterminate Sentence Law and the Parole System in Illinois. Report by the Committee on the Study of the Workings of the Indeterminate-Sentence Law and of Parole in the State of Illinois.

The Bulletin of the Society for Social Research, University of Chicago. University of Chicago, Regenstein Library, Special Collections.

Bulmer, M., 1980, 'The Early Institutional Establishment of

Social Science Research: The Local Community Research Committee at University of Chicago, 1923-30', **Minerva**, 18, pp. 51-110

Bulmer, M., 1981, 'Charles S. Johnson, Robert E. Park and the Research Methods of the Commission on Race Relations, 1919-22: An Experiment in Applied Social Research', **Ethnic and Racial Studies**, 4, pp. 289-306

Bulmer, M., 1981a, 'Quantification and Chicago Social Science in the 1920s: A Neglected Tradition', **Journal of the History of the Behavioral Sciences**, 17, July.

Bulmer, M., 1983, 'The Society for Social Research: An Institutional Underpinning to the Chicago School of Sociology in the 1920s', **Urban Life**, 11, pp. 421-39

Bulmer, M., 1983a, 'The Methodology of the Taxi-Dance Hall: An Early Account of Chicago Ethnography from the 1920s', **Urban Life**, 12, p. 95.

Bulmer, M., 1984, **The Chicago School of Sociology:** Institutionalization, Diversity and the Rise of Sociological Research. Chicago, University of Chicago Press.

Bulmer, M., 1984a, 'The Chicago School of Sociology: What Made It a 'School' ?', Paper to the American Sociological Association, Annual Conference, San Antonio, Texas, 27-31st August.

Burgess, E. W., 1916, 'The Social Survey: A Field for Constructive Service by Departments of Sociology', **American Journal of Sociology**, 21, pp. 492-500.

Burgess, E. W., 1925, Correpondence between Burgess and Marshall, 27. 2. 1925. University of Chicago, Regenstein Library, Special Collections, Burgess Papers.

Burgess, E. W., 1926a, 'The Natural Area as the Unit for Social Work in the Large City', **Proceedings of the National Conference on Social Work.** Fifty-third annual session. Chicago, University of Chicago Press, pp. 504-10

Burgess, E. W., 1926b, 'The Family as a Unit of Interacting Personalities', **The Family**, 7, pp. 3-9

Burgess, E. W., 1926c, 'The Romantic Impulse and Family Disorganization', **Survey**, 57, pp. 290-4

Burgess, E. W., 1927, 'Statistics and Case Studies as Methods of Sociological Research', **Sociology and Social Research**, 12, pp. 103-21

Burgess, E. W., 1931, Letter to R. L. Goodman, 30. 1. 1940. University of Chicago, Regenstein Library, Special Collections, Burgess Papers, Box 19, File 2

Burgess, E. W., 1932, 'Introduction' to Cressey, 1932, **The Taxi-Dance Hall**. Chicago, University of Chicago Press.

Burgess, E. W., 1934, **The Adolescent in the Family:** A Study of the Personality Development in the Home Environment (Report of W H C on Child Health and Protection. Section 3: Education and Training. Committee on the Family and Parent Education). New York, Appleton-Century.

Burgess, E. W., 1935a, 'Trends In Growth And Social Characteristics of Chicago By Local Communities and Principal Sectors'. Enclosure with a Letter to D. Schlesinger, dated 10.
1. 1935, requesting funding from S. S. R. C. University of
Chicago, Regenstein Library, Special Collections, Ogburn
Papers, Box 31.

Burgess, E. W., 1935b, 'A Study of Prediction of Marriage
Adjustment'. Enclosure with letter to Wirth dated 2. 12. 1935
requesting funding from Social Science Research Committee.
University of Chicago, Regenstein Library, Special Collections, Ogburn Papers, Box 31.

Burgess, E. W., 1935c, 'The Family in the Urban Community'.
Enclosure with letter to Wirth dated 2. 12. 1935 requesting
funding from Social Science Research Committee. University of
Chicago, Regenstein Library, Special Collections, Ogburn
Papers, Box 31.

Burgess, E. W., 1939, 'The Human Document', University of
Chicago Regenstein Library Special Collections, Burgess
Papers, Box 20, File 5.

Burgess, E. W., 1941, Social Science Research Committee Request
for Research Support to the Rockefeller Foundation, 11. 3.
1941. University of Chicago, Regenstein Library, Special
Collections, Burgess Papers, Box 21, File 1.

Burgess, E. W., 1944a, 'Research Methods', Undated but attached
to a copy of 'Tea Tattler' of 15. 6. 1944. University of
Chicago, Regenstein Library, Special Collections, Burgess
Papers, Box 194, File 1.

Burgess, E. W., 1944b, Note appended to a Circular letter from
E. B. Wilson to members of the Committee on Future Council
Relationships. University of Chicago, Regenstein Library,
Special Collections, Burgess Papers.

Burgess, E. W., 1952, A Biography of Ernest Watson Burgess.
(The author may not have been Burgess, it is unattributed).
University of Chicago, Regenstein Library, Special Collect-
ions, Burgess papers, Box 3, File 3.

Burgess, E. W. and Cottrell, L. S., 1936, 'The prediction of
Adjustment in Marriage', **American Sociological Review**, pp.
737-51

Burgess, E. W. and Cottrell, L. S., 1939, **Predicting Success or
Failure in Marriage.** New York, Prenctice-Hall.

Burgess, E. W. and Newcomb, C., eds., 1931, **Census Data of the
City of Chicago 1920.** Chicago, University of Chicago Press.

Burgess, E. W. and Newcomb, C., eds. 1933, **Census Data of the
City of Chicago 1930.** Chicago, University of Chicago Press.

Burgess, E. W. and Tibbits, C. 1928, 'Factors Making For Success or Failure on Parole', **Journal of Criminal Law and
Criminology**, 19, p. 239.

Burns, 1924, Letter to Burgess, 22. 11. 1924, with enclosure
relating to the study of the interview by M. L. Mark of Ohio

State University. University of Chicago, Regenstein Library, Special Collections, Burgess Papers.

Burns, L. R., 1980, 'The Chicago School and the Study of Organization-Environment Relation', **Journal of the History of the Behavioral Sciences**, 16, pp. 342-58

Bushnell, C. J., 1901, 'A Study of the Stock Yards Community at Chicago, as a Typical Example of the Bearing of Modern Industry upon Democracy, with Constructive Suggestions', Ph.D., University of Chicago.

Butler, 1925, **Annual Report of the President: 1925.** New York, Columbia University.

Butterfield, H., 1931, **The Whig Interpretation of History.** London.

Butters, S., 1973, 'Participant Observation and "Qualitative Methods"', Unpublished paper, Birmingham Polytechnic. incorporated into 'The Logic of Enquiry of Participant Observation: A Critical Review', in Hall, S. and Jefferson, T., eds, 1976, **Resistance Through Rituals:** Youth subcultures in post-war Britain, London, Hutchinson, pp. 253-73.

Caldarovic, O., 1979, 'Some Classical Dilemmas with Regard to the Validity of the Environmental Approach to Deviant Behaviour', **Revija za Sociologije**, 9, pp. 93-102.

Campisi, P. J., 1947, 'A Scale for the Measurement of Acculturation', Ph.D., University of Chicago.

Carabana, J. and Lamo de Espinosa, E., 1978, 'The Social Theory of Symbolic Interactionism: Critical Analysis and Evaluation', **Revista Espanola de Investigaciones Sociologicas**, 1, pp. 159-203.

Carey, J. T., 1975, **Sociology and Public Affairs:** The Chicago School. Beverley Hills, Sage.

Carter, W. P., 1972, Interview with James Carey; 17. 3. 1972. University of Chicago, Regenstein Library, Special Collections.

Castells, M., 1977, **The Urban Question.** Cambridge, MIT Press.

Cavan, R. S., 1928, **Suicide.** Chicago, University of Chicago Press.

Cavan, R. S., 1972, Interview with James Carey; 28. 4. 1972. University of Chicago, Regenstein Library, Special Collections.

Cavan, R., 1983, 'The Chicago School of Sociology, 1918-1933', **Urban Life**, 11, pp. 407-20

Celinski, A., 1974, 'Critique of Merton's Theory of Deviant Behaviour', **Studia Socjologiczne**, 54, pp. 117-40

Centre For Contemporary Cultural Studies, 1978, On **Ideology.** London, Hutchinson.

Chalmers, A. F., 1978, **What Is This Thing Called Science.** Milton Keynes, Open University Press.

Chapin, F. S., 1920, **Field Work and Social Research.** New York, Century.

Chapin, F. S., 1936a, Letter to Wirth. 20. 10. 1936. University of Chicago, Regenstein Library, Special Collections, Wirth Papers, Box 2, File 4.

Chapin, F. S., 1936b, Letter to G. H. Mink (Manager Auditorium Hotel, Chicago). 28. 11. 1936. University of Chicago, Regenstein Library, Special Collections, Wirth Papers, Box 2, File 4.

Chicago Civic Agencies, 1927, **A Directory of Associations of Citizens of Chicago Intersted in Civic Welfare.** Social Science Studies No. 6. Chicago: University of Chicago Press.

Chicago Commission on Race Relations, 1922, **The Negro in Chicago:** A Study of Race Relations and a Race Riot in 1919. Chicago, University of Chicago Press.

Choldin, H. M., 1980, 'Electronic Community Fact Books', **Urban Affairs Quarterly,** 15, pp. 269-89.

Ciacci, M., 1972, 'The Chicago School: G. H. Mead and Symbolic Interactionism', **Rassegna Italiana di Sociologia,** 13, pp. 263-95.

Clark, H. B., 1897, 'The Public Schools of Chicago: A Sociological Study', Ph.D., University of Chicago.

Cloward, R. and Ohlin, L., 1960, **Delinquency and Opportunity:** A Theory of Delinquent Gangs. Chicago, Free Press.

Coleman, J., 1969, 'The Methods of Sociology' in Bierstedt, R., ed., 1969, **A Design for Sociology:** Scope Objectives and Method. Philadelphia, AAPSS, Monograph, 9, pp. 86-114

Coleman, J., 1980, Personal Interview, 30. 3. 1980.

Cohen, A. K., 1955, **Delinquent Boys:** The Culture of the Gang. Chicago, Free Press.

Conway, P. R., 1926, 'The Apartment House Dweller: A Study of the Social Change in the Hyde Park Community', M.A., University of Chicago.

Cook, G. A., 1977, 'G. H. Mead's Social Behaviorism', **Journal of the History of the Behavioral Sciences,** 13, pp. 307-16

Cooley, C. H., 1920, **Social Process,** New York, Scribner.

Cooley, C. H., 1928, 'Case Study of Small Institutions as a Method of Research', **Publications of the American Sociological Society,** 18, pp. 147-55.

Cooley, C. H., 1930, **Sociological Theory and Social Research:** Selected Papers. (Introduced by R.C. Angell). New York, Holt.

Coser, L. A., 1971, **Masters of Sociological Thought:** Ideas in Historical and Social Context. New York, Harcourt, Brace Jovanovich

Coser, L. A., ed., 1975, **The Idea of Social Structure:** Papers in Honor of Robert K. Merton. New York, Harcourt Brace Jovanovich.

Coser, L. A., 1976, 'Sociological Theory from the Chicago Dominance to 1965', **Annual Review of Sociology,** pp. 145-55.

Coser, L. A., 1978, 'American Trends', in Bottomore, T. and Nisbet, R., eds., 1978, **History of Sociological Analysis.**

London, Heinemann, pp. 321-61.

Cothran, T. C., 1949, 'Negro Stereotyped Conceptions of White People', Ph.D., University of Chicago.

Cottrell, L. S., 1933, 'The Reliability and Validity of A Marriage Study Schedule', Ph.D., University of Chicago.

Cottrell, L. S., 1971, 'Covert Behavior in Interpersonal Interaction', **Proceedings of the American Philosophical Society,** 115, pp. 462-9

Cottrell, L. S., 1972, Interview with James Carey; 28. 3. 1972. University of Chicago, Regenstein Library, Special Collections.

Cottrell, L. S., Hunter, A. and Short, J. F., eds, 1973, **Ernest W. Burgess on Community, Family and Delinquency.** Chicago, University of Chicago Press

Cox, O. C., 1938, 'Factors Affecting the Marital Status of Negroes in the United States', Ph.D., University of Chicago.

Crane, D., 1972, **Invisible Colleges:** Diffusion of Knowledge In Scientific Communities. Chicago, University of Chicago Press.

Cressey, D. R., 1962, 'Role Theory, Differential Association and Compulsive Crimes', in Rose, A. M., ed, 1972, **Human Behavior and Social Processes:** An Interactionist Approach. Boston, Houghton Mifflin, pp. 443-67.

Cressey, P. G., 1929, 'The Closed Dance Hall in Chicago', Ph.D., University of Chicago.

Cressey, P. G., 1932, **The Taxi Dance Hall.** Chicago, University of Chicago Press.

Cressey, P. G., 1983, 'A Comparison of the Roles of the "Sociological Stranger" and the "Anonymous Stranger" in Field Research', **Urban Life,** 13, p. 102.

Dai, B., 1937, 'Opium Addiction in Chicago', Ph.D., University of Chicago.

Daniel, V. E., 1940, 'Ritual in Chicago's South Side Churches for Negroes',' Ph.D., University of Chicago.

De Bernart, M., 1982, 'Personal Documentation: "Proper Research" and the "Methodological Mentality" in American Social Science, 1938-1945', **Sociologia,** 16, pp. 67-98.

DeGraff, H. O., 1926, 'A Study of the Juvenile Court of Iowa with Special Reference to Des Moines', Ph.D., University of Chicago.

Denzin, N. K., 1970, **Sociological Methods:** A Sourcebook. London, Butterworths

Denzin, N. K., 1978, **The Research Act:** A Theoretical Introduction to Sociological Methods, (2nd edn). New York, McGraw-Hill.

Denzin, N. K., 1984, 'On Interpreting an Interpretation', **American Journal of Sociology,** 89, pp. 1426-33.

Detweiler, F. G., 1922, 'The Negro Press in the United States', Ph.D., University of Chicago.

Deutscher, I., 1973, **What We Say, What We Do.** San Francisco,

Foresman.

Devinney, L. C., 1941, 'Some Relationships Between Educational Achievement and Social Stratification', Ph.D., University of Chicago.

Dibble, V. K., 1972, **The Legacy of Albion Small.** Chicago, University of Chicago Press.

Diner, S. J., 1975, 'Department and Discipline: The Department of Sociology at the University of Chicago, 1892-1920', **Minerva**, 13, pp. 514-53

Diner, S. J., 1980, **A City and Its Universities: Public Policy in Chicago, 1892-1919.** Chapel Hill, University of North Carolina Press.

Dodd, S. C. 1940, **Dimensions of Sociology.** New York, Macmillan.

Dollard, J., 1931, 'The Changing Functions of the American Family', Ph.D., University of Chicago.

Dollard, J., 1972, Interview with James Carey; 14. 4. 1972. University of Chicago, Regenstein Library, Special Collections.

Dotter, D. L., 1978, 'Beyond the Chicago School: Deviance and Social Conflict', MiSSA

Dotter, D. L., 1980, 'The Social Construction of Territory: Metaphor, Self and the Meaning of Space', **Sociological Forum**, 3, pp. 19-30.

Doyle, B., 1934, 'The Etiquette of Race Relations in the South', Ph.D., University of Chicago.

Dreitzel, H. P., ed, 1970, **Recent Sociology No. 2.** New York, Macmillan.

Duddy, E. A., 1929, **Agriculture in the Chicago Region.** Chicago, University of Chicago Press.

Duncan, H. D., 1948, 'Chicago as a Literary Center: Social Factors Influencing Chicago Literary Institutions from 1885 to 1920', Ph.D., University of Chicago.

Duncan, H. G., and Duncan, W. L., 1934, 'Interests of American Sociologists', **Social Forces**, 12, pp. 209-12

Duncan, O. D., 1949, 'An Examination of the Problem of Optimum City Size', Ph.D., University of Chicago.

Dunham, H. W., 1941, 'The Character of the Interrelationship of Crime and Schizophrenia', Ph.D., University of Chicago.

Dunn, A. W., 1895, An Analysis of the Social Structure of a Western Town: After the Method of Small and Vincent. Chicago, University of Chicago Press.

Easthope, G., 1974, **History of Social Research Methods.** London, Longman.

Eckberg, D. L. and Hill, L., 1979, 'The Paradigm Concept and Sociology: A critical review.' **American Sociological Review**, 44, p. 925.

Edwards, G. F., 1952, 'Occupational Mobility of A Selected Group of Negro Male Professionals', Ph.D., University of Chicago.

Edwards, L. P., 1927, The Natural History of Revolution. Chicago, University of Chicago Press.

Elmer, M. C., 1914, 'Social Surveys of Urban Communities', Ph.D., University of Chicago.

Eubank, E. E., 1915, 'A Study of Family Desertion', Ph.D., University of Chicago.

Evers, H-D., 1975, 'Urban Expansion and Landownership in Under-developed Societies', Urban Affairs Quarterly, 11, pp. 117-29.

Farberman, H. A., 1979, 'The Chicago School: Continuities in Urban Sociology', Studies in Symbolic Interaction, 2, pp. 3-20.

Faris, E., 1936, 'On Psychological Elements', American Journal of Sociology, 42, pp. 159-76.

Faris, E., 1936a, 'Review of 'Mind, Self and Society'', American Journal of Sociology, 41, p. 6.

Faris, R. E. L., 1945, 'American Sociology' in Gurvitch, G. and Moore, W. E., eds., 1945, Twentieth Century Sociology, New York, McGraw Hill, pp. 538-61.

Faris, R. E. L., 1972, Interview with James Carey; 24. 5. 1972. University of Chicago, Regenstein Library, Special Collections.

Faris, R. E. L., 1967, Chicago Sociology, 1920-1932. San Francisco, Chandler.

Faw, V. E., 1948, 'Vocational Interests of Chicago Negro and White High School Junior and Senior Boys', Ph.D., University of Chicago.

Ferrarotti, F., 1977, 'Marginalization in an Urban Environment', La Crittica Sociologia, 43, p. 225

Feyerabend, P., 1975a, 'On The Critique of Scientific Reason', in Howson, C., ed., 1976, Method and Appraisal in the Physical Sciences. Cambridge, Cambridge University Press, pp. 309-39.

Feyerabend, P., 1975b, Against Method: Outline of an Anarchistic Theory of Knowledge. London, New Left Books.

Filmer, P., Phillipson, M., Silverman D., and Walsh, D., 1972, New Directions In Sociological Theory. London, Collier-Macmillan.

Filstead, W. J., 1970, Qualitative Methodology. Chicago, Markham.

Firey, W., 1945, Sentiment and Symbolism as Ecological Variables', American Sociological Review, 10, pp. 140-48.

Fish, V., 1981, 'Annie Marion MacLean: A Neglected Part of the Chicago School', Journal of the History of Sociology, 3, pp. 43-62.

Fisher, B. and Strauss, A., 1978, 'Interactionism' in Bottomore, T. and Nisbet, R. eds., 1978, History of Sociological Analysis. London, Heinemann, pp. 457-98.

Fisher, B. and Strauss, A., 1979, 'George Herbert Mead and the

Chicago Tradition of Sociology', **Symbolic Interaction**, 2, vol 1, pp. 9-26, part 1, and vol 2, 9-20, part 2,.

Fleming, H. E., 1905, 'Some Phases of the Production and Consumption of Literature in Chicago', Ph.D., University of Chicago.

Frazier, E. F., 1931, 'The Negro Family in Chicago', Ph.D., University of Chicago.

Friedrichs, R. W., 1970, **A Sociology of Sociology**. New York, Free Press.

Fryxell, F. M., 1927, **The Physiology of the Region of Chicago**. Chicago, University of Chicago Press.

Furner, M. O., 1975, **Advocacy and Objectivity**: A Crisis in the Professionalism of American Social Science 1865-1905. Lexington, University of Kentucky Press.

Gans, H., 1968, 'Urbanism and Suburbanism as ways of Life', in Pahl, R. E., ed, 1968, **Readings in Urban Sociology**. Oxford, Pergammon.

Geer, B., 1964, 'First Days in the Field', in Hammond, P., ed., 1964, **Sociologists at Work**, New York, Basic Books.

Giddings, F. H., 1911, 'Outline For A Beginner's Course in Sociology', **American Journal of Sociology**, 17, pp. 628-31.

Gillette, J. M., 1901, 'The Culture Agencies of A Typical Manufacturing Group, South Chicago', Ph.D., University of Chicago.

Giner, S., 1972, **Sociology**. London, Robertson.

Glaser, B., and Strauss, A., 1967, **The Discovery of Grounded Theory**. Chicago, Aldine.

Glick, C. E., 1928, 'Winnetka: A Study of A Residential Suburban Community'. M.A., University of Chicago

Goddijn, H. P. M., 1972a, 'American Classics: Cooley and Mead', **Tijdschrift voor Sociale Wetenschappen**, 17, pp. 263-77

Goddijn, H. P. M., 1972b, 'The Chicago School', **Tijdschrift voor Sociale Wetenschappen**, 17, pp. 397-418

Goffman, E., 1959, **The Presentation of Self in Everyday Life**. Garden City, Doubleday.

Goode, J. P., 1926, **The Geographic Background of Chicago**. Chicago, University of Chicago Press.

Gordon, M. M., 1964, **Assimilation in American Life**. New York, Oxford University Press

Gosnell, H. 1927, **Getting Out the Vote**: An Experiment In The Stimulation of Voting. Chicago, University of Chicago Press.

Gough, H. G., 1942, A Short Analysis of the Sociological Writings of Graham Sumner and W. F. Ogburn. M.A., University of Minnesota.

Gouldner, 1973, 'Introduction', to Taylor, I., Walton, P. and Young, J., 1973, **The New Criminology**. London, Routledge and Kegan Paul.

Greeley, A. M., 1977, 'Anti-Catholicism in the Academy', **Change**, 1977, pp. 40-43

Family and Delinquency. Chicago, University of Chicago Press.

Inskeep, K., 1977, 'Christian Sociology in the Chicago School: 1895-1920', American Sociological Review, 42.

Janowitz, M., 1948, 'Mobility, Subjective Deprivation and Ethnic Hostility', Ph.D., University of Chicago.

Janowitz, M., 1966, 'Introduction' to Thomas, W. I., 1966, On Social Organization and Social Personality. Chicago, University of Chicago Press

Janowitz, M., 1968 'Preface' to Suttles, G., 1968, The Social order of the Slum. Chicago, University of Chicago Press.

Janowitz, M., 1975, 'Sociological Theory and Social Control', American Journal of Sociology, 81, pp. 82-108.

Janowitz, M., 1978, The Last Half-Century: Societal Change and Politics in America. Chicago, University of Chicago Press.

Janowitz, M., 1980, Personal Interview, 24. 3. 1980

Jensen, Mrs. H. E., 1972, Interview with James Carey; 16. 3. 1972. University of Chicago, Regenstein Library, Special Collections.

Jeter, H. R., 1927, Trends of Population in the Region of Chicago. Chicago, University of Chicago Press.

Joas, H., 1985, G.H. Mead: A Contemporary Re-examination of his Thought. Cambridge, Polity Press.

Johnson, C. O., 1928, Carter Henry Harrison I: Political Leader. Chicago, University of Chicago Press.

Johnson, G. B., 1972, Interview with James Carey; 27. 3. 1972. University of Chicago, Regenstein Library, Special Collections.

Kando, T. M., 1977, Social Interaction. St. Louis, Mosby.

Karpf, F. B., 1972, Interview with James Carey; 1. 5. 1972. University of Chicago, Regenstein Library, Special Collections.

Kincheloe, S. C., 1972, Interview with James Carey; 6. 27. 1972. University of Chicago, Regenstein Library, Special Collections.

Kitagawa, E. M., and Taeuber, K. E., eds., 1963, Local Community Fact Book: Chicago Metropolitan Area 1960. Chicago, University of Chicago, Chicago Community Inventory.

Komorowski, Z., 1978, 'The Need for Interdisciplinary Approach and Social Ecology', Kultura i Spoleczenstwo, 22, pp. 157-64.

Krantz, D. L., 1971a, 'Schools and Systems: The Mutual Operation of Operant and Non-operant Psychology as a Case Study', Journal of the History of the Behavioral Sciences, 7.

Krantz, D. L., 1971b, 'The Separate Worlds of Operant and Non-operant Psychology', Journal of Applied Behavioral Analysis, 4, pp. 61-70

Kuhn, M., 1964, 'Major Trends in Symbolic Interaction Theory in the Past Twenty Five Years', Sociological Quarterly, 5, pp. 61-84.

Kuhn, T. S., 1962, The Structure of Scientific Revolutions.

Chicago, University of Chicago Press.

Kuhn, T. S., 1969, 'Reflections On My Critics', in Lakatos, I. and Musgrave, A., eds., 1970, **Criticism and the Growth of Knowledge**. Cambridge, Cambridge University Press, pp. 231-78.

Kuhn, T. S., 1970, The Structure of Scientific Revolutions. (Second Edition, with Appendix). Chicago, University of Chicago Press.

Kuklick, H., 1973, 'A 'Scientific Revolution': Sociological Theory in the United States 1930-1945', **Sociological Inquiry**, 43, pp. 3-22.

Kuklick, H., 1980, 'Chicago Sociology and Urban Planning Policy: Sociological Theory as Occupational Ideology', **Theory and Society**, 9, pp. 821-45

Kuklick, H., 1984, 'The Ecology of Sociology', **American Journal of Sociology**, 89, pp. 1433-40.

Kurtz, L. R., 1982, 'Robert E. Park's "Notes on the Origins of the Society for Social Research" with an introduction by Lester R. Kurtz', **Journal of the History of the Behavioral Sciences**, 18, pp. 332-340.

Kurtz, L. R., 1984, **Evaluating Chicago Sociology**: A Guide to the Literature, with an Annotated Bibliography. Chicago, University of Chicago Press.

Labovitz, S. and Hagedorn, R., 1971, **Introduction to Social Research**. New York, McGraw Hill.

Ladewick, E., 1929, **Scholarships for Children of Working Age.** Chicago, University of Chicago Press.

Lakatos, I., 1970, 'Falsification and the Methodology of Scientific Research Programmes', in Lakatos, I. and Musgrave, A., eds., 1970, **Criticism and the Growth of Knowledge**. Cambridge, Cambridge University Press, pp. 315-417.

Lakatos, I., 1975, 'History of Science and Its Rational Reconstructions', in Howson, C., ed., 1976, **Method and Appraisal in the Physical Sciences**. Cambridge, Cambridge University Press, pp. 1-39.

Landesco, J., 1929, **Organized Crime In Chicago.** Chicago, University of Chicago Press.

Lang, R. O., 1936, 'The Relation of Educational Status to Economic Status in the City of Chicago, by Census Tracts, 1934', Ph.D., University of Chicago.

Laperriere, A., 1982, 'Toward an Empirical Construction of Theory: The New Chicago School', **Sociologie et Societes**, 14, pp. 31-41

Lapiere, R., 1964, Correspondence with Irwin Deutscher, 23. 10. 1964, reprinted in Deutscher, I., 1973, **What We Say/What We Do**. San Francisco, Foresman, pp. 36-37

Larrain, J., 1979, **The Concept of Ideology**. London, Hutchinson.

Lauer, R. H. and Handel, W. H., 1977, **Social Psychology**: The Theory and Application of Symbolic Interactionism. Boston, Houghton Mifflin

Ph.D., University of Chicago.

Hiller, E. T., 1933, **Principles of Sociology**. New York, Harper.

Hinkle, R. C. and Hinkle, G. J., 1954, **The Development of American Sociology**. New York, Random House.

Hirschi, T. and Selvin, H. C., 1972, 'Principles of Causal Analysis', in Lazarsfeld et al., eds., 1972, **Continuities in the Language of Social Research**. New York, Free Press, pp. 126-33.

Holton, G., 1973, **Thematic Origin of Scientific Thought:** Kepler to Einstein. Cambridge, Mass., Harvard University Press.

Horak, J., 1920, 'The Assimilation of the Czechs in Chicago', Ph.D., University of Chicago.

Horrowitz, I., ed, 1964, **The New Sociology:** Essays in Social Science and Social Theory in Honor of C. Wright Mills. New York, Oxford University Press.

Houghteling, L., 1927, **The Income and Standard of Living of Unskilled Laborers in Chicago**. Chicago, University of Chicago Press.

House, F. N., 1924, 'Industrial Morale: An Essay in the Sociology of Industrial Control', Ph.D., University of Chicago.

Howson, C., ed., 1976, **Method and Appraisal in the Physical Sciences:** The Critical Background to Modern Science, 1800 - 1905. Cambridge, Cambridge University Press.

Huber, J., 1973a, 'Symbolic Interaction as A Pragmatic Perspective: The Bias of Emergent Theory', **American Sociological Review**, 38, pp. 274-84

Huber, J., 1973b, 'Reply to Blumer: But Who Will Scrutinize the Scrutinizers ?', **American Sociological Review**, 38, pp. 798-800.

Huber, J., 1974, 'The Emergence of Emergent Theory', **American Sociological Review**, 39, p. 463.

Hughes, E. A. and Stuenkel, F., 1929, The Social Service Exchange in Chicago. Chicago, University of Chicago Press.

Hughes, E. C., 1928, 'A Study of a Secular Institution: The Chicago Real Estate Board', Ph.D., University of Chicago.

Hughes, E. C., 1958, **Men and their Work**. Glencoe, The Free Press

Hughes, E. C., 1970, 'Humble and the Proud: The Compartive Study of Occupations', **Sociological Quarterly**, 11, p. 147-56.

Hughes, E. C., 1980, Contribution to 'Reminiscences of Classic Chicago: The Blumer-Hughes Talk' 1. 9. 1969', **Urban Life**, 9, pp. 254-81

Hunter, A., 1980, 'Why Chicago: The Rise of the Chicago School of Urban Social Science', **American Behavioral Scientist**, 24, pp. 215-27

Hunter, A., 1983, 'The Gold Coast and the Slum Revisited: Paradoxes in Replication Research and the Study of Social Change', **Urban Life**, 11, pp. 461-76.

Hunter, A. and Goldman, N., 1973, 'Introduction' to part I of Cottrell, et al. eds, 1973, **Ernest W. Burgess on Community,**

Gumperz, J., 1981, 'Conversational Inference and Classroom Learning', in Green, J. L. and Wallat C., eds., 1981 **Ethnography and Language in Educational Settings.** Norwood, N.J., Ablex.

Haimowitz, M. L., 1951, 'The Development and Change of Ethnic Hostility', Ph.D., University of Chicago.

Hale, W. H., 1949, 'The Career Development of the Negro Lawyer in Chicago', Ph.D., University of Chicago.

Hall, O., 1944, 'The Informal Organization of Medical Practice: Case Study of a Profession', Ph.D., University of Chicago.

Hammersley, M. and Atkinson, P., 1983, **Ethnography:** Principles in Practice. London, Tavistock.

Hammond, P., ed., 1964, **Sociologists at Work,** New York, Basic Books.

Harvey, L., 1981, 'Misconceptions of the Chicago School', Birmingham Polytechnic, Research Unit, Discussion Paper, 6.

Harvey, L., 1982, 'Use and Abuse of Kuhnian Paradigms in the Sociology of Knowledge', **Sociology,** 16, pp. 85-101.

Harvey, L., 1983, 'Myths of the Chicago School', Birmingham Polytechnic, Research Unit Occasional Paper, 1.

Harvey, L., 1985, 'The Chicago School: A Metascientific Study', Ph.D., Open University

Harvey, L., 1986, 'Schools in the Sociology of Knowledge: The Chicago School as a Case Study', **Sociological Review,** forthcoming.

Harvey, P. A., 1982, 'Expansions and Contractions: Sociology Labor Pains', **Free Inquiry in Creative Sociology,** 10, pp. 29-34.

Hathway, M., 1928, **The Young Cripple and His Job.** Chicago, University of Chicago Press.

Hauser, P., and Kitagawa, E. M., eds., 1953, **Local Community Fact Book of Chicago, 1950.** Chicago, University of Chicago, Chicago Community Inventory.

Haussermann, H. and Kramer-Badoni, T., 1980, 'Urban Sociology by Means of Yardsticks ? A Contribution to the Understanding of Social Ecology', **Soziale Welt,** 31, pp. 140-55.

Hayner, N. S., 1923, 'The Sociology of Hotel Life', Ph.D., University of Chicago.

Hayner, N. S., 1972, Interview with James Carey; 24. 5. 1972. University of Chicago, Regenstein Library, Special Collections.

Henderson, 1899, 'The Ministry Today - It's New Experience', **University of Chicago Record,** 43, p. 281.

Heritage, J. 1981 'Reassessing a 'Founding Father'', **Times Higher Education Supplement,** 7. 8. 1981

Hill, M. C., 1946, 'The All-Negro Society', Ph.D., University of Chicago.

Hiller, E. T., 1924, 'The Strike as Group Behavior: A Study in the Process and Technique of Control of the Striking Group',

Leiffer, M. H., 1928, 'The Boys' Court of Chicago', M.A., University of Chicago.

Lemert, E. M., 1951, Social Pathology. New York, McGraw-Hill.

Lemert, E. M., 1967, Human Deviance, Social Problems and Social Control. New York, Prentice-Hall.

Lengermann, P. M., 1979, The Founding of the American Sociological Review: The Anatomy of a Rebellion', American Sociological Review, 44, pp. 185-98

Lewis, D.J., 1976, 'The Pragmatic Foundation of Symbolic Interactionism', Ph.D. University of Illionois.

Lewis, D. J. and Smith, R. L., 1981, American Sociology and Pragmatism: Mead, Chicago Sociology, and Symbolic Interactionism. Chicago, University of Chicago Press.

Lewis, H. G., 1951, 'The Social Life of the Negro in a Southern Piedmont Town', Ph.D., University of Chicago.

Lincourt, J. M., and Hare, P. H., 1973, 'Negelected American Philosophers in the History of Symbolic Interactionism', Journal of the History of the Behavioral Sciences, 9, pp. 333-8

Lindeman, E. C., 1924, Social Discovery. New York, Republic.

Lindesmith, A. R., 1937, 'The Nature of Opiate Addiction', Ph.D., University of Chicago.

Lindesmith, A. R., Strauss, A. and Denzin, N. K., 1977, Social Psychology (fifth edition). New York, Holt, Rinehart, Winston.

Littlejohn, S. W., 1977, 'Symbolic Interactionism as an Approach to the Study of Human Communication', Quarterly Journal of Speech, 63, pp. 84-91

Lofland, L. H., 1980, 'Introduction to 'Reminiscences of Classic Chicago: The Blumer-Hughes Talk'', Urban Life, 9, pp. 251-4.

Lofland, L. H., 1983, 'Understanding Urban Life', Urban Life, 11, pp. 491-511.

Lunday, G. A., 1949, 'A Study of Parole Prediction', Ph.D., University of Chicago.

Lundberg, G. A., 1929, Social Research: A Study in Methods of Gathering Data. New York, Longman.

Lundberg, G. A., 1936, 'Quantitative Methods in Social Psychology', American Sociological Review, 1, pp. 38-60.

Lundberg, G. A., 1942, Social Research: A Study in Methods of Gathering Data. (Re-write of all but four chapters of Lundberg, 1929). New York, Longman.

Lutz, F.W., 1981, 'Ethnography - The Holistic Approach to Understanding' in Green, J. C. and Wallat, C., eds., 1981 Ethnography and Language in Educational Settings. Norwood, N.J., Ablex.

Lynd, R. S. and Lynd, H. M., 1929, Middletown: A Study in Contemporary Culture. New York, Harcourt Brace

Lynd, R. S., 1939, Knowledge For What ? The Place of Social

Science in American Culture. Princeton, Princeton University Press.

Lynd, R. S., 1941a, Letter to Louis Wirth, 2. 1. 1941, with enclosure 'Memorandum of Future Developments in the Department of Sociology'. University of Chicago, Regenstein Library Special Collections, Wirth Papers, Box 7.

Lynd, R. S., 1941b, Letter to Louis Wirth, 24. 2. 1941. University of Chicago, Regenstein Library, Special Collections, Wirth Papers, Box 7.

MacLean, A. M., 1910, **Wage Earning Women.**

Madge, J., 1963, **The Origins of Scientific Sociology.** London, Tavistock.

Manis, J. G. and Meltzer, B. N., eds., 1978, **Symbolic Interaction:** A Reader in Social Psychology (third edition). Boston, Allyn and Bacon.

Mannheim, K., 1936, **Ideology and Utopia.** (Trans. L. Wirth & E. Shils). London, Routledge & Kegan Paul.

Marcson, S., 1950, 'The Prediction of Intermarriage', Ph.D., University of Chicago.

Martin, J. G. and Franklin, C. W., 1973, **Minority Group Relations.** Columbus, Merrill.

Martindale, D., 1960, **Nature and Types of Sociological Theory.** Boston, Houghton Mifflin.

Martindale, D., 1976, 'American Sociology Before World War II', **Annual Review of Sociology,** 1976, pp. 121-41.

Martins, H., 1972, 'The Kuhnian Revolution and its Implications for Sociology', in Nossiter, J., ed., 1972, **Imagination and Precision in the Social Sciences.**

Matthews, F. H., 1977, **Quest for An American Sociology.** Montreal, McGill-Queens University Press.

Matza, D., 1969, **Becoming Deviant.** Englewood Cliffs, Prentice-Hall.

McCluer, F. L., 1972, Interview with James Carey; 15. 3. 1972. University of Chicago, Regenstein Library, Special Collections.

McGill, H. E. G., 1927, Land Values: An Ecological Factor in the Community of South Chicago. M.A., University of Chicago

McGrath, D. and Geruson, R., 1977, 'Linking Sociological and Economic Analyses of Neighborhood Change', Unpublished paper.

MacIver, R. M, 1968, **As A Tale That Is Told.** Chicago, University of Chicago Press.

McPhail, C. and Rexroat, C., 1979 'Mead Vs. Blumer: The Divergent Methodological Perspectives of Social Behaviorism and Symbolic Interactionism', **American Sociological Review,** 44, p. 449

McPhail, C. and Rexroat, C., 1980 'Ex Cathedra Blumer or ex Libris Mead ?', **American Sociological Review,** 45, p. 420.

Mead, G. H., 1934, **Mind, Self and Society.** Chicago, University of Chicago Press.

Mead, G. H., 1938, **The Philosophy of the Act.** (Editied with intro by C. Morris). Chicago, University of Chicago Press.

Mead, G. H., 1964, **On Social Psychology.** Chicago, University of Chicago Press.

Meltzer, B. N., and Petras, J. W., 1970, 'The Chicago and Iowa Schools of Symbolic Interactionism', in Shibutani, ed., 1970, **Human Nature and Collective Behavior.** Englewood Cliffs, Prentice-Hall, pp. 3-17

Meltzer, B. N., Petras, J. W. and Reynolds, L. T., 1975, Symbolic Interactionism: Varieties and Meanings. London, Routlege and Kegan Paul.

Meroney, W. P., 1922, 'The Town Church and the Modern Home', M.A., University of Chicago.

Merriam, C. E. and Gosnell, H. F., 1924, **Non-Voting: Causes and Methods of Control.** Chicago, University of Chicago Press.

Merton, R. K., 1945, 'Sociological Theory', **American Journal of Sociology,** 50, pp. 462-73

Merton, R. K., 1948, 'The Bearing of Empirical Research Upon the Development of Social Theory', paper read to American Sociological Society in Cleveland in 1946, Publication No. A-89, Bureau of Applied Social Research, Columbia University

Merton, R. K., 1949, **Social Theory and Social Structure.** Glencoe, The Free Press.

Merton, R. K., 1973, **The Sociology of Science, Theoretical and Empirical Investigations** (edited with introduction by N.W. Storer). Chicago, University of Chicago Press.

Messinger, S., 1980, Contribution to 'Reminiscences of Classic Chicago: The Blumer-Hughes Talk' 1. 9. 1969', **Urban Life,** 9, pp. 254-81

Millis, S., (undated), **The Juvenile Detention Home in Relation to Juvenile Court Policy:** A Study of Intake in the Cook County Chicago Juvenile Detention Home. Published by the Citizens' Advisory Committee on the Cook County Juvenile Detention Home.

Mills, C. W., 1959, **The Sociological Imagination.** Harmodsworth, Penguin.

The Minutes of the Society for Social Research, University of Chicago, Regenstein Library, Special Collections.

Molotch, H., 1976, 'The City as a Growth Machine', **American Journal of Sociology,** 80.

Montgomery, R. E., 1927, **Industrial Relations in the Chicago Building Trades.** Chicago, University of Chicago Press.

Mowrer, E. R., 1924, 'Family Disorganization - An Introduction to a Sociological Analysis', Ph.D., University of Chicago.

Mowrer, E. R., 1927, **Family Disorganization:** An Introduction to a Sociological Analysis. Chicago, University of Chicago Press.

Mowrer, E. R., 1972, Interview with James Carey; 17. 4. 1972. University of Chicago, Regenstein Library, Special Collections.

Mulkay, M., 1972, The Social Process of Innovation: A Study in the Sociology of Science. London, Macmillan.

Mullins, N. C., 1973, Theory and Theory Groups in Contemporary American Sociology. New York, Harper and Row.

Myrdal, G., ed., 1968, Value in Social Theory. London, Routledge and Kegan Paul

Myrdal, G., 1970, Objectivity in Social Research. London, Duckworth.

National Commission on Law Enforcement and Observance, 1931, Report on the Cost of Crime. Washington.

Nelson, C. W., 1949, 'Development and Evaluation of a Leadership Attitude Scale for Foremen', Ph.D., University of Chicago.

Neumeyer, M. H., 1929, 'Conscience: A Socio-Psychological Study', Ph.D., University of Chicago.

Neumeyer, M. H.., 1972, Interview with James Carey; 2. 5. 1972. University of Chicago, Regenstein Library, Special Collections.

Newcomb, C. S., 1972, Interview with James Carey; 22. 5. 1972. University of Chicago, Regenstein Library, Special Collections.

Newcomb. C. and Lang, R., eds., 1934, Census Data of the City of Chicago 1934. Chicago, University of Chicago Press.

Nims, E., 1928, The Illinois Adoption Law and Its Administration. Chicago, University of Chicago Press.

Nisbet, R., 1962, 'Sociology as an Art Form', Pacific Sociological Review, 5, p. 67

North, C. C, 1908, 'The Influence of Modern Social Relations Upon Ethical Concepts', Ph.D., University of Chicago.

O'Toole, R. and Dubin, R., 1968, 'Baby Feeding and Body Sway: An Experiment in George Herbert Mead's 'Taking the role of the other', Journal of Personality and Social Psychology, 10, p. 59

Odum, H., 1951, American Sociology: The Story of Sociology in the United States through 1950. New York, Longmans.

Official Publications of the University of Chicago.

Ogburn, W. F., (Journal). The Journal of W. F. Ogburn is in the University of Chicago, Regenstein Library, Special Collections Department.

Ogburn, W. F., (undated). Untitled., draft comments about the popular attitudes of Americans. University of Chicago, Regenstein Library, Special Collections, Box 35, file 10

Ogburn, W. F., 1912, 'Progress and Uniformity in Child Labour Legislation', Studies in History, Economics and Public Law, 48, No. 2. New York, Collier.

Ogburn, W. F., 1917, 'Causes and Remedies of Labor Unrest in the Lumber Industry'. Attatched to a letter of introduction dated 19. 11. 1917. University of Chicago, Regenstein

Library, Special Collections, Ogburn Papers Box 34, File 9.

Ogburn, W. F., 1917a, 'Statistics of American Cities', Reed College Record, 27, Dec.

Ogburn, W. F., 1922, Social Change. New York, Heubsch.

Ogburn, W. F., 1927, ed, Recent Social Changes in the United States. Chicago, University of Chicago Press.

Ogburn, W. F., 1928, 'Preliminary Draft of the Statistics Proposal', undated but c. 1928. University of Chicago, Regenstein Library, Special Collections, Ogburn Papers.

Ogburn, W. F., 1929, Letter to Ruth Newcomb, 17. 10. 1929. University of Chicago, Regenstein Library, Special Collections, Ogburn Papers.

Ogburn, W. F., 1929b, Letter to Woodward. 3. 6. 1929. University of Chicago, Regenstein Library, Special Collections, Ogburn Papers.

Ogburn, W. F., 1930, Letter to F. H. Hankins, 18. 4. 1930. University of Chicago, Regenstein Library, Special Collections, Ogburn Papers.

Ogburn, W. F., 1933, Living With Machines. Chicago, American Library Association.

Ogburn, W. F., 1934, Social Change and the New Deal. Chicago, University of Chicago Press.

Ogburn, W. F., 1934b, You and Machines. Chicago, University of Chicago Press.

Ogburn, W. F., 1937, ed, Technological Trends: Report of Sub-committee of Technology to National Resources Committee. Washington D.C., Government Printing Office.

Ogburn, W. F., 1942, 'You Are Being Bossed and Don't Know It', Draft manuscript. (Under pseudonym, Fielding Williams). University of Chicago, Regenstein Library, Special Collections, Ogburn Papers, Box 35, File 4.

Ogburn, W. F., ed., 1943, American Society in Wartime. Chicago, University of Chicago Press.

Ogburn, W. F., 1952, 'Why We Have A McCarthy'. Draft manuscript. University of Chicago, Regenstein Library, Special Collections, Ogburn Papers, Box 34, File 14. Original undated. Content points to c. 1952.

Ogburn, W. F., 1964, On Technology and Social Change. Chicago, University of Chicago Press.

Ogburn, W. F. and Nimkoff, M. F., 1955, Technology and the Changing Family. Boston, Houghton Mifflin.

Ogburn, W. F. and Nimkoff, M. F., 1960, Handbook of Sociology. London, Routlege and Kegan Paul, fourth edition. (First published in the United States in 1940, adapted for Britain and published in 1947 by Paul, Treach, Trubner and Co. of London).

Ogburn, W. F. and Talbot, N. S., 1929, 'A Measurement of the Factors in the Presidential Election of 1928', Social Forces, 8, pp. 175-83.

Ogburn, W. F. and Thomas, D. 1922 'Are Inventions Inevitable?',

Political Science Quarterly, pp. 83-98.

Ogg, F. A., 1928, **Research In the Humanities and Social Sciences:** Report to the American Council of Learned Societies. New York, Century.

Oliven, R. G., 1978, 'The City as Sociological Category', **Dados,** 19, pp. 135-46.

Palmer, V. M., 1928, **Field Studies in Sociology:** A Student Manual. Social Science Studies No. 12. Chicago, University of Chicago Press.

Park, R. E., 1915, 'The City: Suggestions For the Investigation of Human Behavior in the City Environment', **American Journal of Sociology,** 20, pp. 557-612.

Park, R. E., 1920, quoted in Lofland, 1971, **Analyzing Social Settings.** Belmont, Wadsworth, p. 2. The comment is supposed to have been made around 1920

Park, R. E., 1926, 'Our Racial Frontier on the Pacific', **Survey Graphic,** 1. 5. 1926, pp. 192-196 and **Race and Culture,** pp. 138-51.

Park, R. E., 1927, 'Editor's Preface' to Thrasher, 1927, **The Gang:** A Study of 1,313 Gangs in Chicago. Chicago, University of Chicago Press.

Park, R. E., 1929, 'Sociological Research', in W. Gee, ed, 1929, **Research in the Social Sciences.** New York, Macmillan.

Park, R. E., 1936, Letter to Blumer. 24. 2. 1936. University of Chicago, Regenstein Library, Special Collections, Wirth Papers, Box 7, File 7.

Park, R. E., 1938, Letter from Park (at Fisk U., Nashville, Tennessee) to Wirth, 12. 10. 1938. University of Chicago, Regenstein Library, Special Collections, Wirth Papers.

Park, R. E., 1939, 'Notes on the Origin of the Society for Social Research', University of Chicago, Regenstein Library, Special Collections, Wirth Papers, Box 36, Folder 1. Reprinted in Kurtz, 1982.

Park, R. E., 1941, Letter from Park (from Roaring Brook, Harbor Springs Michigan) to Wirth 12. 8. 41. University of Chicago, Regenstein Library, Special Collections, Wirth Papers.

Park, R. E., 1944, Letter from Park to Horace Cayton, quoted in **Pittsburgh Courier,** 26. 2. 1944, and probably written in 1943.

Park, R. E., 1967, **On Social Control and Collective Behavior.** Chicago, University of Chicago Press.

Park, R. E., 1972, **The Crowd and the Public and Other Essays.** (Edited with an introduction by H. Elsner). Chicago, University of Chicago Press.

Park, R. E. and Burgess, E. W. 1925. **The City.** (with McKenzie, R. D.) Chicago, University of Chicago Press.

Park, R. E. and Burgess, E. W., 1921, **Introduction to the Science of Sociology.** Chicago, University of Chicago Press.

Parrish, C. H., 1944, 'The Significance of Color in the Negro

Community', Ph.D., University of Chicago.

Parsons, T., 1937, **The Structure of Social Action**. New York, McGraw-Hill.

Parsons, T., 1937a, Letter to Louis Wirth, 6. 12. 1937, with enclosure 'The Role of Ideas in Social Action'. University of Chicago, Regenstein Library, Special Collections, Wirth Papers.

Parsons, T., 1939, Letter to Louis Wirth, 6. 10. 1939. University of Chicago, Regenstein Library, Special Collections, Wirth Papers.

Parsons, T., 1951, **The Social System**. London, Routledge and Kegan Paul.

Petras, J. W., 1966, 'The Gensis and Development of Symbolic Interactionism in American Sociology', Ph. D., University of Connecticut.

Petras, J. W. and Meltzer, B. N., 1973, 'Theoretical and Ideological Variations in Contemporary Interactionism', **Catalyst**, 7, pp. 1-8.

Phelps, H. A., 1937, Letter to Bernhard Hormann, 16. 3. 1937. University of Chicago, Regenstein Library, Special Collections, Wirth Papers.

Philpott, T. L., 1978, **The Slum and the Ghetto:** Neighbourhood Deterioration and Middle Class Reform, Chicago, 1880-1930. New York, Oxford University Press.

Platt, J. A., 1981, 'Whatever Happened To Case Study ? or from Znaniecki to Lazarsfeld in one generation', draft manuscript.

Platt, J. A., 1982, 'The Origin Myth of 'Participant Observation', American Sociological Association paper, 1982.

Platt, J. A., 1982a, Personal correspondence.

Polsky, N., 1971, **Hustlers, Beats and Others**. Harmondsworth, Penguin.

Polsky, N., 1980, Contribution to 'Reminiscences of Classic Chicago: The Blumer-Hughes Talk' 1. 9. 1969', **Urban Life**, 9, pp. 254-81

Polya, G., 1954, **Mathematics and Plausible Reasoning**, 2 volumes. Princeton, Princeton University Press.

Presidents' Research Committee on Social Trends, 1933, **Recent Social Trends**. New York, McGraw-Hill.

Price, D. J. de Silva, 1963, **Little Science, Big Science**. New York. Columbia University Press.

Price, D. J. de Silva, 1965, 'Networks of Scientific Papers', **Science**, 149, pp. 510-15.

Pusic, V., 1973, 'Presentation of the Application of Qualitative Methodology to William Whyte's Study "Street Corner Society", **Revija za Sociologije**, 3, 103-108

Quinn, O. W., 1950, 'Racial Attitude and the Conforming Personality', Ph.D., University of Chicago.

Radnitzky, G., 1973, **Contemporary Schools of Metascience**. (Three volumes in one). Chicago, Regnery.

Raushenbush, W., 1979, **Robert E. Park:** Biography of a Sociologist. Durham, North Carolina, Duke University Press.

Reckless, W. C., 1925, 'The Natural History of Vice Areas in Chicago', Ph.D., University of Chicago.

Reckless, W. C., 1933, **Vice In Chicago.** Chicago, University of Chicago Press.

Reckless, W. C., 1972, Interview with James Carey; 28. 6. 1972. University of Chicago, Regenstein Library, Special Collections.

Reeden, E. A., 1939, 'Embezzelement: A Study of One Kind of Criminal Behavior with Prediction Tables Based on Fidelity Insurance Records', Ph.D., University of Chicago.

Region of Chicago Base Map, 1926, Chicago, University of Chicago Press.

Reiss, A. J., 1950, 'The Accuracy, Efficiency, and Validity of a Prediction Instrument', Ph.D., University of Chicago.

Reitzes, D., 1950, 'Collective Factors in Race Relations', Ph.D., University of Chicago.

Reuter, E. B., 1919, 'The Mulatto in the United States: A Sociological and Psychological Study', Ph.D., University of Chicago.

Rex, J., 1973, **Discovering Sociology.** London, Routledge and Kegan Paul.

Rhoades, E. L., 1929a, **The Chain Store and the Packing Industry.** Chicago, University of Chicago Press.

Rhoades, E. L., 1929b, **The Management of Chain Meat Markets.** Chicago: University of Chicago Press.

Rhoades, E. L., 1929c, **Chain Stores and the Independent Meat Retailer.** Chicago: University of Chicago Press.

Rhoades, M. C., 1906 'A Case Study of the Delinquent Boys in the Juvenile Court in Chicago', Ph.D., University of Chicago.

Rice, S.A., 1930, Foreword to 'Statistics in Social Studies'. Proofs located in University of Chicago, Regenstein Library, Special Collections, Burgess Papers, attatched to a letter from Phelps Soule to Burgess, dated, 9. 6. 1930

Rice, S. A., ed, 1931, **Methods in Social Science:** A Case Book. Chicago, University of Chicago Press.

Riley, T. J., 1904, 'A Study in the Higher Life of Chicago', Ph.D., University of Chicago.

Ritzer G., 1975a, 'Sociology: A Multiple Paradigm Science', **The American Sociologist,** 10, 156-167.

Ritzer G., 1975b, **Sociology:** A Multiple Paradigm Science. Boston, Allyn and Bacon

Ritzer, G., 1978, 'The Paradigmatic Status of the Sociological Study of the Professions', ISA

Rock, P., 1979, **The Making of Symbolic Interactionism.** London, Macmillan.

Ross, E. A., 1901, **Social Control:** A Survey of the Foundations of Order. New York, Macmillan.

Rucker, D., 1969, **The Chicago Pragmatists.** Minneapolis, University of Minnesota Press.

Russell, D., 1931, 'The Roadhouse: A Study of Commercialized Amusements in the Environs of Chicago', M. A., University of Chicago.

Schmitt, R.L., 1974, 'Symbolic Interactionism and Emergent Theory: A Reexamination', **American Sociological Review,** 39, p. 453.

Schnore, L. F., 1958, 'Morphology and Human Ecology', **American Journal of Sociology,** 63, 620-34.

Schultz, H., 1928, **Statistical Laws of Demand and Supply with Special Application to Sugar.** Chicago, University of Chicago Press.

Schwendinger, H., and Schwendinger, J. R., 1974, **Sociologists of the Chair:** A Radical Analysis of the Formative Years of North American Sociology. New York, Basic Books.

Scott, C. C., 1929, 'A Study of the Boys' Work Program of a Social Settelement in Its Relation to Delinquency', M.A., University of Chicago.

Scott, M. B., 1968, **The Racing Game.** Chicago, Aldine.

Shanas, E., 1949, 'The Personal Adjustment of Recipients of Old Age Assistance: With Special Consideration of the Methodology of Questionaire [sic] Studies of Older People', Ph.D., University of Chicago.

Shaw, C. H., 1930, **The Jack Roller.** Chicago, University of Chicago Press.

Shaw, C. H., 1931, 'Case Study Method', **Publications of the American Sociological Society,** 21, pp. 149-57.

Shaw, C. H., 1931a, **The Natural History of a Delinquent Career.** Chicago, University of Chicago Press.

Shaw, C. H., 1938, **Brothers in Crime** (assisted by H. D. McKay and J. F. MacDonald). Chicago, University of Chicago Press.

Shaw, C. H. and McKay, H. D., 1931, 'Social Factors in Juvenile Delinquency', National Commission on Law Observation and Enforcement, Washington.

Shaw, C. H. and McKay, H. D., 1942, **Juvenile Delinquency and Urban Areas.** Chicago, University of Chicago Press.

Shaw, C. H., McKay, H. D., Zorbaugh, F. M. and Cottrell, L. S., 1929, **Delinquency Areas:** A Study of the Geographic Distribution of School Truants, Juvenile Delinquents and Adult Offenders in Chicago. Chicago, University of Chicago Press.

Shibutani, T., 1949, 'The Circulation of Rumors as a Form of Collective Behavior', Ph.D., University of Chicago.

Shonle, R., 1926, 'Suicide - A Study of Personal Disorganization', Ph.D., University of Chicago.

Short, J. F., 1971, **The Social Fabric of the Metropolis:** Contributions of the Chicago School of Urban Sociology. Chicago, University of Chicago Press.

Short, J. F., 1973, 'Introduction' to part III of Cottrell, et al. eds, 1973, Ernest W. Burgess on Community, Family and Delinquency. Chicago, University of Chicago Press.

Simpson, E. N., 1926, 'Wishes: A Study in Social Psychology', Ph.D., University of Chicago.

Slattery, M., 1985, 'Urban Sociology', in Haralambos, M., ed, 1985, Sociology: New Directions. Ormskirk, Causeway Press.

Small, A. W., 1891, Letter to Harper. University of Chicago, Regenstein Library, Special Collections, W. R. Harper Papers, Box 15, File 3.

Small, A. W., 1895, Small to Harper, quoted in Matthews, F. H., 1977, Quest for an American Sociology. Montreal, McGill-Queens University Press, pp. 95-6.

Small, A. W., 1911, 'Views of Professor Small, Univerity of Chicago', American Journal of Sociology, 17, pp. 634-5.

Small, A. W. and Vincent, G. E., 1894, An Introduction to the Study of Society. New York, American Book Co.

Smith, H. L., 1949, 'The Sociological Study of Hospitals', Ph.D., University of Chicago.

Smith, R. L., 1971, 'Reflexive Behavior: An experimental examination of G.H. Mead's Treatment of Vocal Gestures', M.A., University of South Carolina, Dept. of Sociology.

Smith, T. V., 1936, 'The Chicago School', International Journal of Ethics, 46, pp. 378-87.

Smith, T. V. and White, L. D., eds., 1929, Chicago: An Experiment in Social Science Research. Chicago, University of Chicago Press.

Smith, W. C., 1920, 'Conflict and Fusion of Cultures as Typified by the Ao Nagas of India', Ph.D, University of Chicago.

Smith, W. D., 1979, 'The Emergence of German Urban Sociology, 1900-1910', Journal of the History of Sociology, 1, pp. 1-16.

Snodgrass, J., 1983, 'The Jack Roller: A Fifty-Year Follow Up', Urban Life, 11, pp. 440-60

Social Science Research Council, 1939, An Appraisal of Thomas and Znaniecki's "The Polish Peasant in Europe and America", New York, Social Science Research Council, Bulletin, 44.

Spiegelberg, H., 1976, The Phenomenological Movement: A Historical Introduction. Second Edition. Two Volumes. The Hague, Nijhoff.

Spradley, J. P., 1980, Participant Observation. New York, Holt Rinehart and Winston.

Staley. E. A., 1929, The Illinois State Federation of Labor. Chicago: University of Chicago Press.

Star, S. A., 1950, 'Interracial Tension in Two Areas of Chicago: An Exploratory Approach to the Measurement of Interracial Tension', Ph.D., University of Chicago.

Steiner, J. F., 1917, The Japanese Invasion: A Study in the Psychology of International Contacts. Chicago, McClurg

Stephan, F. F, 1926, 'Some Social Aspects of the Telephone', M.A., University of Chicago.

Stewart, R. L. 1975, 'What George Mead Should Have Said: Exploration of a Problem of Interpretation'. Paper at Annual Meeting of North Central Sociological Society, Columbus.

Stone, G. P. and Farberman, H. A., 1967, 'Further Comment on the Blumer-Bales Dialogue concerning the Implications of the Thoughts of George Herbert Mead', American Journal of Sociology, 72, p. 409.

Stone, G. P. et al., 1974, 'On Methodology and Craftsmanship in the Criticism of Sociological Perspectives', American Sociological Review, 39, p. 456.

Stonequist, E. V., 1930, 'The Marginal Man: A Study in the Subjective Aspects of Cultural Conflict', Ph.D., University of Chicago.

Stonequist, E. V., 1972, Interview with James Carey; 15. 4. 1972. University of Chicago, Regenstein Library, Special Collections.

Stouffer, S. A., 1930, 'An Experimental Comparison of Statistical and Case History Methods of Attitude Research' Ph.D., University of Chicago.

Stouffer, S. A., 1945, Letter to Walter Bartky, 9. 6. 1945. University of Chicago, Regenstein, Library Special Collections, Burgess Papers, Box 19, File 2

Strauss, A., 1964, 'Introduction' to G. H. Mead, 1964, Collected Papers. Chicago, University of Chicago Press.

Strong, S. M., 1940, 'The Social Type Method: Social Types in the Negro Community of Chicago', Ph.D., University of Chicago.

Stryker, S., 1977 'Developments in Two Social Psychologies: toward an appreciation of mutual relevance', Sociometry, 40, pp. 145-60.

Sutherland, E. H., 1937, The Professional Thief. Chicago, University of Chicago Press.

Sutherland, E. H. and Cressey, D. R., 1966, Principles of Criminology (seventh edition). Philadelphia, Lippincott.

Suttles, G. D., 1968, The Social Order of the Slum: Ethnicity and Territory in the Inner City. Chicago, University of Chicago Press.

Szacki, J., 1975, 'Scientific Schools: An Outline of the Subject Matter', Studia Socjologiczne, 4, pp. 5-27

Taylor, I., Walton, P. and Young, J., 1973, The New Criminology. London, Routledge and Kegan Paul.

Thomas, J., 1983a 'An Introduction', Urban Life, 11.

Thomas, J., 1983b 'Towards A Critical Ethnography: A Re-examination of the Chicago Legacy', Urban Life, 11, pp. 477-90.

Thomas, W. I., 1896, 'On Differences of the Metabolism of the Sexes', Ph.D., University of Chicago.

Thomas, W. I., 1909, Source Book for Social Origins. Chicago, University of Chicago Press.

Thomas, W. I., 1917, 'The Need for A Social Science' in Jennings, H. S., ed., 1917, Suggestions of Modern Science Concerning Education. New York, Macmillan.

Thomas, W. I., 1924, The Unadjusted Girl: With Cases and Standpoint for Behavior Analysis. New York, Little Brown.

Thomas, W. I., 1928, Letter to Park written in 1928, read by Wirth at the 'Polish Peasant Conference' and quoted in, Social Science Research Council, 1939, An Appraisal of Thomas and Znaniecki's "The Polish Peasant in Europe and America", New York, Social Science Research Council, Bulletin, 44, p. 166

Thomas, W. I., 1966, On Social Organization and Social Personality. Chicago, University of Chicago Press.

Thomas, W. I. and Znaniecki, F., 1918, The Polish Peasant in Europe and America. Boston, Gohram Press, 5 Vols.

Thompson, E. T., 1972, Interview with James Carey; 27. 3. 1972. University of Chicago, Regenstein Library, Special Collections.

Thrasher, F. M., 1926, 'The Gang: A Study of 1,313 Gangs in Chicago', Ph.D., University of Chicago.

Thrasher, F. M., 1927, The Gang: A Study of 1,313 Gangs in Chicago. Chicago: University of Chicago Press.

Tiryakian, E. A., 1979a, 'The Significance of Schools in the Development of Sociology', in Snizek, W. E., et al., eds., 1979, Contemporary Issues in Theory and Research. London, Aldwych, pp. 211-34.

Tiryakian, E. A., 1979b, 'The School as The Unit of Analysis: Rethinking the History of Sociology', Mimeograph.

Turner, R. H., 1948, 'Some Factors in the Differential Position of Whites and Negroes in the Labor Force of the United States in 1940', Ph.D., University of Chicago.

Turner, R. H., 1967, 'Introduction' to Park, R. E., 1967, On Social Control and Collective Behavior. Chicago, University of Chicago Press.

Tuttle, W. M., 1970, Race Riot: Chicago in the Red Summer of 1919. New York, Atheneum.

Vergati, S., 1976, 'Louis Wirth and the Chicago School of Sociology', La Critica Sociologia, 38, pp. 164-172

Vincent, G. E., 1896, 'The Province of Sociology', American Journal of Sociology, 1, pp. 473-91

Vincent, G. E., 1896a, 'Sociology and the Integration of Studies', Ph.D., University of Chicago.

Vold, G., 1958, Theoretical Criminology. New York, Oxford University Press.

Walker, H. J., 1945, 'Changes in Race Accommodation in a Southern City', Ph.D., University of Chicago.

Walker, R., 1981, 'On The Uses of Fiction in Educational Research' in Smetherham, D., ed., 1981, Practicing Evaluation. Driffield, Nafferton.

Waller, W. W., 1925, 'Fluctuations in the Severity of Punishment of Criminals from the XI to XX Centuries', MA., University of Chicago.

Waller, W. W., 1936, 'Discussion: of Lundberg (1936)', **American Sociological Review**, 1, pp. 54-60.

Ware, C. M., 1935, **Greenwich Village**, Boston, Houghton Mifflin.

Warne, C. E., 1926, **The Consumers' Co-operative Movement in Illinois**. Chicago: University of Chicago Press.

Warshay, L., 1971, 'The Current State of Sociological Theory: Diversity, Polarity, Empiricism and Small Theories' **Sociological Quarterly**, 12, pp. 23-45

Waskow, A. I., 1967, **From Race Riot to Sit-In**: 1919 and the 1960s. New York, Doubleday.

Webb, E. J., Campbell, D. T., Schwartz, R. D., and Sechrest, L., 1966, **Unobtrusive Measures**: Non Reactive Research in the Social Sciences. Chicago, Rand McNally

Weber, M., 1947, **The Theory of Social and Economic Organization**. New York, Free Press. (Trans and ed., Henderson and Parsons: original German title, Wirtschaft and Gesellschaft.)

Weinberg, S. K., 1935, 'A Study of Isolation Among Chicago Shelterhouse Men', M. A., University of Chicago.

White, L. D. 1925, **Conditions of Municipal Employment in Chicago**: A Study in Morale. Chicago, Higgins.

White, L. D. 1927, **The City Manager**. Chicago, University of Chicago Press.

White, L. D. 1929, **The Prestige Value of Public Employment in Chicago**. Chicago, University of Chicago Press.

White, L. D., 1929a, 'The Local Community Research Committee and the Social Science Research Building', in Smith, T. V., and White, L. D., eds., 1929, **Chicago**: An Experiment in Social Science Research. Chicago, University of Chicago Press, pp. 20-32.

White, L. D., 1929b, 'Co-operation With Civic and Social Agencies', in Smith, T. V., and White, L. D., eds., 1929, **Chicago**: An Experiment in Social Science Research. Chicago, University of Chicago Press, pp. 33-46.

White, L. D., 1969, **The Science of Culture** (second edition). New York, Farrar, Straus and Giroux.

Whitridge, E. R., 1946, 'Art in Chicago', Ph.D., University of Chicago.

Whyte, W. F., 1943, 'Street Corner Society: The Social Structure of an Italian Slum', Ph.D., University of Chicago.

Whyte, W. F., 1943a, **Street Corner Society**, Chicago, University of Chicago Press.

Whyte, W. F., 1955, **Street Corner Society**, (revised edition including methodological appendix). Chicago, University of Chicago Press.

Wiley, N. 1979 'The Rise and Fall of Dominating Theories in American Sociology', in Snizek, W. E., et al, eds., 1979,

Contemporary Issues in Theory and Research, London, Aldwych, pp. 47-80.

Willer, D., 1967, **Scientific Sociology:** Theory and Method. Englewood Cliffs, Prentice-Hall

Williams, R., 1973, **The Country and the City.** London, Chatto and Windus.

Williams, D. and Skinner, M. E., undated, **Work of Children on Illinois Farms.** United States Department of Labor, Children's Bureau, Bulletin No. 168.

Wilson, E. B., 1940, Letter to E. W. Burgess, 19. 1. 1940. University of Chicago, Regenstein Library, Special Collections, Burgess Papers Box 20, File 7

Wirth, L., 1926, 'The Ghetto: A Study in Isolation', Ph.D., University of Chicago.

Wirth, L., 1928, **The Ghetto:** A Study in Isolation. Chicago: University of Chicago Press.

Wirth, L., 1935, Minutes of the Meetings of the Divisional Seminar in Race and Culture Contacts, University of Chicago, 1935', University of Chicago, Regenstein Library, Special Collections, Wirth papers, Box 10, File 5.

Wirth, L., 1936a, Letter to F. S. Chapin. 31. 10. 1936. University of Chicago, Regenstein Library, Special Collections, Wirth Papers, Box 2, File 4

Wirth, L., 1938, Confidential circular to the Sociology Department, original undated but circulation list of staff points to 1938. University of Chicago, Regenstein Library, Special Collections, Wirth Papers.

Wirth, L., 1939, 'Memorandum Regarding the General Study of The Negro Community in Chicago'. Attatched to a letter to Horace Cayton, dated 24. 5. 1939. University of Chicago, Regenstein Library, Special Collections, Wirth Papers.

Wirth, L., 1941, Letter to Park, 2. 9. 1941. University of Chicago, Regenstein Library, Special Collections, Wirth Papers.

Wirth, L., 1941a, Letter to Robert Lynd, 21. 2. 1941. University of Chicago, Regenstein Library, Special Collections, Wirth Papers, Box 7.

Wirth, L., 1944, Wirth's comments on Park at the memorial meeting in 1944. University of Chicago, Regenstein Library, Special Collections, Wirth Papers, Box 7, File 7.

Wirth, L., 1947, 'American Sociology 1915-1947', **American Journal of Sociology Cumulative Index Vols 1 to 52,** pp. 273-81.

Wirth, L., 1948, Letter to Howard Odum, 27. 4. 1948. University of Chicago, Regenstein Library, Special Collections, Wirth Papers, Box 7, File 2.

Wirth, L., 1949, Document on the Committee on Organization of Research in the Social Sciences. University of Chicago, Regenstein Library, Special Collections, Wirth Papers, Box

53, File 6.

Wirth, L., and Bernert, E. H., eds., 1949, **Local Community Fact Book of Chicago, 1940**. Chicago, University of Chicago Press.

Wirth, L., and Furez, M., eds., 1938, **Local Community Fact Book**. Chicago, Chicago Recreation Commission.

Witzgall, O., 1978, 'Tamotsu Shibutani in the Tradition of Symbolic Interaction', **Soziologenkorrespondenz**, 5, pp. 67-88.

Woelfel, J. 1967 'Comment on the Blumer-Bales Dialogue concerning the Interpretation of Mead's Thought', **American Journal of Sociology**, 72, p. 409

Wolf, H. D., 1927, **The Railroad Labor Board**. Chicago, University of Chicago Press.

Wooddy, C. H., 1926, **The Chicago Primary of 1926: A Study In Election Methods**. Chicago, University of Chicago Press.

Woodhead, H., 1907, 'The Social Significance of the Physical Development of Cities', Ph.D., University of Chicago.

Young, E. F., 1924, 'Race Prejudice', Ph.D., University of Chicago.

Young, K., 1949, **Sociology: A Study of Society and Culture**,(Second edition). New York, ABC.

Young, K., and Freeman, L., 1966, 'Social Psychology and Sociology', in Becker, H. S., and Boskoff, A., eds., 1966, **Modern Sociological Theory**. New York, Holt, Rinehart Winston, pp. 50-73.

Young, P., 1932, **The Pilgrims of Russian Town**. Chicago, University of Chicago Press.

Zorbaugh, H. W., 1929, **The Gold Coast and the Slum**. Chicago, University of Chicago Press.

Index

A
Abbott, E., 15, 56
Abel, T., 207
Abstracted empiricism, 126, 145
Acculturation, 120
Addams, J., 25
Adler, A., 149
Agocs, C., 110, 122
Alexander, C. S., 121
Alienation, 120
Alihan, M. A., 208
Allport, G.W., 129, 135, 142
Amelioration, 18, 23-46, 127
American Council of Learned Societies, 198
American Council on Race Relations, 121
American Journal of Sociology, 20, 27, 38, 101, 121, 123, 177, 179, 181, 186, 187, 191
American Sociological Review, 107, 134, 181, 182, 184
American Sociological Society, 74, 177, 179, 181, 182, 184, 186, 191, 192, 203, 209
American Statistical Association, 74, 82, 106
Anderson, N., 9, 36, 50, 55, 58-60, 71, 112, 116, 119, 157, 180, 184
Anomie, 120, 124, 149
Anthropology, 64, 72, 100, 117
Arensberg, C. M., 67, 72
Armchair theorising, 127, 134, 145

Assimilation, see Race relations cycle
Atkinson, P., 48, 49, 108
Attitudes, 52-54, 66, 73, 75, 77, 78, 93, 101, 104, 118,
   122, 129-134, 138, 141, 193, 210

B
Babcock, J. O., 184, 193
Bain, R., 129-133, 151, 184, 185, 211
Baker, A., 150
Baldwin, J. M., 155
Bales, R.F., 161-163, 167
Barnes, B., 220
Barnhardt, K. E., 25, 30, 180, 208
Barthes, R., 22
Bartky, W, 102
Bartlett, H. M., 178
Barton, A., 140
Bauhaus School, 18
Becker, H. P., 185
Becker, H. S., 6, 9, 10, 13, 16, 24, 49, 55, 58, 64, 65, 68,
   70, 104, 124, 138, 174, 205, 206, 211
Bedford, S. W., 14, 15, 21, 30
Behaviourism, 167, 169, 207, 208
Belleville Survey, 87, 127
Bell, C., 47
Bemis, E. W., 14
Bentley, A. F., 15
Berger, B., 23, 47, 110, 113
Berger, P. L., 23, 47, 110, 113, 154
Bernard, J., 28, 187
Bernard, L. L., 8, 19, 28, 159, 185, 186, 207
Bernert, E. H., 88
Besnard, P., 2, 18
Bierstadt, R., 113, 114
Big picture, 33, 43, 55, 145, 195
Blackmar, F. W., 87, 127
Blake, J. A., 125
Blumenthal, A. B., 60, 62, 64-66, 73
Blumer, H., 10, 11, 16, 21, 30, 31, 32, 48, 68, 69, 77, 80, 83,
   95, 97, 103, 105, 114, 119, 126, 129-131, 133, 134, 136-139,
   144, 146, 150, 153-175, 178, 185, 188, 189, 192, 195, 196,
   205, 207, 208, 211
Bogardus, E. S., 80, 95, 122
Bogdan, R., 5, 47, 150, 172
Booth, C., 68, 80, 127
Bossard, J., 185
Boudon, R., 92
Bowerman, C. E., 207
Bowley, A. L., 101

Box, S., 123
Bracey, J., 32
Bradbury, W., 17
Brake, M., 23, 110
Brandeis University, 21
Brannigan, A., 123
Breckinridge, S. P., 25, 31, 37
Breton, A., 18
Brown University, 179
Brown, W. O., 77, 114, 121
Bruere, H., 190
Buffalo, University of, 144
Bulletin of the Society for Social Research, 8, 19, 40, 59, 60,
    64, 78, 83, 85, 88, 96,-98, 118, 168, 184, 191, 193, 215
Bulmer, M., 2-5, 10, 12, 18, 21, 30, 32, 38-40, 61, 74, 80, 84,
    88, 92, 101, 177, 179, 181, 195-197, 200, 213
Burgess, E. W., 7-12, 14-16, 24, 26, 33-39, 42, 44, 51, 59, 69,
    70, 77, 80, 81, 83, 87-95, 100, 101, 106, 114-116, 124-127,
    131, 134-137, 142, 143, 146-149, 152, 154, 157, 167, 178,
    184, 186, 189, 192, 194, 196, 200, 203, 204, 211
Burke, K., 13
Burns, L. R., 124
Bushnell, C. J., 111
Butterfield, H., 217
Butters, S., 49, 50, 136

C
Caldarovic, O., 110, 124
California, University of, 21, 137, 172, 198-200, 204, 205
Campbell, D. T., 69
Campisi, P. J., 207
Carabana, J., 11, 45, 158, 162, 175
Carey, J. T., 9, 13, 20, 26, 41, 45, 117, 119, 155
Carter, W. P., 155
Castells, M., 23, 117
Case study, 50-52, 54-57, 61, 62, 70, 75-78, 80, 88-99, 101,
    103, 104, 107, 134, 152, 213
Cavan, R. S., 6, 8, 11, 24, 25, 55, 56, 77, 80-82, 94, 112-114,
    116, 119, 124, 148, 158, 178, 180, 184
Cavan, S., 21
Cayton, H., 43
Celinski, A., 124
Central value system, 143, 153
Centre For Contemporary Cultural Studies, 2, 22, 153
Chalmers, A. F., 151, 218
Chapin, F. S., 70, 185, 211
Chicago Area Project, 34
Chicago Commons, 25
Chicago Community Inventory, 16

Chicago Fact Books, 80, 88
Chicago Irregulars, 20, 21
Chicago Juvenile Protection Agency/Protective Association, 36, 60, 63
Chicago Real Estate Board, 124
Chicago School of Civics and Philanthropy, 15
Chicago Women's Club, 36
Choldin, H. M., 110
Ciacci, M., 154
Cincinnati, University of, 200
City of Chicago, 11, 43, 106, 111-112, 116, 178, 179, 191, 195, 197
Civic reform, 23, 25, 39
Clark, H. B., 111
Clark Street, 62
Clark University, 208
Clasification schemes, see Typification
Cloward, R., 124
Cohen, A. K., 124
Coleman, J., 68, 69, 99, 204, 205
Collective behaviour, 121, 125, 135
Columbia University, 8, 13, 17, 20, 30, 47, 67, 75, 81, 83, 87, 92, 99, 101, 127, 150, 176-181, 188, 189, 190, 192, 198, 200, 201, 204-209
Committee for Social Thought, 205
Committee on Organisation for Reseach in the Social Sciences, 202, 210
Committee on Social Thought, 153
Committee on University Social Science Research Organisations, 188, 200
Community, 63-67, 88, 100, 106, 120, 127, 138, 148, 159
Community Studies Inc., 16, 205, 212
Comte, A., 135
Concentric zone, 18, 35, 104, 115-117, 119, 120, 124
Conway, P.R., 38
Cooley, C. H., 7, 24, 28, 77, 127, 135, 149, 152, 154-157, 159, 164, 167, 168, 170-172, 175, 179, 183, 207
Cornell University, 200, 208
Cornell University, 107
Coser, L. A., 4, 15, 31, 167, 173, 174, 176, 182, 183, 187
Cothran, T. C., 121
Cottrell, L. S., 31-35, 39, 70, 77, 79, 82, 88, 89, 91, 107, 117, 119, 124, 126, 138, 165, 180, 184, 207
Coup in the American Sociological Society, 19, 102, 104, 176, 181-190, 203, 204, 206, 211
Cox, O. C., 121, 207
Crane, D., 3
Cressey, D. R., 123
Cressey, P.G, 36, 38, 50, 55, 60, 61, 112, 116, 119,

Criminology, see Deviance
Cultural lag, 122, 123
Culture, 100, 117, 122, 123, 125, 130, 131, 133
Cumulative-falsificationist approach, see Falsificationism

D
Dai, B., 104
Daniel, V. E., 49, 67, 121, 150
Darwin, 26, 44, 71
Davie, M., 185
Davis, J., 185
Davis, M. M., 16
Dawson, C.A., 207
DeGraff, H. O., 65, 71
Dealey, J., 179
Decline of Chicago School, 18
Definition of the situation, 119, 120, 190
Delinquency, 76, 88, 90, 93, 117, 124, 138
Demography, 107, 111
Denzin, N. K., 22, 48, 136, 155, 167
Detweiler, F. G., 121
Deutscher, I., 47, 155
Deviance, 4, 57, 68, 76, 77, 107, 110, 117, 123-125, 171, 174
Devinney, L. C., 207
Dewey, J., 147, 154, 155, 161, 162, 168, 171-175
Dibble, V. K., 9, 27, 41, 112, 143
Dillingham Commission, 44
Diner, S., 9, 15, 25
Dittmer, C., 185
Dodd, S. C., 95
Dollard, J., 34, 64, 70, 81, 83, 114, 119, 126, 184
Dotter, D. L., 13, 115-117, 123
Douglas, P., 102
Dowd, J., 179
Doyle, B., 121
Dramaturgical approach, 13
Dreitzel, H.P., 5
Dubin, R., 165
Duncan, H. D., 13, 125
Duncan, H. G., 74, 75
Duncan, O. D., 16, 87, 102, 185, 205
Duncan, W. L., 74, 75
Dunham, H. W., 138, 207
Dunn, A. W., 111
Durkheim, E., 2, 135, 147, 149, 152
De Bernart, M., 187

E
Easthope, G., 4, 109, 116, 117

Ecclesiatical Sociology, Dept. of, 14, 26
Eckberg, D. L., 118
Ecology, 87, 90, 100, 116, 117, 123-125, 148, 149, 153, 167, 207
Edwards, G. F., 121
Edwards, L. P., 125
Elinson, J., 16
Ellwood, C., 179
Elmer, M. C., 185
Empirical research, 27-41, 53-55, 66, 93, 109, 111, 114-115, 124, 126, 128-133, 145, 146, 151, 152, 165, 166, 183, 218
Empiricism, 4, 126, 132, 144, 146
Epistemology, 98, 103, 128, 135, 140, 144, 161, 166-168, 171, 173, 206
Espinosa, E. Lamo de, 11, 45, 158, 162, 175
Ethnography, 5, 11-13, 20, 21, 47-73, 74, 77, 82, 108, 137, 140, 177, 205, 213
Ethnology, 122, 159
Ethnomethodology, 104, 137, 141, 172
Eubank, E. E., 184, 185
Evans, W. A., 36, 60
Evers, H-D., 115

F
Fairchild, H. P., 179
Falsificationism, 54, 75, 78, 103, 128-144, 150, 151, 160
Family, 81, 89, 117, 119, 124, 125, 179
Farberman, H. A., 42, 149, 163, 164, 167
Faris, E., 9, 11, 14, 15, 39, 71, 81, 83, 88, 97, 119, 126, 154, 155, 157-160, 170, 175, 178, 184, 189, 195, 203
Faris, R. E. L., 4, 9, 10, 14, 24, 31, 33, 37, 65, 71, 77, 79, 85, 119, 126, 127, 149, 154, 156-158, 179, 182, 187, 195
Farm Study Center, 16
Faw, V. E., 121
Federal Employment Relief Agency, 192, 193
Feldman, J., 16
Ferrarotti, F., 122
Feyerabend, P., 218
Field, J. A., 80
Field studies, 110, 139, 140
Field work, see field studies
Filmer, P., 141
Filstead, W. J., 136
Firey, W., 117
Fisher, B., 72, 109, 155, 156, 158, 172, 174
Fisher, R. A, 101, 102, 105
Fish, V., 56
Fiske University, 189, 203, 208
Fleming, H. E., 111

Foot, N., 17
Frankfurt School, 2
Franklin, C. W., 122
Frazier, E. F., 38, 42, 117, 121
Freeman, F. N., 97
Freeman, L., 155
Freud, S., 70, 125, 126, 149
Friedrichs, R. W., 23
Functionalism, 124, 128, 143, 144, 182
Functionalist-interactionist, 118, 128, 141, 189
Furez, M., 88
Furner, M. O., 28, 41, 127

G
Gangs, 56, 57, 76, 111, 119
Gans, H., 117
Garfinkel, H., 69
Geer, B., 13, 49, 138, 140, 141, 205, 212
Geruson, R., 115
Ghetto, 65, 111, 120, 148
Giddings, F. H., 127, 135, 176, 179, 180
Gillette, J. M., 111
Giner, S., 109
Glaser, B., 47, 48, 205
Glueck, L., 131
Goddijn, H. P. M., 156, 175, 176, 179, 187
Goffman, E., 10, 13, 137, 141, 172
Golden era, 10, 24, 25, 57, 80, 82, 112, 114-115, 127
Goldhamer, H., 121
Gold Coast, 61-65, 111, 113
Goldman, N., 35
Goodman, L., 17, 87, 205
Gordon, M. M., 122
Gosnell, H. F., 84, 101, 102, 157
Gough, H. G., 122,
Gouldner, A., 24
Grand theory, 110
Greeley, A. M., 23, 44
Guggenheim Foundation, 143
Gumperz, J., 48
Guttman, L., 102

H
Hagedorn, R., 92
Haimowitz, M. L., 121
Hale, W. H., 121
Hall, O., 124
Hammersley, M., 48, 49, 108
Hammond, P., 140

Handel, W. H., 155
Handman, M. S., 15
Hankins, F. H., 185, 206, 207, 211
Hare, P. H., 161, 172
Harper, W. R., 27
Hart, C. W., 16, 87
Harvard University, 17, 67, 178, 181, 188, 190, 192, 199, 200, 204-206
Harvey, L., 2, 3, 12, 17, 55, 118, 172, 175, 214, 217
Harvey, P. A., 128
Hauser, P., 16, 87, 88, 98, 192, 193, 205
Haussermann, H., 110, 117
Hayes, E., 179
Hayner, N. S., 29, 34, 42, 79, 114, 116, 149
Healey, W., 93
Henderson, C. R, 9, 14, 24-27, 56, 111, 112, 179
Henderson, L. J, 190
Heritage, J., 167
Hermeneutic, 104, 131, 141, 143
Hiller, E. T., 120
Hill, L., 118
Hill, M. C., 121
Hirschi, T., 92
Historicism, 215, 218
Hobo, 58-60, 111, 119
Holcombe, 209
Holton, G., 220
Horak, J., 42, 65
Hormann, B., 192
Horowitz, I., 144
Horst, P., 107
Horton, D., 17
House, F., 15, 175, 185, 207
Howerth, I., 15
Howson, C., 220
Huber, J., 109, 155
Hughes, C. S., 184
Hughes, E. C., 6, 10, 13, 16, 19, 21, 80, 81, 124, 125, 154, 196, 207, 208, 212
Hull House, 25
Human document, 66, 90, 129-131
Hunter, A., 5, 10, 23, 35, 55, 62
Hunter, J., 60

I
Idealism, 141, 154, 161, 162
Ideal types, 95, 115, 135, 143, 146, 147
Ideology, 143, 153
Illinois, University of, 179, 200, 207

338

Illinois Board of Pardons and Parole, 35
Illinois Institute for Juvenile Research, 35, 86
Illinois Lodgings House Register, 63
Impressionists, 18
In-depth interviews, 49, 59, 105
Indiana, University of, 91, 179, 208
Inductivism, 127, 130, 145, 150
Industrial Relations Center, 16
Informal interviews, 100, 101
Inskeep, K., 26
Instincts, 70
Institutes of the Society for Social Research, 40, 78, 85, 98,
    186, 191, 196, 204, 215
Institute for Social and Religious Affairs, 32
Institute of Pacific Relations, 81
Interaction(ism), 50, 52-55, 69-71, 95, 99, 118, 120, 122, 125,
    126, 128, 134, 135, 138, 144-146, 148, 154, 155, 158-160,
    163, 168-170, 173
Interpretive sociology, see Phenomenology
Interviews, 55, 67, 68, 73, 75, 78, 90, 92, 95, 100, 101, 104,
    153
Inventions, 122, 123
Invisible College, 3, 214
Iowa, State University of, 208
Iowa, University of, 211
Iowa Association of Economists and Sociologists, 93
Iowa School, 11, 158
Irwin, J., 21

J
James, W., 154, 155, 161, 162, 171, 172
Janowitz, M., 6, 10, 12, 24, 28, 32, 121, 138, 158, 166, 205
Jensen, H., 77
Joas, H., 175
Johns Hopkins University, 208
Johnson, J. H., 150
Johnson, C. O., 32, 80, 184, 203
Johnson, E. S., 16, 184
Johnson, G. B., 34, 58
Johnstone, J. W., 16
Journal of the American Statistical Association, 82, 105

K
Kando, T. M., 155
Kansas, University of, 127, 211, 212
Kant, E., 141, 168
Kattagawa, E., 16
Kelly, E. L., 91, 107
Kelvin, Lord, 85

Kilpatrick, C., 91
Kimball, S. T., 72
Kingsbury, S., 185
King, W. I., 209
Kitagawa, E. M., 87, 88
Kleeck, M. Van, 210
Kolb, J. H, 184
Komorowski, Z., 116
Kramer-Badoni, T., 110, 117
Krantz, D. L., 3
Kreuger, E., 180
Kriesberg, L., 16
Kuhn, M., , 154, 155
Kuhn, T. S., 2, 118, 215, 217-219
Kuklick, H., 23, 44, 47, 156-158, 161, 167, 182, 187
Kurtz, L. R., 5, 9, 30, 214

L
Labelling theory, 13, 110, 123, 124
Labovitz, S., 92
Lakatos, I., 2, 3, 131, 150, 217-219
Lake Michigan, 62
Landesco, J., 35, 112
Lang, R., 207
Lang, R. O., 88, 89
Laperriere, A., 13
Lapiere, R., 24, 127, 177, 180
Larrain, J., 22
Lasswell, H, 157
Lauer, R. H., 155
Laura Spelman Rockefeller Memorial Foundation, 38, 198-200
Lawrence Social Survey, 87, 127
Laws of society, 27-29, 51, 53, 131, 132, 136, 151, 152, 164
Lazarsfeld, P. F., 17, 87, 140, 175, 183, 192, 204, 211
LePlay, F., 93
Leiffer, M. H., 38
Lemert, E. M., 124
Lengermann, P. M., 18, 183-186, 206
Lerner, M, 95, 129, 130, 136
Lewis, D. J., 12, 22, 134, 156, 157, 161, 162, 167, 172
Lewis, H. G., 121
Leyland Stanford University, 17
Life history, 47, 50-52, 55, 62, 66-68, 74, 76-77, 95-98,
    100, 104, 132, 142, 152, 208
Lincourt, J. M., 161, 172
Lindeman, E. C., 49, 60
Lindesmith, A. R., 105, 155
Line, W., 190
Linton, R., 121, 174

Littlejohn, S. W., 11, 13, 155
Little Italy, 62
Litwak, E., 16
Local Community Research Committee, 38-40, 83, 92, 189, 197
Locke, H. J., 91, 193
Lofland, J., 21, 115
Lofland, L. H., 17, 20, 21, 64
Lohman, J. D., 16, 150
Longitudinal studies, 101
Lord, J., 185
Louis, J., 194
Lower North Community Council, 62
Lunday, G. A., 207
Lundberg, G. A., 78, 95, 105, 134, 145, 185, 211
Lutz, F. W., 45
Lynd, H. M., 62, 65, 72
Lynd, R. S., 62, 65, 72, 192, 204, 211

M
MacIver, R., 178, 205, 210, 211
MacLean, A. M., 15, 25, 56
Madge, J., 5, 10, 23, 45, 47, 56, 57, 60, 62, 110, 114, 115,
   117, 187
Malinowski. B., 150
Manis, J. G., 11
Mannheim, K., 143
Mapping, 73, 90, 120
Marcson, S., 121
Marginal 'man', 120, 122, 134, 151
Marks, E. S., 16
Marriage, 89-91, 107
Marriage Adjustment Index, 89
Martindale, D., 4, 109, 122, 176, 181, 182, 187
Martins, H.,, 118, 219
Martin, J. G., 122
Marxism, 2, 153, 208
Mass society, 120, 125
Matthews, E., 25
Matthews, F. H., 4, 10, 15, 25, 32, 41, 69, 80, 121, 177, 181,
   187-190, 195, 196, 207, 208
Matza, D., 124
Mayhew, H., 68
McCarthyism, 144, 194, 208
McCormick, T. C., 97
McGill University, 16, 200
McGrath, D., 115
McKay, H. D., 35, 117
McKenzie, R. D., 7
McPhail, C., 161, 162, 164, 165, 167

Mead, G. H., 11, 16, 18, 22, 103, 147, 154-175, 183, 213, 218
Medvedev, Z. A.,
Meltzer, B. N., 5, 11, 47, 155, 158, 173
Merlant, J., 150
Meroney, W. P., 185
Merriam, C. E., 101, 190
Merton, R. K., 96, 123, 124, 126, 128, 130, 146, 151, 152, 174,
    183, 192, 211
Messinger, S., 21
Metascience, 2-5, 18, 213-220
Methodology, 4, 41, 47-108, 132-134, 137, 139, 141, 144, 145,
    151, 153, 161, 164, 165, 171, 174, 180-182, 185, 187, 188,
    190, 201, 203, 205-210, 218
Michigan, University of, 82, 127, 179, 200, 204, 205, 207, 208
Middletown, 65
Middle range theory, 96, 110, 126, 130, 137, 139, 140, 151, 152
Miller, H., 185
Mills, C. W., 53, 55, 98, 128, 144-146
Minnesota, University of, 82, 91, 112, 200, 207, 208, 211
Missouri, University of, 179, 208
Molotch, H., 23
Montreal, University of, 207
Moore, D. G., 17
Moreno, J. L., 95
Morris, C., 156
Mowrer, E. R., 35, 81, 117, 119, 184
Mulkay, M., 220
Mullins, N. C., 2, 3, 5, 47, 99, 128, 138, 141, 155, 156, 176,
    213, 215, 217, 219
Myrdal, G., 66, 121

N
Naive falsificationism, see Falsificationism
Nash, P., 150
National Opinion Research Center, 16, 87
Naturalism, 26, 47, 49, 50, 68, 108, 164
Natural areas, 35, 44, 116, 123
Near North Side, 62
Nebraska, University of, 208
Nelson, C. W., 16, 207
Networks, 3, 214
Neumeyer, M. H., 114
New School of Social Research, 144
Newcomb, R., 83
Newcomb. C. S., 88, 174, 193
New Chicago School, 13
Nimkoff, M. F., 122, 123
Nisbet, R., 120
Nominalist, 134, 135, 161, 164, 167, 168

Non-participant observation, see observation
Norm, 143
North, C., 185
Northwestern University, 200, 208
North Carolina, University of, 189, 192, 199, 200, 204, 208

O
O'Toole, R., 165
Oaklahoma, University of, 179
Oberlin College, 207
Objectivity, 13, 24-33, 40-42, 53, 55, 91, 129-136, 142, 143,
   145, 152, 162, 187, 193
Observation, 4, 13, 47-73, 100, 101, 103, 113, 137, 138, 164,
   171, 206
Odum, H., 187, 192
Official Publications of the University of Chicago, 14
Ogburn, W. F., 9, 11, 16, 20, 38-40, 69, 81-89, 91, 97, 101,
   102, 105, 113, 122-127, 133, 143, 178, 184, 189, 190, 193-
   196, 202, 211
Ogg, F. A., 30, 189, 198
Ohio State University, 208
Ohlin, L., 124
Oliven, R. G., 110, 117
Operationalisation, 75, 77, 92, 105, 134, 145, 161, 186
Oral tradition, 109, 155, 215
Organisations, sociology of, 124, 125

P
Palmer, V. M., 80, 106
Paradigm, 2, 117, 118, 124, 145, 215
Pareto, V., 147
Park, R. E., 7, 9-11, 14, 15, 20, 28-34, 39, 42-44, 48, 52, 55-
   57, 59, 63, 67, 69, 70, 76, 78-81, 83, 86, 88, 93, 97, 99,
   103, 110-111, 113-114, 116, 119, 121, 123, 125-127, 135, 144-
   150, 154, 157-160, 167, 168, 172, 175, 177, 178, 180, 183,
   184, 186-189, 192, 193, 195, 196, 203, 207, 208, 211, 215
Parmelee, M., 185
Parrish, C. H., 121
Parsons, T., 2, 17, 93, 141, 143, 144, 147, 153, 174, 182, 183,
   188, 192, 211
Participant observation, see observation
Pearson, K., 101
Peirce, C. S., 161, 162, 172
Pennsylvania, University of, 200, 208
Personality, 124, 138, 158, 159
Personal Documents, 73, 77, 95, 142, 147
Petras, J. W., 155, 158
Phelps, H. A., 185, 192
Phenomenology, 50, 54, 70, 103, 104, 108, 128, 137-142, 144,

150, 165, 166, 169, 172, 208
Philpott, T. L., 12, 23, 44, 109
Pierson, R. D., 150
Pittsburgh, University of, 185
Pittsburgh Survey, 80, 127
Platt, J. A., 50, 55, 171
Polish Peasant, Conference on, 128-137, 144, 147, 151, 160
Polish Peasant in Europe and America, 11, 52, 67, 68, 93, 94,
    107, 111, 112, 118-120, 128-137, 144-147, 151, 160, 178
Polish School, 2
Polsky, N., 64, 68, 124
Polya, G., 140
Popper, K. R., 53, 130, 139, 217
Population Research and Training Center, 16
Positivism, 48, 50, 103, 108, 117, 128, 137, 150, 172, 181,
    183, 206
Practical Sociology, Dept. of, 14, 26
Pragmatism, 71, 102, 141, 154, 161, 162, 168-173, 183, 188, 218
Prediction studies, 89-92, 94, 101, 107, 131, 142, 148, 188
Presentism, 5, 166-168, 172, 217, 219
Presidents' Research Committee on Social Trends, 7, 83, 97,
    101, 194
Price, D. J. de Silva, 3
Princeton University, 208
Problems and Policy Committee of the SSRC, 203, 210
Professions, sociology of 124
Progressive movement, 18
Psychoanalysis, 125, 126, 208
Public opinion polling, 73, 75, 87, 210
Purdue University, 107
Pusic, V., 47

Q
Qualitative approach, 13, 18, 24, 47-73, 78, 80, 88, 99, 101-
    103, 136, 138-140, 154, 181, 190, 216
Quantitative approach, 12, 18, 38, 39, 47-50, 74-108, 125, 126,
    132, 140, 147, 148, 175, 177, 181, 182, 185-187, 190, 205,
    206, 216
Questionnaires, 68, 73, 79, 82, 98, 100, 101, 138, 151
Quinn, O. W., 121

R
Race relations cycle, 43, 120-122, 148
Race riots, 32, 80
Race studies, 32, 43, 44, 100, 117, 120-122, 125, 150, 208
Radcliffe-Brown, A. R., 64
Radnitzky, G., 2, 18
Rainwater, C., 15
Rationalisation, 120

Raushenbush, W., 4, 10, 15, 195
Raymond, J. H., 15
Realist, 131, 134, 135, 161, 162, 167, 168
Reckless, W. C., 38, 56, 57, 120, 180
Redfield, R., 65, 73, 117, 150
Reeden, E. A., 207
Reform, 4, 23-46, 80, 82, 127, 213, 218
Regenstein Memorial Library, 7, 19, 20
Reiss, A. J.,, 188
Reitzes, D., 121
Reliability, 14, 69, 130, 142, 188
Religious sects, 3, 8
Reuter, E. B., 121, 150, 184, 211
Rexroat, C., 161, 162, 164, 165, 167
Rex, J., 110, 115, 117
Rhoades, E. L., 111
Rhyne, J. J., 185
Rice, S. A., 57, 74, 77, 86, 127, 185, 211
Richardson, E. E., 107
Riley, T. J., 111
Ritzer G., 124, 155
Rockefeller Foundation, 15, 37, 150, 200
Rock, P., 11, 47, 71, 109, 111, 141, 143, 146, 168-171
Rossi, P., 16
Ross, E. A., 17, 28, 145, 179, 185
Rowntree, B. S., 80
Royce, J., 161, 172
Rucker, D., 41, 173
Ruml, B., 190
Russell, D., 116

S
Sage Foundation, 127
Sapir, E., 209
Scaling, 95, 101
Scheler, M., 143
School of Social Science Administration, 15
Schmidt, E. P., 155
Schmitt, R.L.,
Schnore, L. F., 208
School, concept of 1-3, 8, 22, 213, 214, 220
Schools of art, 3
School of Social Science Administration, 34
Schultz, H., 39, 84, 102
Schutz, A., 141, 154, 172
Schwartz, R. D., 69
Schwendinger, H., 28, 127
Schwendinger, J. R., 28, 127
Scientific Research Programmes, methodology of, 2, 150, 219

Scientific social research 24-42, 54, 57, 59, 70, 129-133, 135-137, 148, 152, 165, 171, 177, 182, 183, 186-188, 200, 203, 213, 218
Scott, C. C., 38
Scott, M. B., 137, 141
Sechrest, L., 69
Secrist, H., 209
Self, 159, 162, 163, 169, 170
Sellin, T., 211
Selvin, H. C., 92
Sensitizing concepts, 78, 164, 166
Shanas, E., 16, 207
Shaw, C. H., 16, 35, 36, 76, 77, 99, 100, 112, 116, 117
Shibutani, T., 125
Shils, E. A., 17, 21, 125, 143, 204
Shonle, R. see Cavan, R.
Short, J. F., 36, 37
Simmel, G., 54, 135, 146, 168
Simpson, E. N., 15, 114
Sims, N., 185
Sippey, J. J., 87
Slattery, M., 12, 115, 117
Slight, D., 91
Slums, 61-63, 65, 111, 113
Small, A. W., 6, 9, 14, 25-29, 33, 42, 56, 80, 82, 111-112, 127, 135, 147, 158, 159, 178-180, 195, 207
Smith, W.C., 185
Smithsonian Institute, 17
Smith, H. L., 124
Smith, R. L., 12, 22, 134, 156, 157, 161, 162, 165, 167, 172
Smith, T. V., 38
Smith, W. D., 112
Smith University, 207
Snodgrass, J., 11
Social change, 82, 106, 122, 123, 125, 143, 195
Social control, 24, 28-37, 42, 52, 135, 149
Social Darwinism, 41
Social disorganisation, 44, 52, 55, 63, 95, 110, 117-125, 134, 145, 149, 190
Social Distance Scale, 80, 95
Social evolution, see social change
Social philosophy, 24
Social reform, see reform
Social Research Committee, 88
Social Science Research Building, 84, 85, 190
Social Science Research Committee, 38, 39, 90, 106, 138, 189, 190, 197, 202
Social Science Research Council, 39, 67, 68, 77, 88, 94, 95, 107, 120, 121, 128-133, 136, 141, 142, 151, 183, 188-191,

197, 200-204, 209-211
Social survey, 79, 87, 101, 103, 111, 127, 205, 210
Social trends, 101, 106
Social work, 24, 31, 34, 36, 37, 57, 75
Society for Social Research, 7, 19, 28, 40-41, 72, 83, 96, 104
 116, 118, 120, 143, 146, 156, 157, 159, 174, 180, 186, 191
 203, 215, 218
Sociological Research Association, 203, 211
Sociology of knowledge, 125, 141, 143, 144, 148, 214
Sociometry, 95, 96
Sophisticated falsificationism, see falsificationism
Sorokin, P. A.,, 146, 152
Southern California, University of, 127
Soviet sociology, 2
Spencer, H., 41
Spiegelberg, H., 144
Spot maps, 47, 65, 99
Spradley, J. P., 48,
Sprengling, M., 150
Springfield Survey, 80
Standard American sociology, 128-144
Stanford University, 200
Star, S. A., 16, 121, 188
Starr, F., 14
Statistics, 70-90, 126, 127, 132, 134, 139, 144, 146, 151, 152
 187, 207, 208
Steiner, J. F., 121
Stephan, F. F., 84, 184, 193
Stewart, R. L., 162
Stinchcombe, A., 68
Stone, G. P., 155, 163, 164
Stonequist, E. V., 114, 121
Stouffer, S. A., 10, 15, 51, 77, 86, 87, 91, 101, 102, 107,
 125, 153 129, 131, 134, 175, 183, 184, 193, 204, 211
Strauss, A., 10, 13, 47, 48, 71, 89, 109, 138, 155-158, 172,
 174, 205, 212
Strong, S. M., 121
Structural, 104, 123, 143, 147, 148, 152, 153, 163, 164, 170
Structural functionalism, 2, 110, 122, 139, 141, 147, 150-152,
 174, 177, 182, 183, 208
Stryker, S., 162
Subjectivity, 53, 55, 66, 79, 129-133, 137, 142, 144, 164, 169,
 187
Sumner, G., 7, 135, 145
Sutherland, E. H., 16, 21, 68, 77, 123, 124, 192
Symbolic interactionism, 5, 11, 18, 68, 71, 102, 136-139, 141,
 144, 154-175
Szacki, J., 18

T

Taeuber, K.E., 88
Talbot, M. S., 14, 25, 111
Tarde, G., 135, 145
Taxi Dance Hall, 36, 60-62, 119
Taylor, G., 15, 25
Taylor, I., 109, 123
Taylor, S. J., 5, 47, 150, 172
Technology, 82, 106, 117, 122, 123, 148
Teggart, F. J., 210
Terman, L., 91
Tetrau, E. D., 193
Texas, University of, 200
Theoretical development at Chicago, 109-153
Thomas, D., 122, 123, 184, 185, 211
Thomas, J., 11, 20, 45, 137, 178
Thomas, W. I., 7, 9, 14, 27-32, 40, 42, 48, 50-56, 68-71, 72
  75-79, 92, 93, 99, 103, 112, 113, 118-120, 125, 127, 129-130
  132, 134, 141, 145-151, 154, 155, 157, 159, 160, 168, 172
  175, 178, 183, 185, 188, 195, 211
Thompson, W., 211
Thorndike, E. L., 190
Thrasher, F. M., 42, 45, 55-57, 76, 81, 112, 116, 119, 184
Thurstone, E. E., 38, 39, 80, 84, 91, 97, 101, 102, 105, 153,
  157, 190, 204, 209
Tibbits, C., 35, 84
Tiryakian, E. A., 2, 3, 5, 9, 10, 18, 23, 47, 116, 149, 176,
  179, 183, 213, 215, 217, 219
Tonnies, F., 146
Toronto University, 190
Towertown, 62
Tulane University, 148, 207
Turner, R. H., 32, 116, 121, 207
Tuskegee Institute, 14, 30, 43, 121
Typification, 61, 108, 121, 146

U

United Charities of Chicago, 60, 63
University of Chicago Press, 115, 178, 181
Urban Life, 20, 21
Urban sociology, 4, 5, 12, 15, 20, 21, 109, 110, 115-117, 121,
  144, 167, 190

V

Validity, 14, 70, 133, 139, 141, 188
Values, 51-55, 75, 93, 118, 129, 132, 134, 138, 141-143, 153
Value freedom, 140, 182, 186, 206
Vergati, S.,, 117
Verstehen, 55, 141, 142

Vidich, B., 205
Vincent, G. E., 9, 14, 27, 28, 112, 178
Virginia, University of, 200, 207, 208
Vold, G. B., 123, 131, 211

W
Walker, H. J., 121
Walker, R., 48
Waller, W., 78, 129, 134, 184, 185
Wallis, A., 105
Walton, P., 109, 123
Ward, L., 17
Ware, C., 72
Warner, L., 62, 64, 65, 68, 150
Warshay, L., 155
Washington University, 208
Weatherly, U., 179
Webb, E. J., 69
Weber, M., 135, 141, 142, 146, 147, 189, 208
Webster, E. J., 193
Weinberg, S. K., 116
West, G. H., 14
White, L. D., 38, 84, 101, 122, 123
Whitridge, E. R., 125
Whyte, W. F., 8, 16, 67, 72, 102
Wickersham Committee, 194
Wiley, N., 47, 182
Willer, D., 7, 128
Willey, M. M., 185, 207
Williams, J. M., 154, 185
Williams, J. J., 87
Williams, R., 117
Wilson, E. B., 8, 68, 99, 102
Winton, C., 21
Wirth, L., 6, 7, 10, 12, 16, 33, 39, 42, 65, 73, 79, 88, 89,
    100, 110, 113, 117, 120-122, 125, 126, 129-131, 133, 134,
    136, 138, 141-144, 148, 150, 153, 154, 160, 178, 184, 188,
    189, 192, 193, 186, 201, 202, 204, 207, 208, 211
Wisconsin, University of, 179, 200, 208
Wiseman, J., 21
Wishes, 51, 71, 118, 119, 149, 158
Witzgall, O., 125
Woodhead, H., 15,
Woolbert, H. G., 193
Works Program Administration, 65, 192
Work, sociology of, 124, 125
Wright, C., 161, 172

Y

Yale University, 67, 178, 179, 185, 198, 199
Young, D., 211
Young, E. F., 42, 114, 121
Young, J., 109, 123
Young, K., 7, 28, 155, 185
Young, P., 55
Yule, G. U., 101

Z

Zeublin, C., 15
Zimmerman, C. C., 184
Znaniecki, F., 15, 30, 51–54, 71, 93, 112, 118, 149–152, 154, 178
Zones, see concentric zones
Zorbaugh, H. W., 23, 50, 56, 61–63, 65, 112, 116, 119, 184